THE LAW OF
ESTATE AGENCY AND AUCTIONS

The Law of Estate Agency and Auctions

Third edition

by

John Murdoch LLB ACIArb

Senior Lecturer in Law
Reading University

1994

A member of Reed Business Publishing

The Estates Gazette Limited
151 Wardour Street, London W1V 4BN

First published 1975
Second edition 1984
Third edition 1994

ISBN 0 7282 0204 2

Typesetting by Amy Boyle Word Processing, Rochester, Kent
Printed in Great Britain at Biddles Ltd, Guildford

To Sandi

Preface

It is now almost ten years since the second edition of this book was published, a decade in which the world of estate agency (and even the more sheltered sphere of auctions) have experienced considerable upheaval. Not only has the nature of the game itself been changed by the intervention of the corporates (though how far that will survive until the next edition remains to be seen); the government has shown an increasing desire to regulate the whole business of land transfer, under the flag of consumer protection.

The most widely publicised result of this governmental interest in the property market has been the Property Misdescriptions Act 1991, which at the time of writing had just produced its first reported conviction of an estate agent. However, in terms of nuisance value to busy practitioners, even that Act must surely concede pride of place to the various Estate Agents Regulations published in 1991, whose requirements, all to be carried out "promptly and in writing", appear designed to bury estate agency in a mountain of paper. Add to this the implications (so far largely unconsidered) for auctioneers of the repeal of section 40 of the Law of Property Act, with the result that a memorandum of sale is no longer required, and the overall extent and importance of these statutory changes is clear to see.

All these developments (and others, such as the new restrictions on estate agents' boards) are duly noted and discussed in this edition, together with the inevitable crop of judicial decisions bearing on such crucial matters as commission, professional negligence and the fiduciary duties which estate agents and auctioneers owe to their clients. In an effort to make room for this material, some harsh pruning has been necessary; those accustomed to the previous edition will note that the treatment of general agency law has been reduced from five chapters to two, and that the section in the final chapter on a vendor's duty to disclose defects of title has been dropped (on the ground that this is not something in any way specific to the sale of land by auction). Out too has gone the treatment of professional negligence claims against surveyors and valuers, in the belief that this subject has now developed to a point where it can no longer be satisfactorily contained within a single chapter, while to extend it beyond that would surely unbalance a book whose primary focus lies elsewhere.

In preparing this edition, my thanks are due to the publishers, and in particular to Audrey Boyle and Colin Greasby, for their unfailing willingness to lighten the load wherever possible. Moreover, it becomes ever more clear to me that authorship demands sacrifices (only some of which are made by the author) and Sandi, Rob and Ailsa have once again demonstrated that charity does indeed begin at home.

St Andrew's Day 1993   John Murdoch

Contents

Table of cases

A

C

D

G

Table of Statutes

Table of Statutory Instruments

CHAPTER 1

General principles of agency

The law of agency is concerned with the activities of three persons:[1] an *agent* who acts on behalf of a *principal*[2] in dealing with a *third party*. And, if these three characters are visualised as standing at the points of a triangle, then the sides of that triangle represent the legal relationships between the parties. This in turn serves to emphasise an important truth, namely that the law of agency deals, not just with one legal relationship (that of principal and agent), but with all three.

There is indeed something to be said for the view that the most important aspect of agency law is the relationship between the principal and the third party. After all, the primary purpose of appointing an agent is to permit the principal to enter into transactions with third parties, without necessarily having to act in person. The fundamental question which has to be addressed, therefore, is how far the agent's acts are to be regarded as equivalent to acts carried out personally by the principal. Other questions (such as the agent's legal position *vis-à-vis* the principal and the third party) are also important, but they may perhaps be regarded as ancillary to the central issue.

Some idea of the kind of legal problems with which the law of agency deals may be obtained by considering the following three situations, each of which concerns an agent representing a client in dealing with a third party:

i The agent fulfils the principal's instructions to the letter, making the existence of the agency clear to the third party. Here a legal relationship comes into existence between the principal and the third party; the agent drops out of the picture, reappearing only to claim from the principal whatever is due under the agency agreement.

---

1 Or four, in cases where a *subagent* is involved.

2 Where estate agents and auctioneers are concerned, the principal is more commonly called a *client*.

ii The agent again makes a contract with the third party, but this time exceeds whatever authority has been given by the principal. Here the principal, who is not bound by the agent's acts, can effectively disclaim all liability on this contract. If the third party is to obtain any form of redress, this can only come from the agent.

iii There are some circumstances, which will be explained later, where the principal can be legally bound by acts of the agent which have not been expressly authorised; indeed, they may have been specifically prohibited. In such a case, the principal, whose legal position *vis-à-vis* the third party has been wrongfully altered, may take action against the agent for breach of duty.

A Agency and authority

If any one concept may be singled out as central to the law of agency, it is surely that of "authority". The scope of the authority given by the principal to an agent is crucial in determining whether or not the third party can hold the principal responsible for what the agent has done. It is also of great importance in deciding whether or not the agent is in breach of duty towards the principal. Again, where the potential personal liability of the agent towards a third party is in issue, the scope of the agent's authority is an important factor to be considered.

In recognising the importance of authority, it is vital to appreciate that the word takes on different shades of meaning in different contexts. As far as the third party is concerned, any act of the agent which is binding upon the principal may be said to have been "authorised" in one way or another. In considering the agent's position, however, "authority" bears a much more restricted meaning; an agent's primary duty is that of obedience to the principal, whose express instructions (as properly interpreted and with any appropriate implications) are paramount.

The first part of this chapter is concerned to identify the various kinds of authority which an agent may possess. As will be seen, these are not all conferred by the principal in any direct sense; they may arise by implication from the parties' actions, or even by operation of law. It is thus all the more important that the types of authority, and the differences between them, are fully understood.

1 Express authority

Agency is a consensual relationship; indeed, it arises most commonly out of a contract entered into between an agent and a principal, under which the agent agrees to perform certain tasks in return for some reward. Even where there is no contract in the full legal sense, as where the agent undertakes to do something for nothing, most (though not all) of the normal incidents of the agency relationship will be present.

Where agency *is* based on a contract, it is subject to all the general rules of law which govern the validity of a contract (such as fraud, misrepresentation, mistake or illegality). In particular, persons such as minors or the mentally incompetent, whose capacity to make contracts is legally restricted, may only appoint agents to carry out such transactions as they could enter into for themselves,[1] and cannot in any event execute a valid power of attorney.[2] Furthermore, an agent's authority will be automatically terminated if an initially sane principal becomes mentally incompetent, although the third party may continue to rely upon the appearance of authority until notified of the principal's condition.[3]

Surprisingly, perhaps, an agent who lacks contractual capacity may none the less bring about a binding contract between the principal and a third party. In such circumstances, however, the agent will not be bound by the contract of agency and will not incur any personal responsibility to the third party, in circumstances where an adult agent would do so.[4]

As to the form of a contract of agency, the general principle is that, apart from certain statutes which require an agent's appointment to be by deed[5] or in writing,[6] no specific formalities are necessary. Thus an agent instructed to execute a contract which must itself be in writing may be validly appointed by word of mouth.[7] However, an agent who is to execute a deed on behalf of the principal must receive authority in the form of a deed (known as a "power of attorney"),[8] except where the agent executes the deed

---

1 *Doyle* v *White City Stadium Ltd* [1935] 1 KB 110.

2 *Zouch d Abbott and Hallet* v *Parsons* (1765) 3 Burr 1794; *Daily Telegraph Newspaper Co* v *McLaughlin* [1904] AC 776.

3 See pp 35, 36.

4 *Smally* v *Smally* (1700) 1 Eq Cas Abr 6.

5 Eg Trustee Act 1925, section 25 (delegation of powers by trustee going abroad).

6 Eg Law of Property Act 1925, sections 53, 54 (creation of interests in land and declaration of trusts).

7 *Re Whitley Partners Ltd* (1886) 32 ChD 337.

8 *Steiglitz* v *Egginton* (1815) Holt NP 141; *Berkely* v *Hardy* (1826) 5 B&C 355.

in the principal's name and presence and at the principal's express request.[1]

The scope of an agent's express authority naturally depends upon the terms of appointment. Where these are contained in a deed, they will be strictly construed.[2] In consequence, general words which appear to confer wide powers upon an agent may well be cut down by special words in another part of the instrument. In *Danby v Coutts & Co*,[3] for example, the plaintiff appointed by deed two persons to be his attorneys, with authority to borrow money on mortgage. The deed did not limit the duration of these appointments; however, it began with a recital that the plaintiff was going abroad for a time and required an attorney to act for him during his absence. When the two agents fraudulently executed a mortgage of the plaintiff's property, in order to raise money for their own purposes, it was held that this was not binding upon the plaintiff, since it was executed after the latter had returned to England. The court ruled that the recital governed the operative part of the deed, so as to limit the agents' powers to the time when the principal was abroad.

Legal interpretation of documents other than deeds is much less strict, far more regard being paid to the surrounding circumstances. As a result, an agent is allowed to exercise a certain amount of discretion for the benefit of the principal, although not to override any express instructions. This principle was applied somewhat generously in *Ireland v Livingston*,[4] where an agent had been instructed to purchase 500 tons of sugar, give or take 50 tons more or less. When the agent found that only 393 tons were available and duly purchased this quantity, the House of Lords held that the transaction lay within the agent's authority. On the other hand, where an agent was instructed to act "in and about the purchase" of a colliery, it was held that this did not include authority to sign a binding contract of purchase.[5]

2   Implied authority

In a number of different situations, the law will imply authority for

---

1 *Ball* v *Dunsterville* (1791) 4 TR 313.
2 *Bryant, Powis & Bryant Ltd* v *La Banque du Peuple* [1893] AC 170 at p 177.
3 (1885) 29 ChD 500; see also *Jacobs* v *Morris* [1902] 1 Ch 816.
4 (1872) LR 5 HL 395.
5 *Vale of Neath Colliery* v *Furness* (1876) 45 LJ Ch 276.

an agent to act on behalf of a principal. Before examining these situations, it is important to emphasise that the authority which they confer is as real as if it were expressly given. Unlike the doctrine of "apparent" or "ostensible" authority,[1] which merely permits a third party to rely on an appearance of authority created by the principal, implied authority also protects an agent who acts within its scope.

Of course, authority will not be implied in the face of express instructions to the contrary from the principal, and an agent who contravenes those instructions will be personally liable to the principal. However, the third party in such circumstances may continue to rely on the agent's apparent authority, unless and until notice of its exclusion or restriction has been given.

(a) *Implication from the parties' conduct*

Where the very appointment of an agent is based upon the parties' actions, rather than upon their words, any resulting authority must by definition be implied. An example of this situation is *Sims v Landray*,[2] in which the defendant bid successfully for property at an auction. The auctioneer's clerk inserted the defendant's name into the memorandum of sale, while the defendant stood beside him without demur. It was held that the defendant must be taken to have authorised the clerk to sign the memorandum on his behalf, and that he was accordingly bound by the contract of sale.

Apart from these (admittedly unusual) cases in which the agency itself rests upon implication, an agent's express authority "implies and includes a right to do all subordinate acts incident to and necessary for the execution of that authority".[3] "Implication" in this sense might equally be regarded as an interpretation of the agent's express authority; either way, it is of a very limited nature, so that for example an agent authorised to sell land has no implied authority to receive the purchase price,[4] although such an agent can accept a deposit.[5]

---

1 See p 9.

2 [1894] 2 Ch 318.

3 *Collen v Gardner* (1856) 21 Beav 540 at p 543; see also *Pole v Leask* (1860) 28 Beav 562 at p 574.

4 *Mynn v Joliffe* (1834) 1 Mood & R 326; *Butwick v Grant* [1924] 2 KB 483; *Petersen v Moloney* (1951) 84 CLR 91.

5 *Boote v RT Shiels & Co* [1978] 1 NZLR 445. This, however, may only apply where the person concerned is an estate agent: see, generally, pp 83-87.

(b) Implication from the business context

The law has long taken the view that, where an agent of a particular type or category is appointed, both the agent and any third party with whom he or she deals should be able to assume (until notified to the contrary) that the agent has been given whatever authority is usual in the circumstances. This view has created a kind of implied authority known as "usual authority", which arises in two rather different situations.

In the first place, an agent may be appointed to a position in the principal's business. Where this is so, it is assumed that the agent has whatever authority is usually conferred upon the holder of such a position. Thus, for example, an agent employed in a general capacity to manage the principal's estate may validly accept a notice to quit from a tenant.[1] By contrast, a notice to quit given by a tenant to a rent collector would not be valid, for it is not within the usual authority of such an agent to receive it.[2] A similar distinction may be found in relation to companies; a managing director has very wide implied powers to commit the company to contracts,[3] whereas the authority of the other individual directors is much more limited in scope.[4]

The second type of "usual authority" consists of what is normal in the *agent's* own trade, business or profession. In this connection it is well established that a principal is bound by any trade custom which is held to be reasonable,[5] and even by an unreasonable custom which was both known and agreed to.[6] The question of what is "usual" for estate agents and auctioneers will be considered in some detail in later chapters; at this stage the point may be illustrated by examples from other areas.

A broker selling goods, unlike an ordinary agent, is impliedly authorised to extend reasonable credit to a buyer.[7] No credit, however, may be given on a sale of *shares*, for this would not be

---

1 See *Papillon* v *Brunton* (1860) 5 H&N 518.

2 *Pearse* v *Boulter* (1860) 2 F&F 133.

3 See *Freeman & Lockyer (a firm)* v *Buckhurst Park Properties (Mangal) Ltd* [1964] 2 QB 480.

4 *Houghton & Co* v *Nothard, Lowe & Wills Ltd* [1927] 1 KB 246.

5 *Bayliffe* v *Butterworth* (1847) 1 Ex 425.

6 *Blackburn* v *Mason* (1893) 68 LT 510.

7 *Boorman* v *Brown* (1842) 3 QB 511.

according to the usual course of business.[1] An insurance broker, in the capacity of agent for an insurance company, has usual authority to enter into a binding contract of interim insurance, albeit orally and in informal or colloquial language.[2] Again, the managing agent of a block of flats has usual authority to make representations to a prospective tenant as to the condition of the property.[3]

As for the legal profession, it was held in *Domb* v *Isoz*[4] that a solicitor authorised to make a contract for the sale of land can effect that contract in any manner recognised by law (in the case itself, this was by an agreement over the telephone between the solicitors that contracts should be deemed to be exchanged). And in *Waugh* v *HB Clifford & Sons Ltd*[5] it was held that, while the implied authority of a solicitor or barrister to compromise a legal action may be limited *vis-à-vis* the client by such things as the agent's knowledge of the client's financial circumstances, this would not prevent the other party from treating any agreed compromise as valid; from the third party's point of view, the only limitation on the agent's usual authority is that the compromise agreement must not contain any matter which is "collateral to the suit".

The last example serves to emphasise the point that a principal seeking to restrict the usual authority of an agent must bring that restriction to the attention of the relevant party. Informing the agent will mean that, if the restriction is exceeded, the agent will be liable to the principal for disobedience. However, in order to prevent a third party from relying on the authority which an agent would normally possess, it is necessary for the principal to inform that third party that this particular agent's authority has been limited.

This focus on what the third party knows makes it clear that the underlying basis of usual authority is some form of estoppel; the principal, having produced the appearance of authority, is not permitted to deny that it actually exists. This makes usual authority very similar to apparent authority and, indeed, many cases could be decided equally well upon either basis. However, the two concepts

---

1 *Wiltshire* v *Sims* (1808) 1 Camp 258.
2 *Stockton* v *Mason* [1979] RTR 130.
3 *Gordon* v *Selico Co Ltd* [1986] 1 EGLR 71.
4 [1980] Ch 548.
5 [1982] Ch 374.

are not entirely coextensive, because of a line of cases[1] in which it has been held that a third party may rely on the "usual authority" of a person *who is not known to be an agent*. In such circumstances it would be completely unrealistic to suggest that the principal has given the agent any "appearance of authority", and so an independent doctrine of usual authority must be recognised.[2]

(c) *Implication from necessity*

In a limited number of cases, where a person's property or interests are threatened by some sort of emergency, another person may be legally justified in acting to protect them. The term "agency of necessity" is often used to encompass these situations, although this is misleading, since it is extremely rare for the so-called "agent" to create a binding relationship between the "principal" and a third party.[3] More commonly, the point arises because the Good Samaritan demands reimbursement of whatever expenses have been incurred, whereupon it must be decided whether or not the intervention was justified.

It should be emphasised at the outset that English law has never looked with much favour upon the providers of unsolicited services, so that, for example, claims in respect of expenses incurred in looking after a stray dog,[4] or in removing timber found on a river bank to a place of safety,[5] have proved unsuccessful. However, the courts are rather more sympathetic where an existing agent oversteps the normal limits of authority in an emergency. Thus, for example, a railway company has been held bound by the actions of employees in ordering medical attention and food for injured passengers following an accident.[6] On the other hand, where a mine manager borrowed money to pay arrears of miners' wages and thus prevent them from distraining upon the mine machinery, it was held that this could not be justified on the ground of

---

1 Of which the best known is *Watteau* v *Fenwick* [1893] 1 QB 346.

2 This doctrine is considered at p 12.

3 The classic example is that of a shipmaster who may, in an emergency, sell both the ship and its cargo: *The Gratitudine* (1801) 3 Ch Rob 240; *Robertson* v *Caruthers* (1819) 2 Stark 571.

4 *Binstead* v *Buck* (1776) 2 W Bl 1117.

5 *Nicholson* v *Chapman* (1793) H Bl 254.

6 *Walker* v *Great Western Railway Co* (1867) LR 2 Ex 228; *Langan* v *Great Western Railway Co* (1873) 30 LT 173.

necessity.[1]

Even in those situations where agency of necessity is capable of being invoked, it is subject to such strict conditions that attempts to rely on it rarely succeed. In the first place, the "agent" must establish that it was impossible in practical terms to obtain instructions from the "principal",[2] a requirement which modern communications have rendered difficult to satisfy. Second, there must be a real emergency, something which the courts have proved reluctant to recognise except in relation to livestock or perishable goods.[3] Finally, it should be noted that inconvenience to the "agent" does not constitute "necessity" for this purpose, so that a person who allowed the plaintiff to store furniture free of charge in her house, but who then sold it because she needed the space and could not contact the plaintiff, was held liable in the tort of conversion.[4]

3 Apparent authority

We have already referred more than once to the doctrine of "apparent authority", under which a principal may be held responsible for what an agent does, even though the agent may have disobeyed explicit instructions. The legal rule which produces this conclusion has been expressed as follows:

> Where a person, by words or conduct, represents or permits it to be represented that another person has authority to act on his behalf, he is bound by the acts of such other person with respect to anyone dealing with him as an agent on the faith of any such representation, to the same extent as if such other person had the authority that he was represented to have, even though he had no actual authority."[5]

(a) *Nature and effect of apparent authority*

The above description of apparent authority makes clear that it is concerned exclusively with the relationship between principal and third party. It is a means by which the principal becomes liable to the third party *as if* the agent had been authorised, when in truth

---

1 *Hawtayne* v *Bourne* (1841) 7 M & W 595.
2 *Springer* v *Great Western Railway Co* [1921] 1 KB 257.
3 See *Prager* v *Blatspiel, Stamp & Heacock Ltd* [1924] 1 KB 566 (no agency of necessity to sell furs which could have been stored without risk of deterioration).
4 *Sachs* v *Miklos* [1948] 2 KB 23; see also *Munro* v *Wilmott* [1949] 1 KB 295.
5 *Bowstead on Agency* (15th ed) p 284.

this was not so. The justification for imposing such liability upon the principal lies in the representation which he or she has made and on which the third party has relied. It is thus based on, or at least closely linked to, the legal doctrine of estoppel. An important conclusion to be drawn from this is that, where the representation of authority comes *from the agent*, the principal will seldom be held liable; it is inherently improbable[1] that an agent, who has no general authority to carry out some act, is none the less authorised to confirm that he or she has been given special authority to carry it out.[2]

The simplest and most straightforward case of apparent authority (albeit one which is seldom encountered) arises out of an express statement made by the principal. In *Trickett* v *Tomlinson*,[3] for example, the principal told a third party that he had authorised his agent to settle a dispute between them, but did not mention that he had placed limits upon the agent's discretion. When the agent reached a settlement outside these limits, the principal was held bound by it.

More commonly, the "representation" on which apparent authority rests is to be inferred from the principal's conduct (which may be purely passive). Thus, for example, a principal who permits an agent to order goods from a particular supplier, in the sense of meeting without demur a series of bills from that supplier, may well find that the agent is clothed with the appearance of authority to continue in this way.[4] In *Townsend Carriers Ltd* v *Pfizer Ltd*,[5] a notice to terminate a business tenancy was served by and on associated companies of the actual landlord and tenant; the service was held to be valid, since it was these companies which had handled all the parties' dealings throughout the lease, and they had therefore been given the appearance of the necessary authority by their respective principals.

In practical terms, perhaps the most important way of "holding out" an agent as having authority consists of appointing that agent to some position in the principal's business. Where this is done,

---

1 But not impossible: see *First Energy (UK) Ltd* v *Hungarian Bank Ltd* [1993] NPC 34.
2 *Armagas Ltd* v *Mundogas SA* [1986] 2 All ER 385.
3 (1863) 13 CBNS 663.
4 *Summers* v *Solomon* (1857) 7 E&B 879.
5 (1977) 33 P&CR 361.

third parties are entitled to assume, until they are notified to the contrary, that the agent is invested with the authority which is usual in that position and, further, that this authority has not been in any way restricted. In the case of a valid appointment, the principal's liability to the third party might equally be based upon the doctrine of implied or "usual" authority;[1] however, the value of apparent authority is that it can be relied on by a third party even where the agent was never properly appointed at all.[2]

Assuming that a "representation" as to an agent's authority has been made, a third party who seeks to hold the principal bound must show that he or she relied on it.[3] This of course means that apparent authority can never be used by a third party who knows that the agent has no real authority.[4] Less obviously, it has been held to mean that, where an agent acts under the authority of a written document, the third party is treated as being aware of any lack of authority which would be revealed by reading that document.[5] Moreover, where a transaction entered into by an agent is so "irregular" as to arouse suspicion, a third party can no longer rely on apparent authority but must make enquiries.[6] Thus, for example, where a solicitor authorised to sign cheques for a client dishonestly used one of these cheques to buy a car for himself, it was held that the car dealers should have checked directly with the client to see that this purchase was authorised.[7]

Where apparent authority exists, it takes effect in a number of different ways. First (although this does not often occur), it may give an appearance of authority to someone who in truth has never been the principal's agent at all.[8] Second, it may serve as a continuation, for the benefit of a third party, of an agency which as between

---

1 See p 6.

2 See *Freeman & Lockyer (a firm)* v *Buckhurst Park Properties (Mangal) Ltd* [1964] 2 QB 480.

3 *Farquharson Brothers & Co* v *King & Co* [1902] AC 325 at p 341.

4 As to the common practice of denying that estate agents or auctioneers are authorised to make statements about property for sale, see pp 91-93.

5 *Jacobs* v *Morris* [1902] 1 Ch 816.

6 *Lloyd's Bank Ltd* v *Chartered Bank of India, Australia & China* [1929] 1 KB 40.

7 *Reckitt* v *Barnett, Pembroke & Slater Ltd* [1929] AC 176: see also *Midland Bank Ltd* v *Reckitt* [1933] AC 1.

8 For an example, see *Mildner (F) & Sons* v *Noble* The Times, March 8 1956; [1956] CLY 32.

principal and agent has ceased to exist.[1] Third, and most commonly, it may prevent a restriction upon the agent's express or implied authority from operating to the detriment of a third party who has no notice of it.[2]

(b) *Analogous forms of authority*

Attention must now be given to two situations in which, although not all the elements of apparent authority were present, the courts have none the less held a principal responsible for what an agent had done. The first of these arose in the notorious and much-criticised case of *Watteau* v *Fenwick*,[3] which concerned a beer-house purchased by the defendant brewers from a Mr Humble. The defendants kept Humble on as manager of the establishment, and it was his name which appeared over the door as licensee; in consequence, third parties had no reason to suspect that he was no longer the owner of the business, but was merely agent for an undisclosed principal. The defendants instructed Humble not to buy supplies for the business but he, in contravention of this instruction, purchased cigars on credit from the plaintiff and failed to pay for them. The Divisional Court of Queen's Bench[4] held the defendants liable to the plaintiff for the price of these cigars, on the basis that:

The principal is liable for all the acts of the agent which are within the authority usually confided to an agent of that character, notwithstanding limitations, as between the principal and the agent, put upon that authority.

The decision in *Watteau* v *Fenwick* cannot be accommodated within the ordinary principles of apparent authority, because it can hardly be said that a person who does not appear to be an agent in the first place has been "held out" as possessing any authority at all. Indeed, had the plaintiff been aware that Humble was merely an agent, the decision would probably have been different, since it was (and is) common for the manager of licensed premises to be restricted in the choice of suppliers.[5] The case has further been

---

1 As in *Summers* v *Solomon* (1857) 7 E&B 879: p 10.
2 As in *Trickett* v *Tomlinson* (1863) 13 CBNS 663: p 10.
3 [1893] 1 QB 346.
4 Relying on *Edmunds* v *Bushell and Jones* (1865) LR 1 QB 97.
5 See *Daun* v *Simmins* (1879) 41 LT 783.

criticised on the ground that there was little reason for allowing the plaintiff, who presumably intended to give credit exclusively to Humble, to hold the undisclosed principal responsible on a transaction which the latter had expressly forbidden. None the less, the decision has been followed on similar facts,[1] and can perhaps best be justified as somewhat analogous to the doctrine of "apparent ownership".[2]

The second judicial extension of apparent authority is based on the decision of the Court of Appeal in *Spiro* v *Lintern*.[3] The defendant there asked his wife to look for a purchaser for a house of which he was the sole owner. The wife, however, went further and, without disclosing that she was acting as an agent, purported to exchange contracts with the plaintiff for the sale of the property. When the existence of the defendant was revealed, he made no reference to his wife's lack of authority; indeed, he appeared to treat the contract as binding, for he allowed the plaintiff to send an architect and a builder to carry out alterations to the property. It was held that the defendant was bound by the contract; by failing to inform the plaintiff to the contrary, he was liable to the same extent as if his wife had been authorised.

Although this decision is clearly not a straightforward application of apparent authority (since there was no such "appearance" when the contract was signed), it might be regarded as an example of ratification,[4] a doctrine by which a principal can give retrospective authority for the act of an agent. However, it is established that there can be no ratification by an undisclosed principal,[5] and so *Spiro* v *Lintern* cannot be justified on that ground. It is rather a case of the defendant being taken to represent that his wife had had authority to make the contract, and then, once the plaintiff had acted upon this representation by incurring expense, being estopped from denying its truth.

The type of authority recognised in *Spiro* v *Lintern* was again

---

1 *Kinahan & Co Ltd* v *Parry* [1910] 2 KB 389; reversed on other grounds [1911] 1 KB 459.
2 See p 24.
3 [1973] 3 All ER 319.
4 See p 14.
5 *Keighley, Maxsted & Co* v *Durant* [1901] AC 240.

utilised by the Court of Appeal in *Worboys* v *Carter*,[1] which arose when the defendant, a tenant farmer, was sent to prison. A land agent representing the defendant purported to arrange an assignment of his tenancy to the plaintiff and the defendant, although never intending to go through with this transaction, allowed the plaintiff to believe that it was valid and that the plaintiff could safely sell his own farm. Again the defendant was held bound by his agent's unauthorised act; not on the basis of ratification (which the Court of Appeal thought inapplicable, given the clear evidence that the defendant had no intention of adopting the agent's acts), but rather on the simple ground of estoppel.

4   Ratification

In certain circumstances an agent's unauthorised act may be subsequently adopted by the agent's principal. The principal in such cases is said to "ratify" the agent's act, and this operates, by and large, to give retrospective authority to the agent. The precise effects of this legal doctrine, and the conditions necessary for its operation, may now be considered.

(a) *Effects of ratification*

As a general rule, ratification operates to place the principal, the agent and the third party in the positions in which they would have been had the agent acted with authority in the first place. If the agent has purported to make a contract on the principal's behalf, the effect of this will be back-dated to the time when it was made. Furthermore, since the agent is now deemed to have acted with authority, there can be no personal liability to either the principal or the third party. The only limitation appears to be that there is no implication of authority for the agent to act similarly in future.[2]

It cannot be denied that the doctrine of ratification is capable of producing some strange results, of which the strangest is perhaps the controversial case of *Bolton Partners* v *Lambert*.[3] The defendant there made an offer to purchase the plaintiffs' property which the plaintiffs' agent, without any authority, accepted. The defendant

---

1 [1987] 2 EGLR 1.
2 *Irvine* v *Union Bank of Australia* (1877) 2 App Cas 366.
3 (1889) 41 ChD 295; much criticised, but followed in *Re Tiedemann and Ledermann Frères* [1899] 2 QB 66.

then notified the plaintiffs that the offer was withdrawn, whereupon the plaintiffs replied that they were ratifying their agent's acceptance of it! The Court of Appeal held that the plaintiffs' ratification operated retrospectively to create a binding contract from the date of the agent's acceptance, and that the defendant's withdrawal was thus of no legal effect.

The difficulty which results from *Bolton v Lambert* is that the third party is placed entirely at the mercy of the principal, who is free to decide whether or not to ratify. The third party can therefore neither ensure that there is a binding contract, nor prevent one from coming into operation. Perhaps in recognition of the hardship which may thus arise, the courts have kept the "retroactivity" principle within fairly strict limits. It has for example been held that, where an agent's action is expressly[1] or impliedly[2] made "subject to ratification", it will take effect only when the principal actually ratifies it. Furthermore, if the agent actually agrees with the third party to cancel a contract which they have purported to make, the principal cannot then revive it by ratification.[3]

(b) Conditions for ratification

The first requirement of a valid ratification is that the principal must exist as a legal person and have the necessary capacity to act, not only at the time of the ratification, but also at the time of the agent's action. It is because of this that a limited company cannot ratify anything done on its behalf before its incorporation.[4] Thus, where a survey of a flat was carried out on behalf of a company which was to be formed to purchase it, the company could not ratify its agent's act so as to sue the surveyor for beach of contract; however, it was held that the surveyor owed the unformed company a duty of care *in tort*, and could be liable for a breach of that duty.[5]

Ratification can only be carried out by the person on whose behalf the agent has purported to act.[6] The most important

---

1 *Watson v Davies* [1931] 1 Ch 455.
2 *Warehousing & Forwarding Co of East Africa Ltd v Jafferali & Sons Ltd* [1964] AC 1.
3 *Walter v James* (1871) LR 6 Ex 124.
4 *Kelner v Baxter* (1866) LR 2 CP 174. The "agent" in such a case is personally liable to the third party: Companies Act 1985, s 36C(1).
5 *Miro Properties Ltd v J Trevor & Sons* [1989] 1 EGLR 151.
6 *Saunderson v Griffiths* (1826) 5 B & C 909.

application of this rule is that there can be no ratification by a principal who, at the time of the agent's act, was undisclosed.[1] The leading case on this point is *Keighley, Maxsted & Co v Durant*,[2] where the defendants authorised an agent to buy wheat on a joint account for the defendants and the agent. The agent bought wheat from the plaintiff without disclosing the joint account, at a price in excess of that which the defendants had authorised. The defendants accepted what their agent had done but, when the plaintiff sued upon the contract, the House of Lords held that the defendants, as undisclosed principals, could not be said to have ratified and were therefore not liable.[3]

Unless the principal is seeking to ratify the agent's execution of a deed (in which case the ratification too must be by deed),[4] there are in general no particular formalities to be observed. Indeed, many if not most cases of ratification are based on some conduct of the principal, as where the principal sells goods which have been purchased by an agent in excess of authority.[5] In accordance with this principle, it has been held that a principal who adopts an unauthorised sale of property will normally also be taken to ratify the appointment of an agent to sell it, so as to incur liability for that agent's commission.[6] However, a court will not infer ratification from the principal's conduct where the principal had no choice whether to accept or reject what the agent had done,[7] nor where the principal did not know all the material facts about the agent's unauthorised act.[8]

In an effort to protect third parties against the hardship which may be caused by the retrospective nature of ratification, the courts have imposed a number of other restrictions upon the use of this doctrine. In the first place, it is settled that, where an act has to be performed within a certain time it must, if performed without

---

1 There are even suggestions that the principal must have been *identified*: see *Watson* v *Swann* (1862) 11 CBNS 756.

2 [1901] AC 240.

3 Note the possibility of estoppel in such circumstances: *Spiro* v *Lintern* [1973] 3 All ER 319; p 13.

4 *Hunter* v *Parker* (1840) 7 M&W 322; *Oxford Corporation* v *Crow* [1893] 3 Ch 535.

5 *Cornwal* v *Wilson* (1750) 1 Ves 509.

6 *Keay* v *Fenwick* (1876) 1 CPD 745; cf *Hughes* v *Hughes* (1971) 221 EG 145.

7 *Forman & Co Proprietary Ltd* v *The Liddesdale* [1900] AC 190.

8 *The Bonita, The Charlotte* (1861) 1 Lush 252.

authority, be ratified within that time.[1] Thus, where a landlord's agent serves a notice to quit on a tenant without authority, this may not be ratified after the last date on which the notice could validly have been served.[2] Second, ratification will not be allowed where its effect would be to divest third parties of proprietary rights which have already vested in them.[3] Finally, where a third party does some act which is lawful when done (such as refusing to hand over the principal's goods on demand by an unauthorised agent), subsequent ratification of the agent's act cannot retrospectively make the third party's act unlawful.[4]

B Agency transactions

Having examined the various types of authority which an agent may possess, we may now consider in rather more detail the ways in which a principal may be held legally responsible for what the agent does. The most important areas concern the making of contracts and the transfer of property, but other matters (notably the commission of torts) are also relevant.

1 Contracts

The extent to which the principal is bound by contracts entered into by an agent may vary according to whether or not the third party was aware of the principal's existence. Moreover, a third party who has some defence against the agent may be able to set up that defence against the principal; and the principal may in some circumstances be able to do likewise against the third party.

(a) *Disclosed and undisclosed principals*

The legal difference between a disclosed and an undisclosed principal turns, not on whether the third party knew the principal's *identity*, but rather on whether the third party was aware of the principal's *existence*. Where the agent is known to be acting as an agent (as will be the case, for example, with an auctioneer), the vendor will be a disclosed (though quite possibly *unnamed*)

---

1 If no time is fixed, then ratification must take place within a reasonable time: *Metropolitan Asylums Board* v *Kingham & Sons* (1890) 6 TLR 217.

2 *Doe d Mann* v *Walters* (1830) 10 B & C 626.

3 *Bird* v *Brown* (1850) 4 Exch 786; *Dibbins* v *Dibbins* [1896] 2 Ch 348.

4 *Solomons* v *Dawes* (1794) 1 Esp 83.

principal. The true undisclosed principal is found in those cases where the agent appears to the third party to be contracting personally, and where the principal only comes into the picture at a later stage.

Where an agent, acting within the scope of his or her authority,[1] enters into a contract on behalf of a *disclosed* principal, the general rule (subject to a few minor exceptions) is that the latter is both liable and entitled on that contract. This is central to the law of agency; indeed it is the fundamental purpose for which agency was designed. The only qualifications relate to contracts made in a particular form, most notably by deed.[2] At common law, a principal could only be a party to such a contract if the deed was executed by the agent in the principal's name,[3] or if the agent could be regarded as a trustee of the principal's rights.[4] This position has been modified by statute;[5] however, it appears that the principal must still be named as a party to the deed in order to acquire any rights or liabilities under it.

The position of a disclosed principal is just as one would expect. What may come as more of a surprise, however, is the fact that an *undisclosed* principal is to a large extent in exactly the same situation. Notwithstanding that the third party has acted throughout on the assumption that the "agent" is dealing personally, the principal becomes both liable and entitled on the contract made.[6] Of course, this will depend upon the agent having acted with authority, and it should be remembered that there can be no question of ratification,[7] although the principal may be estopped by subsequent conduct from denying the agent's authority.[8] Further, the doctrine of apparent authority is not relevant, since the principal cannot be said to "hold out" the agent. However, the principal will be bound by acts falling within the agent's "usual authority", even

---

1 Including *any* of the types of authority described above.

2 There are also special rules governing bills of exchange, cheques and promissory notes: see the Bills of Exchange Act 1882, sections 17, 23 and 91.

3 *Schack* v *Anthony* (1813) 1 M&S 573.

4 *Harmer* v *Armstrong* [1934] Ch 65.

5 Powers of Attorney Act 1971, section 7(1), replacing the Law of Property Act 1925, section 123(1).

6 The agent too remains a party to the contract: *Saxon* v *Blake* (1861) 29 Beav 438.

7 *Keighley, Maxsted & Co* v *Durant* [1901] AC 240.

8 *Spiro* v *Lintern* [1973] 3 All ER 319: see p 13.

where these have been expressly forbidden.[1]

The doctrine of the undisclosed principal appears somewhat anomalous, and the courts have attempted to ensure that it does not operate harshly against third parties. In general, it appears that an undisclosed principal will not be allowed to intervene where this would materially weaken the position of the third party. In *Collins* v *Associated Greyhound Racecourses Ltd*,[2] for example, a company issued shares in order to raise money for the purchase of a number of greyhound racecourses. The plaintiff, attracted by the prospectus, decided to sub-underwrite some of the shares, but did so through agents who did not disclose his existence. When certain statements contained in the prospectus proved to be untrue, the plaintiff claimed to rescind the contract. It was held, however, that since the agents themselves could not rescind (for they had not been misled by the prospectus), the undisclosed principal could not deprive the third party of its rights by rescinding the contract. A similar decision was reached in *Hanstown Properties Ltd* v *Green*,[3] where two tenants of a flat claimed that they had entered into the lease as agents for themselves and a third person. To allow this third person to come into the picture would, of course, be highly detrimental to the landlords, since it would increase the number of persons who might qualify for a statutory tenancy. Accordingly, the undisclosed principal was not permitted to reveal herself as an additional tenant.

In addition to this general regard to the position of the third party, there may be more specific reasons why an undisclosed principal cannot intervene. Where, for example, a certain type of contract may only be made between members of a limited class (such as a trade association), then a non-member cannot claim to have been the undisclosed principal of a member.[4] Moreover, the courts have on occasion held that the contractual description of one of the parties is such as to exclude the possibility that that party is acting as an agent, and thus to rule out any undisclosed principal.[5] It

---

1 *Watteau* v *Fenwick* [1893] 1 QB 346: p 12.
2 [1930] 1 Ch 1.
3 (1977) 246 EG 917.
4 *United Kingdom Mutual Steamship Assurance Ltd* v *Nevill* (1887) 19 QBD 110.
5 Eg "owner" (*Humble* v *Hunter* (1848) 12 QB 310) or "proprietor" (*Formby Bros* v *Formby* (1910) 102 LT 116).

should be acknowledged, however, that this approach is somewhat controversial, and will in any event not apply to more equivocal descriptions of a party, such as "tenant" or "landlord".[1]

It might be thought that, in any case where the third party can show that the agent's identity is a matter of concern, this would be sufficient to keep an undisclosed principal out of the picture. The reality, however, is not quite so simple. It is certainly true that, where the law regards a contract as too "personal" to be assigned (which will be the case, for example, where it involves particular skills or characteristics of a party), it will equally not be possible for an undisclosed principal to take over that contract. However, it appears that the third party may not exclude an undisclosed principal merely by showing that he or she would not have been willing to contract with that person. Thus, surprising though it might seem, a person who knows that he or she would not be acceptable to another as a contracting partner may evade that restriction by operating as an undisclosed principal.

This last point appears from the case of *Dyster v Randall & Sons*,[2] where the plaintiff, who had been employed by the defendants, was dismissed by them in circumstances which left no doubt that they would refuse to do business of any kind with him. Wishing to obtain two plots of land from the defendants, the plaintiff persuaded a friend to buy them as his agent. When the defendants, on learning the truth, purported to cancel the contract, the plaintiff sued for and obtained a decree of specific performance. The court held that there had been no positive misrepresentation as to the purchaser's identity,[3] and that this was not a material ingredient (requiring disclosure) of a contract for the sale of land.[4]

(b) *Principal's defences*

A principal (whether disclosed or undisclosed) who is *prima facie* bound by a contract made by an agent may nevertheless be able to raise one or more defences when sued by the third party. In the

---

1 See *Danziger* v *Thompson* [1944] KB 654; *Epps* v *Rothnie* [1945] KB 562.
2 [1926] Ch 932.
3 Had there been, the contract would not have been enforceable: *Archer* v *Stone* (1898) 78 LT 34.
4 For a contract in which identity *was* held to be material, see *Said* v *Butt* [1920] 3 KB 497.

first place, it is an established rule of common law that a third party who has elected to give credit exclusively to one person may not subsequently choose to proceed against the other. What constitutes an "election" for this purpose is a question of fact, but it may be stated that the courts require evidence that the third party has unequivocally decided to look exclusively for payment to the agent;[1] thus, merely receiving partial payment from the agent,[2] debiting the agent in accounts,[3] or even commencing legal proceedings[4] may all fall short of what is required to release the principal. In any event, there can be no election by someone who does not know all the material facts, which means that the doctrine cannot apply to things done by the third party while the principal remains undisclosed. The third party will not even lose the right to proceed against the undisclosed principal by suing the agent to (unsatisfied) judgment; this was formerly the position under *Kendall v Hamilton*,[5] but that decision has been reversed by statute.[6]

A question which sometimes arises is whether a principal who owes money to the third party may discharge that obligation by paying the agent. At one time this was held to be so, on the general ground that it would be unfair to make the principal pay twice.[7] However, it now appears that the principal may only rely upon a payment to the agent as discharging an obligation to the third party in cases where the principal has been induced by the third party to make the payment (for example where the third party leads the principal to believe that the agent has already paid the debt).[8] An important consequence is that an undisclosed principal can never avoid liability on this ground, since a third party can hardly be said to induce payment by making representations to a person whose very existence is unknown.[9]

---

1 See, for example, *Chestertons v Barone* [1987] 1 EGLR 15.
2 *Ex parte Pitt* (1923) 40 TLR 5.
3 *Young & Co Ltd v White* (1911) 28 TLR 87.
4 *Clarkson Booker Ltd v Andjel* [1964] 2 QB 775.
5 (1879) 4 App Cas 504.
6 Civil Liability (Contribution) Act 1978, section 3.
7 *Armstrong v Stokes* (1872) LR 7 QB 598.
8 *Wyatt v Marquis of Hertford* (1802) 3 East 147.
9 *Irvine & Co v Watson and Sons* (1880) 5 QBD 414, approving *Heald v Kenworthy* (1855) 10 Exch 739.

(c) *Third party's defences*

The converse situation to that described above is where a third party who owes money to the principal claims to have discharged that debt by paying the agent, or by setting off a sum which the agent owes to the third party. The extent to which such claims will succeed depends, among other things, on whether the principal is disclosed or undisclosed.

In the case of a disclosed principal, everything turns on the scope of the agent's authority to receive payment. This is likely to be limited to the receipt of cash, in which case payment in kind (for example a quantity of horse-hair!) will not discharge the debt.[1] Similarly, it is not often that an agent will have authority to set off a personal debt in partial satisfaction of what the third party owes to the principal, although this has occasionally been established.[2]

Where the principal is undisclosed, it might be thought that any payment or set-off by the third party before learning of the principal's existence would validly discharge the debt. This is largely correct, although it is subject to a rather illogical qualification as a result of the decision in *Cooke & Sons* v *Eshelby*.[3] It was held by the House of Lords in that case that, unless the principal has in some way induced the third party to believe that the agent is contracting personally (ie has enabled the agent to appear to deal as principal), the principal will not be bound by any settlement or set-off. While this qualification might seem somewhat unfair, it will not often create hardship for the third party, as the principal will be held to have enabled the agent to appear as principal in any case where the agent is entrusted with actual possession of goods to sell.[4]

As to other defences which the third party may seek to set up, it is clear that a principal who is personally guilty of fraud or misrepresentation runs the risk of losing the contract or having to pay damages. In *Ludgater* v *Love*,[5] for example, the defendant had some sheep for sale which he knew to be diseased. He appointed

---

1 *Howard* v *Chapman* (1831) 4 C&P 508. More importantly, nor will bill of exchange or cheque suffice: *Williams* v *Evans* (1866) LR 1 QB 352.
2 See, for example, *Barker* v *Greenwood* (1837) 2 Y&C Ex 414.
3 (1887) 12 App Cas 271.
4 *Borries* v *Imperial Ottoman Bank* (1873) LR 9 CP 38.
5 (1881) 44 LT 694.

an agent to sell the sheep, but concealed their condition from him. The agent sold the sheep as sound, which was what the defendant had intended, and the purchaser was held entitled to damages from the defendant for this fraud.

Where the third party's defence against contractual liability (for example on the ground of fraud, misrepresentation or illegality) is based on some act of the agent, the legal position depends on whether the principal is disclosed or undisclosed. A disclosed principal is bound by whatever the agent is authorised to do, so that the third party is placed in the same position as if the principal had done the act in person. Thus in *Mullens* v *Miller*,[1] an estate agent's misrepresentation about the property prevented the client from obtaining specific performance of the contract of sale, while in *Gosling* v *Anderson*,[2] on similar facts, a purchaser recovered damages from the vendor. So too, in *Refuge Assurance Co Ltd* v *Kettlewell*[3] the holder of an insurance policy was held entitled to recover from the company premiums which she had paid on the faith of false statements made by the company's agents. Finally, in *Biggs* v *Lawrence*[4] where one of three partners sold goods which he knew to have been packed for the purpose of smuggling, it was held that the firm was prevented by this illegality from suing the purchaser for the price of the goods.

Where the principal is undisclosed, it appears that the third party is in a stronger position for, in addition to the rights outlined above, the third party may rely upon any defences which are obtained against the agent before the principal's existence becomes known.[5]

2 Dispositions of property

The extent to which an agent may dispose of property belonging to the principal, in such a way as to confer good title on a third party, is dependent upon the scope of the agent's authority. If the disposition in question has been expressly authorised by the principal, then the third party will be protected, even if the agent

---

1 (1882) 22 ChD 194.
2 (1972) 223 EG 1743.
3 [1909] AC 243.
4 (1789) 3 TR 454.
5 At least where the principal has enabled the agent to appear to deal in person: see *Cooke & Sons* v *Eshelby* (1887) 12 App Cas 271; p 22.

then fails to hand over the price.[1] Furthermore, it should be remembered that a disposition of the principal's property, no less than the making of a contract, may fall within any of the other types of authority described above, and in fact two of those types of authority are of particular importance in this context. These are, first, the doctrine of apparent authority or ownership (which is now largely contained in section 21(1) of the Sale of Goods Act 1979), and, second, the specialised form of usual authority enshrined in the Factors Act 1889. These two topics merit separate treatment.

(a) *Apparent authority and ownership*

Where a person accepts property, by way of sale or pledge, from someone who is known to be acting as an agent, that person may rely upon any appearance of authority given to the agent by the principal, Where, however, the third party does not know of the principal's existence, it would be unrealistic to speak of apparent *authority*, for the agent does not appear to have "authority" at all; rather it seems that the agent is the owner of the property. To deal with this situation, the courts developed the doctrine of apparent ownership, which runs parallel to that of apparent authority. Under this doctrine, the sort of conduct which, on the part of a disclosed principal, amounts to "holding out" someone as an agent will, on the part of an undisclosed principal, amount to holding out the agent as owner. This idea in fact forms part of a wider rule, contained in section 21(1) of the Sale of Goods Act 1979, which provides:

Subject to this Act, where goods are sold by a person who is not their owner, and who does not sell them under the authority or with the consent of the owner, the buyer acquires no better title to the goods than the seller had, unless the owner of the goods is by his conduct precluded from denying the seller's authority to sell.

As regards the kind of conduct which will preclude the owner of goods from denying the validity of the sale, it is well established that merely giving a person possession of goods or of documents of title does not amount to a representation that that person either owns

---

1 *Lloyds & Scottish Finance Ltd* v *Williamson* [1965] 1 All ER 641.

the goods or is authorised to sell or pledge them.[1] If this were not so, then the fraudulent sale of goods which are being acquired on hire-purchase would operate to confer title on the buyer, something which is not the case.[2]

It appears, then that some additional factor is required, something which goes further towards clothing the seller with the appearance of ownership. In *Rimmer v Webster*,[3] for example, a stockbroker who was asked to sell a mortgage bond for a client persuaded the client to transfer the bond to him. The transfer was duly registered, took the form prescribed by statute and stated that the stockbroker had paid £2,000 for the bond. It was held that the client had clearly given the broker the appearance of ownership so that, when the latter pledged the bond to secure a loan, it was held that the pledgee was entitled to retain it until his advance was repaid.

The decision in *Rimmer v Webster* seems eminently fair and reasonable; it is difficult to see what more the client could have done to enable the broker to masquerade as owner of the bond. Much more difficult are cases where the only positive representation of ownership comes from the dishonest "agent", and where it is argued that the true owner is guilty of negligence in permitting this to occur. As to such cases, all that can be said is that the *possibility* of "estoppel by negligence" has been recognised by both the House of Lords[4] and the Court of Appeal;[5] however, all attempts to establish such an estoppel on the facts of particular cases have so far proved unsuccessful.

(b) *The Factors Act 1889*

The effect of this Act is to confer upon those who fall within its scope a kind of usual authority to dispose of goods. The crucial provision is section 2(1), which provides:

Where a mercantile agent is, with the consent of the owner, in possession of goods or of the documents of title to goods, any sale, pledge, or other

---

1 *Colonial Bank* v *Cady* (1890) 15 App Cas 267; *Central Newbury Car Auctions Ltd* v *Unity Finance Ltd* [1957] 1 QB 371.

2 Except where a motor vehicle is wrongfully disposed of to a private purchaser: Hire-Purchase Act 1964, Part III (as re-enacted by the Consumer Credit Act 1974).

3 [1902] 2 Ch 163: see also *Eastern Distributors Ltd* v *Goldring* [1957] 2 QB 600.

4 *Moorgate Mercantile Co Ltd* v *Twitchings* [1976] AC 890.

5 *Mercantile Credit Co Ltd* v *Hamblin* [1965] 2 QB 242; *Beverley Acceptances Ltd* v *Oakley* [1982] RTR 417.

disposition of the goods, made by him when acting in the ordinary course of business of a mercantile agent, shall, subject to the provisions of this Act, be as valid as if he were expressly authorised by the owner of the goods to make the same; provided that the person taking under the disposition acts in good faith, and has not at the time of the disposition notice that the person making the disposition has not authority to make the same.

It is worth noting that the Act does not refer to the agent as a "factor" but as a "mercantile agent", defined in section 1(1) as "a mercantile agent having in the customary course of his business as such agent authority either to sell goods, or to consign goods for the purpose of sale, or to buy goods, or to raise money on the security of goods". This definition serves to exclude such persons as carriers and warehousemen who, while they may have possession of goods, are not customarily authorised to sell them. However, it is not necessary for the person concerned to be in business as a recognised kind of commercial agent. Thus, an agent may fall within the Factors Act despite acting for only one principal and in only one series of transactions,[1] provided at least that this is not simply a private favour for a friend.[2]

In order for a disposition to be protected under the Act, the person making it must have been in possession of the goods. Moreover, that possession must have been acquired in the capacity of a mercantile agent. In accordance with this principle, a private motor dealer who took possession of a client's car merely to clean and service it with a view of its subsequent sale was held unable to pass title to a third party.[3] Similarly, a self-drive car hire firm which had taken a new car under a hire-purchase agreement was held not to have received it as a mercantile agent; the finance company was accordingly held entitled to recover the car from an innocent purchaser.[4]

As to "the consent of the owner", it has been held that a mercantile agent who obtains possession of goods under an illegal contract cannot rely on this to show the owner's consent.[5] However, consent is not vitiated by fraud upon the agent's part,

---

1 *Lowther* v *Harris* [1927] 1 KB 393.
2 *Budberg* v *Jerwood & Ward* (1934) 51 TLR 99.
3 *Henderson* v *Prosser* [1982] CLY 21.
4 *Astley Industrial Trust Ltd* v *Miller* [1968] 2 All ER 36.
5 *Belvoir Finance Co Ltd* v *Harold G Cole & Co Ltd* [1969] 2 All ER 904.

unless it is established that the owner never intended to part with possession at all.[1]

An aspect of the Factors Act which has given rise to some difficulties of interpretation is the requirement that the agent be acting "in the ordinary course of business of a mercantile agent". This, it has been held, means mercantile agents in general, rather than the one concerned in the actual case, so that a disposition may be validated by what is common in commercial transactions generally, even if it is not usual in the particular trade concerned.[2] More importantly, it has been held that what matters is not whether a disposition appears to the third party to be in the ordinary course of business, but whether objectively speaking it is so. In *Pearson* v *Rose & Young Ltd*,[3] a car owner consented to a mercantile agent having possession of the car; he did not, however, intend to let the agent have the registration book. The agent, having obtained the registration book by a trick, sold the car to the defendants. It was held that, since the sale of a second-hand car without its registration book is not "in the ordinary course of business",[4] the sale of such a car together with the book is equally not protected where the book has been obtained without the owner's consent.

The reasoning of this decision seems somewhat suspect, but it was followed by a differently constituted Court of Appeal in *Stadium Finance Ltd* v *Robbins*.[5] Here the car was left at a dealer's showroom without its ignition key, but with the log-book locked inside the glove compartment. The dealer, having obtained a duplicate key, was in a position to offer to a buyer the car together with its registration book and a key. Nevertheless, the sale was held not to be within the ordinary course of business, so that the buyer did not acquire a good title to the car.

The final requirement of the Factors Act is that the buyer must have acted in good faith. As to this, it has been held that where a transaction is of an inherently suspicious nature, it may lead to the conclusion that the third party should have made enquiries about

---

1 *Pearson* v *Rose & Young Ltd* [1951] 1 KB 275; *Stadium Finance Ltd* v *Robbins* [1962] 2 QB 664.
2 *Oppenheimer* v *Attenborough & Son* [1908] 1 KB 221.
3 [1951] 1 KB 275.
4 *Henderson* v *Prosser* [1982] CLY 21.
5 [1962] 2 QB 664.

the agent's authority. For example, a pledgee who charged an unusually high rate of interest might raise doubts as to his honesty;[1] and it has been suggested that the absence of a log-book should put the purchaser of a second-hand car upon enquiry.[2] In such a case, however, the book must actually be missing; a purchaser cannot be blamed for not realising that it was obtained without the owner's consent.[3]

3 Torts

It may be stated at the outset that a person who expressly authorises or subsequently ratifies the commission of a tortious act by an agent will incur liability in respect of it. Such liability is regarded as "personal", in the sense that the elements of whatever tort is in issue (particularly in relation to knowledge or state of mind) must be proved against the principal.

Leaving aside cases of this kind, there is no general rule of law by which an agent's tort serves to impose liability upon the principal. Such vicarious liability is normally found where there is a relationship of employer and employee; however, the client of an independent contractor is only liable where the contractor's actions amount to a breach of some non-delegable duty which the law imposes personally upon that client. Thus, since the category of "agents" embraces both employees and independent contractors, it is clear that there is no single principle to govern agents' torts.

Notwithstanding what has been said, there are two areas in which, for very different reasons, the law holds a principal liable for the torts of an agent. These may now be considered.

(a) *Misrepresentation*

Actions for deceit and negligent misstatement are undoubtedly tortious in nature. Nevertheless, the statements which give rise to such actions are frequently made by agents who are employed either to make a contract or at least to negotiate one. Perhaps because of this interweaving of the rules of tort and contract, it is well established that a principal is liable for fraudulent[4] statements

---

1 *Janesich* v *Attenborough & Son* (1910) 102 LT 605.
2 *Pearson* v *Rose & Young Ltd* [1951] 1 KB 275.
3 *Stadium Finance Ltd* v *Robbins* [1962] 2 QB 664.
4 And presumably negligent.

made by the agent within the scope of authority, which, it should be remembered, includes implied usual authority.[1] Thus in *Gordon v Selico Co Ltd*,[2] where a builder deliberately covered up dry rot in a flat which was about to be let, it was held that the landlords could not be held directly responsible for this, since it is not within a builder's authority to make statements about a property.[3] However, the evidence showed that the managing agents of this block of flats knew what the builder had done and were thus also guilty of fraud; the landlords *were* therefore responsible, since the making of statements about a property undoubtedly falls within the usual authority of managing agents.

The liability which is thus imposed upon the principal may arise even where the fraudulent statement is made for the agent's own purposes. In *Lloyd v Grace, Smith & Co*[4] the plaintiff sought advice from the defendant solicitors about two properties which she owned. She dealt entirely with the defendants' managing clerk, who fraudulently induced her to transfer the properties to him; he then disposed of them and misappropriated the proceeds. The House of Lords held that, by allowing the managing clerk to deal with clients, the defendants had given him apparent authority to conduct certain types of business. The fraud which was committed fell within the scope of this apparent authority and the defendants were accordingly liable for it, notwithstanding that the clerk had acted entirely for his own benefit.

The tort of deceit, which consists of knowingly making a false statement with the intention that it should be acted upon, raises one particular problem in relation to agency. This is where the agent makes a false statement innocently, while the principal, who knows the truth, is unaware that the statement is being made.[5] In *Cornfoot v Fowke*,[6] an agent told the prospective tenant of a house that there was nothing objectionable about it. In truth, as the principal (though not the agent) knew all too well, the house was next door

---

1 See *Mullens v Miller* (1882) 22 ChD 194: p 89.
2 [1986] 1 EGLR 71.
3 Deliberate concealment of defects is regarded in law as a "statement" that none exist.
4 [1912] AC 716.
5 If the principal intends that the agent should make the offending statement, he is personally guilty of fraud: *Ludgater v Love* (1881) 44 LT 694.
6 (1840) 6 M&W 358.

to a brothel. The tenant sued the principal for fraud, but the action failed. A similar point arose in the case of *Armstrong* v *Strain*,[1] which concerned the sale of a much-underpinned bungalow. The vendor did not mention this fact to the estate agents, who innocently misrepresented its condition to the purchaser. Devlin J, whose decision was affirmed by the Court of Appeal, concluded that neither vendor nor estate agent was liable for fraud, since "you cannot add an innocent state of mind to an innocent state of mind and get as a result a dishonest state of mind".[2]

The vicarious liability of a principal for statements made by his agent has, in England, been restricted to cases of misrepresentation. The High Court of Australia, however, has imposed liability upon a principal whose agent, in canvassing for business, systematically and maliciously defamed the principal's business rivals, by whom the agent had previously been employed.[3]

(b) *Motor vehicles*

At a time when the Road Traffic Act provisions for compulsory third-party insurance were far less comprehensive than they are today, the courts were concerned that the victims of road accidents should not be left uncompensated if a negligent driver turned out to be insolvent and uninsured. This concern led to the development of a doctrine known as "casual delegation", under which liability may be imposed upon the owner of a motor vehicle for the tortious negligence of a person driving it. The driver, in such a case, is hardly the "agent" of the owner in any generally accepted sense; nevertheless, it is the language of agency which has been used to create this area of liability.

The crucial element of casual delegation is that the vehicle is being driven in the interests of its owner, whether the owner is also in the vehicle at the time[4] or not.[5] It is not sufficient that the driver has the owner's *permission*, as for example where a son borrows

---

1 [1952] 1 KB 232.
2 [1951] 1 TLR 856 at p 872.
3 *Colonial Mutual Life Assurance Society Ltd* v *Producers and Citizens Co-operative Assurance Co of Australia Ltd* (1931) 46 CLR 41.
4 As in *Pratt* v *Patrick* [1924] 1 KB 488.
5 As in *Ormrod* v *Crosville Motor Services Ltd* [1953] 2 All ER 753.

his father's car in order to drive two of his own friends home.[1] Indeed, the House of Lords even refused to impose liability where a husband asked a friend to drive him home in a car which was owned by his wife; it was held that English law would not treat this as a "family" or even a "matrimonial" car, even though the two spouses used it indiscriminately.[2]

4 Other matters

The "transactions" described above probably represent the most significant aspects of an agent's power to render the principal liable, but they do not exhaust the possibilities. For example, there are certain criminal offences (mainly those involving "strict" or "absolute" liability) in which the misconduct of the agent may expose the principal to prosecution.

Of more general commercial importance is the question of serving notice on[3] an agent under some statute, rule of common law or contractual provision. Whether this constitutes a valid service on the principal depends ultimately on the extent of the agent's authority to receive the notice, and it may be noted that the usual authority of an estate agent or surveyor in this respect is extremely limited.[4] More surprisingly, perhaps, there is no general assumption that a solicitor has authority to receive notice on behalf of a client,[5] although evidence that such authority has in fact been given may not be too hard to find.[6]

C Termination of agency

It remains in this chapter to consider the various ways by which an agency relationship may be brought to an end, and the effect which this has on the rights and oblations of the parties.

---

1 *Hewitt* v *Bonvin* [1940] 1 KB 188.
2 *Morgans* v *Launchbury* [1973] AC 127.
3 Or, occasionally, by an agent: see *Lawrence Chemical Co Ltd* v *Rubenstein* [1982] 1 All ER 653.
4 See *Robert Baxendale Ltd* v *Davstone (Holdings) Ltd* [1982] 3 All ER 496.
5 *Saffron Walden Second Benefit Building Society* v *Rayner* (1880) 14 ChD 406; *Tate* v *Hyslop* (1885) 15 QBD 368; *Singer* v *Trustee of the Property of Munro* [1981] 3 All ER 215.
6 See, for example, *Westway Homes Ltd* v *Moores* [1991] 2 EGLR 193.

1   Termination by agreement

The agency relationship is based upon agreement of the parties, and it is their agreement (properly interpreted) which primarily determines its duration. In *Danby* v *Coutts & Co*,[1] for example, the plaintiff executed a power of attorney which, after reciting that the plaintiff was going abroad for a time and wished representatives to act for him during his absence, appointed two persons to be his attorneys. It was held that the authority conferred upon these attorneys was only operative while the plaintiff was abroad; he was accordingly not bound by a fraudulent transaction carried out by the attorneys after his return.

In interpreting an agency agreement for this purpose, effect should be given to any trade customs which may be applicable. Thus in *Lawford & Co* v *Harris*,[2] where stockbrokers were instructed to sell certain shares for a client at a named price, they carried out this instruction after the end of the current account. The shares subsequently increased in value, and the client successfully claimed that the sale was unauthorised, on the basis of a custom that, in the absence of agreement to the contrary, a broker's authority did not extend beyond the current account.

Where there is no reason to limit an agent's authority to a certain period of time, it nevertheless comes to an end when the agent completes the task for which he or she was appointed. This means, for example, that a selling agent's authority terminates at the moment the sale is completed; the principal will accordingly not be bound by a subsequent agreement between the agent and the purchaser to alter the terms on which payment is to be made[3] or to rescind the sale.[4]

1   Termination by unilateral action

Agency, in common with other relationships which involve the provision of personal services, will not be enforced in court by the grant of an order of specific performance.[5] As a result, while a party who withdraws from the relationship in breach of contract may

---

1 (1885) 29 ChD 500.
2 (1896) 12 TLR 275: see also *Dickinson* v *Lilwall* (1815) 4 Camp 279.
3 *Blackburn* v *Scholes* (1810) 2 Camp 341.
4 *Nelson* v *Aldridge* (1818) 2 Stark 435.
5 *Clarke* v *Price* (1819) 2 Wils Ch 157; *Chinnock* v *Sainsbury* (1860) 30 LJ Ch 409.

have to pay damages, the withdrawal itself will none the less be effective.[1] Indeed, the courts will not lightly impose liability in the form of damages, for there is a presumption that an agency relationship is terminable at the will of either party, even where it was originally created by deed[2] or for valuable consideration.[3]

The presumption of terminability is especially strong in the case of agents who are employed solely upon a commission basis.[4] Where, however, the agency bears a closer resemblance to a contract of employment, the agent will normally be entitled to a period of notice of dismissal (which means in effect that the principal must pay compensation based on what the agent would have earned during that period).[5] Thus, for example, in *Martin-Baker Aircraft Co Ltd* v *Murison*,[6] where the plaintiff manufacturers of ejector seats appointed the defendant as their "sole selling agent for all their products ... on the North American Continent", it was held that the defendant was entitled to 12 months' notice of termination of this agreement. However, an agent who would otherwise be entitled to notice will forfeit that entitlement, and may thus be instantly dismissed, in cases of serious misconduct such as taking bribes,[7] and possibly even where the agent is guilty of causing loss to the principal through negligence.[8]

Problems similar to those caused by the premature dismissal of an agent may also arise where the principal, without actually revoking the agent's authority, effectively nullifies its value to the agent by closing down the business to which it relates. The basic rule in such cases is that the agent, to recover damages for loss of anticipated earnings, must be able to prove a breach by the principal of some express or implied term of the contract of agency. Thus in *Rhodes* v *Forwood*,[9] where a colliery owner appointed a

---

1 *Whitwood Chemical Co* v *Hardman* [1891] 2 Ch 416; *Page One Records Ltd* v *Britton* [1967] 3 All ER 822.
2 *Bromley* v *Holland* (1802) 7 Ves 3 at p 28 *per* Lord Eldon LC.
3 *Chinnock* v *Sainsbury* (1860) 30 LJ Ch 409.
4 *Alexander* v *Davis & Co* (1885) 2 TLR 142; *Motion* v *Michaud* (1892) 8 TLR 253.
5 *Parker* v *Ibbetson* (1858) 4 CBNS 346; *Barrett* v *Gilmour & Co* (1901) 17 TLR 292.
6 [1955] 2 QB 556.
7 *Boston Deep Sea Fishing & Ice Co* v *Ansell* (1888) 39 ChD 339.
8 See *Cussons* v *Skinner* (1843) 11 M&W 161.
9 (1876) 1 App Cas 256: see also *French & Co Ltd* v *Leeston Shipping Co Ltd* [1922] 1 AC 451.

firm of brokers to be sole agents for seven years for the sale of his coal in Liverpool, but sold the colliery after four years, the brokers failed in their claim for damages. It was held that the contract did not expressly bind the colliery owner to supply any coal for sale by the brokers, and there was no reason to imply any term to this effect.

Rhodes v *Forwood* may be contrasted with *Turner* v *Goldsmith*,[1] where a shirt manufacturer expressly agreed to employ a traveller for five years. The principal's factory was destroyed by fire after only two years had elapsed, but this, it was held, did not release him from the specific obligation into which he had freely entered.

It should finally be noted that, even where an agency is terminable at will, this does not mean that the termination can take effect before the agent is notified of it. Indeed the presumption is very much to the contrary.[2] However, this presumption is subject to any contrary intention, express or implied, and it is clear that estate agents form an important exception to the general rule. It was accepted by the Court of Appeal in *EP Nelson & Co* v *Rolfe*[3] that the authority given to an estate agent, to find someone willing to purchase the client's property, would automatically terminate if the client exchanged contracts with another purchaser; hence, the estate agent would be unable to earn commission on an introduction made after that time, even if the agent was unaware that the property had already been sold.

3   Termination by operation of law

An agency relationship may be brought to an end automatically by certain supervening events, which serve to incapacitate the principal or the agent in either a legal or a practical sense. In the case of the principal, such events include death (whether known to the agent or not),[4] and winding up, which is the equivalent of death where the principal is a limited company.[5] The mental incompetence of the principal will also operate to terminate

---

1 [1891] 1 QB 544: see also *Warren & Co* v *Agdeshman* (1922) 38 TLR 588.
2 *Re Oriental Bank Corporation, ex parte Guillemin* (1884) 28 ChD 634.
3 [1950] 1 KB 139: see also *AA Dickson & Co* v *O'Leary* (1979) 254 EG 731: p 141.
4 *Blades* v *Free* (1829) 9 B&C 167.
5 *Salton* v *New Beeston Cycle Co* [1900] 1 Ch 43.

agency,[1] although it should be noted that, under the Enduring Powers of Attorney Act 1985, it is now possible for a principal to execute a power of attorney which will survive the principal's subsequent insanity.[2] To achieve this effect, various prescribed formalities must be complied with and the agent, on realising that the principal is becoming mentally incapable, must register the power of attorney with the Court of Protection, having first given notice to certain of the principal's relatives.

Where the principal becomes bankrupt, this will normally bring the agency to an end,[3] although it will not deprive the agent of authority formally to complete a transaction already binding on the principal.[4]

As for the agent, death[5] and mental incompetence are again established as terminating events. However, the agent's bankruptcy will only be so where its effect is to prevent the agent from carrying out what he or she was appointed to do.[6]

Apart from these specific examples of personal catastrophe, a contract of agency will be terminated under the doctrine of frustration wherever its continuance would be impossible, illegal or completely impracticable. Thus, when war is declared, the agent's conscription[7] or internment as an enemy alien may have this effect, provided that it is sufficiently long-term to frustrate the purpose of the agency.[8]

4 Limitations on termination

Where an agent is given authority, by deed or for valuable consideration, in order to effect a security or protect an interest of the agent, the authority cannot be revoked by the principal while the security or interest continues in existence.[9] Furthermore, the authority in these circumstances will not be terminated by the death,

---

1 *Yonge* v *Toynbee* [1910] 1 KB 215.
2 For the mental capacity required to execute such a power: see *Re K; Re F* [1988] Ch 310.
3 *Dawson* v *Sexton* (1823) 1 LJOS 185.
4 *Dixon* v *Ewart* (1817) Buck 94.
5 *Farrow* v *Wilson* (1869) LR 4 CP 744.
6 *McCall* v *Australian Meat Co Ltd* (1870) 19 WR 188.
7 *Marshall* v *Glanvill* [1917] 2 KB 87.
8 *Nordman* v *Rayner & Sturges* (1916) 33 TLR 87.
9 *Gaussen* v *Morton* (1830) 10 B&C 731.

insanity or bankruptcy of the principal.[1] However, authority is only irrevocable on this basis where it is given specifically to protect the agent's interest; it is not sufficient merely to show that the agent was owed money by the principal at the time.[2]

The common law rules described above are now largely repeated in the Powers of Attorney Act 1971, section 4. However, this provision is of somewhat narrower scope in that it only applies to authority given in the form of a deed and only where that authority is actually *expressed* to be irrevocable. If these conditions are not met, there appears to be nothing to prevent the agent from relying on the principles of common law.

5 Effects of termination

Although the termination of an agency relationship in any of the ways described above will serve to deprive the agent of any express or implied authority to act on the principal's behalf, a third party who is unaware of the terminating event may continue to rely on the agent's apparent authority. This is certainly so where the termination results from the parties' actions[3] or from the principal's insanity,[4] although it seems that apparent authority too will cease to operate on the principal's death.[5] Further protection for innocent third parties, at least where the agent's authority is conferred by deed, is given by the Powers of Attorney act 1971, section 5(2).

Termination may bear harshly upon an agent who, being unaware of it, continues to act. If the agent's actions are binding on the principal under the doctrine of apparent authority, then the agent will be liable for any loss caused on the basis that, as between principal and agent, the act was unauthorised.[6] Conversely, if the principal is not bound, then the agent will be personally liable to the third party for breach of warranty of authority.[7] However, statute has again provided some protection for the innocent, at least those whose authority is conferred by deed. Section 5(1) of the Powers of

---

1 *Alley* v *Hotson* (1815) 4 Camp 325; *Carter* v *White* (1883) 25 ChD 666.
2 *Raleigh* v *Atkinson* (1840) 6 M & W 670; *Smart* v *Sandars* (1848) 5 CB 895.
3 *Trueman* v *Loder* (1840) 11 A&E 589.
4 *Drew* v *Nunn* (1879) 4 QBD 661.
5 *Blades* v *Free* (1829) 9 B&C 167.
6 *Re Overweg, Haas* v *Durant* [1900] 1 Ch 209.
7 *Yonge* v *Toynbee* [1910] 1 KB 215.

Attorney Act 1971 provides:

A donee of a power of attorney who acts in pursuance of the power at a time when it has been revoked shall not, by reason of the revocation, incur any liability (either to the donor or to any other person) if at that time he did not know that the power had been revoked.

As to the rights which are normally enjoyed by agents, these are presumed to cease at the moment of termination, so that the agent will not be entitled to remuneration,[1] or even to an indemnity,[2] in respect of transactions effected after that time. However, termination cannot deprive an agent of rights which have already accrued, such as the right to be reimbursed for expenses incurred on the principal's business.[3]

The question of accrued rights has given rise to particular difficulties in relation to those selling agents whose contracts entitle them to "continuing commission" in respect of orders placed after the termination of their agency by customers whom they have introduced. In deciding whether such a right exists, the courts pay great attention to the actual words of the agreement[4] and appear generally reluctant to imply a term to this effect where none is expressed.[5] Indeed, even express mention of "repeat orders" is not conclusive, since that could mean those repeat orders placed prior to the termination of the agency.[6] However, it may be noted that, where an agent *is* entitled to continuing commission, this can be a most valuable right, since the entitlement may last until the "crack of doom".[7]

---

1 *Farrow* v *Wilson* (1869) LR 4 CP 744.
2 *Pool* v *Pool* (1889) 58 LJP 67.
3 *Chappell* v *Bray* (1860) 6 H&N 145.
4 In the light of the course of dealing between the parties: *Roberts* v *Elwells Engineers Ltd* [1972] 2 QB 586.
5 See *Sellers* v *London Counties Newspapers* [1951] 1 KB 784.
6 *Crocker Horlock Ltd* v *B Lang & Co Ltd* [1949] 1 All ER 526.
7 *British Bank for Foreign Trade Ltd* v *Novinex Ltd* [1949] 1 KB 623.

CHAPTER 2

The legal position of agents

The previous chapter, in considering the concept of authority on which much of the law of agency is based, concentrated mainly on the relationship between the principal and a third party with whom the agent deals. This chapter, on the other hand, is concerned with the legal position of the agent. Attention will therefore be given to the rights and obligations of the agent *vis-à-vis* the principal, and also to the legal relationship (if any) which exists between the agent and the third party. Finally, the position of subagents will receive separate consideration.

A Duties to the principal

1 Positive action

As a general rule, an agent whose appointment is contractual (and who is therefore to be paid for carrying out services) owes a positive duty to the principal to carry out those services.[1] If this cannot be done, then the agent must at least inform the principal, in order that the latter's interests can be safeguarded. The only exception to this is that the agent is not obliged to enter into any transaction which would be contrary to law.[2] Thus, an agent who failed to place bets as instructed was held not liable for the amount which the principal would have won, for these "winnings" would have been legally irrecoverable.[3]

A gratuitous agent does not, it appears, owe any duty of positive action to the principal.[4] In legal terms, such an agent is liable only

---

1 *Smith* v *Lascelles* (1788) 2 Term Rep 187; *Turpin* v *Bilton* (1843) 5 Man & G 455.
2 *Webster* v *De Tastet* (1797) 7 Term Rep 157.
3 *Cohen* v *Kittell* (1889) 22 QBD 680.
4 *Coggs* v *Bernard* (1703) 2 Ld Raym 909; *Elsee* v *Gatward* (1793) 5 Term Rep 143; *Balfe* v *West* (1853) 13 CB 466.

for misfeasance and not for nonfeasance.[1] Indeed, there are strong suggestions that an estate agent is in a similar position, that is to say, under no positive obligation to seek a purchaser for a client's property, at least where there is no "sole agency". This possibility is considered in detail in chapter 4.[2]

2 Obedience

As we saw in the last chapter, it is quite possible for a principal to be held responsible for something done by an agent, even where there has been a direct contravention of the agent's instructions.[3] In terms of the relationship between principal and agent, however, the express instructions are paramount; an agent who disobeys these will be automatically liable for any loss which is thereby caused to the principal. Thus in *Lilley* v *Doubleday*,[4] for example, where the defendant undertook to deposit the plaintiff's goods in his own warehouse, but in fact stored some of the goods elsewhere, he was held liable when they were destroyed in a fire, even though the fire was not caused by any fault on the defendant's part.

An agent's duty of obedience takes precedence over the duty to exercise all reasonable care and skill in the principal's interests. Thus in *Bertram, Armstrong & Co* v *Godfray*,[5] where stockbrokers were instructed to sell stock "when the funds should be at 85 per cent or above that price", they delayed in selling at that price because they believed that it would rise further. The stock fell and the brokers were held liable for the client's losses; the instructions here were so clear as to leave no discretion in the matter. The only valid excuse for outright disobedience is that the instructions are unlawful, so that, where an auction sale is stated to be "without reserve", the auctioneer is entitled to ignore a secret reserve which the vendor seeks to impose.[6]

The strict principle which was applied in *Bertram* v *Godfray* assumes that the agent's instructions are capable of only one

---

1 Whether there is any obligation to warn the principal is a difficult and so far unresolved issue.
2 See p 98.
3 This will apply, for example, to cases of apparent or usual authority.
4 (1881) 7 QBD 510.
5 (1830) 1 Knapp 381: see also *Fray* v *Voules* (1859) 1 E&E 839.
6 *Bexwell* v *Christie* (1776) 1 Cowp 395: p 270.

interpretation. If they are ambiguous, an agent who acts upon a reasonable interpretation is not liable merely because it later transpires that it is not the correct one. In *Weigall & Co v Runciman & Co*,[1] for example, a foreign shipowner sent a telegram to a firm of shipbrokers instructing them to "fix steamer", by which he meant them to hire one for him. The shipbrokers, interpreting "fix" as meaning "let", let one of the shipowner's vessels to a third party at the rate specified in the telegram. It was held that, since the interpretation of the shipbrokers was reasonable, the fact that it was incorrect did not entitle the shipowner to repudiate the charter.

It should also be noted that an agent's instructions may actually be intended to confer a degree of discretion on the agent. Where this is so, the agent will not be liable provided that the discretion is exercised in a fair and reasonable manner;[2] at this point, the agent's "duty of obedience" effectively merges with the duty to exercise reasonable care and skill.

3 Care and skill

In acting on behalf of a principal, an agent is under a duty to exercise such care and skill as is reasonable in all the circumstances of the case. If the agency is based on a contract (which means that the agent is being paid for services rendered), the common law implied term as to care and skill is now contained in section 13 of the Supply of Goods and Services Act 1982, at least as regards services carried out by the agent "in the course of a business".[3] However, statutory instruments have specifically excluded certain categories of services from the operation of section 13. These are the services rendered by an arbitrator;[4] "the services of an advocate in court or before any tribunal, inquiry or arbitrator and in carrying out preliminary work directly affecting the conduct

---

1 (1916) 85 LJKB 1187.
2 *Boden* v *French* (1851) 10 CB 886; *Ireland* v *Livingston* (1872) LR 5 HL 395.
3 The Act also imposes a duty to carry out services within a reasonable time: section 14.
4 SI 1985 No 1.

of the hearing";[1] and "the services rendered to a company by a director of the company in his capacity as such".[2]

It is worth noting that what section 13 implies into contracts for services is described as a *term* rather than a *condition*. As a result, while a breach of this provision renders the agent liable to pay damages for any loss suffered by the client, it does not inevitably disentitle the agent to payment. Whether or not it will have this effect depends upon the seriousness of the agent's breach.

Where there is no contractual relationship between the parties (as where the agency is gratuitous), any duty of care must arise in tort.[3] That a duty can arise in such circumstances, even between private individuals, was recognised by the Court of Appeal in *Chaudhry* v *Prabhakar*. The plaintiff[4] there, who knew nothing about cars, asked the defendant, a close friend, to find a suitable car for her to purchase. The plaintiff stressed that she did not want a vehicle which had been involved in an accident; the car which she bought on the defendant's recommendation turned out to have been crashed and rebuilt, as the defendant ought reasonably to have known. Counsel for the defendant conceded that in such circumstances a duty of care was owed (though arguing about the standard of their duty), and a majority of the Court of Appeal regarded the concession as properly made.

We noted above that an agent's duty of care is subordinate to the duty of obedience, so that the agent cannot excuse disobedience by claiming to have acted in the principal's best interests. This principle may on occasion work in the agent's favour, in that an agent who carries out the principal's imprudent instructions will not normally be liable for negligence. In *Overend, Gurney & Co* v *Gibb*,[5] where a company was formed for the express purpose of taking over an existing business, the directors were held not liable for negligence in failing to perceive that this was not a sound investment, since they were merely carrying out the terms of their

---

1 Confirming and extending the immunity of barristers (and probably other advocates) conferred by the House of Lords in *Rondel* v *Worsley* [1969] 1 AC 191 and *Saif Ali* v *Sydney Mitchell & Co* [1980] AC 198.
2 SI 1982, No 1771.
3 Under *Hedley Byrne & Co Ltd* v *Heller & Partners Ltd* [1964] AC 465.
4 *Chaudhry* v *Prabhakar* [1988] 3 All ER 718.
5 (1872) LR 5 HL 480.

authority. It should, however, be noted that, where an agent is employed in a general capacity because of professional expertise, there may well an implied obligation to warn the principal that certain instructions are clearly unwise.

As far as the *standard* of skill and care demanded of an agent is concerned, the law at one time drew a sharp distinction between gratuitous agents and those paid for their services.[1] It was said that, while a paid agent must be judged by the standards of the trade in which he or she practised, a gratuitous agent would be subject to a more flexible standard. Where such agents claimed to possess the skill necessary for a particular enterprise, they would be judged accordingly; in the absence of any representation of ability, however, they need exhibit no greater degree of care and skill than they would use in their own affairs.

A neat example of this highly subjective test may be found in *Shiells* v *Blackburne*,[2] where the defendant entered two parcels of leather at the Customs for export. The parcels, one of which belonged to the defendant and the other to his principal, were wrongly described and, as a result, both were impounded. It was held that the defendant was not liable to his principal for, while acting gratuitously, he had clearly exercised as much skill in the principal's affairs as in his own!

There may be something to be said for the view that a person who obtains the services of an agent free of charge should take them as they are, and should thus bear the risk of the agent's incompetence. However, such a subjective approach would be out of keeping with modern trends in the law of tort, and it seems that a court today would prefer to enquire whether an agent had exercised the degree of care and skill which could reasonably to be expected in the circumstances, while recognising that the agent's status (paid or gratuitous) might be a relevant factor in this objective equation.[3]

4 Duty of loyalty

Every agent owes to the principal a duty of loyalty which arises automatically out of the fiduciary nature of their relationship. This

---

1 See *Beal* v *South Devon Railway Co* (1864) 3 H&C 337.
2 (1789) 1 HBL 158.
3 See *Chaudhry* v *Prabhakar* [1988] 3 All ER 718.

duty appears in a vast range of circumstances, but the underlying principle always remains the same: the agent must not allow personal interest, or the interest of a third party, to come into conflict with the interests of the principal, except where the principal has full knowledge of the facts and gives consent. The duty thus imposed is sometimes referred to as a "duty of fidelity" or "duty of good faith", but this should not be taken to mean that a breach of the duty requires bad faith on the agent's part. The truth is that liability here is strict; an agent is in breach of the duty of loyalty wherever a conflict of interest is permitted to arise, although the agent's "innocence" may have a bearing on the remedies available to the principal.[1]

Although, as mentioned above, the duty of loyalty arises in many different circumstances, it is convenient to classify these into three main groups. It should be borne in mind, however, that this formulation is not at all rigid; indeed, and many of the reported cases might be regarded as falling under two or even all three headings.

(a) *Personal interest of agent*

An agent who is instructed to carry out a particular transaction must make full disclosure to the principal of any personal interest which the agent may have in the matter. The most important illustration of this lies in the rule that an agent may neither acquire property from,[2] nor transfer property to,[3] the principal, unless the agent's position is made perfectly clear. Other, less direct, examples of prohibited conflicts are discussed in later chapters dealing specifically with estate agents and auctioneers.

The duty to disclose any personal interest is an extremely strict one. In the first place, it is clear that disclosure must be full (in the sense that all material facts must be revealed); it is not enough for the agent merely to put the principal on inquiry.[4] Again, it makes no difference that the agent may have made no direct profit out of

---

1 See p 53.
2 *McPherson* v *Watt* (1877) 3 App Cas 254.
3 *Gillett* v *Peppercorne* (1840) 3 Beav 78; *Headway Construction Co* v *Downham* (1974) 233 EG 675.
4 *Dunne* v *English* (1874) LR 18 Eq 524.

the transaction,[1] nor that the transaction is fair or even for the principal's benefit;[2] an agent who has not disclosed a personal interest is in breach of duty, and the principal is entitled to redress. The duty may even extend so as to prevent an ex-agent from contracting with the ex-principal, at least where the ex-agent has concealed material facts at the time of termination[3] or is making improper use of confidential information acquired during the agency.[4]

The principal's remedies in cases of non-disclosure include having the offending transaction set aside. This right to rescission is not affected by any intervening fall in the value of the property, which must be borne by the agent;[5] however, rescission may be ruled out by other matters, for example by the fact that the property concerned is now in the hands of an innocent third party. Alternatively, the principal may choose to affirm the transaction and to demand that the agent hand over any profit made from it. Thus, where an agent has in breach of duty acquired property from the principal, the latter may claim whatever profit the agent has made by reselling that property.[6] So too, where an agent buys property in order to sell to the principal, the latter is entitled to have it at cost price.[7] It appears, however, that if the agent sells to the principal property which the agent already owned, the principal must either rescind or establish that the property has been sold above its true value; if it has not, the agent is not accountable for any profit made.[8]

(b) *Secret profits*

The foregoing discussion makes it clear that an agent's duty to avoid conflicts of interest applies whether or not the agent profits from any conflict. However, the making of an undisclosed profit is

1 *Salomons* v *Pender* (1865) 3 H&C 639.
2 *Aberdeen Railway Co* v *Blaikie Bros* (1854) 1 Macq 461.
3 *Regier* v *Campbell-Stuart* [1939] Ch 766.
4 See *Nordisk Insulin-laboratorium* v *Gorgate Products Ltd* [1953] Ch 430.
5 *Armstrong* v *Jackson* [1917] 2 KB 822.
6 *De Bussche* v *Alt* (1878) 8 ChD 286.
7 *Regier* v *Campbell-Stuart* [1939] Ch 766. In *Headway Construction Co* v *Downham* (1974) 233 EG 675, the principal also recovered damages for the loss of a chance to have bought the property for even less than the agent paid for it.
8 *Re Cape Breton Co* (1885) 29 ChD 795.

itself a breach of an agent's duty, whether this arises out of dealing with the principal or less directly. The general rule is that an agent is entitled only to whatever remuneration has been agreed; all other benefits arising out of the agency belong in equity to the principal.

The position was clearly stated by Lord Denning MR in *Phipps* v *Boardman*:[1]

It is quite clear that if an agent uses property, with which he has been entrusted by his principal, so as to make a profit for himself out of it, without his principal's consent, then he is accountable for it to his principal ... So also if he uses a position of authority, to which he has been appointed by his principal, so as to gain money by means of it for himself, then also he is accountable to the principal for it ... Likewise with information or knowledge which he has been employed by his principal to collect or discover, or which he has otherwise acquired, for the use of his principal, then again if he turns it to his own use, so as to make a profit by means of it for himself, he is accountable ....

The law reports contain many examples of the kind of "secret profits" which must be handed over to the principal. A shipmaster who used the principal's empty vessel to carry his own cargo was held accountable for the entire profit on resale of that cargo;[2] auctioneers were obliged to pass on to their vendor client the benefit of a reduced rate for advertising which they obtained from newspapers;[3] and even a gratuitous agent, asked to purchase a cavalry outfit for the principal's son, could not charge the principal the full price when he succeeded in negotiating a discount.[4]

These examples may appear fairly obvious; however the case of *English* v *Dedham Vale Properties Ltd*[5] serves as a reminder both of the potential range of the "secret profit" rule and of its strictness. The defendants there, who were negotiating to purchase land from the plaintiff, applied before contracts were exchanged for planning permission to develop the site. The defendants purported to submit this application "as agent" for the plaintiff, but the application was in fact made without the plaintiff's knowledge. Planning permission

---

1 [1965] Ch 922, 1018; affirmed [1967] 2 AC 46.
2 *Shallcross* v *Oldham* (1862) 2 Johns & H 609.
3 *Hippisley* v *Knee Bros* [1905] 1 KB 1.
4 *Turnbull* v *Garden* (1869) 20 LT 218.
5 [1978] 1 All ER 382.

was granted between the exchange of contracts and completion of the sale, and the value of the land was thus considerably enhanced. It was held that the defendants, as "self-appointed agents", were bound to account to the plaintiff for the whole of the profits which had accrued to them out of the grant of planning permission.

The decision in the *English* case was based firmly upon the ruling of the House of Lords in *Boardman* v *Phipps*,[1] which, though not actually a case of agency, laid down principles governing fiduciary relationships generally which are of great importance in the agency context. That case concerned a will trust which included among its assets a substantial shareholding in a private company. The defendants, one of the beneficiaries and the trustees' solicitor, were dissatisfied with this company's financial management, believing that a large part of its assets could be distributed without affecting its profitability as a going concern. Such a course of action necessitated a take-over of the company and, since the trustees did not wish to take this action, the defendants personally acquired a controlling interest. The transaction proved extremely profitable, both to the trust and to the defendants, but one of the other beneficiaries, claiming that the defendants were in a fiduciary position, sued for an account of their profits.

The House of Lords, by a bare majority, held that this claim was entitled to succeed. This was despite the fact that the defendants had acted throughout in good faith, that they had personally taken on the risk of loss in the venture, and that the result of the decision was to give the trustees the benefit of a course of action which they themselves had not been willing to undertake. The only crumb of comfort for the defendants lay in the court's agreement that, having acted honestly for the benefit of the trust, they should be both reimbursed for their expenses and paid a reasonable sum for the work and skill involved in realising this profit.

(c) *Bribes*

In the context of criminal law (for example under the Prevention of Corruption Act 1916), the meaning of the word "bribe" includes an element of corruption, in the sense of a payment made to an agent for an improper purpose. However, it must be appreciated that what

---

1 [1967] 2 AC 46.

the civil law of agency means by a bribe goes very much wider. As was stated in *Industries & General Mortgage Co Ltd* v *Lewis:*[1]

For the purposes of the civil law a bribe means the payment of a secret commission, which only means (i) that the person making the payment makes it to the agent of the other person with whom he is dealing; (ii) that he makes it to that person knowing that that person is acting as the agent of the other person with whom he is dealing; and (iii) that he fails to disclose to the other person with whom he is dealing that he has made that payment to the person whom he knows to be the other person's agent.

As the same judgment went on to explain, once these three elements are proved against the third party, "the law will presume against him that he has acted corruptly, that the agent has been influenced by the payment to the detriment of his principal, and that the principal ... has suffered damage to at least the amount of the bribe". Furthermore, these three presumptions are irrebuttable.[2] The only defence in a case where a payment of this nature has been made is that the principal expected it, for example where the agent was not paid by the principal but was left to look elsewhere for remuneration.[3]

Since it is obvious that any bribe taken by an agent must also constitute a "secret profit", it may be wondered why this topic is given separate treatment. The reason is that, where a bribe has been paid, the principal has a greater range of remedies available. In the first place, the principal may immediately dismiss the agent. Indeed, in *Boston Deep Sea Fishing and Ice Co* v *Ansell*,[4] where a company director received bonuses from two other companies in which he was a shareholder in return for placing orders with them, these bribes were held to justify his dismissal, although they were not discovered until after he had been dismissed for an insufficient reason. Second, the agent loses any right to remuneration, so that an agent who attempts to obtain commission from both sides may well end up with none at all.[5] Third, the principal may elect to repudiate any transaction in respect of which the agent has been

---

1 [1949] 2 All ER 573 at p 575.
2 *Hovenden & Sons* v *Millhoff* (1900) 83 LT 41.
3 *Great Western Insurance Co of New York* v *Cunliffe* (1874) LR 9 Ch App 525.
4 (1888) 39 ChD 339.
5 *Andrews* v *Ramsay & Co* [1903] 2 KB 635; *Fullwood* v *Hurley* [1928] 1 KB 498.

bribed. Thus, in *Shipway* v *Broadwood*[1] a purchaser of two horses was held entitled to avoid the contract upon discovering that the veterinary surgeon, upon whose certificate of soundness the sale depended, had agreed to accept a sum of money from the seller provided that the sale took place.

It is in relation to the bribe itself that the principal's remedies are most valuable. Since the bribe in the hands of the agent is a secret profit, it is recoverable by the principal in an action for money had and received, and it bears interest from the date of its receipt by the agent.[2] Where the bribe takes the form of property, the agent is liable to account for the highest value which the property has had while in the agent's possession.[3] It has further been held that, although a principal who repudiates the tainted transaction must hand back to the third party all benefits received under the contract, this does not include the bribe itself; this the principal may keep.[4] However, the old rule[5] which permitted the principal both to recover damages (from either the agent or the third party) for any loss suffered *and* to demand the amount of the bribe no longer applies; the principal must elect which remedy to pursue.[6]

5   Duty of personal performance

The common law maxim *delegatus non potest delegare* indicates that, as a general rule, an agent may not entrust performance of the agency to any other person.[7] This is based on the law's view of agency as a relationship which involves some trust placed in the agent by the principal. In consequence, as was stated by Buckley J in *Allam & Co Ltd* v *Europa Poster Services Ltd*:[8]

Where the principal reposes no personal confidence in the agent the maxim has no application, but where the principal does place confidence in the

---

1 [1899] 1 QB 369.
2 *Boston Deep Sea Fishing and Ice Co* v *Ansell* (1888) 39 ChD 339.
3 *Re Morvah Consols Tin Mining Co, McKay's Case* (1875) 2 ChD 1.
4 *Logicrose Ltd* v *Southend United Football Club Ltd* [1988] 1 WLR 1256.
5 Under *Salford Corporation* v *Lever* [1891] 1 QB 168; *Hovenden & Sons* v *Millhoff* (1900) 83 LT 41.
6 *Mahesan s/o Thambiah* v *Malaysia Government Officers' Co-operative Housing Society Ltd* [1979] AC 374.
7 *De Bussche* v *Alt* (1878) 8 ChD 286.
8 [1968] 1 All ER 826, 832.

agent, that in respect of which the principal does so must be done by the agent personally unless either expressly or inferentially he is authorised to employ a subagent or to delegate the function to another.

Whether or not an agent is entitled to delegate depends, therefore, on the scope of the agent's authority. If the principal has expressly authorised such a procedure it will obviously be valid; so too where the principal ratifies an unauthorised delegation.[1] Apart from this, authority to delegate may in certain circumstances be implied from the nature of the transaction (for example where the acts concerned are purely ministerial and involve no element of skill or discretion),[2] or from the conduct of the parties. Thus, for example, a principal who appoints an agent to carry out certain tasks, knowing that the agent does not intend to act personally, will be taken to have authorised the appointment of a subagent.[3] Authority may also be implied on the basis of what is usual in a particular trade or profession, although this does not appear to apply in the case of an estate agent.[4] Finally, there seems no reason to doubt that, in principle at least, delegation may be justified in an emergency.[5] although, as noted earlier, the doctrine of "agency of necessity" is one of extremely limited scope.[6]

The complex rights and duties which arise where a subagent is appointed are considered at the end of this chapter.

6 Other duties

An agent who is in possession of money to the use of the principal must pay that money over on demand or account for it in some other way.[7] This obligation attaches to money which the agent receives from the principal, that which is received from a third party to be handed over to the principal, and that which the agent

---

1 As in *Keay* v *Fenwick* (1876) 1 CPD 745.

2 Such as signing a notice to terminate an agreement: *Allam & Co Ltd* v *Europa Poster Services Ltd* [1968] 1 All ER 826.

3 *Quebec & Richmond Railway Co* v *Quinn* (1858) 12 Moo PCC 232; *De Bussche* v *Alt* (1878) 8 ChD 286.

4 See p 95.

5 See *De Bussche* v *Alt* (1878) 8 ChD 286, 310-11.

6 See p 8.

7 For example by setting it against sums to which the agent is entitled by way of commission or expenses: *Dale* v *Sollet* (1767) 4 Burr 2133.

is deemed to receive on behalf of the principal (eg a secret profit or bribe). It matters not that the money comes to the agent by virtue of a void or illegal transaction,[1] although the principal cannot claim where the entire contract of agency is unlawful.[2] Nor can the principal lay claim to money which the agent has with legal justification repaid to a third party (for example because the contract under which it was paid is voidable). Indeed, in *Murray v Mann*,[3] an agent successfully resisted a claim by the principal for the price of a horse, which had been returned to the purchaser on the grounds of the agent's own fraud!

Where a principal can be said to have a proprietary interest in money which is in the agent's possession, the agent will be regarded as a constructive trustee. This will give the principal certain advantages over other creditors of the agent in that the principal takes priority in the agent's bankruptcy, may trace the money in certain circumstances and may demand from a mixed fund everything which cannot be positively identified as belonging to the agent.[4] Unfortunately, in view of the importance of these remedies, the case law does not clearly indicate the circumstances in which they apply;[5] however, it now appears that, as regards a bribe, the relationship between principal and agent is that of beneficiary and trustee.[6]

An agent's overriding duty to account to the principal prevents the agent from setting up competing claims to the money in question.[7] A similar rule has traditionally been applied to other forms of property (land and goods) held by an agent on behalf of the principal, so as to estop the agent from disputing the principal's title.[8] However, the impact of this latter rule has been somewhat reduced by the Torts (Interference with Goods) Act 1977, section 8,

---

1 *De Mattos v Benjamin* (1894) 63 LJQB 248.
2 *Parker (Harry) Ltd v Mason* [1940] 2 KB 590.
3 (1848) 2 Exch 538.
4 *Lupton v White* (1808) 15 Ves 432.
5 See, for example, *Henry v Hammond* [1913] 2 KB 515; *Kingscroft Insurance Co Ltd v HG Weavers (Underwriting) Agencies Ltd* [1993] 1 Lloyd's Rep 187.
6 *A-G for Hong Kong v Reid* (1993) 143 NLJ 1569, refusing to follow *Metropolitan Bank v Heiron* (1880) 5 Ex D 319 and *Lister & Co v Stubbs* (1890) 45 ChD 1.
7 *Blaustein v Maltz, Mitchell & Co* [1937] 2 KB 142.
8 *Williams v Pott* (1871) LR 12 Eq 149; *Lyell v Kennedy* (1889) 14 App Cas 437.

which in certain circumstances permits an agent to raise third-party claims when faced with a demand from the principal for goods. The application of this statutory provision is considered in the context of auctioneers, for whom it is a matter of considerable practical importance.[1]

B Rights against the principal

1 Remuneration

The most important right of an agent, that of remuneration, may take a variety of forms, ranging from the salary or wages of one who is employed full-time in the principal's business to the fees or commission charged by an independent professional. Whatever form it takes, however, an agent's entitlement will depend upon the terms of the agency agreement. As to express terms, those which commonly apply to estate agents and auctioneers will be considered later; for the moment, attention will be given to the general question of an agent's *implied* right to be paid.

As a general rule, a request for the provision of services by a professional person raises a presumption that those services will be paid for.[2] Further, it is presumed that payment will be at the normal professional rate, so that an auctioneer, for example, may rely on the evidence of other auctioneers[3] or on a recommended scale.[4] However, the courts have shown considerable reluctance to uphold any professional "custom" which purports to relate a fee for professional *services* (as opposed to the bringing about of an event) to the value of the property involved, believing that such fees should instead reflect the time and trouble involved. The extent of this reluctance may be shown by reference to the old case of *Upsdell* v *Stewart*[5] in which a surveyor who checked the bills of workmen involved in building a house claimed 5% of the amount as his fee according to professional custom. Lord Kenyon CJ exclaimed: "As to the custom offered to be proved, the course of

---

1 See p 304.

2 *Manson* v *Baillie* (1855) 2 Macq 80; *Miller* v *Beal* (1879) 27 WR 403; see now the Supply of Goods and Services Act 1982, section 15.

3 *Re Page* (1863) 32 Beav 487.

4 *Newman* v *Richardson* (1885) 1 TLR 348.

5 (1793) Peake 255.

robbery on Bagshot Heath might as well be proved in a court of justice". Similar views have been expressed (although not so strongly) in relation to surveyors' charges for appearing at arbitration.[1]

The implication that a professional agent is to be paid a reasonable sum for services rendered is, like other implications, powerless to override an express term of the agreement. Thus, if the contract provides in clear terms that commission is payable only on the occurrence of a certain event, and that event does not occur, there is no room for an implied term that the agent should receive a reasonable recompense for the work done. Moreover, the express terms of an agency agreement may show that the agent's services are to be performed gratuitously or at a fixed rate of payment, in which case again no term for reasonable remuneration can be implied. Indeed, it has been held in a number of cases that an agent who agrees to leave the question of remuneration entirely to the discretion of the principal can have no complaint if the principal decides that nothing at all is to be paid![2] However, such an apparently unjust ruling is not inevitable; thus in *Bryant* v *Flight*,[3] where an agent was employed full-time under an agreement which provided "the amount of payment I am to receive I leave entirely for you to determine", a majority of the Court of Exchequer held that some payment was clearly envisaged, and that the court could therefore assess what was reasonable in the circumstances.

The circumstances in which an agent may successfully claim a *quantum meruit* (or reasonable sum) from the principal may be summarised as follows:

i Where, although payment is clearly intended, the parties have not expressly said so, or have not stated the amount.

ii Where the amount of commission has expressly been left for future agreement, and no agreement has been reached.[4]

iii Where the express agreement may be ignored as being too vague to be enforceable, or where it is void.[5]

---

1 *Drew* v *Josolyne* (1888) 4 TLR 717; *Faraday* v *Tamworth Union* (1917) 86 LJ Ch 436.
2 *Taylor* v *Brewer* (1813) 1 M & S 290; *Kofi Sunkersette Obu* v *Strauss & Co Ltd* [1951] AC 243; *Re Richmond Gate Property Co Ltd* [1964] 3 All ER 936.
3 (1839) 5 M&W 114; see also *Powell* v *Braun* [1954] 1 All ER 484.
4 *British Bank for Foreign Trade Ltd* v *Novinex Ltd* [1949] 1 KB 623.
5 *Craven-Ellis* v *Canons Ltd* [1936] 2 KB 403.

iv Where the express agreement has been rescinded.[1]

A claim for remuneration which appears to satisfy the rules described above will none the less fail if it relates to a void or illegal transaction.[2] Thus, for example, no fees can be claimed by an unqualified person who purports to act as a solicitor,[3] an agent employed to make an illegal wager form the principal,[4] or one who acts illegally as a secret "puffer" for the vendor at an auction sale.[5]

An agent will also be unable to recover any remuneration in respect of an unauthorised transaction (unless, of course, the principal ratifies it), or where the agent has been guilty of a breach of duty. In accordance with this latter principle, agents have forfeited their commission on the grounds of wrongful delegation (at least where the subagent could not be expected to have the principal's interest at heart);[6] negligence;[7] secret profit;[8] and failure to disclose a personal interest.[9] It has, however, been held that an agent who acts in good faith may remain entitled to commission, notwithstanding an inadvertent technical breach of duty to the principal,[10] even though the agent may have to pay damages for that breach[11] or hand over a secret profit.[12] Furthermore, an agent who has been guilty of fraud in respect of some transactions, but who has acted honestly in others, may claim commission in respect of the honest dealings,[13] provided at least that these are severable and that the fraud has not tainted the entire agency agreement.[14]

---

1 *Faraday* v *Tamworth Union* (1917) 86 LJ Ch 436.
2 Unless the illegality is incidental, and the agent is unaware of any it: *Haines* v *Busk* (1814) 5 Taunt 521.
3 Solicitors Act 1974, section 25.
4 Gaming Act 1892, section 1.
5 *Walker* v *Nightingale* (1726) 4 Bro PC 193.
6 *Beable* v *Dickerson* (1885) 1 TLR 654.
7 *Denew* v *Daverell* (1813) 3 Camp 451.
8 *Andrews* v *Ramsay & Co* [1903] 2 KB 635.
9 *Salomons* v *Pender* (1865) 3 H&C 639.
10 *Harrods Ltd* v *Lemon* [1931] KB 157.
11 *Keppel* v *Wheeler* [1927] 1 KB 577.
12 *Hippisley* v *Knee Bros* [1905] 1 KB 1.
13 *Nitedals Taendstikfabrik* v *Bruster* [1906] 2 Ch 571.
14 *Headway Construction Co* v *Downham* (1974) 233 EG 675.

2   Reimbursement and indemnity

As a general rule, an agent is entitled to be indemnified by the principal against any losses and liabilities, and to be reimbursed for any expenses, which are incurred in acting on the principal's behalf. This entitlement, however, is subject to any express or implied agreement to the contrary; consequently, an estate agent who fails to earn commission by finding a purchaser will have no implied right to be reimbursed for expenses incurred in advertising the property, for such expenses are assumed to be covered by the agent's commission on successful transactions.[1]

The right to reimbursement, where it exists, covers all authorised payments made by the agent, not merely those which operate to discharge the principal from some legal liability. Thus in *Adams* v *Morgan & Co Ltd*,[2] where a person carrying on a business as an agent became liable for super tax, it was held that the principal must indemnify him, even though the principal, as a limited company, would not itself have attracted this form of taxation.

As with claims for remuneration, an agent is not entitled to be indemnified against any losses incurred in carrying out an unlawful act,[3] unless the agent's part in the transaction is innocent. In *Adamson* v *Jarvis*,[4] for example, an auctioneer sold goods on behalf of a person who in fact had no right to authorise the sale. The auctioneer, having been successfully sued by the true owner of the goods, was held entitled to recover from his client the damages and costs which the auctioneer had been forced to pay.

An agent who incurs losses or liabilities in performing an unauthorised act cannot claim reimbursement or indemnity in respect of these. Thus in *Warwick* v *Slade*,[5] for example, an agent who effected an insurance policy for a principal after his authority had been revoked was held unable to recover the amount of the premiums. Nor is an agent entitled to an indemnity for any losses

---

1 See p 177.
2 [1924] 1 KB 751.
3 *Ex parte Mather* (1797) 3 Ves 373.
4 (1827) 4 Bing 66.
5 (1811) 3 Camp 127; see also *Barron* v *Fitzgerald* (1840) 6 Bing NC 201.

which result from the agent's own failure to obey the principal's instructions,[1] negligence[2] or other default.[3]

3 Lien

Apart from seeking to enforce claims for remuneration or indemnity through the courts, an agent may be legally entitled to exercise a lien over (ie retain possession of) the principal's goods. If this is done, the agent's rights will not be defected by the principal selling the goods to a third party,[4] nor by the principal's insolvency.[5] However, the agent's rights will be no greater than those of the principal,[6] so that the agent will take the goods subject to any existing third-party rights.[7].

The law of agency recognises two main types of lien. First, every agent has a particular lien, which entitles the agent to retain possession of the principal's goods until all claims in respect of those particular goods are met. In addition, certain classes of agents (notably solicitors, bankers, factors, stockbrokers and insurance brokers) have a general lien, by virtue of which they may retain possession of the principal's goods until the general balance of account between the parties is settled. As a broad principle, it may be stated that the law favours particular liens, whereas general liens are kept within strict limits.

The valid exercise of a lien by an agent is only possible where certain conditions are met:

i The agent must be in actual or constructive possession of the goods in question.[8]

ii The agent's possession of the goods must be both lawful and authorised. Thus, in *Madden* v *Kempster*,[9] an agent who obtained a cheque from the principal by a misrepresentation was not entitled to exercise a lien over it.

---

1 *Ellis* v *Pond* [1898] 1 QB 426.
2 *Lewis* v *Samuel* (1846) 8 QB 685.
3 *Duncan* v *Hill* (1873) LR 8 Ex 242.
4 *West of England Bank* v *Batchelor* (1882) 51 LJ Ch 199.
5 *Robson* v *Kemp* (1802) 4 Esp 233.
6 Except in relation to negotiable instruments, where the agent is unaware of any defect in his principal's title: *Jones* v *Peppercorne* (1858) John 430.
7 *Turner* v *Letts* (1855) 7 De GM&G 243.
8 *McCombie* v *Davis* (1805) 7 East 5; *Bryans* v *Nix* (1839) 4 M&W 775.
9 (1807) 1 Camp 12; see also *Taylor* v *Robinson* (1812) 2 Moore 730.

iii The agent must have obtained possession of the goods in the same capacity as that in which the lien is claimed.[1] It follows that a lien cannot be exercised in relation to debts which have arisen before the commencement of the agency.[2]

iv The circumstances in which the agent obtained the goods must not be inconsistent with a lien.[3] This will be the case, for example, where the agent is only given possession of the goods for a specific and limited purpose.[4]

Once established, an agent's lien may come to an end in the following circumstances:

i Where the principal duly pays the agent whatever is owed.

ii Where the agent parts with possession of the goods in question, whether by returning them to the principal[5] or by wrongfully selling[6] or pledging[7] them. However, this will not apply where the agent has been induced to part with possession by the principal's fraud[8] and, moreover, it appears that the agent may release the goods to the principal for a specific limited purpose without losing the lien.[9]

iii Where the agent acts in such a way as to indicate that the lien is waived or abandoned.[10] In practice, this is most likely to occur where the agent accepts an alternative form of security for what is owed,[11] provided that this would be inconsistent with the continuance of the lien.[12]

C The agent's relationship with third parties

In considering the legal position of an agent *vis-à-vis* the third parties with whom the agent deals on the principal's behalf, it should be made clear from the outset that an agent who is guilty of

---

1 *Dixon* v *Stansfield* (1850) 10 CB 398.

2 *Houghton* v *Matthews* (1803) 3 B&P 485.

3 *Re Bowes, Earl of Strathmore* v *Vane* (1886) 33 ChD 586.

4 *Burn* v *Brown* (1817) 2 Stark 272.; *Brandao* v *Barnett* (1846) 12 C&F 787.

5 *Sweet* v *Pym* (1800) 1 East 4.

6 *Siebel* v *Springfield* (1863) 3 New Rep 36.

7 *McCombie* v *Davis* (1805) 7 East 5.

8 *Wallace* v *Woodgate* (1824) R&M 193; *Dicas* v *Stockley* (1836) 7 C&P 587.

9 *Albemarle Supply Co Ltd* v *Hind & Co* [1928] 1 KB 307.

10 *Weeks* v *Goode* (1859) 6 CBNS 367.

11 *Hewison* v *Guthrie* (1836) 2 Bing NC 755.

12 See *Re Morris* [1908] 1 KB 473.

committing a wrong such as a tort or a breach of trust will be personally liable for this. It may be, in accordance with the principles discussed in the previous chapter,[1] that the third party can hold the principal responsible for what the agent has done. If so, this is an additional remedy for the third party, which in no way exonerates the agent as the primary wrongdoer.

As for contracts entered into by agents, the legal position is not quite so clear. In some circumstances the agent will drop out of the picture altogether, so that the resulting contract concerns only the principal and the third party. In other situations, however, the agent will be regarded as a party to the contract, with rights against and obligations towards the third party. It is this problem area which now falls to be discussed, together with the question of an agent's liability to the third party for acting without authority from the principal.

1 Contractual relationships

Where an agent makes a contract without revealing the existence of a principal, the agent is regarded in law as contracting personally.[2] The third party, after all, has intended to contract with the agent, and this contractual link is not to be taken away, even though the undisclosed principal may also be liable and entitled on the contract. As to the agent's right to enforce the contract in such a situation, however, this is subject to any defence (such as fraud) which the third party could have raised against the principal. This might not appear entirely logical (since the third party by definition intended to contract exclusively with the agent), but it was approved in *Garnac Grain Co Inc v H M F Faure & Fairclough Ltd*[3] on the ground that, if this were not so, "the fraudulent principal would indirectly be entitled to enjoy the fruits of his own fraud".

The question whether or not the agent of a *disclosed* principal is to be treated as contracting personally turns, at least in theory, on the intention of the parties in the individual case. However, the reported cases in which this has been held to be so appear on examination to fall into a number of recognisable categories, which may now be described. It should be noted that, in all these cases,

---

1 See pp 28-31.
2 *Sims* v *Bond* (1833) 5 B&Ad 389; *Saxon* v *Blake* (1861) 29 Beav 438.
3 [1966] 1 QB 650 at p 656.

a third party sued by the agent may set up any defence (such as a set off) which could have been used against the principal.[1]

(a) *Matters of form*
As we saw in the previous chapter,[2] the common law rule was that a principal could not be a party to a formal contract (ie one made by deed) which was executed in the agent's name or with the agent's seal. As a natural corollary, the agent in such cases was personally liable.[3] The primary rule has been altered by statute,[4] so as to enable the principal to be regarded as a party; however, whether this means that the agent is no longer liable or entitled has been left unclear.

As for contracts which are made in writing, the law is not so strict as in the case of deeds, but it none the less creates a serious trap for the unwary. The common law rule[5] here is that a person who signs a contract in his or her own name will be liable[6] and entitled[7] upon it, even though it is understood on all sides that that person is merely acting as an agent. To avoid this conclusion, the contract documents themselves must reveal the agent's true status, for example by some qualification to the signature itself.

As to what kind of "qualification" will release the agent, the case law has drawn a crucial distinction between words which clearly show the representative nature of the signature, and those which merely describe the position held by the signatory. Such epithets as "chartered civil engineer"[8] or "director"[9] have been treated as mere description. Nor can the addition of "broker"[10] or "agent"[11] be regarded as conclusive, since these may not show unequivocally

1 *Atkinson* v *Cotesworth* (1825) 3 B&C 647.
2 See p 3.
3 *Appleton* v *Binks* (1804) 5 East 148.
4 Powers of Attorney Act 1971, section 7, replacing the Law of Property Act 1925, section 123(1).
5 Which is given statutory recognition, in relation to negotiable instruments, by the Bills of Exchange Act 1882, section 26(1).
6 *Higgins* v *Senior* (1841) 8 M&W 834.
7 *Short* v *Spackman* (1831) 2 B&Ad 962.
8 *Sika Contracts Ltd* v *BL Gill and Closeglen Properties Ltd* (1978) 9 Build LR 15.
9 *McCollin* v *Gilpin* (1881) 6 QBD 516.
10 *Hutcheson & Co* v *Eaton & Son* (1884) 13 QBD 861.
11 *Parker* v *Winlow* (1857) 7 E&B 942.

that the person is signing the contract in that capacity! It seems that what is required is a phrase equivalent to "for and on behalf of"[1] or "on account of",[2] although it should be noted that even the last of these has not always proved infallible in excluding an agent's personal liability.[3]

Whether such formalistic rules are really appropriate to modern business conditions must be open to doubt, and it is worth pointing out that the Court of Appeal has refused to extend them to oral contracts. In such cases it is for the third party to show that the agent undertook personal responsibility; there is no presumption to this effect merely because the agent made the contract without using the magic words "as agent".[4]

(b) Non-existent principal

Where a person claims to be acting as an agent for someone else (whether named or unnamed), this claim may turn out to have no foundation, either because the "principal" has no existence at law (eg where it is an unformed company or an unincorporated association), or because the "agent" really intends to deal personally but wishes to conceal this fact. In both cases, the law is usually prepared to treat the agent as personally liable and entitled on the contract; whether this is a justifiable approach, however, is a matter of considerable dispute.

Dealing first with the situation of a principal who lacks legal capacity, the presumption in such cases is that the third party must have intended to contract with the agent, since there would otherwise be no enforceable contract at all. Notwithstanding this possibility, however, the presumption is not conclusive; thus in *Jones* v *Hope*,[5] where a solicitor rendered professional services to a volunteer corps, it was held that the solicitor's fees could not be claimed from the commanding officer, for the evidence showed clearly that there had been no intention to make a contract with the colonel personally.

---

1 *Universal Steam Navigation Co Ltd* v *James McKelvie & Co* [1923] AC 492.
2 *Fairlie* v *Fenton* (1870) LR 5 Ex 169; *Gadd* v *Houghton* (1876) 1 ExD 357.
3 *Punjab National Bank* v *de Boinville* [1992] 3 All ER 104.
4 *N & J Vlassopulos Ltd* v *Ney Shipping Ltd, The Santa Carina* [1977] 1 Lloyd's Rep 478.
5 (1880) 3 TLR 247n.

The most common example of this type of case concerns contracts made on behalf of a company which has not yet been formed. The position in such cases is now governed by legislation, which provides that, subject to any agreement to the contrary, the contract shall take effect as one made personally with the "agent", who is accordingly liable on it.[1]

The second situation mentioned above, that of an "agent" who secretly intends to deal personally, is one in which the courts' decisions have been much more controversial. In *Schmaltz* v *Avery*[2] the plaintiff, describing himself as "agent of the freighter", signed a charterparty which provided; "This charter being concluded on behalf of another party, it is agreed that all responsibility on the part of the agents shall cease as soon as the cargo is shipped." Notwithstanding this provision, it was held that the plaintiff, on later revealing that he himself was the true principal, could enforce the contract in his own name.

In reaching this decision, the Court of Queen's Bench clearly believed that the identity of the principal must have been a matter of indifference to the third party, who had not bothered to ask who it was. The court acknowledged that, had the principal's identity been important to the third party, the decision might have been different. However, even this qualification failed to protect the third party in *Harper & Co* v *Vigers Bros*,[3] where the principle of *Schmaltz* v *Avery* was followed and indeed extended. The plaintiffs in the later case signed a charterparty "by authority of and as agents for owners", at a time when they had no principal, but were speculating in freight and also wanted to obtain brokers' fees. The defendants gave evidence that, had they known that the plaintiffs had not already arranged a ship, they would not have made the contract. Notwithstanding this evidence, it was held that the plaintiffs were entitled to sue in their own name, although their concealment of the truth was enough to deprive them of an award of costs.

It is perhaps possible to support these decisions on the basis that a third party who is prepared to contract with an unnamed principal

---

1 Companies Act 1985, section 36C; see *Phonogram Ltd* v *Lane* [1982] QB 938.
2 (1851) 16 QB 655.
3 [1909] 2 KB 549.

cannot be unduly concerned about that principal's identity.[1] However, the same surely cannot be said of the situation where an agent actually names a principal before revealing that the latter does not exist. In such a case it might be assumed that the agent's misrepresentation would render the contract unenforceable, and yet, surprisingly, the law does not appear to adopt this position. Despite a strong *dictum* to the effect that "where a man assigns to himself the character of agent to another whom he names, I am not aware that the law will permit him to shift his situation, and to declare himself the principal, and the other to be a mere creature of straw",[2] an action by such an agent to enforce a contract was successful in *Rayner v Grote*.[3]

It is of course possible that an unexpressed reason for these decisions is the courts' desire to ensure that the "agent" should not escape *liability* on the resulting contract, if the third party wishes to enforce it.[4] If this really is the motive, then it should be pointed out that the agent in all such cases could be held liable instead for breach of warranty of authority.[5]

(c) Trade custom

Agents who act in particular trades are frequently treated as contracting personally by virtue of some usage of the trade in question. This is especially true of brokers, whether of stocks and shares[6] or commodities.[7] The custom may be limited to cases where the agent fails to name the principal at the time of making the contract, or it may even permit the agent to avoid personal responsibility by identifying the principal within a reasonable time thereafter.[8] It should be remembered, however, that no term can be implied into a contract by custom where it would conflict with some

---

1 They have nonetheless been heavily criticised in the Scottish courts: see *Hills SS Co Ltd v Hugo Stinnes Ltd* [1941] SC 324 at p 340.
2 *Bickerton v Burrell* (1816) 5 M&S 383 at p 386.
3 (1846) 15 M&W 359.
4 Liability is readily imposed on the "agent" in such circumstances: see, for example, *Hersom v Bernett* [1955] 1 QB 98; *Savills v Scott* [1988] 1 EGLR 20.
5 See p 63.
6 *Bayliffe v Butterworth* (1847) 1 Exch 425.
7 *Anglo Overseas Transport Co Ltd v Titan Industrial Corporation (UK) Ltd* [1959] 2 Lloyd's Rep 152.
8 *Hutchinson v Tatham* (1873) LR 8 CP 482.

other express or implied term. In *Barrow & Bros* v *Dyster, Nalder & Co*,[1] for example, a contract for the sale of hides between buyers and brokers acting on behalf of unnamed sellers provided that any disputes arising should be settled by the brokers as arbitrators. In these circumstances it was held that, notwithstanding a trade custom to the contrary, the brokers could not be made personally liable on the contract, for this would be inconsistent with their neutral position as arbitrators.

It may be appropriate in this context to mention that, in the last century, there was a presumption that an English agent who made a contract on behalf of a foreign principal (ie one resident outside the jurisdiction of the English courts) was liable and entitled on that contract to the exclusion of the principal. This presumption, although in theory rebuttable, was in practice usually upheld. However, as international trade has increased in size and sophistication, so the need for such a rule has decreased, and it is today recognised that the nationality of the principal is merely one factor to be taken into account when deciding whether the principal or the agent, or both, are liable and entitled on the contract.[2]

(d) *Other cases*

Although an agent is not automatically to be treated as contracting personally wherever the principal's identity is not revealed, there is no doubt that the courts are often influenced by this in their decision as to what the parties must have intended. Indeed, there are signs of an increasing readiness in the courts to conclude that, quite apart from the categories of case discussed above, a contract may well be entered into on the basis that the principal and the agent both undertake to guarantee performance.

A good example of this more flexible approach is provided by *The Swan*,[3] where the defendant formed a company to operate his fishing boat. The company, which hired the boat from the defendant in return for 90% of its profits, was responsible for any repairs which might become necessary. Various repairs were carried out by the plaintiffs at the request of the defendant, and paid for by cheques drawn on the company's account. Eventually extensive repairs and

---

1 (1884) 13 QBD 635.
2 See *Teheran-Europe Co Ltd* v *S T Belton (Tractors) Ltd* [1968] 2 QB 545.
3 [1968] 1 Lloyd's Rep 5.

alterations became necessary, and these were ordered by the defendant (signing himself "director") on company notepaper, after a meeting between the defendant and the plaintiffs at which the work required was agreed. When the company became insolvent, the plaintiffs sued the defendant for the price of the repairs, alleging that he had made the contract either as principal or as agent in such circumstances that he was personally liable for its due performance. Brandon J while rejecting the plaintiffs' first contention, had little hesitation in accepting the second. It was, he said, natural to assume that a shipowner would undertake personal responsibility to pay for repairs. He might disown that responsibility, but only in clear terms; merely pointing out that he was placing the order on behalf of a company did not in itself relieve him of liability.

2 Liability for unauthorised acts

Where an agent purports to act on behalf of a principal, but exceeds whatever authority has been given, it follows that the principal will not be bound to the third party. In such circumstances, the agent may be personally liable to the third party, not on the contract itself (since the third party never intended to contract with the agent),[1] but rather for breach of an implied warranty that the agent had the necessary authority. In *Collen* v *Wright*,[2] the defendant land agent agreed on behalf of his principal to grant a 12½-year lease of a farm to the plaintiff. The plaintiff brought an action against the principal to enforce this agreement, only to discover that the agent was not authorised to grant leases of this length. Accordingly, a second action was brought against the defendant, who was held liable to pay damages. Willes J, delivering the judgment of a majority of the Exchequer Chamber, said:[3]

A person, professing to contract as agent for another, impliedly, if not expressly, undertakes to or promises the person who enters into such contract, upon the faith of the professed agent being duly authorised, that the authority which he professes to have does in point of fact exist.

---

1 This particular fallacy was exposed in *Lewis* v *Nicholson* (1852) 18 QB 503.
2 (1857) 8 E&B 647.
3 At p657.

The liability of an agent in a case of this kind does not depend upon fraud[1] or even negligence, but rather on the fact that "by professing to act as agent he impliedly contracts that he has authority, and it is immaterial whether he knew of the defect of his authority or not."[2] Thus in *Yonge* v *Toynbee*,[3] where a solicitor continued to defend an action on behalf of a client who had been certified as insane, the Court of Appeal held the solicitor personally liable for the costs incurred by the other party, notwithstanding that he neither knew of his client's insanity nor could reasonably have been expected to know of it.

The essence of this form of action lies in the third party's reliance on a representation, usually implied, that the agent possesses the necessary authority.[4] If there is no such representation (for example because the third party is informed as to any limitations on the agent's authority) then the agent cannot be liable. Thus in *Lilly, Wilson & Co* v *Smales, Eeles & Co*,[5] where a firm of shipbrokers signed a contract "by telegraphic authority", they were held not liable when it transpired that the telegram was inaccurate and that they were not in fact authorised to sign. Nor can liability arise where the "representation" is one of law rather than of fact, since the third party is presumed to know what the law is and thus not to have been misled.[6]

The third party's "reliance" in these cases is normally shown by entering into a contract, but this is not the only situation in which liability can arise. In *Starkey* v *Bank of England*,[7] for example, the Bank of England were held to have relied on a stockbroker's power of attorney (which turned out to have been forged) by transferring stock to a purchaser. Again, in *V/O Rasnoimport* v *Guthrie & Co Ltd*,[8] it was held that the agents of a shipowner who signed a bill of lading could be held liable to anyone who subsequently acquired it; the mere acquisition of the bill in the course of business, in the

---

1 If the agent *is* aware of the lack of authority, an action will lie in the tort of deceit: *Polhill* v *Walter* (1832) 3 B&Ad 114.
2 *Yonge* v *Toynbee* [1910] 1 KB 215, at p 227, *per* Buckley LJ.
3 [1910] 1 KB 215.
4 *Halbot* v *Lens* [1901] 1 Ch 344.
5 [1892] 1 QB 456.
6 *Eaglesfield* v *Marquis of Londonderry* (1875) 4 ChD 693; affirmed (1878) 38 LT 303.
7 [1903] AC 114.
8 [1966] 1 Lloyd's Rep 1.

belief that it conferred rights which could be exercised against the shipowners, constituted sufficient "reliance" on the agents' authority to sign it.

The remedy in an action for breach of warranty of authority is an award of damages, assessed with the intention of putting the third party in the position which he or she would have occupied if the agent had been authorised and the principal had therefore been bound. In effect, therefore, the agent is forced to compensate the third party for whatever profitable bargain appeared to have been struck. Conversely, if the third party's rights against the principal would in any event have been worthless (for example because the principal is insolvent), then the damages awarded against the agent should be nominal.[1]

In the simple case of an unauthorised contract of sale or purchase, the appropriate amount of damages will normally be the difference between the contract price and the market price,[2] assessed at the date on which completion should have taken place.[3] In addition to this basic sum, the third party is entitled to recover any foreseeable incidental expenditure. Thus the costs of taking an abortive legal action against the principal,[4] or of investigating the principal's title to land,[5] are recoverable from the agent, as are the costs of defending an action brought by the principal's solicitor without authority.[6] However, the fact that a purchaser has already agreed to resell the property concerned, and is thus liable to the subpurchaser for breach of contract, is regarded as too remote a consequence for the agent to be liable,[7] except where the agent actually knows of the proposed resale.[8]

---

1 *Re National Coffee Palace Co, ex parte Panmure* (1883) 24 ChD 367.
2 *Simons v Patchett* (1857) 7 E&B 568.
3 *Chitholie v Nash & Co* (1973) 229 EG 786.
4 *Collen v Wright* (1857) 8 E&B 647.
5 *Godwin v Francis* (1870) LR 5 CP 295.
6 *Yonge v Toynbee* [1910] 1 KB 215.
7 *Spedding v Nevell* (1869) 4 CP 212.
8 *CH Rugg & Co Ltd v Street* [1962] 1 Lloyd's Rep 364.

D The position of subagents

We noted earlier[1] the limited extent to which an agent is authorised to delegate to a subagent. What must now be considered is the effects which delegation has upon the legal positions of the principal, agent and subagent.

It may be stated at the outset that a delegation which is unauthorised produces no legal relationship whatsoever between principal and subagent. Thus, where the third party seeks to take action in respect of anything done by the alleged "subagent", it is the main agent and not the principal who will be held responsible.[2] Furthermore, the subagent in such circumstances will have no claim against the principal for remuneration,[3] and cannot exercise any kind of lien over the principal's goods.[4]

Where an agent *is* authorised to appoint a subagent, such delegation may take effect in one of two ways. In the first place, the agent may be authorised to create privity of contract between principal and subagent, so that the person appointed becomes an agent of the principal in the full sense and will take on all the appropriate rights and duties.[5] An appointment of this kind may operate in addition to the existing agency or in substitution for it; in the latter case the original agent, having carried out the principal's instructions, drops out of the picture. It should be noted, however, that the courts are not in favour of this type of delegation, and will require clear evidence that this is what was intended. As was pointed out by Wright J in *Calico Printers' Association Ltd* v *Barclays Bank*:[6]

To create privity it must be established not only that the principal contemplated that a subagent would perform part of the contract, but also that the principal authorised the agent to create privity of contract between the principal and the subagent, which is a very different matter requiring precise proof.

---

1 See p 48.
2 *Maloney* v *Hardy and Moorshead* (1970) 216 EG 1582.
3 *Schmaling* v *Tomlinson* (1815) 6 Taunt 147.
4 *Solly* v *Rathbone* (1814) 2 M&S 298.
5 *De Bussche* v *Alt* (1878) 8 ChD 286; *Powell & Thomas* v *Evan Jones & Co* [1905] 1 KB 11; *Foalquest Ltd* v *Roberts* [1990] 1 EGLR 50.
6 (1931) 145 LT 51 at p 55.

The second type of delegation, and the one which the courts will presume to have been intended, is where the subagent is merely an "agent of the agent" and has no personal contractual relationship with the principal. Such a subagent cannot be directly liable to the principal for money received on the principal's behalf; the subagent's duty is to account to the agent alone.[1] The agent is in turn liable to the principal, although the extent of this liability is not altogether clear. In *Mackersy v Ramsays, Bonars & Co*,[2] where an agent in England appointed a subagent in India to obtain payment of a debt, the agent was held automatically liable for the subagent's failure to pass on the amount received to the principal. However, there have been suggestions that an agent should not be liable for the defaults of a subagent in whose selection the agent has used all reasonable care.[3]

A subagent of the kind now under discussion cannot be held liable to the principal in respect of any of the normal "agency" duties which are based upon contract, for there is no contract between them. Moreover, whether liability may arise in other ways is a matter of some controversy. While in principle it might be argued that a subagent should owe a duty of care in tort to the principal, this was denied in *Calico Printers' Association Ltd v Barclays Bank*,[4] so that a principal was unable to claim damages against subagents who negligently failed to insure his goods. Further, the suggestion that the position had been altered by general developments in the tort of negligence[5] was rejected in *Balsamo v Medici*[6] by Walton J, who stated that such liability can arise only where the negligence in question concerns property or money actually held by the subagent on the principal's behalf.

The position with regard to a subagent's possible duty of loyalty is equally unclear. In *New Zealand & Australian Land Co v Watson*[7] the plaintiffs, in seeking to recover from the defendant subagents

---

1 *Stephens v Badcock* (1832) 3 B&Ad 354.
2 (1843) 9 C&F 818. See also *Swire v Francis* (1877) 3 App Cas 106; *Edwards Real Estate v Bamtor* (1978) 11 AR 589.
3 See *Cheshire & Co v Vaughan Bros & Co* [1920] 3 KB 240, 359.
4 (1931) 145 LT 51.
5 Notably the decisions of the House of Lords in *Donoghue v Stevenson* [1932] AC 562 and *Hedley Byrne & Co Ltd v Heller & Partners Ltd* [1964] AC 465.
6 [1984] 2 All ER 304.
7 (1881) 7 QBD 374.

the proceeds of a sale of the plaintiffs' goods, based their claim upon an alleged fiduciary relationship between the parties. The Court of Appeal held that no such fiduciary relationship could exist in a commercial case without privity of contract, so that the plaintiffs' claim failed. In *Powell & Thomas* v *Evan Jones & Co*,[1] on the other hand, a subagent employed to raise finance made a secret profit in the form of a commission from the company supplying the loan. The Court of Appeal held that, on the facts, privity of contract existed between the principal and the subagent, so that the latter was accordingly liable to hand over the secret profit. However, the court went on to say (without mentioning *Watson*'s case, although it had been cited in argument) that, even without such privity, the subagent would have been under a fiduciary duty to account for this money to the principal. It is submitted that this latter view should now prevail.[2]

As far as the rights of a "true" subagent are concerned, it may safely be assumed that any claims for remuneration or indemnity must lie against the agent rather than the principal. In pressing these claims, however, the subagent may well be able to exercise a lien over goods of the principal, although this will not apply where the appointment of the subagent was unauthorised.[3] The extent of an authorised subagent's lien depends upon whether or not the subagent was aware of his or her status at the time of appointment. If the existence of the principal was not disclosed, then the subagent may exercise any lien, whether particular or general, to the same extent as this could have been exercised against the agent.[4] If the principal's existence was disclosed, on the other hand, then the subagent may still exercise a particular lien;[5] any general lien, however, may not exceed the scope of the lien (if any) which the agent could have exercised against the principal.[6] It may finally be noted that a subagent who, having parted with possession of the goods, discovers the existence of the principal before

---

1 [1905] 1 KB 11.
2 See *Anangel Atlas Compania Naviera SA* v *Ishikawajima-Harima Heavy Industries Co* [1990] 1 Lloyd's Rep 167, where the principal's claim failed on the facts.
3 *Solly* v *Rathbone* (1814) 2 M&S 298.
4 *Mann* v *Forrester* (1814) 4 Camp 60; *Westwood* v *Bell* (1815) 4 Camp 349.
5 *Fisher* v *Smith* (1878) 4 App Cas 1.
6 *Ex parte Edwards* (1881) 8 QBD 262.

regaining possession, cannot rely on this new possession as reviving a general lien in its original form; the subagent's present rights are the more limited ones which would have applied if the principal had originally been disclosed.[1]

1 *Near East Relief* v *King, Chasseur & Co Ltd* [1930] 2 KB 40.

CHAPTER 3

Estate agents' authority

The essence of agency lies in the ability of the agent to affect the legal position of the principal. As we have already seen, this ability exists wherever the agent acts with authority, whether it be express, implied or apparent. An estate agent will of course be authorised to act in accordance with whatever instructions are given to him by the client. The purpose of this chapter, however, is to consider the extent of the *implied* authority which the estate agent is deemed to possess merely by being an estate agent. Thus, the question to be answered is this: where property is put into the hands of an estate agent for the purpose of sale, to what extent will the client be responsible for the agent's acts connected with the sale?

As we shall see, the courts take a rather limited view of the implied authority of an estate agent, particularly in relation to the making of a contract of sale. However, in certain other matters the estate agent may be treated as having authority, so that the client will incur legal responsibility for the agent's actions; these particular spheres of operation will be considered in due course.

A Authority to make a contract

1 Implied authority

It has long been the view of the English courts that the sale of land, with all its accompanying technicalities, is not something to be entered into lightly and without proper consideration. This judicial attitude has found expression in, among other things, a reluctance to construe informal or casual agreements as intended to be legally binding (hence the eagerness with which such phrases as "subject to contract" are seized upon) and, more important to the present discussion, a requirement that any person claiming to sell land on behalf of another shall show clear evidence of authority to do so.[1]

An early manifestation of this latter requirement is found in the case of *Godwin* v *Brind*[2] where the five joint owners of an estate advertised it for sale, naming Benjamin Francis, one of the five, as a person to whom anyone interested could make application "to treat and view". Francis purported to make a contract for the sale of the property to the plaintiff who, when the other four owners denied liability, brought an action against them. It was held that, notwithstanding the definition of "treat" in a leading dictionary as "negotiate, settle, come to terms", Francis had no authority to conclude a contract on behalf of his co-owners. Two years later the disappointed plaintiff succeeded in recouping his loss from Francis himself, in an action for a breach of warranty of authority.[3]

The first reported case in which the authority of an estate agent as such was called in question was *Hamer* v *Sharp*,[4] where an agent was requested to "procure a purchaser" for certain property at a price of £2,800. The agent accepted a deposit of £280 from the plaintiff and signed a receipt which described the money as paid "on account of purchase". The corresponding acknowledgement signed by the plaintiff stipulated a date for completion of the contract and stated that the vendor was to supply an abstract of title; it did not, however, contain any special conditions as to the title and to this extent, therefore, it was an "open contract". It was held that the making of such a contract was beyond the scope of the estate agent's authority so that his client was not legally bound by it. Hall V-C, concerned at the burdens placed upon a vendor of land by open contracts, said of the agent: "If he had a right to enter into any contract at all, it was one of a different description."

The actual decision in *Hamer* v *Sharp* is thus of fairly limited application. A later *dictum* of the judge has, however, been used to support a much more general proposition:

---

1 Even a solicitor has no implied authority to exchange contracts on a client's behalf: see *Suleman* v *Shahsavari* [1989] 2 All ER 460.
2 (1868) LR 5 CP 299n.
3 *Godwin* v *Francis* (1870) LR 5 CP 295.
4 (1874) LR 19 Eq 108.

I state my opinion to be, that when instructions are given to an agent to find a purchaser of landed property, he, not being instructed as to the conditions to be inserted into the contract as to title, is not authorised to sign a contract on the part of the vendor.

Four years later, in the case of *Wilde* v *Watson*,[1] an Irish court based its decision firmly upon the general principle expounded in *Hamer* v *Sharp*. In holding that an estate agent, who was instructed to procure an offer of £2,900 by a certain date, had no authority to make an open contract of sale, the judge said that, were this not so, the common practice of instructing a number of agents could lead to the owner becoming bound to sell to several different parties at the same time.

The opinion of Hall V-C quoted above was enthusiastically endorsed by Kekewich J in two cases which came before the Chancery Division. In *Prior* v *Moore*[2] an estate agent was instructed to place certain property on his books for sale and informed that the lowest price which would be acceptable to the vendor was £1,600. In due course the estate agent purported to sell the property and the purchaser sued for specific performance of the contract. The actual decision was that the agent had no authority to make the contract in question (it is not clear from the report what sort of contract this was) but the judge went on to consider the apparent "loophole" left by Hall V-C in *Hamer* v *Sharp*, that is, the insinuation that some contracts might be within the scope of the agent's authority: "His Lordship was sorry the Vice-Chancellor did not state what contract the agent was entitled to enter into. The general result seemed to be that the agent was not entitled to enter into any contract."

In *Chadburn* v *Moore*,[3] an English court was able for the first time to reach a decision based on an estate agent's lack of *any* implied authority to contract on behalf of a client. The defendant there instructed a firm of estate agents to find a purchaser for leasehold property consisting of thirty-four houses. On receiving an offer from the plaintiff, the owner instructed the agents to withdraw five of the houses, and named the lowest price which he would accept for the

1 (1878) 1 LR Ir 402.
2 (1887) 3 TLR 624.
3 (1892) 61 LJ Ch 674.

remainder. It was held that the agents had no authority to accept the offer which the plaintiff then made and that the defendant was accordingly not bound by the open contract which they had purported to make. Kekewich J said:

Unless express authority is given to the agent to sell, and for that purpose to enter into a binding contract, the principal reserves his final right to accept or refuse.

After this decision, the courts appeared to accept the general principle as valid and no longer found it necessary to inquire into the type of contract which the estate agent had purported to make. The few cases in which a vendor was held to be bound turned very much on their own peculiar facts[1] and, in *Lewcock v Bromley*,[2] Sargant J was able to say:

The law on this point is quite settled that a general authority to an agent to find a purchaser does not authorise the agent to sign a contract binding on the vendor.

All the cases so far mentioned concerned the sale of property by an estate agent, but it is worth noting that the same principle applies to the creation of a lease. In *Thuman v Best*[3] the defendant put his flat into the hands of a number of estate agents and one of these introduced the plaintiff, who expressed himself willing to pay the required rent of £195 per year for "a usual West End lease". The estate agent purported to accept this offer and the plaintiff brought an action against the owner for specific performance. It was held that the alleged agreement could not possibly be enforced since, even if it did not fail for uncertainty, it lacked the written evidence necessary to satisfy the provisions of the Statute of Frauds. Furthermore, the estate agent had, by purporting to sign a contract on behalf of his client, exceeded his authority, which was no greater in the case of a lease than that of a sale. Parker J stated with admirable clarity and concision the judicial view of an estate agent's function:

---

1 See, for example, *Allen v Whiteman* (1920) 89 LJ Ch 534.
2 (1920) 127 LT 116.
3 (1907) 97 LT 239; see also *Yallop v Fosh* (1953) 161 EG 603.

Estate agents as such have no general authority to enter into contracts for their employers. Their business is to find offers and submit them to their employers for acceptance.

2 Other kinds of authority

It is established, then, beyond any reasonable doubt that the mere placing of property in the hands of an estate agent does not endow that agent with any implied authority to make a contract for the sale or other disposition of the property.[1] This is not to say, however, that authority to that effect can never be conferred upon the agent; what it means is that it must take one of the other forms which we discussed in chapter 1. In the Irish case of *Brennan* v *O'Connell*,[2] for example, an estate agent telephoned clients to tell them that he had signed a contract for the sale of their farm, whereupon they expressed unqualified approval of his (unauthorised) action. What the agent did *not* tell the clients was that another prospective purchaser had shown some interest in the property and, as a result, when sued on the contract, the clients claimed that their lack of knowledge precluded a finding that they had ratified the agent's act.[3] The Irish Supreme Court, however, held that the fact of which the clients had been kept in ignorance was not, objectively speaking, sufficiently material to obviate what appeared to be a clear case of ratification; the sale was therefore binding upon them.

In *Worboys* v *Carter*[4] a land agent representing the tenant of an agricultural holding believed that his client, who was serving a short term of imprisonment, had authorised him to assign the tenancy to the plaintiff. This was not in fact true but the defendant client, on being released from prison, allowed the plaintiff to believe that the contract of assignment was valid and binding. The Court of Appeal was not prepared to follow the trial judge in holding that the defendant had ratified his agent's act (since the evidence showed that he was in truth always opposed to what had been done). However, the court held that the plaintiff was none the less entitled

---

1 The decision of the Irish Supreme Court in *Kelly* v *Park Hall Schools Ltd* (1978) 113 ILTR 9 can only be justified on the basis that the agent was *expressly* authorised to sell.

2 [1980] IR 13; see also *Keen* v *Mear* [1920] 2 Ch 574: p 80.

3 See p 16.

4 [1987] 2 EGLR 1.

to enforce the contract of assignment, on the basis that the defendant was estopped by his conduct from disputing its validity.[1]

The doctrine of apparent authority may well serve to bind a client in this context; a good illustration, and one with serious implications for practising estate agents, is *Walsh* v *Griffiths-Jones*.[2] The plaintiff there, who owned a house divided into three flats, wished these to be occupied pending the sale of the whole property, but did not want any occupier to acquire a protected tenancy. The plaintiff accordingly instructed an estate agent (one who had advertised to the effect that he could avoid the provisions of the Rent Act) to grant a licence (but not a lease) of each of the flats to a suitable applicant. When the defendants went to view one of the flats in question, they were told by the plaintiff herself that the agent would attend to all the details of the agreement. The defendants duly visited the agent and entered into a form of agreement which, it was subsequently held, took effect as a lease (within the Rent Act) and not as a licence. Notwithstanding this finding, the plaintiff claimed that she was not bound, since the agent had exceeded his authority. However, the county court judge, who described the case as "one of the clearest cases of holding out an agent as having full authority to enter into a contractual agreement that I can recall", held that, whatever might be the legal effect of the agreement between the defendants and the agent, the plaintiff was bound by it.

3 Instructions to sell

Where what is in issue is the *express* authority given to an estate agent by a client, it seems from various judicial remarks that, if this is to include the making of a binding contract, very clear evidence will be needed.[3] In order to decide whether the agent has been authorised to do more than carry out the normal function of effecting introductions, the exact instructions given by the client must be ascertained, and the court is then faced with the task of

---

1 Following *Spiro* v *Lintern* [1973] 3 All ER 319: p 13.

2 [1978] 2 All ER 1002; see also *Hayes* v *Douglas* [1976] 5 WWR 308.

3 For an odd case in which the agent's authority was held to extend beyond what either the agent or the client intended, see *Graylaw Investments Ltd* v *J R Bridgford & Sons* (1982) 266 EG 807: p 82.

interpreting these instructions in accordance with past cases and in the light of the parties' own course of dealing, where this exists.

The cases already considered show categorically that the general rule is not displaced by instructing the estate agent to "find a purchaser" or to "procure an offer". Moreover, this applies even where the client mentions a specific price at which he or she is prepared to settle. In *Chadburn* v *Moore*[1] the instructions relating to the property in its revised form were "to find a purchaser and to negotiate a sale", and again the estate agent was held to have no more authority than usual.

The Irish case of *Carney* v *Fair*[2] shows the reluctance of the courts to infer authority from any save the most unequivocal of instructions. In that case a land agent, who looked after certain estates for the defendant, was approached by the plaintiff with a view to buying the land. The agent wrote to the defendant's solicitors saying he "had reason to believe that he could secure a purchaser at £6,000 cash" and the solicitors, having taken instruction, replied that the defendant "will accept a purchaser at £6,000". Once again the court could find no reason to depart from the general rule expressed in *Hamer* v *Sharp*, and the plaintiff was held unable to enforce the contract alleged to have been made with the land agent.

Conflicting expressions of judicial opinion have been provoked by the simple instruction to "sell" property, and the question as to the legal effect of such a request remains unresolved. In *Chadburn* v *Moore*,[3] Kekewich J was of the opinion that an estate agent obtained no extra authority from being instructed to sell, unless the agent was also expressly authorised to enter into a binding contract. This view was endorsed in *Lewcock* v *Bromley*,[4] where Sargant J said: "There must, to justify such a signing, be a special and express authority to sign".

Sargant J treated as depending on its own special circumstances the decision of Buckley J in *Rosenbaum* v *Belson*,[5] where a client requested a firm of estate agents in writing: "Please sell for me my

---

1 (1892) 61 LJ Ch 674.
2 (1920) 54 Ir LT 61.
3 (1892) 61 LJ Ch 674.
4 (1920) 127 LT 116.
5 [1900] 2 Ch 267.

houses ..." and named a price of £800. The estate agents obtained an offer of £785 which the client agreed to accept and, on the facts of the case, the estate agent was clearly empowered to sign the open contract in question. However, Buckley J, after reviewing all the previous English cases, came to the conclusion that, even without the specific consent of the client, the instruction to "sell" would still have empowered the agent to make a contract. As the judge remarked: "A sale *prima facie* means a sale effectual in point of law, including the execution of a contract where the law requires a contract in writing." Noting that the authority in *Hamer* v *Sharp* was to "find a purchaser", Buckley J said:

To my mind there is a substantial difference between those expressions. Authorising a man to sell means an authority to conclude a sale; authorising him to find a purchaser means less than that – it means to find a man willing to become a purchaser, not to find him and also make him a purchaser.

The effect of an authority to sell property arose again in the case of *Keen* v *Mear*,[1] which is discussed in more detail below. Having there considered a number of cases concerning the estate agent's authority, Russell J said:

The result of those cases is, in my opinion, this: that the mere employment by an owner of an estate agent to dispose of a house confers no authority to make a contract; the agent is solely employed to find persons to negotiate with the owner; but, if the agent is definitely instructed to sell at a defined price, those instructions involve authority to make a binding contract and to sign an agreement.

Had the matter rested there, it might well have appeared that the opinions expressed in *Rosenbaum* v *Belson* and *Keen* v *Mear*, coming after a survey of precedent, were preferable to the contrary opinions shown in *Chadburn* v *Moore* and *Lewcock* v *Bromley*. However, in *Wragg* v *Lovett*[2] the Court of Appeal had its first opportunity to express a view upon the question. On the facts of the case, the firm of estate agents were held to have been given express authority to do whatever was best for their client, including making a binding contract on his behalf. Thus the following remarks

---

1 [1902] 2 Ch 574.
2 [1948] 2 All ER 968.

of Lord Greene MR (who delivered the only judgment of the court) were strictly *obiter*:[1]

We must not be understood as suggesting that when a vendor merely authorises a house agent to "sell" at a stated priced he must be taken to be authorising the agent to do more than agree with an intending purchaser the essential (and, generally, the most essential) term, ie, the price. The making of a contract is no part of an estate agent's business, and, although, on the facts of an individual case, the person who employs him may authorise him to make a contract, such an authorisation is not lightly to be inferred from vague or ambiguous language.

The effect of this *dictum* is to confuse still further the legal effect of the instruction to "sell" property. However, the practical lesson to be drawn from the cases is obvious (especially in view of the disappointed purchaser's right of action against the agent for breach of warranty of authority):[2] unless the client's written instructions clearly and unequivocally empower the estate agent to sign a binding contract of sale, the agent should conquer the natural desire to see the property sold and go no further than introducing prospective purchasers to the client.

As a postscript to this discussion, it may be noted that, even where express authority *does* exist, any sale which is effected by the agent must be in strict accordance with its terms. Thus, in *Ludwig* v *Schultze*,[3] where an estate agent was instructed to effect a binding contract of sale, the client was none the less held not to be bound by a sale at a lower price than had been authorised. It was irrelevant that the purchaser knew nothing of the restriction on the agent's authority; there was no implied authority in this situation, so the express terms were all that mattered.

4   Extent of authority

It is clear from what has been said that an estate agent may be given authority to enter into a contract of sale or lease on behalf of the client. Where, however, the court decides that such authority has been given, a further problem of interpretation remains to be

---

1 The passage was however approved by the Privy Council in *Jawara* v *Gambia Airways* [1992] EGCS 54; [1992] NPC 61.
2 As in *Godwin* v *Francis* (1870) LR 5 CP 295.
3 (1885) NZLR 4 SC 247.

solved. The question which must be asked is: do the instructions under which the agent is acting empower the making of any sort of contract at all, or is the agent restricted to making an "open contract", that is, one which leaves all the terms except the price to be implied by law? In particular, is an agent who acts under general instructions "to sell and exchange contracts" permitted to make use, for example, of the National Conditions of Sale, a standard-form document containing most of the detailed conditions subject to which land is commonly sold?

When the courts were first called upon to consider the question of the general authority of estate agents, the conditions which were implied into open contracts by common law placed the vendor under onerous obligations, especially in connection with the satisfactory proof of title. Vendors were accordingly very reluctant to enter into open contracts for the sale of their property, preferring to modify their common law obligations by inserting into the contract of sale express terms, drafted for the purpose by their legal advisers. In *Hamer* v *Sharp*,[1] where an estate agent purported to make an open contract, the actual decision was that he had no implied authority to make such a contract. So too, in *Wilde* v *Watson*,[2] although the decision rested upon a broader principle, the judge was clearly concerned at the idea of the vendor being bound by an open contract. Indeed, considerable weight was attached in that case to the fact that the agent still had in his possession the conditions under which the property was to have been sold at auction; this should have made him more careful to guard against committing his client to anything more burdensome.

The Real Property and Conveyancing Act 1881 greatly improved the position of vendors under open contracts (particularly where leasehold property was being sold) and thus made the use of express conditions less necessary. Although this alteration in the law failed to convince Kekewich J in *Chadburn* v *Moore*[3] that estate agents should now be presumed to have authority to contract, it nevertheless led to a change of judicial attitude regarding the type of contract which might be entrusted to such agents. Hitherto, the protection of the client from the rigours of an open contract had

---

1 (1874) LR 19 Eq 108.
2 (1878) 1 LR Ir 402.
3 (1892) 61 LJ Ch 674.

been of paramount importance; henceforth, more weight could be given to another judicial view, that the drafting of conditions of sale should be left to solicitors. Significantly, in *Saunders* v *Dence*,[1] the first case in which an estate agent was held to have been given authority to make a binding contract on behalf of a client, no special drafting was necessary. In that case the defendant, who had bought a farm at an auction for £6,000, authorised the auctioneer to transfer his interest for £6,600. In holding that this empowered the auctioneer to sign a contract, Field J drew attention to the fact that the property was sold on exactly the same conditions as those on which the defendant had bought it; thus, no complications arose as to title.

The question of the extent of an estate agent's authority arose specifically in *Keen* v *Mear*,[2] which concerned a cottage owned by two brothers, Samuel and Walter Mear. Samuel authorised an estate agent named Cox to "sell" the cottage and Cox, having accepted a deposit from the plaintiff, signed a contract which set a date for completion and contained conditions relating to the title. In considering the effect of the agent's instructions, Russell J said:

In these circumstances, Cox had, in my opinion, authority to sign an open contract on behalf of Samuel Mear to sell the property for £515. But had he authority to sign the particular contract here in question? I think not. It contains a special condition as to title, which might or might not be less favourable to a vendor than the title required under an open contract ...

The agent had therefore exceeded his authority in making this contract. However it was held that, on the facts, Samuel had ratified the agent's act, thus giving him authority in retrospect and making Samuel liable on the contract. The result of the case was that Samuel had to pay damages to the plaintiff; specific performance was out of the question, since the whole transaction had taken place without the consent, or indeed the knowledge, of Walter Mear.

The quotation from the judgment of Russell J given above may appear to suggest that, if the special condition in question could be shown conclusively to be for the benefit of the vendor, an estate agent would have implied authority to include it. This was the view

---

1 (1885) 52 LT 644.
2 [1920] 2 Ch 574.

taken by the trial judge in *Wragg* v *Lovett*;[1] the Court of Appeal, however, concerned at the difficulty of weighing the relative merits and demerits of each individual condition, interpreted this *dictum* rather differently, saying (i) that the words of Russell J:

suggest to our minds that he meant to limit the authorisation in such a case to an authorisation to make an open contract and to exclude a consideration whether a term inappropriate to an open contract was or was not more beneficial to the vendor; (ii) that an open contract is a thing certain, whereas the question whether or not a particular stipulation is more or less beneficial to the vendor may, in the complications of English conveyancing, be a question of great difficulty which could only be resolved by litigation ...

The Court of Appeal was at pains to point out that no concluded opinion was necessary on this matter since, on the special facts of the case, the estate agents had been given express authority to enter into a contract of considerable complexity. Nevertheless, it would be a foolhardy estate agent who, in the teeth of such *obiter dicta*, relied on such general words of authority as "sell" to make anything other than an open contract.

B Authority to sign a document

An agent who is actually authorised to effect a binding contract on behalf of a client will have implied authority to do whatever is necessary to render that contract enforceable.[2] Until recently, this meant that such an agent could sign a memorandum of sale sufficient to satisfy section 40 of the Law of Property Act 1925. Now with the replacement of that provision by somewhat tighter rules regarding contracts for the sale of land,[3] it seems that the agent's implied authority would extend to signing an actual contract.

A more difficult question is whether an agent who is *not* authorised to effect a binding transaction, but who is authorised to carry out some formal act for the client (such as signing a document), can expose the client to legal responsibility if that act turns out to have unexpected consequences in law. Prior to 1989,

---

1 [1948] 2 All ER 968.
2 *Rosenbaum* v *Belson* [1900] 2 Ch 267; see also the position of an auctioneer: p 275.
3 Law of Property (Miscellaneous Provisions) Act 1989, section 2.

for example, it was repeatedly held that the "memorandum" required to make a contract for the sale of land enforceable need not have been drafted with that in mind, and that any document which in fact contained the relevant terms would suffice.[1] The question therefore was whether an agent authorised to sign a document would also be treated as authorised to provide the necessary memorandum.

To hold a client bound by the agent's act in such a case would appear artificial, to say the least, and it is perhaps as well that this particular problem has ceased to be of practical importance with the repeal of section 40 of the Law of Property Act 1925. However, there remain other areas of agency work in which written documents may have unexpected legal effects, and support for the artificial view described above may be found in the case of *Graylaw Investments Ltd* v *JR Bridgford & Sons*.[2] The plaintiffs there, who owned a large building occupied by various tenants, instructed the defendant agents to negotiate surrenders of all the leases, so that they could sell the property with vacant possession. Owing to a mistaken view of the Landlord and Tenant Act 1954, section 38, both the plaintiffs and the defendants believed that any agreement which was reached with a tenant would not be legally enforceable, but would be a commitment of honour only. The defendants accordingly negotiated a number of surrender agreements but, when the property market declined, the plaintiffs sought to resile from one of them. On finding, to everyone's surprise, that the agreement was in fact legally binding, the plaintiffs brought an action against their agents, claiming that they had exceeded their authority. However, it was held by the Court of Appeal that the agents had done precisely what they had been instructed to do, namely to negotiate surrender agreements; it was irrelevant that the legal effect of these was different from what the parties had envisaged.[3]

If this view of the law is correct, so that the "accidental" consequences of an authorised act are also deemed to be authorised, it means that an agent must take extra care to avoid

---

1 *Re Hoyle* [1893] 1 Ch 84 (recital in a will); *Phillips* v *Butler* [1945] Ch 358 (auctioneer's receipt for a deposit); *Elias* v *George Sahely & Co (Barbados) Ltd* [1982] 3 All ER 801 (solicitor's receipt for a deposit "as stakeholder").

2 (1982) 266 EG 807.

3 In *Walsh* v *Griffiths-Jones* [1978] 2 All ER 1002 (p 75, *ante*), on the other hand, where what was intended to be a licence turned out to be a lease, the client was bound only because there was *ostensible* authority.

any such consequences. In particular, it suggests that estate agents should continue to pepper their correspondence with such phrases as "subject to contract", in order to avoid any possibility of inadvertently committing the client to a binding contract.

C Authority to receive payment

The question of an agent's authority to receive payment on behalf of the principal usually arises for decision in cases where the agent has, whether dishonestly or not, lost the money and is either untraceable or insolvent. In such circumstances, the third party's obligation to pay the principal is only discharged if the agent was authorised to receive the money; if not, the loss falls on the third party, who must pay again. The legal position is frequently governed by the express terms of the agreement between principal and third party;[1] where this is not so, however, it is the extent of the agent's implied authority which must be ascertained.

Surprisingly, perhaps, it seems that the mere fact that an agent is authorised to sell property does not of itself impliedly confer authority to receive the purchase price, either of goods[2] or, in the case of an estate agent, of land.[3] Indeed, there is support for the view that an auctioneer does not even have implied authority to receive a deposit from the highest bidder.[4] If correct, this principle would seem equally applicable to the rare case of an estate agent who is authorised to make a binding contract for the sale of a client's property. It is submitted, however, that the better view[5] is that an estate agent instructed to make a contract for the sale of property, on terms which require the payment of a deposit, has in consequence implied authority to receive that deposit on the vendor's behalf.[6]

---

1 This is commonly so at auctions: see p 276.

2 *Butwick* v *Grant* [1924] 2 KB 483.

3 *Peterson* v *Moloney* (1951) 85 CLR 91.

4 *Mynn* v *Joliffe* (1834) 1 Mood & R 326: p 277.

5 Which was taken by a New Zealand court in *Boote* v *RT Shiels & Co* [1978] 1 NZLR 445.

6 As to the capacity (agent or stakeholder) in which such a deposit would be received, see p 224.

1   Pre-contract deposits

The "deposits" referred to in the previous paragraph are *contract* deposits, that is to say, sums paid on or after the making of the contract of sale and in accordance with its terms, as a part payment of the purchase price and a guarantee that the purchaser means business.[1] Rather different considerations apply to *pre-contract* deposits, or "earnest money", which may be demanded and received by an estate agent at the "subject to contract" stage of the transaction.[2] The purpose of this practice is not entirely clear, for the payment of a deposit before contracts are exchanged is of no *legal* effect. The purchaser acquires no rights to the property by virtue of making such a payment; the vendor cannot prevent the purchaser from insisting on the return of the money;[3] and the estate agent cannot use this sum as security for a commission claim unless and until it becomes the vendor's money, which will not be before the sale is completed.[4] Furthermore, it appears that, unless the estate agent accepts this money "as agent for the vendor" with specific authority from the vendor so to do, it must not be paid to the vendor, but must be held at all times on behalf of the purchaser.[5] It was at one time the law that the estate agent was entitled to keep whatever interest might be earned on the money while it was being held,[6] but even this benefit has largely disappeared under the provisions of the Estate Agents Act 1979.[7] As a result, it seems that the only justification for demanding or accepting a pre-contract deposit is a purely practical one, namely that the estate agent is more likely to find out when a prospective purchaser loses interest in a property.

A particular problem which has been caused by pre-contract deposits, and the one with which we are presently concerned, arises when an estate agent absconds with the money. Naturally, a vendor who has actually authorised the agent to receive this sum

---

1 *Soper* v *Arnold* (1889) 14 App Cas 429 at p 435, *per* Lord Macnaghten.

2 The "client's money" provisions of the Estate Agents Act 1979, however, apply equally to both kinds of deposit.

3 *Chillingworth* v *Esche* [1924] 1 Ch 97.

4 *Skinner* v *Trustee of the Property of Reed* [1967] Ch 1194.

5 *Rayner* v *Paskell and Cann* (1948) 152 EG 270.

6 *Potters* v *Loppert* [1973] Ch 399.

7 See p 231.

will be liable to the purchaser for its repayment;[1] in the absence of express authority from the vendor, however, the question is whether such authority is to be implied. In a series of cases which began with the decision of the Court of Appeal in *Ryan* v *Pilkington*,[2] the English courts held that such implied authority did indeed exist. A vendor was thus responsible to the purchaser for money, notwithstanding that the vendor had not asked the agent to collect it, might indeed know nothing about it and certainly had no legal entitlement to it. The legal justification for this extraordinary result was, according to Morris LJ in *Ryan* v *Pilkington*, that the collection of earnest money is reasonably incidental to the function of finding a purchaser and thus within an estate agent's implied authority. The moral justification was summed up by Megaw LJ in the later case of *Burt* v *Claude Cousins & Co Ltd*:[3]

It is the vendor who has chosen the estate agent, who has clothed him with the capacity of agent, and who has enabled him to ask for and receive a deposit in connection with the business to which the agency relates.

In the first edition of this book, this self-perpetuating line of authority was heavily criticised on both legal and moral grounds, and the hope was expressed that a superior court would be able to reverse the trend. This is precisely what happened when the case of *Sorrell* v *Finch*[4] reached the House of Lords. In the opinion of their lordships, the argument that the vendor should be liable on the ground of having chosen the estate agent was "too simplistic"; more important was the point that a pre-contract deposit remains at all times the property of the purchaser. As Lord Edmund-Davies pointed out:[5]

The just solution of the problem of which of two innocent parties should suffer should depend very largely (and possibly conclusively) upon what

---

1 *Duke of Norfolk* v *Worthy* (1808) 1 Camp 337.
2 [1959] 1 All ER 689: of the others, the most important are *Goding* v *Frazer* [1966] 2 All ER 234; *Hassan* v *Varol Agencies Ltd* (1969) 212 EG 39; *Maloney* v *Hardy and Moorshead* (1970) 216 EG 1582; *Burt* v *Claude Cousins & Co Ltd* [1971] 2 QB 426; *Barrington* v *Lee* [1972] 1 QB 326.
3 [1971] 2 QB 426 at p 452.
4 [1977] AC 728.
5 *Ibid*, at p 748.

rights could have been asserted by each of them in respect of the money in the agent's hands at all material times.

The illogicality and injustice of making a vendor responsible for money to which he or she had no claim was equally important in the eyes of Lord Russell of Killowen:[1]

I find it impossible to accept a theory of authority from a vendor to the estate agent to accept a deposit *as agent for the vendor* on terms that so long as all remains in negotiation the estate agent must on no account pay the deposit to the vendor or to the vendor's order, but on the contrary must on demand of the purchaser pay it back to the purchaser without reference to the vendor . . . That appears to me with all respect to be juridically unacceptable.

As a result of the decision in *Sorrell* v *Finch*, it is now clearly established that, unless an estate agent is expressly authorised to receive a pre-contract deposit on behalf of a client, it is the purchaser alone who takes the risk that the agent will default in repayment. Moreover, this applies irrespective of whether the estate agent purports to receive the money "as agent", "as stakeholder" or without specifying any particular capacity. This change from the previous unjust and illogical rule is greatly to be welcomed, but it should not be thought that the problem is thereby completely solved. A lost deposit, notwithstanding *Sorrell* v *Finch*, remains lost; only the identity of the loser is changed. While the major professional bodies to which estate agents belong provide a measure of protection by means of Accounts Rules and Compensation Schemes, these do not cover the kind of agent who appeared in *Sorrell* v *Finch* itself:

The estate agent was, so far as is known, a man with no professional qualifications and a member of no professional organisation. He was, unknown to either the vendor or to any of the possible purchasers concerned, a dishonest rogue and an undischarged bankrupt.[2]

It is greatly to be regretted, therefore, that the Government has so far declined to implement the full range of deposit-protecting

---

1 [1977] AC 728 at p 753.
2 [1977] AC 728 at p 752, *per* Lord Russell of Killowen.

powers which are available to it under the provisions of the Estate Agents Act 1979.[1]

2   Illegal premiums

There is one other area in which a client has been held responsible for the receipt of money by an estate agent. This rests largely upon a single decision of the Court of Appeal, which is somewhat surprising since one suspects that the factual situation involved is not as uncommon as it might (or should) be. Nevertheless, although the case appears as an isolated landmark in the Law Reports and although certain views expressed by Denning LJ are open to criticism, the decision itself has been quoted with apparent approval on subsequent occasions.

The case in question, *Navarro v Moregrand Ltd,*[2] concerned the letting of a flat by an estate agent on behalf of the defendants. The plaintiff, who wanted a tenancy of the flat, was told by the agent that he would have to make a payment of £225 in one pound notes, in addition to the rent. The plaintiff paid this sum to the estate agent, and then sued both landlords and agent to recover the money as an illegal premium under section 2(5) of the Landlord and Tenant (Rent Control) Act 1949. The county court judge found that, although the agent had no authority from the landlords to demand such a sum, he had ostensible authority to conduct the full business of letting this particular property. Nevertheless the judge held that, when the agent demanded an illegal premium, the plaintiff received the clearest possible notice that the agent was exceeding his authority.

The plaintiff appealed to the Court of Appeal, where Somervell LJ took a very different view of the conclusions to be drawn from the evidence. Referring to the fact that the trial judge had treated the payment as a premium, and not as a bribe to the estate agent, he said: "I think that the conclusion which anybody in the tenant's position would have drawn, dealing with a man placed in the position of the second defendant by the landlords, was that the landlords were demanding a premium for the granting of the lease." The agent's illegal action was therefore within the scope of his

---

1 See p 225.
2 [1951] 2 TLR 674.

ostensible authority, and the landlords were liable to the plaintiff for the sum paid.

Denning LJ reached the same conclusion as Somervell LJ, but by a completely different (and, it is submitted, quite erroneous) route. The estate agent, he said, had committed a "statutory wrong" by demanding a premium for the granting of the lease. This wrong had been committed in the course of the agent's employment (and this would be so whether or not the agent had actual or ostensible authority) and the principal was therefore vicariously liable. This analysis of the law can be criticised on two main grounds. First, it represents an application of tort principles to what is in fact a case of quasi-contract, an action to recover a sum of money paid in contravention of a statute. Second, it reveals a confusion between the liability of an employer for the torts of an employee and that of a principal for the torts of an agent. General vicarious liability, with its allied concept of the "course of employment", appears relevant only to the former relationship, where it is well established. No such broad principle covers the second situation where, if the principal is to be made liable, it must be established that the agent acted within the scope of authority.[1]

The precise status of *Navarro* v *Moregrand* today is a matter of some doubt. The judgment of Denning LJ has already been criticised; that of Somervell LJ, with its emphasis on the landlord's placing of the agent in a position to perpetrate the fraud, is strongly reminiscent of the argument in respect of pre-contract deposits which was rejected by the House of Lords in *Sorrell* v *Finch*.[2] Indeed, the latter decision renders it very difficult to claim that the agent in *Navarro* v *Moregrand* had implied authority to collect a premium, or even that such authority would be contained by implication within the ostensible authority to conduct the full business of letting.[3] In short, it may be best to regard the case as turning on its own individual facts which were sufficient to clothe the agent with the appearance of authority to do the very act complained of, namely, to collect an illegal premium.

---

1 See P S Atiyah, *Vicarious Liability in the Law of Torts*, chapter 9.

2 [1977] AC 728: p 85.

3 This none the less appears to have been the view of the Court of Appeal in the similar case of *Saleh* v *Robinson* [1988] 2 EGLR 126, where *Navarro* v *Moregrand* was not mentioned.

D Authority to describe the property

1 Agent's misrepresentation

The law of misrepresentation enables a person to resile from a contract or to claim damages where it can be shown that the other party induced that contract by making a false statement of fact. The position is the same where the offending statement is made by an agent of a contracting party, provided, of course, that the agent is acting with authority.[1]

The possibility that an estate agent's rather restricted authority might not extend to making statements appears to have been canvassed for the first time in *Mullens* v *Miller*,[2] where the plaintiff employed an estate agent to find, first, a tenant and, later, a purchaser for his warehouse. The agent induced the defendant to offer £750 by making wildly exaggerated claims as to the value of the warehouse and by naming, falsely, various persons who were said to be eager to lease it. When the truth was discovered, the defendant refused to complete the purchase; the plaintiff then brought an action for specific performance of the contract, claiming that, since the agent's statements were made without any form of authority whatsoever, they should not prejudice the rights of the seller.

In refusing to award specific performance, Bacon V-C dealt with this contention as follows:

A man employs an agent to let a house for him; that authority, in my opinion, contains also an authority to describe the property truly, to represent its actual situation, and, if he thinks fit, to represent its value.

A similar result was reached in *Wauton* v *Coppard*[3] where, however, the point does not appear to have been specifically raised. There, an auctioneer, selling the defendant's leasehold property by private treaty (and therefore in the same position, legally speaking, as an estate agent) misrepresented the effect of certain restrictions

---

1 An agent acting in excess of authority can be personally liable for breach of warranty of authority, although the innocent party cannot of course rescind the contract.
2 (1882) 22 ChD 194.
3 [1889] 1 Ch 92.

upon the permitted use of the property under the lease. The court, referring throughout to the statements complained of as being made by the defendant's agent, awarded the plaintiff rescission of the contract and the return of the deposit with interest.

These two examples illustrate clearly the liability to which a client may be subjected by an agent's misrepresentation, and it might well be supposed in such circumstances that the client could recover this loss by taking action against the agent. This assumption was proved accurate in *Whiteman* v *Weston*[1] where the defendant, an estate agent instructed to find a tenant for the plaintiff's house, told a music teacher that he could use the property as a school of music. This use in fact constituted a breach of covenant and the plaintiff was in due course compelled, by complaints from the neighbours, to take legal action against his tenant. This action for breach of covenant failed, because the tenant was entitled entirely to rely on the assurances given by the estate agent, and the landlord then succeeded in recovering the costs of his suit from the agent by way of damages for breach of duty.

In two more recent cases concerning estate agents' commission,[2] the effect of an agent's misrepresentation fell to be considered. In each case commission was payable on the signing of a binding contract and in each case the purchaser, incensed at a misstatement made by the estate agent, refused to complete the contract he had signed. The estate agents failed in their claims for remuneration since, as was admitted on all sides, the misrepresentations made these contract unforceable against the purchasers.

Had the line of judicial comment stopped at this point, it would have appeared settled beyond any reasonable argument that clients are responsible for statements made by their estate agents. However, some doubt has been cast upon this proposition by remarks of Roskill LJ in *Gosling* v *Anderson*.[3] In that case the plaintiff bought a flat from the defendant on the faith of an assurance from the defendant's estate agent that planning

---

1 The Times, March 15 1900: see also *Power* v *Atkins* [1921] NZLR 763, and its sequel, *Atkins* v *AD Kennedy & Co Ltd* [1921] NZLR 977.
2 *Gregory* v *Fearn* [1953] 2 All ER 559; *Peter Long & Partners Ltd* v *Burns* [1956] 1 WLR 413 and 1083.
3 (1972) 223 EG 1743.

permission had been obtained for the erection of a garage. The judge at first instance,[1] Graham J, impressed by the fact that the defendant had left all negotiations in the hands of the estate agent, said that he "had ostensible authority to finalise matters and in particular to answer questions and give assurances about the property and the position in regard to planning permission". Nevertheless, the plaintiff failed in her claim for damages under section 2(1) of the Misrepresentation Act 1967 since, in the eyes of the court, she had not relied on the statement to a sufficient extent in deciding to purchase.

This latter finding was reversed by the Court of Appeal, so that the plaintiff was, after all, awarded damages. Only Roskill LJ made any mention of the question of an estate agent's authority, saying: "The learned judge spoke of the agent having ostensible authority from the defendant. In my view he was wrong in so stating. The relevant modern authorities on ostensible authority were not cited to him. The agent had actual authority to make the representation relied on, and the defendant is bound by that representation."

Since Roskill LJ did not identify the "relevant modern authorities", it is difficult to establish exactly why he denied the existence of any ostensible authority in this case. It may indeed be that his reference to "actual authority" was intended to include *implied* authority, in which case his judgment would be in line with the earlier cases to which we have referred. If, however, he meant to suggest that a client will be liable only where the agent has been *expressly* authorised to make the statement in question, it is submitted that this is incorrect. For safety's sake it should be assumed that statements made by an estate agent may be a source of liability for the client as well as for the agent personally.[2]

2 Avoidance of liability

The use of contract terms and extra-contractual notices to exclude or restrict liability for misrepresentation is discussed elsewhere.[3] At this point, however, it is relevant to consider one particular method by which vendors have in recent years sought to avoid liability for false statements made by an estate agent or auctioneer on their

---

1 (1971) 220 EG 1117.
2 See *Hatlelid* v *Sawyer & McClocklin Real Estate* [1977] 5 WWR 481.
3 pp408-410.

behalf. This consists of an announcement to the world at large that the agent concerned has no authority to that effect, so as to preclude any implication of authority which might otherwise be made. The device first came before a court in the case of *Overbrooke Estates Ltd* v *Glencombe Properties Ltd*[1] where the defendants, who had purchased property at an auction, refused to complete the purchase on the ground that the auctioneers, three days before the sale, had made a material misrepresentation about the property. The plaintiff vendors, while not denying this allegation, sought to rely upon a general condition of sale in the following terms:

The Vendors do not make or give and neither the Auctioneers nor any person in the employment of the Auctioneers has any authority to make or give any representation or warranty in relation to these properties.

It was held by Brightman J that the defendants, who must be taken to have bid with knowledge of the condition, were fixed with notice of the auctioneers' lack of authority and were therefore bound by the sale. Further, the condition was held not to be "a provision which would exclude or restrict . . . any liability" within the meaning of section 3 of the Misrepresentation Act 1967, so that it could not be challenged as being unreasonable.

Overbrooke v *Glencombe* was approved and, indeed, extended, by the Court of Appeal in *Collins* v *Howell-Jones*[2] in which estate agents, acting on the instructions of a client, showed a prospective purchaser certain drawings of a property for sale which were misleading (they suggested that a two-storey extension could be built at the rear of the property, whereas the rights to light of adjoining landowners would not in fact permit this). The purchaser, having bought the property, sought compensation from the client on the ground of misrepresentation, but the Court of Appeal held that a "no authority" clause in the estate agents' particulars of sale operated to defeat his claim. In so deciding, the court held that the *Overbrooke* principles applied, even though the clause in this case did not form part of the contract (the sale particulars themselves

---

1 [1974] 3 All ER 511.
2 (1980) 259 EG 331.

made this clear) and even though the agents here had been *expressly* authorised to make the offending statement.

The Court of Appeal in *Collins* v *Howell-Jones* did not have to consider the effect (if any) which section 3 of the Misrepresentation Act 1967 might have upon the clause in question, for section 3, as amended by section 8 of the Unfair Contract Terms Act 1977, now applies only to exemption clauses which form part of a contract. However, the view of Brightman J mentioned above, that an authority-denying clause is in any event outside the scope of the statute, must now be regarded a little more doubtfully in the light of *South Western General Property Co Ltd* v *Marton*.[1] That case concerned the sale of a plot of land at auction, so the conditions of sale formed part of the contract which was made on the fall of the hammer. The purchaser claimed to rescind the contract on the ground of a misrepresentation contained in the auctioneers' catalogue, whereupon he was faced with a variety of exemption clauses set out in the conditions of sale, including one of the kind now under discussion. It was held by Croom-Johnson J that all these clauses should be struck out as failing to satisfy the statutory requirement of "reasonableness"; the possibility that the authority-denying clause was not subject to this test does not appear to have been considered or even mentioned.

3 Warranties

Prior to the passing of the Misrepresentation Act 1967, a person seeking damages for a false statement had to establish either that the statement formed part of a contract or that fraud was involved. If neither of these factors was present, the injured party was limited to the equitable remedy of rescission, a remedy which was defective in a number of respects. In order to alleviate the situation, the courts would sometimes, in deserving cases, construct a second contract collateral to the main one and consisting of, on one side, a guarantee that a pre-contractual promise would be honoured and, on the other, a promise to enter into the main contract. Thus, on the failure of the pre-contractual promise, damages could be obtained for breach of this "collateral warranty".

---

1 (1982) 263 EG 1090.

In *Lawrence* v *Hull*[1] the court was invited to construct such a warranty from an estate agent's newspaper advertisement which described a house as being "in perfect order". The disappointed purchaser, unable to obtain rescission of the contract after completion,[2] sought damages. Rowlatt J, in holding that an estate agent's advertisement could not be treated as a warranty, said "it might be that in equity a vendor whose agent had made a misrepresentation of this kind would not be able to enforce specific performance, but that was a very different thing from holding that the representation was a warranty".

In *Hill* v *Harris*[3] the defendant, who was the tenant of premises on which he carried on the trade of boot and shoe maker and dealer, instructed estate agents to find a subtenant for the premises. The plaintiff wanted the premises for a confectionery and tobacco business and, although the headlease prohibited such a use, the estate agents told him that it would be all right. When the headlessor prevented the plaintiff from using the premises in this way, the plaintiff sought damages for breach of an implied collateral warranty that, if he took a lease of the premises, the defendant would guarantee that he could use them as he intended. The Court of Appeal held that no collateral warranty existed and Diplock LJ said:

It is, I apprehend, clear law that the ostensible authority of an estate agent invited to find a purchaser for premises or a lessee for premises, does not extend to entering into any contractual relationship in respect of the premises on behalf of the person instructing him. It may well be that he has authority to make representations as to the state of the premises, but representations are a very different matter from warranty.

Since the Misrepresentation Act 1967 it is possible to recover damages in respect of a misrepresentation and, accordingly, the pressing need to establish a collateral warranty has to a large

---

1 (1924) 41 TLR 75.
2 *Wilde* v *Gibson* (1848) 1 HL Cas 605. This is no longer a bar to recision: Misrepresentation Act 1967, section 1(b).
3 [1965] 2 QB 601: see also the New Zealand case of *McClure* v *Barth & Smith* [1980] *Recent Law* 38.

extent disappeared.[1] The same may be said of the need to prove fraud, something which has never been an easy thing to do. This is especially true in the field of agency, where "fraud" receives an added dimension. In *Armstrong* v *Strain*,[2] estate agents, employed by the defendant to sell a bungalow, told the plaintiff that it was in a very nice condition and that any building society would lend £1,200 on it, as this represented a small proportion of its value. The estate agents were unaware that the bungalow had a history of unsuccessful underpinnings which made its true value in the region of £1,000. The defendant knew of the underpinnings, but had not authorised the agent to make any statements as to the condition of the property, nor did he know that any statements had been made. The plaintiff bought the property for £2,400 but, within a short time, severe subsidence caused irreparable damage and the plaintiff brought an action for deceit.

Devlin J (whose decision was affirmed by the Court of Appeal) carried out an exhaustive survey of the authorities, many of which were contradictory, and reluctantly decided that the defendant was not guilty of fraud. As the judge put it: "you cannot add an innocent state of mind to an innocent state of mind and get as a result a dishonest state of mind".

E Authority to delegate

The general duty imposed upon every agent, to perform tasks personally and not to delegate them, has already been discussed;[3] we have also considered the legal relationships which may arise where delegation is authorised by the principal.[4] There is little authority upon the application of these principles to the specific case of an estate agent, which is somewhat surprising in view of the frequent use by such agents of commission-sharing agreements. Under these arrangements, an agent instructed to find a purchaser or a property offers a proportion of the commission to another agent in return for a successful introduction, and the courts have on

---

1 However, the device retains some usefulness, for example to circumvent an exclusion clause: see *Couchman* v *Hill* [1947] KB 554.
2 [1951] 1 TLR 856; affirmed [1952] 1 KB 232.
3 p48.
4 p66.

occasion been called upon to settle disputes arising between the two agents.[1]

The extent to which a commission-sharing agreement affects the original client was considered by the Court of Appeal in *Maloney v Hardy and Moorshead*,[2] in which an estate agent, without the client's knowledge, invited several other agents to co-operate in finding a purchaser. The plaintiff, after negotiating with one of the subagents, agreed "subject to contract" to purchase the property and paid a deposit. When the subagent absconded, taking the deposit with her, the plaintiff sued both the main agent and the vendor. The Court of Appeal unanimously held that the main agent was liable for the subagent's default, for it was clear from the evidence that he had authorised and, indeed, expected her to receive such a deposit. The vendor, however, bore no such responsibility, for she had not authorised the appointment of any subagents.[3] The basis of the decision was neatly summed up by Megaw LJ:

It is plain that no express authority was given ... to employ a subagent. There is no pleading or finding, nor is there any warranty in the evidence for a finding, that it is well-known practice, or a custom of the trade, general or local, or that it is a necessary and recognised incident of such agency, that the agent may employ a subagent with authority to collect a pre-contract deposit.

Although these remarks were based upon the evidence brought in the particular case, rather than upon any general legal rule, it is felt that the courts' general disinclination to imply authority to delegate would certainly apply to estate agents. However, this is not to say that a case could not be made out for customary authority if the evidence of usage was sufficiently strong, and this indeed is what happened in the Canadian case of *Carmichael v Bank of*

---

1 See, for example, *Davis* v *George Trollope & Sons* [1943] 1 All ER 501; *Wilkinson v North Suburban Properties Ltd* (1959) 174 EG 213. The former decision shows a court striving to interpret a subagency agreement in such a way that the subagent cannot earn commission unless the main agent is also entitled.
2 (1970) 216 EG 1582.
3 Today the action would fail anyway for lack of any implied authority to accept a pre-contract deposit: see p 86.

Montreal,[1] where the court gave official recognition to the North American practice of "multiple listing".

It is clear from the above case that the actions of a subagent whose appointment has not been authorised are the responsibility of the main agent alone; the client is completely unaffected by them. Indeed, according to a recent decision of the Court of Appeal, this legal liability is not the only misfortune which may befall an estate agent who delegates without seeking the client's authority; such action may lead the agent to forfeit commission. In *McCann & Co v Pow*[2] the plaintiffs, who were appointed "sole agents" for the sale of the defendant's flat, instructed subagents without his knowledge. A prospective purchaser was sent by one of the subagents to view the flat and the defendant, on learning that this purchaser had not come from the plaintiffs, naturally assumed that they could negotiate privately. When the flat was sold to this applicant, the plaintiffs claimed commission, but their claim was unanimously rejected by the Court of Appeal.

While the justice of this decision is not in dispute (because a vendor who believes that he or she is negotiating privately may well reduce the price to take account of the amount of commission saved) it is difficult to agree with the court in basing it upon the rule prohibiting delegation. Surely, so long as the client does not incur legal liability for the acts of a subagent, it is of no consequence whether potential purchasers of the property are introduced directly by the appointed agent, or indirectly through another firm? In either case, the main agent appears equally to be an "effective cause" of the subsequent sale. It is submitted that a much better justification for refusing the agents' commission claim in this case would have been that, by failing to disclose the fact of delegation to their client, and thereby weakening his negotiating position, they were in breach of their duty of loyalty.[3]

---

1 (1972) 25 DLR (3d) 570.
2 [1975] 1 All ER 129; followed in *Robert Bruce & Partners* v *Winyard Developments* [1987] 1 EGLR 20. *Cf* the unreported case of *Britton Poole & Burns* v *Theodosiades* (1983), where delegation was held to have been authorised by virtue of a "confirming letter".
3 See p 110.

CHAPTER 4

Estate agents' duties

A Duties to the client

Most of the duties which an estate agent owes to his client arise by implication from the general law of agency, and their underlying principles were consequently discussed in chapter 2. In this chapter we turn our attention to the way in which these principles have been applied in the context of estate agency.

1 Duty to act

(a) General

The relationship which exists between estate agent and client is, for the most part, treated in law as a normal example of agency for the purpose of determining their mutual rights and duties. However, it is a more loosely knit relationship than that of master and servant, or even that of salaried agent and principal, and this has led to suggestions that not all the normal incidents of agency are applicable. In particular, there is a certain amount of disagreement over the question whether an estate agent who takes on a property is obliged to do anything at all to attempt to secure a sale. The view that an estate agent is completely free to act or not is exemplified by *dicta* from the decision of the House of Lords in *Luxor (Eastbourne) Ltd* v *Cooper*.[1] The best-known remarks, in which are considered the basic nature of commission contracts in general and those of estate agents in particular, come from the speech of Lord Russell of Killowen:[2]

Contracts by which owners of property, desiring to dispose of it, put it in the hands of agents on commission terms, are not (in default of specific provisions) contracts of employment in the ordinary meaning of those words.

---

1 [1941] AC 108.
2 At p124.

No obligation is imposed on the agent to do anything. The contracts are merely promises binding on the principal to pay a sum of money upon the happening of a specified event, which involves the rendering of some service by the agent. There is no real analogy between such contracts, and contracts of employment by which one party binds himself to do certain work, and the other binds himself to pay remuneration for the doing of it.

Lord Romer said:[1]

The respondent was not employed by the appellants to find a purchaser. He was not employed to do anything at all, and would have committed no breach of his agreement with the appellants had he remained entirely inactive.

Finally, Viscount Simon LC said:[2]

I doubt whether the agent is bound, generally speaking, to exercise any standard of diligence in looking for a possible purchaser. He is commonly described as "employed": but he is not "employed" in the sense in which a man is employed to paint a picture or to build a house, with the liability to pay damages for delay or want of skill.

According to the view thus forcibly expressed, the true analogy with an estate agent's mandate is the offer of a reward in return for a specific act. A person is under no duty to seek the reward but, if the act is done, the reward is payable.[3] If this is correct, it leads to the conclusion that the normal relationship between estate agent and client consists of a "unilateral contract", that is to say, one which does not ripen into a contract in the full sense until the agent "accepts" the client's "offer" by bringing about whatever event is specified.

Such a conclusion would have a number of unfortunate consequences. In the first place, it would mean that the terms of the "offer" are fixed at the moment when the client first instructs the agent to act; as a result, a "confirming letter" sent by the agent which in fact alters those terms (or the terms which are implied by law in the absence of express agreement) takes effect as a counter-

---

1 At p153.
2 At p117.
3 See Murdoch: "The Nature of Estate Agency" (1975) 91 LQR 357.

offer and is thus not binding unless specifically accepted by the client.[1] Second, it would cause severe difficulties of interpretation in relation to section 18 of the Estate Agents Act 1979, which requires estate agents to notify their clients in advance of all potential charges, and which was clearly drafted on the assumption that the relationship is contractual from the outset.[2] Third, the statutory duty of care which is imposed by section 13 of the Supply of Goods and Services Act 1982 is expressed in such terms that it can only apply once a contract for the supply of services is in existence; if the relationship consists of a "unilateral contract", therefore, it lies outside the scope of this provision.

Since what we may call the *Luxor v Cooper* view has so many inconvenient implications, it is somewhat reassuring to find that it has not passed wholly without challenge. In the case itself, Lord Wright described the estate agent as having introduced a prospective purchaser "in pursuance of his undertaking" and further stated:[3]

It is well known that in the ordinary course a property owner intending to sell may put his property on the books of several estate agents with each of whom he makes a contract for payment of commission on a sale.

Such comments suggest that an estate agent is not quite as free to remain inactive as the majority of their lordships appear to have thought, and a similar line was taken by two members of the Court of Appeal in the case of *Prebble & Co v West*.[4] In that case a vendor of property made a claim against her estate agents for negligence in relation to the sale. Counsel for the agents, relying on *dicta* from *Luxor v Cooper*, contended that, since an estate agent could not be sued for doing nothing at all, there must equally be immunity for doing something and doing it negligently. This proposition was described as "startling" by Edmund Davies LJ, who asserted that if an estate agent, who had been told that the client required a quick sale, received an offer for the property at the asking price, it would be the agent's duty to pass on this offer to

---

1 See p 174.
2 See p 208.
3 At p139.
4 (1969) 211 EG 831.

the client. Lord Denning MR agreed with this illustration, and said of an estate agent: "So long as he has the house on his books, it is his duty to have regard to the interest of his client and not to do anything contrary to it."

A further attack on the "unilateral contract" concept of estate agency[1] uses as ammunition the earlier decision of the Court of Appeal in *Keppel* v *Wheeler*.[2] In that case a firm of agents whose commission was not earned until matters reached at least the stage of exchanging contracts were held liable to pay damages to their client for failing to disclose certain information *before* that date. The agents' liability *could* in all probability have been based upon breach of their duty of loyalty[3] (a duty which exists whether or not there is a contractual relationship between agent and client[4]) but the Court of Appeal appears to have treated them as guilty of a breach of contract; thus the decision as it stands is undeniably in conflict with the *dicta* (for that is all they are) of the House of Lords in *Luxor* v *Cooper*.

(b) *Sole agency*

In the light of the foregoing it is impossible to say with any degree of certainty whether or not an estate agent may be liable for damaging a client's interests through inaction. However, it may be more confidently suggested, for the reasons outlined below, that such liability could indeed be incurred by a "sole agent".

It is well established that a client who appoints a "sole agent" will be liable in damages for selling the property through another agent. Likewise, a client who gives an agent "sole right to sell" will be liable for selling the property privately.[5] The legal basis of the vendor's undoubted obligation in such cases has seldom been the subject of judicial investigation, but such authority as there is suggests that it rests upon some consideration, in the form of a counter-obligation, moving from the agent. In *Bentall, Horsley & Baldry* v

---

1 By CR McConnell (1983) 265 EG 547.

2 [1927] 1 KB 577.

3 As it was in the Canadian case of *Jackson* v *Packham Real Estate Ltd* (1980) 109 DLR (3d) 277.

4 See p 42.

5 *Chamberlain & Willows* v *Rose* (1924) summarised at [1931] 1 KB 261; *Hampton & Sons Ltd* v *George* [1939] 3 All ER 627: p 161.

Vicary,[1] for example, the agency agreement provided that, in the event of a sale, the expenses incurred in advertising the property should be borne by the client; if no sale resulted, on the other hand, this cost should fall upon client and agent in equal shares. McCardie J held that the arrangement provided "ample consideration" to render a sole agency enforceable against the client, but it is submitted that this reasoning is suspect. Since, as we shall see,[2] the client of an estate agent is not usually responsible for the agent's expenses unless this is specifically agreed, the special arrangement in *Bentall's* case was in truth a *concession* by the client and could hardly therefore be said to constitute consideration on the agent's part.

In cases where there is no special arrangement of the kind found in *Bentall's* case, judges have on occasion found the consideration which they regard as necessary to support a sole agency in an implied undertaking by the agent to use "best endeavours" to bring about a sale. The two cases most commonly cited in this connection are *E Christopher & Co* v *Essig*[3] and *Mendoza & Co* v *Bell*.[4] Unfortunately, neither of these decisions is fully reported and, moreover, certain remarks attributed to Goddard LJ in the latter case cast some doubt upon his line of reasoning. In reply to his own question: "Why should a property owner appoint a sole agent?", his lordship is said to have explained:

If he employed a sole agent it seemed ... that the contract must be that the agent would do his best to find a purchaser and would be committing a breach of his contract if he did not do something, although he might not be successful. Otherwise a property owner was getting no benefit by appointing a sole agent.

Since the vendor in this case had claimed that it was precisely because he was getting no benefit from the appointment of a sole agent that he should not be liable for the breach of the sole agency agreement, it may be objected that the learned judge's reasoning assumes the very thing which it sets out to prove.

---

1 [1931] 1 KB 253.
2 p177.
3 [1948] WN 461.
4 (1952) 159 EG 372.

The idea of an implied obligation on the part of a sole agent to use "best endeavours" is open to two further objections. First, while such an obligation has been examined by the courts in situations beyond the world of property,[1] it is difficult to see how it would operate in the field of estate agency. No doubt some form of positive action would be expected of the agent, but what precisely would this involve? In *Glentree Estates Ltd* v *Gee*,[2] where the client of a sole agent suggested that the agent was under a positive duty to advise as to price and sale, to provide regular "progress reports" and to negotiate with applicants in an effort to raise the price, Ewbank J expressed strong doubts as to whether any such duties were owed. Secondly, it would be extremely difficult for a client to prove any loss flowing from an agent's failure to use best endeavours. Unlike a deprived sole agent, who can always point to the fact that the property has actually been sold as showing that the agent too could have sold it, a frustrated vendor has no such convenient evidence available.

The uncertainty of this area of the law has led many agents to make some express promise in an effort to ensure that their sole agency is enforceable. Such a promise may be in general terms, eg to use one's best endeavours, or it may consist in the provision of some special service denied to ordinary clients. In either case, it appears that an express promise takes the place of any obligation which would otherwise be implied. This, at any rate, is a conclusion which may be drawn from the decision of the Court of Appeal in *Midland Business Agency* v *Apted*,[3] where the plaintiffs were granted the sole right to sell the defendant's business in return for their inclusion of the business in their "sales circulation scheme". Upon proof that there was no such special scheme, it was held that consideration for the sole agency had totally failed and it was, accordingly, unenforceable by the plaintiffs. Although the point was not expressly taken, the decision appears to bear the implication that, if an *express* undertaking is not honoured, the agent cannot seek to support sole agency rights by reverting to an *implied*

---

1 *B Davis Ltd* v *Tooth & Co Ltd* [1937] 4 All ER 118; *Ault & Wiborg Paints* v *Sure Service* The Times July 2 1983.
2 (1981) 259 EG 332.
3 (1971) 218 EG 1727.

promise, such as that the agent will use best endeavours on the client's behalf.

In spite of the difficulties inherent in identifying any positive obligation owed by a sole agent to the client, let alone in discovering precisely what, in practical terms, such an obligation entails, there is no doubt that the English courts hitherto have treated the legal basis of sole agency as being a bilateral contract. It is therefore of interest to note that a Canadian judge has expressed the firm view that sole agency and multiple agency alike consist of unilateral contracts.[1] Since a client who commits a breach of a sole agency agreement is liable under Canadian law just as in England,[2] this view may be met with the objection that there can be no liability for the mere withdrawal of an offer at a time when that offer has not yet been accepted. It is submitted, however, that, since the English law which governs unilateral contracts already recognises that an *implied* promise by the offeror not to revoke an offer becomes legally binding once the offeree acts upon it,[3] there is no reason whatsoever why the client's *express* promise not to sell the property by other means should not become binding in exactly the same way. Such a view, if generally accepted, would ensure the continued enforceability of sole agency agreements, while freeing the law from the artificial and often fictitious constraints of "best endeavours".

2   Duty to comply with instructions

An estate agent's fundamental obligation is to comply with all the client's express instructions, provided only that these are lawful. Thus, an estate agent who disregards a specific prohibition imposed by the client, or who fails to honour an explicit undertaking given to the client, will be liable for any loss which is thereby caused.

Liability of this kind may obviously arise where an agent, despite exceeding whatever actual authority has been given, succeeds in rendering the client legally liable to a third party. For example, a client who loses a sale, or who has to pay damages, because of an

---

1 *Bradley-Wilson (1954) Ltd* v *Canyon Gardens Ltd* (1965) 53 WWR 413 at p417, *per* Sheppard JA.
2 *Galan* v *Alenko* [1950] 3 DLR 9; *Fidelity Trust Co* v *Rudy* (1957) 23 WWR 668.
3 See *Chitty on Contracts* (26th ed, 1983) at p85.

estate agent's misrepresentations, may in turn recoup all the losses from the offending agent.[1] Less commonly, an estate agent may be able to bind a client to a contract of sale, perhaps by virtue of the doctrine of apparent authority; once again, assuming that the agent had no *actual* authority to conclude the deal, he or she will be liable to the client for breach of duty.[2] However, everything turns on the meaning of the instructions given, so that an agent who does no more than write a letter which the client has actually authorised will not be liable to the client if this turns out to have more sweeping legal consequences than either party envisaged.[3]

Cases of the kind mentioned above are relatively rare, perhaps because, as we saw in the previous chapter, the ability of an estate agent to bind the client in law is so restricted. Of the countless other ways in which an agent's straightforward breach of duty may cause loss to the client, three examples must suffice. In *Papé* v *Westacott*,[4] an agent was instructed to give a client's tenant written permission to assign his lease, provided that the tenant first paid off all arrears of rent. The agent in fact gave the licence to the tenant in return for a cheque; when this was subsequently dishonoured, the agent was held liable to account to the client for the money lost. In *Edmunds* v *Andrews & Ashwell*,[5] agents acting for the vendor of a café handed over the keys to prospective purchasers so that they could inspect the premises and stock; once in possession, these applicants refused to leave and proved somewhat difficult to remove. On the evidence before the court, the clients failed to show that they had specifically instructed the agents to retain possession of the keys; however, the judge made it quite clear that, if such an instruction *had* been given, the agents would have been liable for failing to obey it.

Finally, in *Benham & Reeves* v *Christensen*,[6] estate agents were told by their client that no "For Sale" board was to be erected outside the property. The agents complied with the letter of this

---

1 *Whiteman* v *Weston* The Times, March 15 1900; *Atkins* v *AD Kennedy & Co Ltd* [1921] NZLR 977.
2 *Hayes* v *Douglas* [1976] 5 WWR 308.
3 *Graylaw Investments Ltd* v *JR Bridgford & Sons* (1982) 266 EG 807: p 82.
4 [1894] 1 QB 272.
5 (1981) 261 EG 53: p 108.
6 [1979] CLY 31.

instruction but, having introduced an applicant with whom contracts were duly exchanged, they put up a "Sold by" board. It was held that, while an agent would normally be entitled by custom to erect a board, this is subject to any express instructions from the client, so that the agents in this case were guilty of a breach of contract. Since, however, the client here had suffered nothing more than annoyance, he was entitled only to nominal damages of £5.

3 Duty of care

Whether or not the mere appointment of an estate agent imposes any positive obligation to look for a purchaser, there is no doubt that, once the agent takes the first step, a duty of care and skill will be owed to the client. This duty may not arise under the provisions of the Supply of Goods and Services Act 1982,[1] but it is in any case well established at common law.[2] In consequence, an estate agent who is guilty of "professional negligence" will be liable to the client in the same way as any other agent. This form of liability may attach to every aspect of the agent's work. However, in the specific field of estate agency, two areas stand out as being of particular importance.

It has long been settled that an estate agent who is instructed to find a prospective tenant for a client's property must use reasonable diligence to ascertain that the person introduced will be a proper tenant.[3] Failure in this respect may expose the agent to liability, not only for loss of rent, but also for the damage which the "rogue" tenant does to the premises.[4] What constitutes "reasonable diligence" is of course a question of fact; further, in accordance with the normal rule in negligence cases, it is a totally objective standard by which the agent falls to be judged. In *Brutton v Alfred Savill, Curtis & Henson*,[5] for example, a young employee of the defendants allowed a prospective tenant to take possession of premises without payment of a deposit or any rent in advance because he said that he had forgotten his cheque book. Once in possession, the tenant proved extremely difficult to remove and the

---

1 See p 40.
2 *Prebble & Co v West* (1969) 211 EG 831: p 100.
3 *Heys v Tindall* (1861) 30 LJQB 362.
4 Which can be considerable: £2810 in *Murray v Sturgis* (1981) 260 EG 61.
5 (1971) 218 EG 1417: see also *Faruk v Wyse* [1988] 2 EGLR 26.

landlady lost some £770 in unpaid rent and the cost of legal proceedings. It was held that, since the normal worldly estate agent would not have been taken in by this simple confidence trick, the young employee's gullibility amounted to negligence, and the defendants were therefore liable to their client for this loss.

Although the standard required of an agent is thus a fairly high one, the case of *Cunningham* v *Herbert Fulford & Chorley*[1] serves as a useful reminder that liability is not strict. The agents there were absolved by a County Court judge from liability for negligence in accepting a tenant who appeared wealthy but who had no bank account. The Court of Appeal thought that the agents had been "a bit casual" but, although it might have reached a different conclusion on the facts, did not find the evidence strong enough to say that the judge had erred in law.

The second main area in which estate agents have incurred liability for professional negligence is that of advising clients to conclude a transaction upon unfavourable terms. Such errors are no doubt frequently (perhaps most frequently) linked to the valuation of property. However, even where the tie between a specific valuation exercise and the advice given is not so clear, liability may still arise. In *Cuckmere Brick Co Ltd* v *Mutual Finance Ltd*,[2] for example, the defendants were mortgagees of land who had exercised their statutory power of sale. The estate agents employed by them to organise the sale prepared particulars on the basis that planning permission had been granted for 33 houses to be built on the land and that an earlier outline permission for 100 flats had lapsed. This was not in fact so, but the agents were so pessimistic as to the value of flat development in the area that, on learning that this permission had been confirmed, they neither postponed the auction nor readvertised the property. The Court of Appeal held that this constituted a failure to take reasonable care for which the defendants were responsible to the mortgagors.[3]

---

1 (1958) 171 EG 285: see also *Bradshaw* v *Press* (1982) (agents not obliged to check tenant's references, but only to obtain them); *Berkowitz* v *MW (St John's Wood) Ltd* [1993] EGCS 115.

2 [1971] Ch 949.

3 For recent cases in which estate agents successfully refuted allegations of negligence, see *Knight Frank & Rutley* v *Randolph* [1991] 1 EGLR 46; *Lough Eske Holdings* v *Knight Frank & Rutley* [1991] EGCS 18; *Watson* v *Lane Fox & Partners Ltd* [1991] 2 EGLR 21; *Letgain Ltd* v *Super Cements Ltd* [1993] EGCS 184.

In cases where an estate agent is acting on behalf of a prospective purchaser or tenant, negligence may consist of a failure to obtain sufficient information to enable the client to make the right decision. In *Carreras Ltd* v *D E & J Levy*,[1] for instance, agents who were asked to find office accommodation for their clients were held to be guilty of negligence in over-estimating the total floor area of the premises which they recommended. Similarly in *Computastaff Ltd* v *Ingledew Brown Bennison & Garrett*,[2] where estate agents acting on behalf of the landlords of business premises quoted too low a figure for the rateable value, it was held that the tenants could sue both their own estate agents and their solicitors for negligently failing to notice the error. On the other hand, in *GP & P Ltd* v *Bulcraig & Davis*[3] it was held that a surveyor acting for a prospective tenant of office premises was under no obligation to make a personal check of the planning register for the permitted use; a telephone call to the planning office was sufficient, since the clients' solicitors would be expected to carry out more formal enquiries.

Of the other ways in which an estate agent may cause loss to a client, mention may be made of those situations where the agent may, by virtue of implied or apparent authority, render the client liable to a third party. We have already considered such cases as examples of straightforward failure to comply with instructions;[4] most of them, however, might equally well be based upon negligence. Finally, a point of some practical importance arose in the case of *Edmunds* v *Andrews & Ashwell*,[5] where the prospective purchasers of a café, who had been given the keys by the defendant estate agents, took possession of the property and refused to move out. The judge held that the defendants were not guilty of negligence in handing over the keys, since the risk which actually materialised would be regarded as so slight as not to require any precautions to be taken against it. However, it was made clear that to take a similar risk in respect of *residential*

---

1 (1970) 215 EG 707.
2 (1983) 268 EG 906.
3 [1986] 2 EGLR 148; [1988] 1 EGLR 138.
4 p105.
5 (1981) 261 EG 53.

property (where intruders, once installed, are often difficult and expensive to remove) would be a very different matter.

An estate agent who is held to be in breach of the duty of care and skill (or, for that matter, of any other duty) which is owed to the client will be liable for whatever loss or damage can be proved to have resulted. This may on occasion cause problems, as it did in the case of *Dunton Properties Ltd* v *Coles, Knapp & Kennedy Ltd*.[1] The defendants there were held liable for failing to inform the plaintiffs that the sitting tenant who was about to purchase their farm intended to resell it as soon as possible. Wynn-Parry J, at first instance, awarded the plaintiffs £2,000 on the basis that they could, by raising the tenant's rent, have increased the market value of the farm by this amount. The Court of Appeal, however, held that the rent could have been raised in any case and the plaintiffs' failure to raise it was not, therefore, a consequence of the defendants' breach of duty. In view of the difficulty in surmising what action if any the plaintiffs would have taken if the defendants had informed them of the tenant's intention, the Court of Appeal awarded a sum of £250, admittedly as a conjecture.

The case of *Carreras Ltd* v *D E & J Levy*[2] provides another good example of the difficulty which sometimes arises in proving that financial loss has been suffered by the plaintiff as a result of the defendant's negligence or other breach of duty. In that case the plaintiffs asked the defendants to find them office accommodation in London. The defendants suggested premises which, they said, had a net area of almost 27,000 sq ft. In fact the net area was only 26,000 sq ft, the discrepancy being due to negligent calculations by an employee of the defendants. The plaintiffs, who had signed a sublease of the property at £54,000 pa, contended that the true market rent was proportionately less (£52,000), and that the defendants were responsible for the difference. It was held, however, that the true market rent was impossible of exact definition, save within a bracket which included both these figures. Thus, since the plaintiffs could not prove that the rent was based purely on the floor area, they had failed to establish that they had suffered any loss and were entitled only to nominal damages for the defendants' admitted breach of contract. By contrast, where agents

---

1 (1959) 174 EG 723.
2 (1970) 215 EG 707.

(and solicitors) failed to notice that their clients had been quoted too low a figure for the rateable value of premises of which they took a lease, the clients were held entitled to recover as damages the full amount of the extra rates which they had to pay during the tenancy, notwithstanding that the rating assessment was a fair and reasonable one for the premises.[1] This decision was based on the fact that, had they known the truth, the clients would not have taken the lease; it is none the less not easy to reconcile with cases on the measure of damages for negligent valuations.[2]

4 Duty of loyalty

The agency relationship is one of trust and confidence and, as a result, certain equitable duties are imposed upon every agent. These duties are all manifestations of one general principle, that the agent must not allow any personal interest, or the interests of others, to conflict with the obligations which are owed to the client.[3] Where any potential conflict arises, the agent is under a strict duty to make full and frank disclosure to the client of all relevant facts, so as to give the latter an opportunity to decide whether or not to continue with the proposed transaction or with the employment of the agent.[4]

The conduct demanded of an agent in this connection is of a high standard. As Martin, B said in *Salomons* v *Pender*:[5]

The principal bargains, in the employment, for the exercise of the disinterested skill, diligence and zeal of the agent, for his own exclusive benefit. It is a confidence necessarily imposed in the agent, that he will act with a sole regard to the interests of his principal.

---

1 *Computastaff Ltd* v *Ingledew Brown Bennison & Garrett* (1983) 268 EG 906.
2 See *Watts* v *Morrow* [1991] 4 All ER 937.
3 For the various forms in which these duties may appear, see pp 42-48. Further estate agency examples, in which breach leads to forfeiture of the agent's commission, are to be found at pp 165-169.
4 The duty under section 21 of the Estate Agents Act 1979 is not relevant in this context, since it requires disclosure to third parties rather than to clients: see p 214.
5 (1865) 3 H&C 639, at p643, quoting from *Story on Agency*, the leading textbook at that time.

In *Rhodes* v *Macalister*[1] Atkin LJ, having reiterated the basic duty of an agent, continued:

Now that is not an impossible standard of attainment. It is laid down by the law and it is in respect of a practical matter. The remedy is a very simple one and it is well within the compass of any ordinary business man. The complete remedy is disclosure, and if an agent wishes to receive any kind of remuneration from the other side and wishes to test whether it is honest or not, he has simply to disclose the matter to his own employer and rest upon the consequences of that. If his employer consents to it, then he has performed everything that is required of an upright and responsible agent.

Although these duties are sometimes described as "fiduciary", and although they undoubtedly have their origins in ideas of trust, it is well established that a breach of them may be committed notwithstanding that the agent has acted in good faith. Thus in *Harrods Ltd* v *Lemon*,[2] the plaintiffs, through their estate department, were acting on behalf of the defendant in connection with the sale of her house. A prospective purchaser, who was introduced by the plaintiffs, wished to have the property surveyed, and asked the plaintiffs' building department to undertake this. The two departments were housed in different buildings and operated quite independently. Nevertheless it was held that the plaintiffs, by acting for both sides, were in breach of their duty to the defendant.[3]

Acting for both parties to a transaction is perhaps the most obvious example of conflict of interest in an estate agency context, but it is not the only one. In *Eric V Stansfield* v *South East Nursing Home Services Ltd*,[4] for example, the plaintiff agents were retained by no fewer than three clients, all of whom were seeking suitable premises from which to operate a nursing home. When the defendants, one of these clients, duly purchased a property to which they had been introduced by the plaintiffs, they refused to pay commission on the ground that the plaintiffs had not disclosed this conflict. However, it was held that, while a disclosable conflict *could* arise in such circumstances (at least once more than one

---

1 (1923) 29 Com Cas 19, 29.
2 [1931] 2 KB 157.
3 For the result of the case, which depended on further facts, see p 169.
4 [1986] 1 EGLR 29.

client "demonstrates a real intent to buy"), the plaintiffs here had in fact kept the defendants informed as to the actual position.

In one sense it might be said that the very nature of estate agency brings about a potential conflict of interests. After all, it is well known that estate agents act simultaneously for a number of vendors, and there must be many occasions when a prospective purchaser might well be suited by any of a number of different properties on the agent's books. Surprisingly, perhaps, it is only in two recent cases that the potential for this to bring about conflicts of interest has been specifically acknowledged by the English courts.

In *Robinson Scammell & Co* v *Ansell*[1] the plaintiff estate agents, fearing that their vendor client was about to withdraw from a sale which they had arranged, went directly to the purchaser and attempted to interest him in another property. The original sale did not in fact fall through, but the vendor, on discovering what the agents had done, refused to pay their agreed commission. When the agents sued, the Court of Appeal considered that the "conflict of interest" rule must be tempered by the knowledge that estate agents have many clients; none the less, the court was satisfied that the agents were guilty of a serious breach of duty in going directly to the purchaser without first discussing matters with their client. Even so, it was held that the agents were entitled to their commission, since the evidence clearly showed that the agents had acted throughout in good faith.[2]

The problem of multiple clients arose again in *Brent Kelly* v *Cooper Associates*,[3] where a firm of estate agents were acting for the vendors of two neighbouring properties which fronted on to a Bermudan beach. The two properties were acquired (at a total cost of $Ber 4.5 m) by the same purchaser, in order to form a family compound. The vendor of one of the properties sued the estate agents for damages, on the basis that the possibility of such a joint acquisition rendered the property more valuable and that, had the agents informed him of the purchaser's intentions, he would have been able to obtain a higher price. The Privy Council, however, held

---

1 [1985] 2 EGLR 41.
2 In accordance with the principle established in *Keppel* v *Wheeler* [1927] 1 KB 577: p 113.
3 [1992] 3 WLR 936.

that an estate agent's duty to client X cannot possibly require the agent to divulge information which is confidential to client Y and that in consequence the agents were not in breach of their duty.[1]

Since fiduciary duties arise by virtue of the agency relationship, it is to be expected that they will be co-extensive in time with that relationship. This is borne out by the decision of the Court of Appeal in *Pilkington* v *Flack*,[2] which concerned the sale of the defendant's confectionery shop. The plaintiff, a business broker, produced a document containing his terms of business which the defendant, who was engaged in serving customers, signed without reading it. This document, which was described by the Court of Appeal as "scandalous", provided that the plaintiff should have, for 26 weeks, the sole right to sell the business for £500 and that he should receive his commission even if the business was sold by someone else. The commission stipulated was more than double the usual rate and, in addition, the plaintiff was to be entitled to any part of the price in excess of £500. The defendant was held bound by this document since, when it was produced for her signature, the plaintiff was not her agent and owed her no duty of disclosure.[3]

The moment at which an estate agent's duty of disclosure begins is fairly clear; the time at which it ceases to operate has in the past given rise to some problems. In *Keppel* v *Wheeler*,[4] the plaintiff instructed the defendants to find a purchaser for his house, intimating that he would consider favourably offers of £6,000 or more. The defendants almost immediately introduced a Mr Essam, who made an offer of £6,150. This offer was accepted by the plaintiff "subject to contract" but, before contracts were exchanged, a Mr Daniel approached the defendants and told them that he was prepared to pay £6,750 for the house. The defendants, believing that their duty to the plaintiff had been fulfilled, communicated this offer, not to the plaintiff, but to Essam, and a resale to Daniel was arranged at a price of £6,950. The matter eventually reached the ears of the plaintiff, who sued the agents for the difference between

---

1 Ironically, divulging the information would presumably have been of considerable benefit to *both* clients.

2 (1948) 152 EG 366.

3 The position would have been different if the agent had positively misrepresented the contents of the document: see *Jaques* v *Lloyd D George & Partners Ltd* [1968] 2 All ER 187; *Homebuyers Estates (Fylde) Ltd* v *Laycock* CA unreported May 8 1981.

4 [1927] 1 KB 577.

the two prices. The Court of Appeal held that the agents were in breach of duty,[1] since the legal relationship between estate agent and client is not terminated by an agreement made "subject to contract", but only by the execution of a binding contract of sale. Until that time the agent need not positively look for other purchasers, but must communicate to the client any better offers which are in fact received; in addition, the agent must pass on any other relevant information which, for example, shows the property to be more valuable than was supposed, or which casts doubt upon the solvency of the purchaser.

Keppel v *Wheeler* was followed in *Dunton Properties Ltd* v *Coles, Knapp & Kennedy Ltd*,[2] where a farm was being sold to the sitting tenant. Three days before contracts were exchanged, the estate agents discovered that the tenant was contemplating an immediate resale but, believing that they no longer owed any duty to the owners, did not inform them of this fact. The Court of Appeal held that the information was of relevance and should have been passed to the owners; the agents were accordingly liable in damages.[3]

It appears, then, that an estate agent's duty to inform the client of offers received terminates when the property is actually sold, in the sense of contracts being exchanged.[4] However, it should not be thought that the same principle necessarily applies to all the other manifestations of the agent's duty of loyalty. For example, an agent is not permitted to make use, for personal gain, of information gained in the capacity of agent, even after the agency has terminated.[5] What is more, an agent who sees an opportunity of personal gain cannot shrug of this prohibition without making a full disclosure to the principal. In *Regier* v *Campbell-Stuart*[6] the defendant, an estate agent, was asked to find a suitable house for the plaintiff. The defendant bought a house for £2,000 through a nominee, from whom he then purported to buy it for £4,500. Telling the plaintiff only that he had paid £4,500 for the house, he then sold

---

1 Damages were assessed at £600, since it was felt that the plaintiff would have accepted Daniel's original offer of £6,750.
2 (1959) 174 EG 723.
3 As to the assessment of damages, see p 109.
4 The same is true of the agent's statutory duty to pass on offers: see p 212.
5 *Robb* v *Green* [1895] 2 QB 315.
6 [1939] 1 Ch 766.

it to her for £5,000. When the plaintiff discovered the truth and sued for all the profit which the agent had wrongfully obtained, the defendant claimed that, at the time of the sale, he had ceased to be an agent. It was held that, although an agent can terminate the agency and then deal directly with the client, this requires the agent to give the "fullest possible information" to the client. No such disclosure had been made in this case, and the agent was accordingly liable to account.

The client in *Regier* v *Campbell-Stuart* chose to allow the transaction to stand and to claim from her agent the profit which he had made. Had she so wished, she might alternatively have insisted that the sale be set aside. This was the course taken in two Canadian cases[1] where, interestingly, the undisclosed purchaser of the client's property was not the estate agent himself, but one of his employees. In each case it was held by the court that, since the duty of loyalty does not rest upon privity of contract, it applied in full to the employee, who was accordingly not entitled to enforce the contract against the client.[2]

One aspect of an agent's fiduciary duty which is of particular importance is the prohibition against what is termed a "secret profit". This includes any financial advantage whatsoever which the agent receives, over and above the agreed remuneration from the client, provided of course that it is not received with the client's knowledge and consent. An agent who receives a secret profit such as a trade discount[3] or a commission from the other contracting party is strictly liable to account to the client for this money.[4] For example, in *Andrews* v *Ramsay & Co*,[5] an estate agent who received £20 from the purchaser of property, although he was acting on behalf of the vendor, was made to hand over this sum to his client. The same principle was applied in *Price* v *Metropolitan House Investment and Agency Co Ltd*[6] where the plaintiff, an estate agent who was instructed to find a purchaser for some high-street shops

---

1 *Kramer* v *Cooper* [1975] 2 WWR 1; *Palinko* v *Bower* [1976] 4 WWR 118.
2 The employee's breach may also prevent the agent himself from claiming commission: *Edwards Real Estate* v *Bamtor* (1978) 11 AR 589.
3 As in *Hippisley* v *Knee Bros* [1905] 1 KB 1.
4 The agent may also forfeit the right to commission: see p 165.
5 [1903] 2 KB 635.
6 (1907) 23 TLR 630.

owned by the defendants, learned that the local authority intended to purchase a strip of the frontage for road-widening purposes. The plaintiff passed on this information, not to the vendor, but to a prospective purchaser, who was thereby induced to make an acceptable offer for the property. The plaintiff then received commission on the sale of part of the property to the local authority. The Court of Appeal held that the plaintiff had by his conduct not only disentitled himself to commission from the defendants but also incurred liability to hand over to them his commission on the resale, since this constituted a secret profit.

Finally, it should be remembered that a secret profit will, in many cases, amount to a "bribe" as defined by Slade J in *Industries & General Mortgage Co Ltd* v *Lewis*.[1] Where this is so, the principal may take action against the donor as well as against the agent.[2]

B Duties to the purchaser

It is only in exceptional circumstances that an estate agent, having introduced two parties, will be a party to the contract of sale into which they enter.[3] In consequence, any legal duties owed by the estate agent directly to the third party must arise independently of that contract. This rules out, among other things, any liability under the Misrepresentation Act 1967, since that Act applies only to statements made by one contracting party to another.[4] This does not mean that the agent's misrepresentations cannot result in personal liability, but rather that the usual procedure is for the third party to sue the agent's principal in respect of statements made by the agent, and for the principal in turn to seek an indemnity from the agent.

There are none the less certain situations in which an estate agent employed by the vendor undertakes personal responsibility to the purchaser. In particular, an agent who receives a pre-contract deposit from a prospective purchaser "as stakeholder" is personally

---

1 [1949] 2 All ER 573.
2 For the principal's remedies in such a case, see p 47.
3 *Davies* v *Sweet* [1962] 1 All ER 92 is an interesting example of such exceptional circumstances.
4 *Resolute Maritime Inc* v *Nippon Kaiji Kyokai* [1983] 2 All ER 1.

liable to return it on demand.[1] Indeed, this will apply even where the estate agent purports to accept the deposit "as agent" for the vendor, unless the latter has actually authorised this.[2] More generally, any agent who claims to have authority beyond what in fact exists may be liable to a third party for breach of warranty of authority. Thus, where an agent purported to sell land on behalf of a client, something which the client had not authorised, the agent was held liable to pay damages to the disappointed purchaser.[3]

Apart from the foregoing, any action taken by a purchaser against an estate agent employed by the vendor must lie in tort. The agent will clearly be liable in deceit for inducing the purchaser to buy the property by *fraudulently* giving false information about it; of greater practical importance, however, is the question whether there is a "special relationship" between them within the meaning of *Hedley Byrne & Co Ltd* v *Heller & Partners Ltd*,[4] such that the agent will be liable for *negligence*. A possible objection to finding such a relationship is that it might conflict with the estate agent's undoubted duty to identify with the interests of the client. Indeed, a similar argument has been held in a number of cases to prevent an action based on *Hedley Byrne* from being brought by one party to a commercial transaction against the other party's *solicitor.*[5]

Until very recently, there was only one reported case in which the English courts had considered the application of *Hedley Byrne* to the specific case of estate agent and prospective purchaser, and even there the position was not completely straightforward. In *Computastaff Ltd* v *Ingledew Brown Bennison & Garrett*,[6] the plaintiffs retained a firm of agents to seek office accommodation for them to rent. The agents found suitable premises and, taking the information from particulars drawn up by the landlords' estate agents, told their clients that the rateable value was £3,305. The

---

1 *Rayner* v *Paskell & Cann* (1948) 152 EG 270.
2 As a result of *Sorrell* v *Finch* [1977] AC 728: p 85.
3 *Godwin* v *Francis* (1870) LR 5 CP 295.
4 [1964] AC 465.
5 *Cemp Properties (UK) Ltd* v *Dentsply Research & Development Corporation* [1989] 2 EGLR 192; *Gran Gelato Ltd* v *Richcliff (Group) Ltd* [1992] 1 EGLR 297; cf *Wilson* v *Bloomfield* (1979) 123 SJ 860. See also the Commonwealth cases of *Wynston* v *MacDonald* (1979) 105 DLR (3d) 527, affirmed without discussion (1981) 119 DLR (3d) 256, and *Allied Finance & Investment Ltd* v *Haddow* [1980] 2 NZLR 428.
6 (1983) 268 EG 906. See, however, the very recent case discussed at p 120.

correct figure was in fact £8,305 but, when the discrepancy was noticed (the landlords' solicitors quoted the correct figure in reply to a preliminary enquiry), the plaintiffs' solicitors and the two firms of agents investigated the matter in such a negligent fashion that the plaintiffs were still given the wrong answer. The plaintiffs duly took the lease and, on finding that the burden of the rates was far heavier than they had been led to expect, sued their own agents and solicitors in negligence. These defendants brought in the landlords' agents on the ground that, since they too could have been made liable to the plaintiffs under *Hedley Byrne*, they must contribute towards the damages as provided for in the Civil Liability (Contribution) Act 1978. Agreeing with this contention, McNeill J held that, as between the plaintiff's advisers, the solicitors were 40% and the agents 60% to blame; in each case, these defendants were entitled to recoup one-half of what they had to pay from the landlords' agents.

The scarcity of English authority on the applicability of *Hedley Byrne* to estate agents is in striking contrast to the substantial body of case law which exists in a number of Commonwealth jurisdictions. On the whole, this recognises that a duty *can* arise, at least where the information given to the purchaser comes from the agent's own knowledge, rather than merely being passed on from the client. Liability has accordingly been imposed upon agents for negligently misinforming prospective purchasers about the acreage of a property;[1] such physical characteristics as its boundaries,[2] sewerage[3] and soundproofing;[4] the size of the existing mortgage on the property;[5] the use to which it could lawfully be put;[6] and the income and expenditure in which that use might be expected to result.[7]

It is a prerequisite of liability under *Hedley Byrne* that the plaintiff be shown to have relied on information from the defendant, and

---

1 *Komarniski* v *Marien* (1979) 100 DLR (3d) 81.

2 *Richardson* v *Norris Smith Real Estate Ltd* [1977] 1 NZLR 152.

3 *Barrett* v *JR West Ltd* [1970] NZLR 789.

4 *Roberts* v *Montex Development Corporation* (1979) 100 DLR (3d) 660.

5 *Avery* v *Salie* (1972) 25 DLR (3d) 495.

6 *Bango* v *Holt* (1971) 21 DLR (3d) 66; *Alessio* v *Jovica* (1973) 34 DLR (3d) 107; *Hauck* v *Dixon* (1975) 64 DLR (3d) 201.

7 *Dodds & Dodds* v *Millman* (1964) 45 DLR (2d) 472; *Olsen* v *Poirier* (1980) 111 DLR (3d) 512.

claims against estate agents have thus failed where the purchaser did not *in fact* rely[1] and where a court held that it was not *reasonable* to rely[2] on an agent's statement. Further, the courts have linked this principle to the question of whether the subject-matter of the statement was such that it could be said to fall within the agent's special skill and competence. In *Presser v Caldwell Estates Pty Ltd*,[3] for example, the plaintiff bought an individual building plot on a 50-acre development after being assured by the vendor's estate agents that no "filling" had taken place on this plot. This was not true, but the agents had acted honestly and the court held that, in these circumstances, honesty was all that was required of them. As one of the judges pointed out, it was not part of an estate agent's ordinary business to advise on the geological structure of land, nor had the agents here claimed to possess the special skill and competence necessary to do so.

The *Presser* case raises the question whether an estate agent should not be under a duty at least to make careful enquiries of the client before answering a purchaser's question. The court there held that no such duty existed, and a similar decision was reached in *Alessio v Jovica*.[4] However, in several of the cases noted above, liability was imposed upon an agent who did no more than pass on to a prospective purchaser information provided by the client. Indeed, in *Bango v Holt*,[5] it was held that a negligent agent was not entitled in such circumstances to claim an indemnity from the client in respect of the damages which the agent had to pay to a purchaser, even though the client had been guilty of fraud! The cases are thus not entirely consistent, but it is submitted that the true position is as suggested in *Barrett v J R West Ltd*.[6] The estate agent there, when asked about something on the back lawn which looked like a septic tank cover, told the prospective purchaser what his client had told him, namely that the house had once been on a septic tank but was now on main drainage. This turned out to be

---

1 *Hatlelid v Sawyer & McClocklin Real Estate* [1977] 5 WWR 481.
2 *John Bosworth Ltd v Professional Syndicated Developments Ltd* (1979) 97 DLR (3d) 112.
3 [1971] 2 NSWLR 471: see also *Jones v Still* [1965] NZLR 1071.
4 (1973) 34 DLR (3d) 107.
5 (1971) 21 DLR (3d) 66.
6 [1970] NZLR 789.

untrue and the agent was duly held liable for negligence. The judge took the view that, in normal circumstances, an agent may safely rely upon information from the client; where, however, there is any reason to suspect that this may not be accurate, the agent's duty of care towards the purchaser demands further inquiries, of the client or elsewhere, before any answer is given.

The foregoing discussion must now be read in the light of *McCullagh* v *Lane Fox & Partners Ltd*,[1] the decision in which was unfortunately reported too late to be incorporated properly into this chapter. The plaintiffs there purchased an expensive house on the bank of the River Thames in West London, after a senior member of the defendant estate agents had orally confirmed what was stated in the sale particulars, namely, that it overall plot size was 0.92 acres. On discovering that the true area was only 0.48 acres, and finding that terms in the contract of sale prevented them from taking legal action against the vendors, the plaintiffs sought damages for negligence from the agents. Their claim in fact failed because Colman J, despite holding that the plaintiffs had indeed relied upon this misstatement in deciding to purchase the house, nevertheless concluded that they had paid no more than the property was worth and had thus suffered no loss. However, the importance of this case in the present context lies in the judge's ruling that estate agents would undoubtedly owe a duty of care to purchasers in what they said about the property, at least where (as in the case itself) they were aware that the purchasers did not intend to have a survey carried out.

In reaching this important decision, Colman J did not simply follow the *Computastaff* case,[2] but relied on more recent general rulings concerning negligent misstatements.[3] Moreover, the judge specifically knowledged those cases cited above[4] which denied that the vendor's *solicitor* would be liable to a purchaser, but held that an estate agent was in a different position.

---

1 [1994] EGCS 2.

2 *Computastaff Ltd* v *Ingledew Brown Bennison & Garrett* (1983) 268 EG 906: p 117.

3 Notably *Smith* v *Eric E Bush; Harris* v *Wyre Forest DC* [1990] 1 AC 831 and *Caparo Industries plc* v *Dickman* [1990] 2 AC 605.

4 See p 117 note 5.

CHAPTER 5

Estate agents' rights

A Remuneration

The work which is done by estate agents, valuers and surveyors on behalf of their clients falls neatly into two categories. First, it may consist of *services* which are of value in themselves, irrespective whether or not they produce any particular end result. This would include such things as surveys, valuations, expert witness work or the representation of a client before an arbitrator or a tribunal. Second, the professional services may be geared much more closely to the achievement of a desired *result*, irrespective of the means used to achieve it. This would apply to the sale of property, the introduction of suitable tenant or the procurement of a loan of money.

It is usual to find that the form which remuneration takes is different for the two types of work. In relation to services pure and simple, charges are usually based on the time and trouble involved. True, where the client specifically agrees to it, or where there is a legally binding custom, the agent's fees may be based upon the value of the property concerned[1] or upon some contingency, such as a reduction in the rateable value of the client's property or the obtaining of planning permission.[2] However, the courts lean heavily against such an interpretation and consequently, if a term as to remuneration has to be implied,[3] it will invariably be for payment of a sum to be assessed on a "time and trouble" basis.[4]

---

1 *Wilkie* v *Scottish Aviation Ltd* 1956 SC 198.

2 Provided that the rule which prohibits "contingency fees" in litigation work is not contravened: see *Pickering* v *Sogex Services (UK) Ltd* (1982) 262 EG 770; *Picton Jones & Co* v *Arcadia Developments Ltd* [1989] 1 EGLR 43.

3 Because there is no express agreement (Supply of Goods and Services Act 1982, section 15) or for other reasons: see p 52.

4 *Upsdell* v *Stewart* (1793) Peake 255; *Drew* v *Josolyne* (1888) 4 TLR 717; *Faraday* v *Tamworth Union* (1917) 86 LJCh 436: see generally, Murdoch: "Professional Fees – How Much is Reasonable?" [1981] Conv 424 at pp 425-428.

Where what is in issue is *commission* payable on the occurrence of a certain *event*, rather different considerations apply. It is well established that, in the absence of a clear express provision to the contrary, agents who work on a commission basis are not entitled to any remuneration in respect of abortive work. As Lindley LJ explained in *Lott* v *Outhwaite*:[1]

It was said that there was an implied contract to pay the agent a "quantum meruit" for his services. The answer was that there could be no implied contract when there was an express contract.

The consequences were clearly spelled out by McCardie J in *Howard Houlder & Partners Ltd* v *Manx Isles Steamship Co Ltd*:[2]

It is a settled rule for the construction of commission notes and the like documents which refer to the remuneration of an agent that a plaintiff cannot recover unless he shows that the conditions of the written bargain have been fulfilled. If he proves fulfilment he recovers. If not, he fails. There appears to be no halfway house, and it matters not that the plaintiff proves expenditure of time, money and skill.

This firm principle, which applies to an auctioneer as well as to an estate agent,[3] means that an agent who intends to charge a client for a valuation, if no purchaser is found for the property, must ensure that this is expressly stated in the terms of agency.[4]

Since an unsuccessful agent normally receives neither commission nor expenses, it may be said that in a sense the agent shares in the risks of the client's venture; as a result, if that venture proves successful, the agent will expect to be paid on a participation basis. Of course, this rate of payment will usually be higher than one which is geared to "time and trouble", but this is logically inevitable. After all, if a professional adviser's time is "worth" a certain amount, and one-half of that time is spent on work which is unsuccessful and which therefore earns nothing, it follows that the remainder must be charged at double rates. Thus, where an adviser is paid commission under a "no sale, no pay" arrangement,

---

1 (1893) 10 TLR 76 at p 77: see also *Rosenthal* v *Allan* (1975) 238 EG 797.
2 [1923] 1 KB 110 at p113 (shipbroker).
3 *John Meacock & Co* v *Abrahams* [1956] 3 All ER 660.
4 See *Gross Fine & Krieger Chalfen* v *Clifton* (1974) 232 EG 837.

the satisfied clients effectively pay for the work which is done on behalf of the unsatisfied ones.[1]

The claims of estate agents to be paid commission for their services have proved a remarkably fertile field of litigation, both at first instance and in the Court of Appeal. Many of the cases have turned on the correct interpretation to be given to the relevant agent's instructions in order to ascertain whether the event has occurred on which commission is made payable. We shall accordingly look first at this particular problem, before considering a further requirement imposed by law, namely that the agent must be an "effective cause" of the transaction which takes place. The special rules applicable to "sole agents" will be discussed, and the circumstances in which an agent's misconduct may lead to the forfeiture of commission which would otherwise be earned. Finally, attention will be given to the amount of commission which will be awarded in cases where this is not specified at the outset, and to the formalities with which an agent may have to comply in order to ensure that commission is legally recoverable.

1   Fulfilment of instructions

It must be emphasised at the outset that the question whether or not an estate agent has fulfilled the client's instructions is one which can only be answered by examining and interpreting those instructions. Further, this interpretation must take place in the context of the particular case, a factor which serves to reduce the importance of previously decided cases when a claim arises for adjudication. The individuality of each case was stressed by Lord Wright in *Luxor (Eastbourne) Ltd* v *Cooper*,[2] the leading case on this subject:

I deprecate in general the attempt to enunciate decisions on the construction of agreements as if they embodied rules of law. To some extent decisions on one contract may help by way of analogy and illustration in the decision of another contract, but, however similar the contracts may appear, the decision as to each must depend on the consideration of the language of the particular contract, read in the light of the material circumstances of the parties in view of which the contract is made.

---

1 As to whether this view of estate agency is shared by the courts, see pp 170-172.
2 [1941] AC 108 at p130.

Nevertheless, in spite of the clear warning, decisions on the construction of agreements are undoubtedly often treated, especially by litigants, as expositions of some universally valid principle, a fact of life remarked upon rather wryly by Atkin LJ in *James* v *Smith*:[1]

As a matter of fact, the result depends so often on the terms of the contract, and nothing but the terms of the contract, that it is very seldom that one case really is a guide in respect of future cases; nevertheless, it is our experience in every commission case, and necessarily so, to find about half-a-dozen cases cited on one side, and very often half-a-dozen other cases upon the other.

Indeed, this tendency to rely upon past cases is not without its exponents among the judiciary. As Denning LJ put it:[2]

So many cases have now come before the courts on claims by house agents to commission that the document cannot, I think, be interpreted in vacuo. It must be interpreted in the light of the general law on the subject.

Before plunging into the welter of cases which comprise "the general law on the subject", a point should be made which, if borne in mind, may help to explain, though not to justify, some of the anomalies and conflicts which will be encountered. Much of the confusion in this part of the law (and in particular the vexed question whether commission can be "earned" at one moment but not "payable" until later) arises from a failure, by and large, on the part of the courts to distinguish between an agent's right to commission and the right to damages where the client wrongfully prevents the agent from earning commission. The former, by definition, depends upon the fulfilment of the agent's instructions; if these are not carried out then, however reprehensible the client's conduct, and whatever liability for breach of contract may ensue, the client cannot possibly be liable to pay commission as such.

Lest it should be thought that this is mere semantics and that it matters not what the money is called, so long as it is awarded, brief mention may be made of a possible consequence of some practical importance. It by no means necessarily follows that an award of

---

1 (1921), [1931] 2 KB 317n.
2 *Dennis Reed Ltd* v *Goody* [1950] 2 KB 277 at p 284.

damages for wrongfully preventing an agent from earning commission will be equal in amount to the commission itself. The damages are designed to compensate the agent for loss of an opportunity and, where there is no certainty that the opportunity would have been taken, the sum to be awarded should be reduced accordingly. However, while this method of assessment has on occasion been adopted in "sole agency" cases,[1] the judicial tendency, in cases where an estate agent successfully sues a client, is still to speak of "commission", thereby implying that the agent has carried out the client's instructions. As we shall see, this implication quite frequently imposes a severe strain upon the English language, and it is submitted that a simpler approach would be to extend the analysis used by Lord Russell of Killowen in *Luxor's* case. This would involve an acknowledgment that, while "commission" depends upon completion, damages are available to the agent whenever the client wrongfully withdraws from the transaction in question.

Be this as it may, the purpose of this chapter is not to seek academic analyses, nor to attempt a theoretical reconciliation between judicial ideas which are patently irreconcilable, but to investigate the practical effects of various types of commission agreement. Thus, for the most part, the question: "damages or commission?" will be, if not ignored, at least subordinated to the question: "Is the agent entitled to be paid?"

(a) *Commission on completion*

With the foregoing in mind, we may now move to a consideration of the various forms of words used by estate agents in attempting to secure their commission. Any inquiry into this area of law must really begin with the seminal decision in *Luxor (Eastbourne) Ltd* v *Cooper*[2] of which mention has already been made and of which the facts were as follows:

The appellant companies, who wished to sell four cinemas, told the respondent that, if he introduced a person who bought the cinemas for at least £185,000, they would pay him a "procuration fee" of £10,000 on completion of the sale. The respondent introduced a potential purchaser who made an offer of £185,000

---

1 See p 163.
2 [1941] AC 108.

"subject to contract" and who remained at all material times both willing and able to proceed with the transaction. The appellants, however, for reasons which are not important in this context, decided not to sell to the person introduced and so no binding contract was ever signed. It was clear from these facts that the respondent could not claim to be paid commission, for this was expressly made payable on completion, and there had been no completion. Nevertheless, the respondent argued that he was entitled to damages for breach of a term which, he said, was to be implied into the commission agreement. This term was said to be that the appellants would "do nothing to prevent the satisfactory completion of the transaction so as to deprive the respondent of the agreed commission".

The respondent's claim, which was accepted by the Court of Appeal, was that the appellants had broken this implied term by refusing to make and complete the contract with the willing and able person whom he had introduced. The House of Lords, however, unanimously rejected this argument and the previous decisions on which it was based.[1] The House of Lords pointed out that terms are only implied into contracts where it is necessary to do so in order to give business efficacy to the contract. In this case no such need arose, since the contract as it stood bore the following, perfectly reasonable, construction: "The agent takes the risk [of the sale failing to materialise] in the hope of a substantial remuneration for comparatively small exertion ... A sum of £10,000, the equivalent of a remuneration of a year's work by a Lord Chancellor, for work done within a period of 8 or 9 days is no mean reward, and is one well worth a risk."[2] Lord Romer further criticised the cases which supported the implication of such a term on the grounds that, if the vendor was thus prevented from withdrawing from negotiations for any reason whatsoever, the implied term was wholly unreasonable; if it only prohibited the vendor from withdrawing "without just cause or reasonable excuse" it was so vague as to be void for uncertainty.

---

1 The Court of Appeal decisions in *Trollope (George) & Sons* v *Martyn Bros* [1934] 2 KB 436 and *Trollope (George & Sons)* v *Caplan* [1936] 2 KB 382 were overruled; *Prickett* v *Badger* (1856) 1 CBNS 296 was treated as resting on its own facts.
2 Per Lord Russell of Killowen at p125.

Taken at face value, the decision in *Luxor's* case appears to mean that an estate agent who is to be paid commission on completion will have no right of action if the sale falls through for any reason. In fact, however, a qualification referred to in two of the speeches goes a long way towards mitigating this apparent harshness. Lord Russell of Killowen, having explained his refusal to imply into the contract the term which the respondent sought, went on to say:[1]

The position will not doubt be different if the matter has proceeded to the stage of a binding contract having been made between the principal and the agent's client. In that case, it can be said with truth that a "purchaser" has been introduced by the agent. In other words, the event has happened upon the occurrence of which a right to the promised commission has become vested in the agent. From that moment, no act or omission by the principal can deprive the agent of that vested right.

Similarly, Lord Wright said:[2]

If the negotiations between the vendor and the purchaser have been duly concluded and a binding executory agreement has been achieved, different considerations may arise. The vendor is then no longer free to dispose of his property. Though the sale is not completed, the property in equity has passed from him to the purchaser. If he refused to complete, he would be guilty of a breach of agreement *vis-à-vis* the purchaser. I think, as at present advised, that it ought then to be held that he is also in breach of his contract with the commission agent – that is, of some term which can properly be implied.

These *dicta*, which were made the basis of the Court of Appeal's decision in *Alpha Trading Ltd* v *Dunnshaw-Patten Ltd*,[3] mean that, in the type of commission agreement exemplified by *Luxor's* case, the vendor will not be able to avoid paying the agent remuneration by resiling from a binding contract which the agent has procured.

Luxor's case is an example of an agreement which provides expressly for the payment of commission only on completion of the sale. The same result is reached by implication wherever reference is made to the payment of commission out of the purchase price.

---

1 At p126.
2 At p142.
3 [1981] QB 290.

In *Beningfield* v *Kynaston*,[1] the plaintiff was instructed to find a purchaser for the defendant's estate in return for "the usual commission out of the purchase money". A person introduced by the plaintiff signed a contract and paid a deposit, only to forfeit this on his subsequent failure to complete. It was held that the true meaning of the agreement was that the agent should be paid out of the total purchase price only when this was received by the vendor.

A similar decision was reached in the case of *Beale* v *Bond*,[2] where the owner of some houses told an estate agent that he could retain as commission anything in excess of £1,150 for which the property might be sold. As in the previous case, a contract was signed which the purchaser then failed to complete, forfeiting his deposit. It was held, once again, that commission could not be paid until completion.

As a timely reminder that every case depends on its own facts and particularly upon the actual wording of the agreement, mention may be made of the case of *Passingham* v *King*.[3] Here an agent was instructed to find a purchaser of a public house in return for £100 "upon the purchase money". The facts were very similar to those of the two cases already discussed, but in this case the Court of Appeal awarded the agent his commission. A majority of the court[4] based their decision upon the ground that, in the circumstances of this contract, the words "upon the purchase money" meant "upon the money contracted to be paid". Thus completion of the sale was not a pre-requisite of payment to the agent.

(b) *Find a purchaser*

We may now consider a second group of commission cases in which, although the legal analysis is somewhat different from those already discussed, the practical results appear indistinguishable. These cases turn upon the construction of the phrase "find a purchaser" and other similar instructions. In *Raymond* v *Wootton*[5]

---

1 (1887) 3 TLR 279.
2 (1901) 17 TLR 280.
3 (1898) 14 TLR 392.
4 Vaughan Williams LJ concurred in the result on different grounds.
5 (1931) 43 TLR 606.

the plaintiff, whose sole agency for the sale of the defendant's house had expired, nevertheless kept the property on his books and introduced a person interested in purchasing it. An agreement was reached "subject to contract" and a deposit paid. The defendant then received a higher offer from a person introduced by other agents and sold the house to him. It was held that, in the absence of a binding contract between the defendant and the person introduced by the plaintiff, the plaintiff was not entitled to commission; nor had the defendant committed any wrongful act which would render him liable in damages. A similar decision was reached in *Jones* v *Lowe*[1] where the agent was to receive commission in the event of his "introducing a purchaser". Hilbery J, applying the principle of *Luxor's* case, held that this condition would not be satisfied until someone introduced by the agent "goes so far as to sign a legal contract binding him to go through with the purchase".

To be a "purchaser", then, a person must sign a binding contract of purchase; however, the mere fact that this has been done is not sufficient to entitle the agent to commission under the clauses now in question. In *Poole* v *Clarke & Co*[2] the defendants, a firm of business transfer agents, were retained by the plaintiff in the following terms: "I hereby instruct you to find a purchaser for my business ... I also instruct you to receive any deposit paid by such purchaser and to apply the same, on the signing of the contract, as far as possible, towards payment of your expenses and commission." The defendants introduced someone who signed a contract to purchase the business, but who failed to raise sufficient money to complete and so forfeited the deposit which he had paid to the agents. The agents claimed to retain this deposit in part payment of their commission, but the plaintiff was held entitled to recover the money from them. Although a contract had undoubtedly been procured, they could not claim to have found a "purchaser" since, as Singleton J said: "I think it must be taken that in the ordinary way the meaning of 'purchaser' in such a document is a purchaser who is willing and able to complete."

The legal position where this particular form of words is used also applies to a number of other fairly common clauses including: "on

---

1 [1945] KB 73.
2 [1945] 2 All ER 445.

a sale being effected";[1] "in the event of business resulting";[2] "find someone to buy";[3] and "if the property is sold".[4] It is perhaps ironic that in *James* v *Smith*,[5] a Court of Appeal decision often relied upon to support the above views, both Bankes and Atkin LJJ, appeared to suggest that an agent who was to receive commission "if the business is sold" could satisfy the condition by introducing a person willing and able to purchase, even if the vendor then refused to enter into a contract with that person. Since, however, the person introduced by the agent in that case was not financially "able" to purchase, the question did not fall to be decided; these observations were, therefore, strictly *obiter* and, in the light of subsequent decisions, may safely be ignored.

(c) *The basic rule*

It may be helpful at this point to summarise the legal requirements imposed upon an estate agent by the commission agreements so far discussed. These requirements, it is submitted, are the same, regardless of whether the agreement is of the "find a purchaser" type or the "completion" type.

(a) The estate agent must introduce a person who actually enters into a legally binding contract.[6] This rule is inflexible; if the vendor declines, however arbitrarily, to contract with the person introduced, the agent can have no claim to commission or damages.

(b) The "purchaser" must be both willing and able to carry on and complete the purchase.

The point of time at which a purchaser's willingness and ability must be proved to exist is normally the date fixed for completion, and the best method of proof is naturally to show that completion has taken place as arranged. However, where the vendor resiles

---

1 *Martin* v *Perry & Daw* [1931] 2 KB 310.

2 *Murdoch Lownie Ltd* v *Newman* [1949] 2 All ER 783.

3 *McCallum* v *Hicks* [1950] 2 KB 271.

4 *Bavin* v *Bunney* (1950) 13 WN 181.

5 (1921), unreported, but extensively noted at [1931] 2 KB 317.

6 For a Scottish case in which an estate agent was held to have brought about a "sale" on conclusion of missives, notwithstanding that there was no completion because of a suspensive condition, see *Chris Hart (Business Sales)* v *Currie* 1991 SLT 544.

from a binding contract and thus prevents completion from taking place, this form of evidence is not available to the agent, who may none the less claim commission. As Denning LJ explained:[1]

The reason why the vendor is liable in such a case is because, once he repudiates the contract, the purchaser is no longer bound to do any more towards completion: and the vendor cannot rely on the non-completion in order to avoid payment of commission, for it is due to his own fault ... But if the vendor could show that the purchaser would not in any event have been able or willing to complete, he would not be liable for commission.

The requirement stated above, that the contract must be "binding", was considered by the Court of Appeal in *Peter Long & Partners* v *Burns*.[2] The plaintiffs there introduced a potential purchaser of the defendant's garage business contracts were exchanged, but it was then discovered that the plaintiff's representative, acting on information received from the defendant, had innocently misrepresented the effect upon the property of a local town and country planning scheme. On discovering the truth, the applicant sought rescission of the contract and was released from his obligations by the defendant. The Court of Appeal held that, as the present contract was voidable, it could not be described as "binding" and the agents had not earned their commission.

The decision seems a rather harsh one, since the flaw in the contract had after all resulted from information provided by the client. However, it was followed by *Blake & Co* v *Sohn*,[3] where a contract of sale negotiated by the plaintiffs was rescinded by the purchasers on the ground that the vendor could not prove title to the whole of the property. Nield J recognised that, if the failure of the sale was due to the vendor's "default", the plaintiffs would be entitled to their commission.[4] Nonetheless, he held that the client's action, in instructing the plaintiffs to sell property which he did not own, did not amount to "default" for this purpose (no doubt the result would have been different if the client had *known* that his title was defective).

---

1 *Dennis Reed Ltd* v *Goody* [1950] 2 KB 277 at p285.
2 [1956] 1 WLR 413 and 1083; see also *Gregory* v *Fearn* [1953] 2 All ER 559.
3 [1969] 3 All ER 123; see also *C & S Realties of Ottowa* v *McCutcheon* (1978) 84 DLR (3d) 584.
4 See *Luxor (Eastbourne) Ltd* v *Cooper* [1941] AC 108: p 127.

An important point, on which there appears to be no direct authority, is whether estate agent's entitlement to commission depends on the contract of sale being, not just legally binding, but specifically enforceable. In *Murdoch Lownie Ltd* v *Newman*[1] Slade J said:

I think that "binding contract" means a contract which binds both parties, ie, which is a contract and is clothed with the necessary form required to make in an enforceable contract in law. But whether that be so or not, I am satisfied that the expression envisages a contract which, as against the party introduced by the agent, the vendor is entitled to have specifically performed or for whose breach he is at least entitled to recover damages.

The view that, where specific performance would not be available, the estate agent does not qualify for commission, has been expressed on a number of occasions, notably by Denning LJ in *Fowler* v *Bratt*[2] and *McCallum* v *Hicks*.[3] However, in *Sheggia* v *Gradwell*,[4] commission was expressed to be payable in any of a number of events, one of which was: "if within the said period of three months any person introduced by the agents enters into a legally binding contract to purchase the said business and property." The agents introduced a person who signed a contract to purchase the property, which was leasehold; since, however, the landlord was not satisfied with this person's references, he was forced to break the contract. The Court of Appeal, by a majority (Lord Denning MR dissenting) held that this contract could properly be described as "legally binding" notwithstanding that specific performance might not have been obtainable.

As we have seen, a vendor whose agent has procured a binding contract cannot, by breaking that contract, avoid paying for the agent's services. However, the vendor's obligation extends no further than that; where it is the purchaser who resiles from the binding contract, "[t]he vendor is not bound to bring an action for specific performance or for damages simply to enable the agent to

---

1 [1949] 2 All ER 783 at p789.

2 [1950] 2 KB 96 at p105.

3 [1950] 2 KB 271, at p274; see also *Dennis Reed Ltd* v *Goody* [1950] 2 KB 277 at p283, *per* Bucknill LJ.

4 [1963] 3 All ER 114. For the criticism which this decision has attracted, see p 136.

get commission; but, if he does get his money, he will probably be liable to pay the commission out of it."[1]

The first part of this *dictum* came before the Court of Appeal in the case of *Boots* v *E Christopher & Co*,[2] where the defendant agents were to introduce "a person who is willing and able to purchase" the plaintiff's shop in return for a commission "at the rate of 5 per cent of the total purchase price obtained". The defendants introduced a person who signed a contract to purchase and paid a deposit to the agents. Subsequently, however, this person, although financially able to complete the purchase, refused to do so and forfeited the deposit. The defendants, who claimed to have earned their commission, deducted this from the deposit and handed only the balance to the plaintiff. It was held that the words "total purchase price obtained" meant that commission would not be earned until completion, since only then would the money be "obtained" by the vendor. Further, the plaintiff was not at fault in merely forfeiting the deposit and choosing not to seek specific performance or damages. Thus, the defendants were not entitled to commission and were ordered to pay over what they had wrongfully retained.

There appears to be no authority on the second point raised by Denning LJ, as to the liability of a vendor who successfully sues a recalcitrant purchaser. Clearly, if specific performance is awarded, the agent is entitled to commission under the clause used, for completion will then take place.[3] So, too, if the vendor obtains an award of damages, it would seem equitable that the agent should receive something, although in this case it cannot be commission as such. In a case of this nature, it has been suggested[4] that the agent would succeed in an action for reasonable remuneration. This suggestion, although open to objection on technical grounds,[5] would seem to do substantial justice.

---

1 *Dennis Reed Ltd* v *Goody* [1950] 2 KB 277 at p285, *per* Denning LJ.

2 [1952] 1 KB 89.

3 The argument that, even so, the purchaser is not "willing" is unlikely to attract the sympathy of the courts.

4 By Denning LJ in *Boots* v *E Christopher & Co* [1952] 1 KB 89 at p98. Indeed, the principle might well have been applied in the case itself had the defendants claimed on that basis (see p99).

5 It forces the client to pay for something not originally agreed between the parties (unless consent can be implied).

The principles discussed above are undoubtedly regarded by the courts as the norm, so that any new clause is presumed to fall into the same category unless and until it is established that the language used indicates a clearly contrary intention. A good example of the prevailing judicial attitude is to be found in the speech of Lord Russell of Killowen in *Luxor (Eastbourne) Ltd* v *Cooper*:[1]

It is possible that an owner may be willing to bind himself to pay a commission for the mere introduction of one who offers to purchase at the specified or minimum price, but such a construction of the contract would, in my opinion, require clear and unequivocal language.

Similar views have been expressed on a number of occasions by Lord Denning MR. Thus: "in the absence of express terms to the contrary, the commission of the agents is to be paid out of the proceeds of sale"[2] and, likewise: "The common understanding of mankind is that commission is only payable by the vendor when the property is sold."[3] Indeed, Lord Denning has taken this principle a stage further:[4]

When a house is in the hands of more than one agent, it cannot be supposed that the vendor is to be made liable for double commission. In the ordinary way commission is payable to the agent who is the first to find a purchaser who enters into a binding contract which both parties accept. If a binding contract is made before another agent has produced "a person able, ready and willing to purchase" – or before any contract is made with that person – the first agent gets commission, the second does not. It is a race as to which agent wins. He wins who first gets the binding contract.

Whether or not this view, that it is impossible for a vendor to become liable to more than one agent, can be supported is closely linked to the problem of whether or not commission can ever be

---

1 [1941] AC 108 at p129.

2 *Fowler* v *Bratt* [1950] 2 KB 96 at p104.

3 *Jaques* v *Lloyd D George & Partners Ltd* [1968] 2 All ER 187 at p 190; see also *McCallum* v *Hicks* [1950] 2 KB 271 at p274 and *Dennis Reed Ltd* v *Goody* [1950] 2 KB 277 at p284.

4 *AA Dickson & Co* v *O'Leary* (1979) 254 EG 731. Contrast the views expressed by Sir David Cairns at p733, and by Orr LJ in *Christie Owen & Davies Ltd* v *Rapacioli* [1974] 1 QB 781 at p790.

recoverable in the absence of a contract between vendor and purchaser. This question will shortly be considered.[1]

(d) *Exchange of contracts*

The remarks of Lord Russell of Killowen quoted above have been said to have "inspired estate agents to set about devising formulae intended to ensure that principals should not be able to escape liability by refusing to accept offers by persons willing to purchase".[2] Before evaluating the results of this inspiration, however, we may consider another form of words which is designed to make the agent's right to commission rest solely upon the formation of a binding contract between vendor and purchaser, thus ruling out any discussion of the "purchaser's" subsequent willingness or ability to complete the transaction. In *Midgley Estates Ltd* v *Hand*[3] the agreement between the agents and their client was contained in a letter from the agents which provided for the payment of commission as soon as "our purchaser shall have signed a legally binding contract, effected within a period of three months from this date". A person was introduced who signed a contract within the stipulated time, but this applicant proved financially unable to complete and so forfeited the deposit to the vendor. The Court of Appeal held that, as the terms of the agreement were clear and unambiguous, there was no reason for not enforcing them; accordingly the agents were entitled to their commission.

This decision is perhaps open to objection on the ground that the use of the word "purchaser" should, in accordance with established principles, have raised the question of that person's willingness and ability to complete. However, it was said by Jenkins LJ that the rest of the agreement so clearly qualified the word "purchaser" that such questions were rendered irrelevant. The case was followed by a majority of the Court of Appeal in *Sheggia* v *Gradwell*,[4] a decision

---

1 pp136-147.
2 *Graham & Scott (Southgate) Ltd* v *Oxlade* [1950] 2 KB 257 at p262, *per* Cohen LJ.
3 [1952] 2 QB 432.
4 [1963] 3 All ER 114: p 132.

which has itself attracted a considerable amount of criticism.[1] The present position seems to be that these decisions remain of authority where commission is unequivocally made dependent upon the signing of a contract and nothing more; however, the principle will not be applied in cases where there is any ambiguity.

(e) *Willing to purchase*

The most important commission clauses to have been inspired by Lord Russell of Killowen's *dictum* are those which make commission payable "on the introduction of a person willing and able to purchase" the property. This formula, with the addition or substitution of the words "ready" and "prepared", was much in vogue in the 1950s, its object being to prevent the vendor not only from breaking a binding contract, but also from refusing to enter into such a contract with a suitable prospective purchaser. Although, once again, the individuality of each case must be stressed, the particular epithets attached to the potential purchaser have been interpreted sufficiently often by the courts for a number of principles to have emerged.

In *Graham & Scott (Southgate) Ltd* v *Oxlade*[2] the plaintiff estate agents introduced to the defendant vendor a person who made an offer for the property "subject to contract" and "subject to satisfactory survey". This person was financially able to purchase the property and anxious to do so, the qualifications to her offer being added as a prudent precaution. The defendant, however, received a better offer from someone else, to whom the property was thereupon sold. The Court of Appeal held that the conditions attached to the first offer prevented the person making it from being described as "willing" to purchase the property; accordingly the terms of the commission agreement were not fulfilled and the agents' claim failed.

The Court of Appeal in *Oxlade's* case overruled the decision of Lewis J in *Giddy & Giddy* v *Horsfall*,[3] where a person introduced by the plaintiffs was held to be "willing" notwithstanding that his offer

---

1 Lord Denning MR dissented. Further criticism has come from Salmon LJ in *A L Wilkinson Ltd* v *Brown* [1966] 1 All ER 509 at p515 and Edmund Davies LJ in *Jaques* v *Lloyd D George & Partners Ltd* [1968] 2 All ER 187 at p192.
2 [1950] 2 KB 257.
3 [1947] 1 All ER 460.

was made "subject to contract".[1] Two other decisions at first instance, those of Lynskey J in *Dennis Reed Ltd* v *Nicholls*[2] and Hilbery J in *EH Bennett & Partners* v *Millett*,[3] were also viewed with some suspicion. Nevertheless, it is at least doubtful whether they were actually overruled,[4] since it was not clear in either case whether the qualification "subject to contract" was introduced by the prospective purchaser or by the vendor. If the vendor had accepted conditionally an offer which was unqualified, then, as was acknowledged by Cohen LJ in *Oxlade's* case, the agent would be entitled to claim commission.[5]

The principle underlying *Oxlade's* case was applied by the Court of Appeal to a different form of words in *Bennett, Walden & Co* v *Wood*.[6] The agents in that case wrote to the vendor confirming that " in the event of our securing for you an offer of £2,900 or some such offer as shall be acceptable to you our commission will be at the recognised ... scale". A person was introduced who made an offer "subject to contract". The vendor accepted this offer but changed his mind before contracts were exchanged, with the result that the sale did not go through. It was held that the agents were not entitled to commission, for the "offer" which they were to obtain had to be a firm offer, not one made "subject to contract".

Where a person introduced by an estate agent actually enters into a binding contract to purchase property, that person's "willingness" to do so is placed beyond dispute.[7] The problem inherent in the "willing to purchase" cases, however, is whether, in the absence of such a contract, the estate agent may establish an applicant's willingness by means of alternative evidence. This question has

---

1 The commission agreement in fact used the term "prepared", but Lewis J treated this as synonymous with "willing".

2 [1948] 2 All ER 914.

3 [1949] 1 KB 362.

4 This was assumed to be so by Denning LJ in *Dennis Reed Ltd* v *Goody* [1950] 2 KB 277 at p289.

5 This point was applied in the County Court case of *Lucas & Sons* v *Mayne* (1954) 164 EG 441.

6 [1950] 2 All ER 134.

7 The argument that "willingness" and "ability" were to be judged at the time of introduction, rather than at the point of sale, was rejected in *Knight Frank & Rutley* v *Fraser* 1974 SLT 50.

received a remarkable divergence of judicial answers, and the two main views expressed must now be examined.

The leading proponent of what we may term the "narrow view", that is, the view that no other evidence will suffice, is Lord Denning MR, whose determination that clients should never be made to pay more than one commission upon a single property has led him to distrust any clause which awards the agent commission on less than a completed sale. The opinion of the learned Master of the Rolls is effectively illustrated by his assertion in *McCallum* v *Hicks*[1] that:

A person may not properly be said to be "willing" to purchase, so as to entitle an agent to commission, unless he is irrevocably willing, that is, unless he has given irrevocable proof of his willingness by entering into a binding contract to purchase.

If correct, "this interpretation means that the special clause has practically the same effect as the usual terms on which an estate agent is employed"[2] thus making a binding contract and continued willingness to complete prerequisites of the agent's claim. Support for this view is to be found in *Martin Gale & Wright* v *Buswell*[3] where commission was expressed to be payable on the introduction of a person "prepared to purchase on the terms of your instructions, or on terms acceptable to you". After an initial offer made "subject to contract", a price was agreed and the parties instructed their solicitors. The prospective purchaser's solicitor, having received a draft contract, returned it marked "approved" and sent an engrossment to his client for signature. Before this was signed, however, the vendor withdrew from the sale. Upon these facts the Court of Appeal rejected the estate agent's claim for commission, and there are undoubtedly passages in the judgments which suggest that it was the absence of a binding contract which prevented the applicant from being described as "prepared". However, the case may also be explained upon the ground that the applicant's original offer remained "subject to contract" until such

---

1 [1950] 2 KB 271 at p276; see also *Dennis Reed Ltd* v *Goody* [1950] 2 KB 277 at p288.
2 *Dennis Reed Ltd* v *Goody* [1950] 2 KB 277 at p287 *per* Denning LJ.
3 (1961) 178 EG 709; see also *Mustafa* v *K G Palos* (1972) 224 EG 35.

time as it could clearly be shown to have become unconditional (presumably when he returned the signed contract to his solicitor).

The "broad view", which permits an estate agent to prove an applicant's willingness merely by showing that the latter has made an unqualified offer to purchase, was clearly taken by Bucknill LJ in *Dennis Reed Ltd v Goody.*[1] Although the agents' claim in that case failed, because their applicant withdrew from negotiations before contracts were exchanged, Bucknill LJ stated that they could have succeeded by showing "that he was ready, able and willing to purchase up to the time when either an enforceable contract for the purchase of the house is made between the parties, or, alternatively, up to the time when the vendor refuses to enter into such a contract on terms on which the purchaser is willing to purchase and the vendor was at one time willing to sell".

The opinion of Bucknill LJ was clearly *obiter*, as were the similar views expressed by the Court of Appeal in *EP Nelson & Co v Rolfe.*[2] The court there was satisfied as to the "willingness" of a person who never in fact made an offer, even conditionally, for the property, but the point in that case was conceded by counsel for the client. Direct authority for the broad view is thus confined to the following three cases.

In *John E Trinder & Partners v Haggis,*[3] the plaintiffs introduced a person who signed his part of a contract to purchase the property; when the vendor refused to exchange contracts, the Court of Appeal held by a majority that he was liable to pay commission. A more extreme case is *AL Wilkinson Ltd v O'Neil,*[4] in which commission was made payable upon the introduction of "an applicant willing and able to sign a contract to purchase" at a named price or such other price as the vendor would accept. Negotiations reached the point at which the prospective purchaser received a draft contract; this he returned with a number of small verbal amendments and one of more substance. The Court of Appeal accepted evidence that the applicant would have waived this amendment if pressed to do so and, stressing that "willingness"

---

1 [1950] 2 KB 277 at p283.
2 [1950] 1 KB 139.
3 (1951) 158 EG 4.
4 (1961) 181 EG 137.

is a matter of fact, found it to be satisfactorily established in this case.

The third, and most important, case is *Christie Owen & Davies* v *Rapacioli*[1] in which, to earn commission, the agents were to effect "an introduction either directly or indirectly of a person ready able and willing to purchase" the defendant's restaurant for £20,000 or an acceptable lower price. The plaintiffs introduced a person who, having agreed a price with the vendor, signed his part of the contract and paid a deposit. The Court of Appeal, after considering the cases already referred to, decided that this person clearly fitted the description and therefore awarded the plaintiffs their commission.

The weight of authority thus appears to favour the broad view[2] and, at least at first sight, it seems perfectly reasonable that this should be so. As Ormerod LJ said in *Ackroyd & Sons* v *Hasan*:[3] "I can find no justification for holding that the words 'prepared to enter into a contract' mean the same as, 'introduction of a party who does enter into a contract'." However, there is one argument in favour of the narrow view, put forward by writers on this subject,[4] which is extremely difficult to answer. The main lines of this argument are as follows: an applicant's willingness to purchase is only legally relevant if the terms upon which he or she is willing are acceptable to the vendor: the vendor's state of mind can seldom be ascertained before contracts are exchanged, because until that time the vendor is free (at least as against the applicant) to reject the offer outright or modify the terms for acceptance: the commission agreement should not be interpreted in such a way as to fetter this freedom, for "the commission agreement is, however, subordinate to the hoped for principal agreement of sale. It would be strange if what was preliminary or accessory should control the freedom of action of the principal in regard to the main transaction which everyone contemplates might never materialise."[5]

---

1 [1974] 2 All ER 311.
2 Inferential support may be also found in the drafting of the Estate Agents (Provision of Information) Regulations 1991: see pp 205-206.
3 [1960] 2 QB 144 at p163.
4 Ash, *Willing to Purchase*, Heriot Press, 1963; *Bowstead on Agency*, 15th ed, art 58.
5 *Luxor (Eastbourne) Ltd* v *Cooper* [1941] AC 108 at pp138-9, *per* Lord Wright.

This argument does not appear to have been specifically canvassed in the courts; it is significant, however, that in *Ackroyd & Sons* v *Hasan*,[1] where the commission agreement expressly required the vendor's assent to the terms of purchase, the Court of Appeal held this to be lacking despite the fact that the parties' solicitors had reached agreement. If, then, the vendor's assent is impliedly required in the normal "willing to purchase" case, it is difficult to resist the conclusion that this requires an exchange of contracts, or at least the signature by the parties of their respective parts.

The question of "willingness" to purchase is thus in a state of extreme uncertainty, and the most recent pronouncements of the Court of Appeal have done little to dispel the general confusion. In *AA Dickson & Co* v *O'Leary*[2] the defendant, who wished to sell his flat, put it in the hands of more than one firm of agents. The plaintiffs, who were to receive commission on "either directly or indirectly introducing a person ready, able and willing to purchase on terms authorised by [the defendant]", introduced an applicant who seriously intended to purchase and who, on October 28, actually signed her part of a contract and returned it to her solicitors. On receiving this document on October 29, the solicitors immediately telephoned the defendants' solicitors, only to be told that contracts had been exchanged on October 28 with a rival applicant. The plaintiffs nevertheless claimed to be entitled to their commission, but it was held by the Court of Appeal[3] that commission is not payable unless the agent carries out his instructions before the property is sold to someone else (whether or not the agent is aware of that fact).

As to precisely *when* the plaintiffs' applicant might have been described as "willing", Lord Denning MR thought that this would be when the part of the contract which she had signed reached her solicitors (why this should be preferred to the moment of signature was not made clear). Sir David Cairns, however (in a discussion with counsel on costs which is not contained in the published report of the case), suggested that a person's willingness would not be established until the transaction was beyond recall, which would be

---

1 [1960] 2 QB 144.
2 (1979) 254 EG 731.
3 Following *EP Nelson Co* v *Rolfe* [1950] 1 KB 139.

when that person's solicitors actually *sent* the signed part of the contract to the other side.

(f) *Ready, able and prepared*

Whether or not a person is "able" to purchase property is regarded by the courts as depending primarily upon questions of finance. In this connection the following words of Atkin LJ[1] have often been quoted:

I think that "ability" does not depend upon whether the purchaser has got the money in hand at the time or the balance at his bank. To my mind it is a question of fact. I do not think it depends on whether he has a binding agreement by which some third person is obliged to provide him with resources to carry out the contract. I think it is sufficient if it is proved by the agent or by the purchaser the circumstances are such that if the vendor had been willing and ready to carry out his contract he on his part at the proper time could have found the necessary money to perform his obligation.

This *dictum* was applied by Lynskey J in *Dennis Reed Ltd* v *Nicholls*[2] where, after hearing evidence as to the potential purchaser's earnings and the value of the house which he owned, the learned judge found that he was clearly able to purchase the property in question.

"Ability" was extended to include matters other than finance in the case of *Dellafiora* v *Lester; Lester* v *Adrian Barr & Co Ltd*.[3] In that case the agents, in return for a commission of 10% of the purchase price, were instructed to find a person willing and able to purchase property which consisted of the remaining 11 years of a lease on a café. The agents introduced a person who signed a contract and paid a deposit. However, the sale went off because the landlords refused their consent to the assignment, and the purchaser's deposit was returned in accordance with the conditions of sale. The agents, who earned commission on a subsequent sale of the property, claimed to be entitled in addition to commission on this abortive introduction. The Court of Appeal held that the person whom the agents introduced could not be described as "able" in the

---

1 *James* v *Smith* [1931] 2 KB 317n at p322.
2 [1948] 2 All ER 914.
3 [1962] 3 All ER 393.

face of the landlord's refusal to allow her to purchase the property; accordingly the agents' claim failed.

There is little authority upon the meaning, if any, which is to be given to the word "ready" where this is used in addition to, or in substitution for, "willing and able". The view of Denning LJ that a person who is ready "must have made all necessary preparations by having the cash or a banker's draft ready to hand over"[1] does not appear to be based on previous decisions; nor has it been followed. It is submitted that "ready" adds nothing to the requirement already discussed, a view which is supported, for example, by the judgment of Atkin LJ in *James* v *Smith*[2] where the terms "ready" and "able" are used interchangeably.

As a variation upon the "willing and able" theme, some estate agents stipulate that commission shall be payable on the introduction of a person "prepared to enter into a contract" to purchase. The Court of Appeal in *Ackroyd & Sons* v *Hasan*[3] had no difficulty in finding that the prospective purchasers were "prepared", since they had gone so far as to sign their part of the contract. No general consideration of the meaning of "prepared" took place, however, and for guidance on this matter one must turn to the later case of *AL Wilkinson Ltd* v *Brown*,[4] which concerned the sale of a leasehold property. The plaintiff estate agents introduced a person who was undoubtedly eager to purchase, but whose references at first failed to satisfy the landlord. This obstacle was later removed, but the potential purchaser could not exchange contracts until he was sure of selling his own property and raising the purchase price. Before his expectations were fulfilled, the defendant sold the property elsewhere. The Court of Appeal, in holding that the agents were not entitled to commission because the person they had introduced was never "prepared" to purchase, considered the meaning of that term. Harman LJ said:

"[P]repared", as I think is conceded, means something more, generally speaking, than "willing". It means a person who is ready and willing. It may involved the qualification "able", but in many circumstances one would not

---

1 *Dennis Reed Ltd* v *Goody* [1950] 2 KB 277 at p287.
2 [1931] 2 KB 317n at p322.
3 [1960] 2 QB 144.
4 [1966] 1 All ER 509.

look beyond whether the person was a genuine person ready and willing to sign a contract.

The meaning of this *dictum* is somewhat obscured by the use of the word "ready" which, as we have already seen, means "able" if it means anything at all. Salmon LJ, on the other hand, would not concede that the agent's position was in any way improved by the use of the word "prepared": "In my judgment a person is not prepared to enter into a contract who is not ready, willing and able to do so."

(g) *Willing purchaser*

The commission clauses which we have so far considered draw a clear distinction between a "purchaser" and a "person willing to purchase". Since, however, it is not uncommon to find estate agents using commission terms which envisage the introduction of a "willing purchaser", it is relevant to consider into which category such a clause falls. As we have already seen, a "purchaser" is treated by the courts as meaning one who actually purchases, and it is therefore strongly arguable that "willing purchaser" cannot mean less than this; if it means anything at all, it suggests that the purchaser must be shown to have purchased willingly! As against this, there are at least two decisions in which the normal meaning of "purchaser" was held to have been qualified by the context in which it was found. In *EH Bennett & Partners* v *Millett*,[1] a clause requiring an agent to introduce "a purchaser who is able and willing to complete the transaction" was held to have been satisfied by the introduction of someone who never in fact signed a contract, but who remained at all times willing and able to do so. And in *Midgley Estates Ltd* v *Hand*,[2] the characteristics usually required of a "purchaser" (continued willingness and ability to complete the purchase) were held to have been rendered irrelevant by making commission payable as soon as "our purchaser shall have signed a legally binding contract".

In so far as these decisions suggest that the meaning of "purchaser" may vary, they lend support to the view that "willing purchaser" is to be equated with "person willing to purchase".

---

1 [1949] 1 KB 362.
2 [1952] 2 QB 432.

However, in what appears to be the only reported case in which the phrase itself required interpretation, the Court of Appeal took a much stricter line. The case in question, *Davis* v *George Trollope & Sons*,[1] in fact concerned, not a straightforward commission clause, but an agreement between an agent and a subagent. The plaintiff, an estate agent, thought that he could find a purchaser for a property which was on the defendants' books, and (in the words of the county court judge), "the defendants agreed to pay the plaintiff one-half of the sum which they would earn if he introduced to them a willing buyer" at an agreed price. The plaintiff made his introduction, but the vendor sold the house elsewhere and the defendants did not therefore earn any commission. This did not prevent the plaintiff from claiming against the defendants and, in the county court, the claim succeeded. The Court of Appeal, however, reversed this decision on two grounds: first, the term "willing buyer" meant, not "person willing to buy" but "person who actually becomes a buyer", something which had clearly not happened; second, in the view of Scott LJ, a contract of this nature must mean: "If through your bringing a willing buyer I earn my commission, I will then pay you half of it."

Although the true meaning of "willing purchaser" is thus open to doubt, it may well be that this uncertainty will not henceforth be a source of problems, thanks to the Estate Agents (Provision of Information) Regulations 1991. According to those regulations, which were made under section 18 of the Estate Agents Act 1979, any estate agent using the term "ready, willing and able purchaser" is obliged to give the client a written definition of that term, using words provided by the regulations themselves. And, since the statutory definition is a person who "is prepared and is able to exchange unconditional contracts for the purchase of your property", and since it is further made clear that commission must be paid "even if you subsequently withdraw and unconditional contracts for sale are not exchanged, irrespective of your reasons", it must be assumed that an agent who complies with the regulations will be entitled to payment in these circumstances, *Davis* v *Trollope* notwithstanding.

---

1 [1943] 1 All ER 501.

(h) *Other clauses*

From all that has gone before, it is clear that an estate agent may stipulate for the payment of commission notwithstanding that no contract has been made, (eg the "willing and able" cases) and notwithstanding the inability of a purchaser to complete a contract which has been made (where commission is linked merely to the contract). It remains for us now to consider two attempts which have been made to provide for the payment of commission without reference to either of these conditions. In *Drewery* v *Ware-Lane*[1] the defendant, who owned a leasehold house, put it into the hands of the plaintiffs and signed an agreement to pay them commission "if and when (a) a prospective purchaser signs your 'purchaser's agreement' and (b) I sign your 'vendor's agreement' (receipt of a copy of a form of each of the above agreements is hereby acknowledged)". The agents introduced a person, a price was agreed, and the two "agreements" were signed "subject to contract". The person introduced was not, at that stage, able to purchase the property, as he had first to obtain a mortgage; however, since he wished to buy the freehold from the landlord, he did not intend to apply for a mortgage until his negotiations with the landlord had terminated, successfully or otherwise. Nine days after the signing of the agreements, the defendant sold the property to someone else and the agents sued for their commission. The Court of Appeal held that the terms of the commission agreement were clear and had been fulfilled by the agents. In considering whether the applicant could properly be described as a "prospective purchaser", Ormerod LJ said:

The word "prospective" does not connote necessarily either the term "ready" or "willing" or "able"; it means a man who has the question of buying this property in prospect or in contemplation and is prepared to make an offer with regard to it.

The second attempt by estate agents to cross the usual barriers met with a good deal less success. In *Jaques* v *Lloyd D George & Partners Ltd*[2] the plaintiff agreed that he would pay commission to agents "should you be instrumental in introducing a person willing

1 [1960] 3 All ER 529.
2 [1968] 2 All ER 187.

to sign a document capable of becoming a contract to purchase at a price, which at any stage of the negotiations has been agreed by me". As we shall see,[1] the agents were not allowed to rely on this clause since they had misled the plaintiff as to its effect. However, Lord Denning MR and Cairns J provided a further ground for the decision, holding the clause unenforceable by reason of its vagueness and uncertainty. As Cairns J pointed out, one possible reading of this clause would entitle the agents to commission if the person introduced signed a blank piece of paper, since this could then be completed so as to form a contract of sale!

2 Substantial performance

In this chapter we have so far tended to assume that, once the event on which commission is payable has been satisfactorily identified, the question whether or not it has taken place is a simple and straightforward one. In practice, however, cases frequently arise in which what has actually occurred is *not* the stipulated event but something which resembles it to a greater or lesser degree. The problem which confronts the court in such a case is to decide whether the agent's entitlement to commission depends upon the *exact* fulfilment of the client's instructions or whether *substantial performance* will suffice and, if the latter applies, whether what has been produced is sufficiently akin to what was envisaged for it to be said that the agent's instructions have been substantially performed.

A simple example of this principle in operation, and one with which every practising estate agent will be familiar, is that of a sale of property which goes through only upon the agreement of the vendor to reduce the asking price. In *Jack Windle Ltd v Brierley*[2] the plaintiffs introduced a prospective purchaser for the defendant's bakery business, but he was unable to raise the purchase money and negotiations ceased. A short time later, after the plaintiffs' instructions had been withdrawn, the defendant agreed to reduce the price to this applicant and to allow a part of the money to remain outstanding on the security of a second mortgage. It was held that the plaintiffs were not entitled to commission, for they had

---

1 p173.
2 [1952] 1 All ER 398. Like many such cases, this might equally well be dealt with under the heading of "effective cause": p152.

not fulfilled their instructions; the sale which actually took place was effectively brought about by the vendor himself.

This, it must be said, seems a very harsh decision and one, moreover, which is somewhat out of line with previous authority.[1] Indeed, it has been criticised in subsequent cases,[2] and it now seems safe to assume that a price reduction in itself will not affect an agent's right to claim commission for an effective introduction.

A second group of cases raising the question of substantial performance concerns limited companies. Where, for example, the property which is to be sold represents virtually the only assets of a company, it sometimes happens that a person introduced by an estate agent buys, not the property, but the company itself, by acquiring all (or nearly all) its shares. Common sense suggests that, where this occurs, the agent should be entitled to commission and, despite one decision to the contrary,[3] the majority view is indeed in the agent's favour.[4] However, an agent whose client is a company may still be worse off in one situation, namely where the property is subject to a mortgage. It has always been accepted that commission on the sale of mortgaged property is based, not merely on the price paid for the equity, but on the "grossed up" value. Where, however, mortgaged property is put on the market by a company, and an applicant introduced by the agent then buys the company's shares at a price which is depressed because of the mortgage, it has been held that the agent's commission can only be based upon the actual price of the shares; here no "grossing up" is possible.[5]

Problems can also arise where an agent introduces a company as a potential purchaser of the client's property, for the labyrinthine ways of the business world may well mean that the property is ultimately transferred, not to the company actually introduced, but to another company which may be its subsidiary or linked to it in some other way. In the Australian case of *LJ Hooker Ltd* v *WJ*

---

1 *Price Davies & Co* v *Smith* (1929) 45 TLR 542.
2 *Levers* v *Dunsdon* (1967) 206 EG 979; *Glentree Estates Ltd* v *Gee* (1981) 259 EG 332.
3 *Harris & Gillow* v *Kelly* (1953) 162 EG 622.
4 *Levers* v *Dunsdon* (1967) 206 EG 979; *Allen* v *Anderson* [1969] NZLR 951.
5 *Way & Waller Ltd* v *Ryde* [1944] 1 All ER 9.

Adams Estates Pty Ltd,[1] for example, a company introduced by the plaintiffs made an agreement with another company which had already been negotiating with the vendor on terms that, no matter which of them ultimately purchased the site, they would join together in its development. When the land was actually sold to the other company, which then allotted shares to the plaintiffs' applicant, it was held that the plaintiffs were not entitled to any commission from the vendor; they could not be said to have *caused* the sale, nor could their applicant be described as a "purchaser". However every case turns on its own facts, so that, in another Australian case[2] concerning the sale of a leasehold farm, commission was held to be payable when the vendor and purchaser set up a joint company to manage the property for a period. Similarly, in *Gunn* v *Showell's Brewery Co Ltd*,[3] where the plaintiff was retained by the defendants to find a suitable brewery for them to purchase, it was held that they could not avoid the payment of commission by arranging for the property to be bought by one of their subsidiary companies.[4]

Apart from these identifiable groups, variations on the theme of substantial performance are endless. In *Griffin & Son* v *Cheesewright*,[5] where agents were instructed to let a house for three years, the applicant whom they introduced decided instead to purchase the vendor's entire interest in the property. In *Battams* v *Tompkins*,[6] the terms of a sale effected by the plaintiff were materially different from those envisaged by the client's instructions. In *Mason* v *Clifton*,[7] it was the terms of the stipulated loan which differed. In all these cases, the agents failed in their claims for commission.

---

1 (1977) 138 CLR 52.
2 *Lord* v *Trippe* (1977) 51 ALJR 574.
3 (1902) 18 TLR 659; see also *Druce Investments Ltd* v *Thaker* [1988] 2 EGLR 229; *Kinney & Green* v *Johns* (1985) 276 EG 799.
4 In *Peter Yates & Co* v *Bullock* [1990] 2 EGLR 24, estate agents successfully claimed commission when an applicant whom they had introduced purchased the property jointly with another party.
5 (1885) 2 TLR 99.
6 (1892) 8 TLR 707.
7 (1863) 3 F&F 899.

In *GT Hodges & Sons* v *Hackbridge Park Residential Hotel Ltd*,[1] the plaintiffs, in attempting to find a purchaser for the defendants' hotel, introduced a representative of the War Department which, however, was not prepared to pay the price which the defendants wanted. The following year, as a result of their representative's report, the War Department acquired the hotel by compulsory purchase at a price even lower than their original offer. The Court of Appeal held that, in the absence of a voluntary sale, there was no contractual relationship between the agents' acts and the transfer of the property. The plaintiffs were not entitled to commission, for all they had done was "to start a train of causes which ultimately led to the defendants' property being taken away from them against their will",[2] at a price considerably less than they were willing to accept.

While most agents would probably regard the decision in the *Hodges* case as entirely reasonable, the same can hardly be said of a much more recent decision of the Court of Appeal, that in *Spiers (trading as "Garmans")* v *Taylor*.[3] The plaintiffs there, on being instructed to market the defendant's house, stated that the it would be "entered on the Agent's list of properties for sale at the asking price of £34,500". Commission would then be payable, it was said, on a sale at or above that price, or at any price subsequently agreed. For reasons which are not at all clear, the plaintiffs never marketed the property at £34,500; they told the first serious applicant to appear that he need offer no more than £33,500 (while telling the client that a sale had been agreed at the asking price) and the client, in order to avoid breaking a chain of sales, agreed to sell at the lower price. The Court of Appeal held (quite rightly, it is submitted) that the agents must pay damages for depriving their client of the chance of obtaining a higher price. The court also held (quite wrongly, it is submitted) that the essential term which must be satisfied in order for commission to be earned was the marketing of the property at the correct price; since this had not occurred, no commission was payable, even though the house had been sold at (presumably) a fair price.

---

1 [1940] 1 KB 404.
2 At p412 *per* Clauson, LJ.
3 (1984) 271 EG 196.

Further examples of transactions too far removed from the original instructions to entitle an estate agent to commission may be found in *Barnett* v *Isaacson*,[1] where a business was bought by someone whom the agent had introduced *as a subagent*, and *Richard Ellis* v *Pipe-Chem (Holdings) Ltd*,[2] where agents acting for prospective tenants of business premises were only able to obtain an underlease, rather than the specified lease, since the landlords refused to lease the property directly to the agents' clients. Finally, as a monument to the eternal optimism of those who work on commission terms, we may look at the case of *Tufnell* v *Richard Costain Ltd*.[3] The plaintiff there, who was commissioned to procure finance for a large development project contemplated by the defendants' client, found himself unable to obtain the necessary loans. The plaintiff thereupon persuaded the client to use his own resources and duly claimed his commission for so doing! Not surprisingly, the claim failed, Paul J holding that the availability of this source of finance was due to the client's own decision rather than to the efforts of the agent.

The foregoing selection of unsuccessful commission claims serves to indicate that an agent who seeks to be paid for producing something different from what was originally called for faces something of an uphill struggle. However, the task is not an impossible one. In *Rimmer* v *Knowles*,[4] for example, an agent instructed to find a purchaser was held entitled to commission for introducing someone who took a 99-year lease of the property with an option to purchase the reversion. In *Hegarty* v *Bryant Homes Ltd*,[5] an agent seeking development sites earned commission for an introduction, even though the client then purchased the property by tender.[6] Again, in *Connell Estate Agents* v *Begej*,[7] an agent employed to bring about a "sale" of the client's property recovered commission on a part-exchange; the amount of commission,

---

1 (1888) 4 TLR 645.
2 (1980) 258 EG 329.
3 (1968) 209 EG 705.
4 (1874) 30 LT 496.
5 (1983, unreported).
6 In *Taplin* v *Barrett* (1889) 6 TLR 30, by contrast, no commission was payable *by a vendor* where the agent introduced someone who purchased the property at a subsequent auction.
7 [1993] 39 EG 125.

moreover, was assessed on the full value of the transaction and not merely on the cash element.[1]

From an agent's point of view, the most generous decision is surely that of the Court of Appeal in *Chamberlain & Willows* v *HBS (Trust) Ltd*.[2] The plaintiffs there introduced a prospective tenant for their clients' property but, before a lease could be signed, the clients sold the freehold. When the plaintiffs' applicant subsequently leased the property from the new owners, the Court of Appeal[3] held that the agents could be said to have "introduced a tenant" in accordance with their instructions; the clients were therefore liable to pay commission.

3   Effective cause[4]

In order for an agent to claim commission it is necessary to show, not only that a specified event has occurred, but also that the agent has caused it to occur.[5] This, like all questions of causation, is a matter of fact which is to be determined upon the evidence available. Moreover, it is a question of common sense whether what the agent has done is sufficiently closely connected with the subsequent transaction for it to be said effectively to have caused the transaction, wholly or in part.

In this connection it should be noted that it is not enough for the agent's activities to be a *causa sine qua non*, that is to say, that the event would not have taken place without the agent's intervention (for example because the parties would never have met). It must further be established that the agent is an "effective" or "efficient" cause or, to put it another way, that the result has been achieved through the instrumentality of the agent. All these forms of words have been used in cases, by judges seeking to explain the legal position. The basic rule may be better understood, however, in the light of a hypothetical example. Let us suppose that an estate agent, who has been instructed to find either a tenant or a

---

1 According to the Court of Appeal, a pure exchange of properties would not have satisfied the requirement of a "sale".

2 (1962) 184 EG 849.

3 Rather surprisingly, perhaps, reversing the trial judge: (1962) 183 EG 417.

4 See Murdoch: "The Principle of Effective Cause" (1985) 276 EG 742 and 877.

5 In "willing to purchase" cases, the agent must have caused the applicant's "willingness": *Hartnell, Taylor, Cook* v *Bromwich* (1982) 264 EG 440.

purchaser of a client's property, introduces a tenant, and that this tenant, many years later, purchases the reversion. The agent's act is clearly a *causa sine qua non* of the purchase since, in the final analysis, this depends on the original introduction. However, common sense dictates that, for practical purposes, the agent cannot be treated as having "caused" the sale to take place and so the agent will not receive commission on it. If, however, in similar circumstances, a tenant introduced by the estate agent agreed in a matter of days to become a purchaser, the agent might well be treated as an "effective cause" and thus entitled to commission.

The general rule stated above has to be applied by the courts to the infinitely variable facts of actual cases. Since, as already mentioned, it is a question of fact whether or not the agent is an effective cause, decisions on this point are not of binding authority for the future. Nevertheless, a consideration of some of these cases is instructive for two reasons: first, because certain general principles emerge from even the most empirical of inquiries, and. second, as a guide to the types of case in which this point is likely to arise and the circumstances in which the agent may stand to lose commission which at first sight appears to have been earned.

For an agent's act to rank as an effective cause of the event which earns commission, it must be carried out in pursuance of a commission agreement. It follows that there can be no successful claim in respect of an introduction made by the agent before the commission agreement is entered into; to hold otherwise would mean allowing the agent to rely on past consideration to enforce the client's promise.[1] Nor can an agent rely on an introduction made by a subagent, where the client has given the agent no authority to subinstruct.[2]

However, an introduction may be treated as the effective cause of a sale whether or not the client is aware of it, as for example where a prospective purchaser deceives the vendor by pretending to have come privately.[3] Furthermore, if a potentially effective introduction

---

1 *Samuel & Co* v *Sanders Bros* (1886) 3 TLR 145, *per* Lord Esher: see also *Mote* v *Gould* (1935) 152 LT 347 at p348, *per* du Parcq J; *Robert Bruce & Partners* v *Winyard Developments* [1987] 1 EGLR 20.
2 *McCann & Co* v *Pow* [1975] 1 All ER 129; *Robert Bruce & Partners* v *Winyard Developments* [1987] 1 EGLR 20.
3 See *Warman* v *Newmans Ltd* (1901) 17 TLR 509.

is made by an agent acting under a commission agreement, it will not be rendered ineffective by the vendor's decision to take over the negotiations in person[1] or through another agent.[2] Nor can the vendor avoid liability to pay commission by terminating the agent's instructions before concluding the deal,[3] although a sole agent may not be entitled to claim on a sale to someone introduced within that period, where contracts are not exchanged until after the sole agency has expired.[4]

The question whether or not an introduction ranks as the "effective cause" of a transaction is one which is answered objectively. Thus, in *Burchell* v *Gowrie & Blockhouse Collieries Ltd*,[5] an agent was held entitled to commission on a sale to a person introduced, notwithstanding that the agent had advised the client against selling to this person. However, where an agent's reason for advising the client not to accept an offer from X was a secret agreement between the agent and Y, a rival applicant, one of the court's reasons for rejecting the agent's claim to be paid commission on a sale to X was that this sale had not been brought about by the agent.[6]

A situation which frequently gives rise to an effective cause dispute is that in which an agent "introduces" a person who has already been in negotiation with the vendor. In order to succeed in such a case, the agent must show that the previous negotiations had come to nothing and that it was only because of the agent's intervention that they were revived.[7] An agent who is unable to establish this is unlikely to convince a court that things done subsequently, such as persuading the client to reduce the asking price, is decisive enough to earn commission.[8]

1 *Wilkinson* v *Martin* (1837) 8 C&P 1.
2 *Bow's Emporium Ltd* v *AR Brett & Co Ltd* (1927) 44 TLR 194 at p 197, *per* Lord Shaw of Dunfermline.
3 *Green* v *Bartlett* (1863) 14 CBNS 681; *Christie & Co* v *Jones* (1966) 198 EG 1093.
4 So held in *Fairvale Ltd* v *Sabharwal* [1992] 2 EGLR 27 (p 336), where the commission clause spoke of sales "effected". See also the doubts expressed by Simon Brown J in *Brodie Marshall & Co* v *Carpenter* [1985] 1 EGLR 24.
5 [1910] AC 614.
6 *Henry Smith & Son* v *Muskett* (1977) 246 EG 655.
7 *Thompson, Rippon & Co* v *Thomas* (1895) 11 TLR 304; *Hampton & Sons* v *Trade & General Securities Ltd* (1978) 250 EG 451.
8 *Lewis* v *Calder* (1957) 170 EG 5.

In many cases of this kind, a client is faced with claims from two or more agents. The strongly held (and strongly expressed) view of Lord Denning was that there could only ever be one commission per transaction, and that this would be earned by whichever of the agents found the ultimate purchaser.[1] However, there seems no reason in principle why more than one agent should not be entitled to commission in respect of the same transaction and, as a result, the courts will not allow a client to interplead, that is, pay one amount of commission into court and leave the competing agents to fight over it.[2] How such double liability might come about was discussed by Drake J in *Lordsgate Properties Ltd* v *Balcombe*:[3]

It appears to me that there is no good reason in law why a vendor may not be liable to two agents in respect of the same transaction, provided either (a) both parties were instrumental in causing the sale; or (b) the different contracts entitle each of the agents to commission for different reasons.

Taking the second of these possibilities first, it is clear that an agent instructed on "willing to purchase" terms may succeed in earning commission for having made a suitable introduction, even where the property is ultimately sold to an applicant introduced by another agent. Again, it was held in the *Lordsgate* case itself that, where one agent was instructed to "introduce an applicant who purchases" the property, and another to be "instrumental in negotiating a sale", their claims were not mutually exclusive and indeed that both agents were entitled.

The first of the possibilities mentioned by Drake J is, however, rather more problematical. While in theory a court might decide that a purchaser has been introduced by the combined efforts of two or more competing agents, and that these agents must therefore share the commission, this approach does not appear to have been adopted in any reported case. More typical is the blunt statement of Lopes LJ in *Barnett* v *Brown*[4] that: "The question to be decided was: Whose introduction had brought about the purchase?", although the modern judicial tendency is to pay lip service to the

---

1 See, for example, *AA Dickson & Co* v *O'Leary* (1979) 254 EG 731.
2 *Greatorex* v *Shackle* [1895] 2 QB 249; *Moss Kaye & Roy Frank & Co* v *Jones* [1979] CLY 37.
3 [1985] 1 EGLR 20.
4 *Barnett* v *Brown* (1890) 6 TLR 463.

possibility of a double claim, while denying it on the facts of a particular case.[1]

When called upon to select an "effective cause" from two or more competing claims, the courts profess to be completely open-minded. As Harman LJ put it in *Bartlett v Cole:*[2]

I do not think you can answer the question by saying: "Who was first on the list?" I think you can answer the question by saying: "Whose introduction was the effective introduction?"

Notwithstanding such expressions of opinion, however, it cannot be denied that the decisions have a tendency to favour the first introduction,[3] unless there is some very clear reason for this to be displaced.[4] Indeed, at first instance in *John D Wood & Co v Dantata,*[5] Forbes J said:

I do not consider than an agent who effects a second introduction to the property (if that is not a contradiction in terms) can succeed in demonstrating that such an introduction was the effective cause of the sale, unless he can show that the interest aroused in the purchase by the first introduction has evaporated by the time of the second.

Although this *dictum* was referred to without apparent disagreement when the *John D Wood* case reached the Court of Appeal, and was endorsed by Garland J in *Chesterfield & Co Ltd v Zahid,*[6] it was disapproved by the Court of Appeal in the recent case of *Chasen Ryder & Co v Hedges.*[7] According to Staughton LJ, the true position is rather more open:

---

1 See, for example, *Lordsgate Properties Ltd v Balcombe* [1985] 1 EGLR 20; *John D Wood & Co v Dantata* [1985] 2 EGLR 44; [1987] 2 EGLR 23.

2 (1963) 188 EG 397.

3 See, in addition to *Bartlett v Cole* (1963) 188 EG 397, *Moss Kaye & Roy Frank & Co v Jones* [1979] CLY 37; *Glentree Estates Ltd v Gee* (1981) 259 EG 332; *Bentleys Estate Agents Ltd v Granix Ltd* [1989] 2 EGLR 21.

4 See *Taplin v Barrett* (1889) 6 TLR 30 (where the applicant subsequently bought the property at auction); *Robert Drummond v Mangles* (1981) 260 EG 1039; *Chesterfield & Co Ltd v Zahid* [1989] 2 EGLR 24; *Cobbs Property Services Ltd v Liddell-Taylor* [1990] 1 EGLR 49.

5 [1985] 2 EGLR 44; affirmed by the Court of Appeal [1987] 2 EGLR 23.

6 [1989] 2 EGLR 24.

7 [1993] 1 EGLR 47.

The burden is on the plaintiff to show that his introduction in any case was the effective cause of the purchase. If, however, he shows that he was the first to introduce the purchaser, and that a purchase followed, then it may well be that the judge will infer that the plaintiff was the effective cause. It can therefore be said that the evidential burden in such a case passes to the defendant, whether the other agent or the vendor, to prove more facts which displace that inference. But even in such a case, I do not think that the further facts which the defendant then has to prove must be such as to show that interest aroused by the first introduction has evaporated, that is to say, entirely disappeared. It will be a matter for consideration in each case, how far the defendant has to go before he has displaced an inference which might arise from the mere fact of the introduction followed by the purchase.

Most of the "two agent" cases cited above arose when applicants who had been shown a property by one agent lost interest, but were subsequently reintroduced to it by a second agent. However, an unusual example occurred in *Calloway & Co* v *Peters*,[1] where the plaintiffs and another firm of estate agents had both erected "For Sale" boards outside the defendant's house. A prospective purchaser, having made some enquiries through the plaintiffs, told a member of her staff to contact "the agents" and negotiate a purchase. The employee inadvertently telephoned the other firm, the sale was concluded through them, and it was held that the plaintiffs were not entitled to commission.[2] Even more bizarre is the case of *Bloom* v *Yefet*[3] where, it appears, a Saudi Arabian princess was shown round a property for sale by two rival agents at the same time, each agent being blissfully unaware of the other's presence!

The "effective cause" problem arises in a rather different form where there is a substantial delay between the original introduction and the ultimate transaction. Sometimes the break in causation is clear, as it was in the New Zealand case of *Lewis* v *Wong*.[4] The agents there showed a prospective purchaser several properties, one of which he duly bought. Not surprisingly, they were held not to be entitled to commission when, after negotiating directly with the vendor, he later bought one of the other properties. Less obvious

---

1 [1954] 164 EG 353.

2 It is possible that a "two board" case might today be decided according to which board was covered by deemed planning consent: see p 261.

3 (1982) 264 EG 142.

4 [1982] *Recent Law* 336: see also *Barnett* v *Brown* (1890) 6 TLR 463.

are those cases in which a person introduced by the agent as a *tenant* of the client's property later purchases the freehold. In *Toulmin* v *Millar*[1] the agent's claim failed because, it was found, the authority given by the client was limited to finding a tenant. The question arose in a pure form in *Nightingale* v *Parsons*,[2] where the plaintiff was asked to find either a tenant or a purchaser for the defendant's house. A tenant was introduced who, after three years, purchased the freehold instead of exercising his option to renew the lease. It was held that the agent, who had played no part in the negotiations leading up to the sale, could not claim to be an "effective cause" of it. In the county court case of *Poulter* v *Doggett*,[3] on the other hand, where the estate agent's instructions were similar, the lease itself gave the tenant an option to purchase the freehold. It was held that, when this option was exercised by an assignee of the original tenant, the estate agent was entitled to commission on the sale, less, of course, the amount which the client had already paid.

The question of commission on a subsequent transaction arose in rather different circumstances in *Tribe* v *Taylor*,[4] a case which emphasises the factual nature of this whole matter. The plaintiff there, who was commissioned to find capital for the defendant's business, introduced a person who lent £10,000, on which the plaintiff duly received commission. A few months later this person entered into partnership with the defendant and injected a further £4,000 into the business. It was held that this further loan resulted, not from the plaintiff's introduction, but from the partnership negotiations and that, accordingly, no commission was payable.

Before leaving the subject of "effective cause", it should be noted that an agent's chances of succeeding on this point may be enhanced by the drafting of wide commission terms. In *Brian Cooper & Co* v *Fairview Estates (Investments) Ltd*,[5] for example, the plaintiff agents were instructed to market an office development on terms that commission would be payable "should you introduce a tenant ... with whom we have not been in previous communication

---

1 (1887) 3 TLR 836.
2 [1914] 2 KB 621: see also *Millar, Son & Co* v *Radford* (1903) 19 TLR 575.
3 (1964) 115 LJ 76.
4 (1876) 1 CPD 505.
5 [1987] 1 EGLR 18.

and who subsequently completes a lease". The plaintiffs introduced a company which ultimately took a lease of the property, but only after its negotiations with the clients had ceased and been revived by another firm of agents. The plaintiffs were clearly not the effective cause of the lease; but the Court of Appeal held that, on the wording of their commission terms, they were not required to be.

As to other attempts to outflank the effective cause principle, it has been held that a term that commission is payable "should a sale be effected" still requires that sale to be effected by the agent;[1] not so, however, where commission is tied to a sale "whether arranged by the auctioneers or not".[2] Even less explicit wording may play its part. In *Bayley* v *Chadwick*,[3] for example, where the plaintiff was employed to sell a ship by auction, his client agreed to pay commission if a private sale came about "in consequence of your mention or publication for auction purposes". Information obtained from the plaintiff was passed on to a person who bought the ship direct from the client. The House of Lords held that, on the wording of this clause, the plaintiff was entitled to commission.[4]

4 Negotiation

The commission clauses which we have so far considered in this chapter, although depending upon a variety of events, nevertheless have one thing in common. Implicit in them all is the assumption that it must be the estate agent who actually makes the introduction of the applicant to the client. We must now turn our attention to a rather different function which an estate agent is not infrequently employed to carry out, namely to *negotiate* on behalf of a client in circumstances where the parties have already been introduced, either privately or by another agent.[5] Many of the commission terms in common use (for example the former RICS scales) make express provision for this situation, and the precise requirements for

---

1 *Sadler* v *Whittaker* (1953) 162 EG 404.
2 *Bernard Thorpe & Partners* v *Snook* (1982) 266 EG 440; *Barnard Marcus & Co* v *Ashraf* [1988] 1 EGLR 7.
3 (1878) 39 LT 429.
4 Contrast *Coles* v *Enoch* [1939] 3 All ER 327, where the ultimate purchaser merely overheard the agent discussing the property with someone else.
5 This does not constitute "estate agency work" for the purposes of the Estate Agents Act 1979; see p 186.

a claim on such terms to succeed have been considered by the Court of Appeal on two occasions. In *FP Rolfe & Co v George*[1] the plaintiffs, who had the defendant's grocer's shop on their books, were called on by the defendant to negotiate on his behalf with a person who had been introduced by someone else. The plaintiffs explained both the business and the accounts to this applicant and persuaded him to go through with the deal, but their claim to commission was rejected by the county court judge on the ground that they had not *introduced* the purchaser. When the plaintiffs appealed (successfully) to the Court of Appeal, Lord Denning MR had this to say about the phrase "negotiating a sale by private contract" which formed part of the plaintiffs' terms of business:

Those words mean, as I understand it, that the agent must be, by reason of his negotiation, the efficient cause of the sale; or ... he must have produced the sale by his negotiation. There was clear evidence that the agent did this.

It may at first sight seem odd that an agent who by definition has not introduced the parties must nevertheless show that he or she is the "effective cause" of the sale, but it is submitted that this requirement is in fact a perfectly reasonable one. After all, what the agent is claiming is not a *fee* for professional services, but *commission* based on the value of the property; and this, as discussed earlier,[2] depends upon the achievement of a result.

The second requirement for success under a clause of this type is more controversial. In *Hoddell v Smith*,[3] an agent's claim for commission was rejected by the Court of Appeal for reasons which the following extracts from the judgments make clear. First, in the opinion of Geoffrey Lane LJ:

"Negotiation" must, to my mind, mean conferring with the prospective purchaser, or his representatives, with a view to agreeing a sale, and cannot include the simple giving of advice to the agent's own principal, the seller.

Sir John Pennycuick was even more explicit:

---

1 (1969) 210 EG 455: see also *Anscombe & Ringland Ltd v Watson* [1991] 2 EGLR 28.
2 p122.
3 (1975) 240 EG 295.

I do not think the word "negotiate" is apt to cover (i) the giving of advice by an agent to his principal where the principal is conducting personally or through another agent the negotiations with the other party concerned; (ii) preparing plans and the like in connection with such negotiations being carried on by the principal or another agent; (iii) acting as a mere channel of communication between the principal and his prospective purchaser; or (iv) a mere willingness to enter into negotiations if so required by the principal.

It is submitted that to require the agent to "negotiate" in this formal sense is both illogical and unjust, for an agent may be wholly effective in bringing about a sale while standing behind, rather than in front of, the client. Nevertheless, the principle has been applied in two subsequent cases,[1] where agents acting on behalf of companies wishing to rent business premises were to be remunerated for "seeking and negotiating a tenancy or lease". In each case the agents found suitable premises and a lease was duly signed, but the absence of any positive "negotiations" was held to mean that there could be no claim for commission as such. True, the court in each case was able to award the agents a "reasonable sum" for their work but, as we shall see,[2] these sums fell far short of what would have been payable under the agents' scales.

5 Sole agency

A "sole agency" agreement is one where, in return (it appears) for an express or implied promise of services,[3] an estate agent is granted the exclusive right to introduce a purchaser for the vendor's property.[4] The extent of the rights given to an estate agent by such an agreement, which of course restricts the vendor's freedom of contract, has been considered by the courts on a number of occasions. A straightforward example is provided by the case of *Hampton & Sons Ltd v George*[5] in which the plaintiffs were appointed sole agents for the sale of the defendant's leasehold

---

1 *Reiff Diner & Co v Catalytic International Inc* (1978) 246 EG 743; *Sinclair Goldsmith v Minero Peru Comercial* (1978) 248 EG 1015.
2 p171.
3 The estate agent's obligations are considered at pp101-104.
4 The mutual obligations of "joint sole agents" were considered by the Court of Appeal in *Hampton & Sons v Garrard Smith (Estate Agents) Ltd* [1985] 1 EGLR 23.
5 [1939] 3 All ER 627.

hotel. Another firm had had the property on their books for some time but their authority was determined on the appointment of the plaintiffs. Nevertheless the other firm introduced an applicant whose offer was accepted by the defendant. The plaintiffs sued for and were awarded damages for the defendant's breach of the sole agency agreement.

In *Bentall, Horsley & Baldry* v *Vicary*[1] the plaintiffs were appointed sole agents for a period of six months for the sale of the defendant's house. During this period the defendant sold the house privately, not through any agent. It was held that, in the absence of an express prohibition, the defendant was quite entitled to do this, and so the agents could not recover either commission or damages. McCardie J distinguished the earlier case of *Chamberlain & Willows* v *Rose*,[2] which concerned the sale of a cinema. The plaintiffs in that case were appointed to sell the property by auction or otherwise under an agreement which stated: "The property to be left solely in your hands for sale from this date until the auction and for a further period of three months". It was held that the defendant was liable in damages for breach of this agreement when, during the period in question, he sold the cinema privately.

It is clear, then, that an agent who is given "sole selling rights" is in a better position than one who is appointed "sole agent", since the former is protected, not only against sales through other agents, but also against private sales by the vendor. The category into which a particular agent falls is to be determined by interpreting his instructions, and it is suggested that the commonly used phrase "sole selling agent"[3] should in principle be interpreted as conferring merely a sole agency and not sole selling rights.[4] Where either category is concerned, however, it is submitted that, notwithstanding certain remarks of Ewbank J in *Glentree Estates Ltd* v *Gee*,[5] a mere withdrawal of the property by the vendor is not a breach; it is only a *sale* which may be wrongful.

---

1 [1931] 1 KB 253.
2 (1924), unreported but summarised at [1931] 1 KB 261.
3 Or "sole letting agent": see *Folioshield Ltd* v *Pleamere Ltd* [1990] 2 EGLR 1.
4 Although certain remarks in *Brodie Marshall & Co (Hotel Division) Ltd* v *Sharer* [1988] 1 EGLR 21 lend some support to the opposite view.
5 (1981) 259 EG 332 at p336.

A claim for breach of a "sole agency" or "sole right to sell" is a claim for damages, not commission. As a result, such questions as whether the agent's instructions have been fulfilled, or whether the agent is the effective cause of the sale, do not arise. Moreover, since the agent's complaint is of being deprived of the opportunity to sell the property, the damages awarded should reflect the value of that lost opportunity, and will thus not necessarily equal the full commission which would have been earned. In *Hampton & Sons Ltd* v *George*,[1] for example, the plaintiffs' commission on the sale of the lease would have amounted to £104. However, due to the difficulties surrounding the sale of licensed premises, in that the landlords, a brewery company, had to give their consent, it was by no means certain that a suitable purchaser would have been found. Accordingly damages were assessed at £80.[2]

The case of *Morris Oddy Ltd* v *Hayles*[3] appears rather at odds with these principles of compensation. The defendant in that case, who was developing an estate, appointed the plaintiffs as his selling agents under an agreement, the important terms of which were as follows: "Upon a sale being effected by you, I hereby agree to pay you a commission at the rate of £75 for each bungalow sold ... You are to be sole agent in the sale of the said properties ... All inquiries received by me will be referred to you, and I shall not have any rights of direct negotiations with purchasers." The agreement was expressed to be irrevocable for a period and thereafter terminable by notice of a specified length. A number of bungalows were sold in clear contravention of this agreement and the plaintiffs accordingly sued. It seems reasonably clear from the judgment of Thesiger J that he awarded the plaintiffs their agreed commission on all sales up to the date on which the agreement was validly terminated. If this is so, it is submitted that the award is incorrect, since by no stretch of the imagination can these sales be said to have been "effected" by the plaintiffs, as the agreement called for. However, the sum awarded could also be reached by another route, which would avoid this logical inconsistency: since the agreement

---

1 [1939] 3 All ER 627.
2 In *Newton* v *Eriksson* (1951) 157 EG 414, where commission would have been £115, damages of £75 were awarded. In *HM Rendall* v *Lammas* [1967] CLY 36 the "discount" was a mere £10.
3 (1971) 219 EG 831.

stipulated that all inquiries should be referred to the plaintiffs, it was a near certainty that those which led to a sale would have done so anyway; thus damages based on the full commission could validly be awarded.[1]

What is effectively a sole agency or sole right to sell may on occasion be created without using these actual terms. A device frequently encountered is a stipulation that commission shall be payable upon any sale which takes place during the currency of the sole agency agreement. Less widely used, but successful before the Court of Appeal in *Property Choice Ltd* v *Fronda*,[2] was an express undertaking by the client not to "consent to sell the property to anyone not introduced by [the agents]". This, it was held, entitled those agents to damages on any such sale, whether negotiated through another agent or privately by the client.

Such variations on the sole agency theme require careful drafting. It has for example been held that, where an agent was to receive commission "should a sale be effected", this meant "effected *by the agent*"; there was accordingly no right to claim when the vendor sold the property privately.[3] However, this problem can be overcome by making commission payable "if a sale of the property, whether arranged by the [agents] or not, is effected" within a stated time.[4] Such wording is today commonly found in auctioneers' commission clauses, and is further discussed in that context.[5]

Everything which has so far been said about sole agency and its variants must henceforth be read in the light of the Estate Agents (Provision of Information) Regulations 1991, which were made under section 18 of the Estate Agents Act 1979. Those regulations require any estate agent using the term "sole agency", "sole selling rights" or an equivalent to explain to the client in writing what the term means, using form of explanation contained in the regulations themselves. What is significant is that the explanations given in fact put the agent in a more favourable position than would be the case

---

1 See *Gross Fine & Krieger Chalfen* v Gaynor (1974) 233 EG 1015, where a buoyant market justified an award of damages equivalent to the full commission.
2 [1991] 2 EGLR 249.
3 *Sadler* v *Whittaker* (1953) 162 EG 404.
4 *Bernard Thorpe & Partners* v *Snook* (1982) 266 EG 440; *Barnard Marcus & Co* v *Ashraf* [1988] 1 EGLR 7. See, however, *Fairvale Ltd* v *Sabharwal* [1992] 2 EGLR 27.
5 See p 336.

under the general law, by providing for example that the agent will be paid commission rather than damages on any breach.[1]

6 Forfeiture of commission

We considered in the previous chapter the duties which estate agents owe to their clients by virtue of the agency relationship. In that context, our inquiry was concerned with the liability of the agent to pay damages for breach of duty and, naturally, one of the points in issue was whether the client had suffered any financial loss. The purpose of the present chapter is to discover the effect of a breach of duty upon the estate agent's claim for commission and to this the question of damage is not relevant. As Scrutton LJ said in *Rhodes* v *Macalister:*[2]

Whether it causes damage or not, when you are employed by one man for payment to negotiate with another man, to take payment from that other man without disclosing it to your employer and getting his consent is a dishonest act.

The general legal position is clearly shown by the case of *Fullwood* v *Hurley*[3] where the plaintiff, a hotel broker, was approached by the defendant as an interested purchaser. The plaintiff gave the defendant an "order to view" a particular hotel, which provided for a payment to the plaintiff in the event of a sale. The defendant bought the hotel but, on discovering that the plaintiff was in receipt of commission from the vendor, refused to pay the agreed sum. The Court of Appeal upheld the defendant in this refusal and Scrutton LJ said:[4]

An agent who wants to make two contracts for double commission must do so in the clearest possible terms and with the clearest possible information to each of his principals what he is doing, otherwise he cannot sue under an alleged agreement.

---

1 This and other "bonuses" in the statutory wording are discussed at pp 204-206.
2 (1923) 29 Com Cas 19 at p 28.
3 [1928] 1 KB 498. In *Andrews* v *Ramsay & Co* [1903] 2 KB 635 and *Price* v *Metropolitan House Investment and Agency Ltd* (1907) 23 TLR 630 (p 115) the agents also failed in their claims for commission.
4 At p 504.

The principle thus expressed seems clear, and yet the courts in more recent cases have permitted estate agents to recover commission where, notwithstanding a potential conflict of interest, it is plain that the client has not been in any way disadvantaged. In *Meadow Schama & Co v C Mitchell & Co Ltd*,[1] for example, the plaintiffs were retained by the defendants to find them business premises in the West End of London. The plaintiffs found a suitable property but the defendants, in the hope of paying less commission, claimed to terminate the plaintiffs' authority and asserted that the introduction had been made by another firm (who were engaged in selling the defendants' existing premises). Fearing that they were to be "squeezed out", the plaintiffs reached an agreement with the vendors' agent whereby they were to receive one-third of the latter's commission. When this agreement (which was never in fact implemented) came to the notice of the defendants, they claimed that it constituted a secret profit which disentitled the plaintiffs to commission. This argument succeeded at first instance, but was unanimously rejected by the Court of Appeal. Lord Denning MR stated that, while not wishing to derogate in any way from the principle established in *Rhodes* v *Macalister*,[2] he did not regard it as applicable to the present case. The plaintiffs had in effect completed their work so that when, faced with the dishonesty of their principals, they made a sensible and reasonable arrangement to protect their own interests, this could not be said to conflict in any way with their duty as agents.

The *Meadow Schama* case might seem a particularly strong one from the point of view of the agents, but a similar conclusion has been reached in less extreme circumstances. In *Christie Owen & Davies* v *Brown*,[3] for instance, the plaintiffs changed their status from subagents of the vendor to agents of the purchaser; in *Druce Investments Ltd* v *Thaker*,[4] two firms of agents acting for vendor and purchaser agreed to divide their combined commission equally. In each of these cases the agents' conduct was judicially described

---

1 (1973) 228 EG 1511.
2 (1923) 29 Com Cas 19.
3 (1983, unreported).
4 [1988] 2 EGLR 229.

as unwise and likely to provoke suspicion, but the agents were none the less successful in their claims for commission.[1]

Although the cases under discussion are commonly concerned with "secret profits" obtained by the agent, the principle expounded is of wider application, covering the full range of agents' fiduciary duties.[2] In *Salomons* v *Pender*,[3] one of the leading cases in this field of law, the plaintiff, who was instructed to sell land for the defendant, obtained an offer from a company in which he had a substantial shareholding and of which he became a director just before contracts were exchanged. The plaintiff received nothing from the company in respect of this transaction, nor was there any evidence that the land had not realised is full price; none the less, it was held that the plaintiff's undisclosed interest disentitled him to commission.[4] A similar decision was reached in *Henry Smith & Son* v *Muskett*,[5] where the plaintiffs were instructed by the defendant to sell a plot of land which was ripe for development. Of the various development companies interested in the site, one promised to reinstruct the plaintiffs on the sale of the houses which were to be built, and the plaintiffs duly tried to persuade their client to sell to this company. In the event, the plaintiffs' advice was not taken and the property was sold to a rival applicant. This applicant, too, had been introduced by the plaintiffs, but it was held that their conduct in placing the interests of a prospective purchaser above those of their client was sufficient to deprive them of their right to commission.

The principle was extended in the case of *Hocker* v *Waller*[6] where the plaintiff, who owned a leasehold flat, instructed the defendant to find either a purchaser or a subtenant. The defendant was unable to do so but, since he himself was looking for a flat, it was agreed that he should take a sublease. It was held that, in view of

---

1 As to the position of estate agents who act for more than one prospective purchaser (and the inevitability of acting for more than one vendor) see pp 111-112.
2 For a particularly glaring example, see *Ian Scott & Co* v *Medical Installations Co Ltd* (1981) 258 EG 556.
3 (1865) 3 H&C 639.
4 See also *Edwards Real Estate* v *Barntor* (1978) 11 AR 589, where a claim to commission was defeated on proof that the (undisclosed) purchaser was the estate agent's employee.
5 (1977) 246 EG 655.
6 (1924) 29 Com Cas 296.

the changed circumstances, commission would only be payable if this had been expressly agreed and, since there was no evidence of this, the defendant's claim failed.

The overriding duty of an agent, which embraces both the "secret profit" and the "personal interest" cases, is always to act in the best interests of the client. As a final example we may look at the rather unusual case of *Heath* v *Parkinson*,[1] where an estate agent broke this duty in a way which did not fall within either of the above categories. In that case the defendant, a music seller, asked the plaintiff to find a purchaser for leasehold premises at a price of £2,500. It was known that large tailoring firms, who had been introduced through other channels, would pay this price but the defendant, believing that the landlord would not consent to this change of use, had rejected their offers. The plaintiff discovered that the landlord would in fact raise no objection and, concealing both this and the identity of his applicants, introduced a small tailoring firm which purchased the lease for £2,250. It was held that the plaintiff was not entitled to commission, since he had knowingly caused the defendant to sell his property for £250 less than could have been obtained.[2]

The principle underlying all these cases is that "A principal is entitled to have an honest agent, and it is only the honest agent who is entitled to any commission."[3] However, since it is possible for a breach of these fiduciary duties to occur without any dishonest intention on the part of the agent, the qualification has emerged that in such circumstances the agent, although liable to pay damages, may still be able to claim commission. This relaxation of the normally harsh rules governing an agent's conduct originated in the case of *Keppel* v *Wheeler*,[4] where a firm of estate agents, believing that any duty to the client ended on the introduction of a suitable prospective purchaser, failed to pass on a subsequent higher offer. The Court of Appeal, while holding the agents liable to pay damages based on the difference between the sale price and the amount which could have been obtained, nevertheless allowed the

---

1 (1926) 42 TLR 693.
2 It is surprising, to say the least, that the client did not counter-claim for damages in respect of this loss.
3 *Andrews* v *Ramsay & Co* [1903] 2 KB 635 at p638, *per* Lord Alverstone CJ.
4 [1927] 1 KB 577.

recovery of commission, since the agents' breach of duty was based, not on an improper motive, but on a genuine misconception of their legal obligations.[1]

The position of the agents was even stronger in *Harrods Ltd* v *Lemon*,[2] where the plaintiffs inadvertently acted for both vendor and purchaser in the same transaction. On discovering this, the plaintiffs suggested to the defendant vendor that the purchaser should obtain an independent survey. The defendant did not accept this suggestion and completed the sale at a price which was reduced because of the plaintiffs' adverse report to the purchaser on the condition of the drains. The Court of Appeal held that the plaintiffs' breach of duty did not disentitle them to commission since the defendant had, with full knowledge of the facts, elected to continue with them as her agents.

There is little authority on the effect of an estate agent's negligence upon a claim to commission. The general principle of agency law is that commission will be forfeited where the effect of the agent's negligence is to render useless the work done. It is submitted that this principle, which has been applied to surveyors,[3] valuers[4] and architects,[5] would also govern the position of an estate agent.

7 Amount of commission

Once it is established that an estate agent has done what is necessary to earn commission, and has done nothing to forfeit the right to receive it, all that remains to be decided is the amount which is to be paid. This is normally a matter for express agreement between agent and client, although in some circumstances their freedom of contract may be restricted. In particular, where land is sold by order of the Chancery Division, Family Division, Court of Protection or a divorce county court, the specific authorisation of the court is needed if the estate agent's charges (which must be

---

1 This was followed in *Robinson Scammell & Co* v *Ansell* [1985] 2 EGLR 41: p 112.
2 [1931] 2 KB 157.
3 *Moneypenny* v *Hartland* (1826) 1 C&P 352.
4 *Whitty* v *Lord Dillon* (1860) 2 F&F 67.
5 *Nye Saunders* v *Bristow* (1987) 37 BLR 92.

inclusive of everything except surveys) are to exceed either that agent's normal sole agency rate or 2.5% of the sale price.[1]

Estate agents' commission agreements commonly provide for reference to a printed scale of charges in order to determine the amount payable in a particular case. These printed scales, which are frequently the work of the professional societies governing estate agents, usually make provision for the assessment of commission as a percentage of the sale price. The use of the scales is widespread, but it should be noted that, as a result of The Restriction on Agreements (Estate Agents) Order 1970,[2] which was passed to give effect to recommendations contained in a report of the Monopolies Commission, it is unlawful for estate agents to accept restrictions in respect of their charges in connection with the sale or purchase of unfurnished dwellings. Thus, although members of a professional body may *choose* to adhere to a recommended scale of charges in respect of residential property, no sanctions may be taken against them if they prefer not to.

In certain circumstances an agent may be entitled to claim a *quantum meruit* or "reasonable sum" for services rendered. This may arise, for example, where an express commission agreement has become unenforceable for some reason. In principle it may also occur because there is no express agreement at all,[3] although cases of this kind should in future be rare, in view of the statutory obligation on estate agents to give clients written notice of their charges.[4]

Where a *quantum meruit* claim arises, the appropriate amount will be assessed by a court. In accordance with the principles discussed earlier,[5] the sum awarded should logically be based on the idea of "participation" rather than on that of "time and trouble", and this method of assessment receives support from a number of cases concerning commission agents in the field of commerce.[6]

---

1 Practice Direction [1983] 1 All ER 160.

2 SI 1970 No 1696.

3 A term to this effect would be implied at common law: *Miller* v *Beal* (1879) 27 WR 403. It will also be implied under the Supply of Goods and Services Act 1982, section 15, assuming that the Act applies to estate agents' agreements (see p100).

4 Estate Agents Act 1979, section 18: see p201.

5 p122.

6 *Way* v *Latilla* [1937] 3 All ER 759; *Campbell* v *National Trust Co Ltd* [1931] 1 WWR 465; 1 DLR 705.

For estate agents, too, a "reasonable sum" has frequently been geared to professional scales, at least where the evidence shows clearly that the parties intended remuneration to take the form of *commission* rather than a *fee*.[1] However, a certain amount of confusion has been caused in this connection by judicial remarks suggesting that what an estate agent has done is not "worth" the amount of commission claimed. In *Hampton & Sons v Trade & General Securities Ltd*,[2] Pain J (who was forced reluctantly to concede that the plaintiffs had bound their client to pay in accordance with the RICS scales) said that what they had done, "although undoubtedly valuable, would from most people's point of view hardly seem to be £27,500 worth of work". So too, in *Lewis & Graves v Harper*,[3] where the plaintiffs claimed commission of £276, the Court of Appeal thought that a "reasonable sum" for their services would have been £60.

The remarks so far mentioned were all *obiter*, so that the views expressed did not actually affect the amount of commission awarded. In a number of other cases, however, estate agents who had undeniably achieved what their clients wanted were remunerated on a much lower basis than the relevant professional scale. In two such cases,[4] agents had found suitable business premises for their clients but failed to qualify for commission in accordance with their terms of business, as they had not "negotiated" on their clients' behalf.[5] Having held that the relevant clause, on its true interpretation, expressly provided for the agents to receive a reasonable sum in this situation, the judge in each of these cases was faced with the problem of assessing that sum. In *Reiff Diner*, the possibility was considered that the fee for merely "seeking" (and finding) a tenancy should be 2.5% of one year's rent, which was the difference between the scale fees for "seeking and negotiating" and simply "negotiating". While rejecting this interpretation, the deputy judge nevertheless assessed the plaintiffs'

---

1 See, for example, *Turner v Reeve* (1901) 17 TLR 592; *Lewis & Graves v Harper* (1978) 250 EG 1287; *Michael Elliott & Partners Ltd v UK Land plc* [1991] 1 EGLR 39.
2 (1978) 250 EG 451: see also *Luxor (Eastbourne) Ltd v Cooper* [1941] AC 108 at p125, *per* Lord Russell of Killowen.
3 (1978) 250 EG 1287.
4 *Reiff Diner & Co v Catalytic International Inc* (1978) 246 EG 743; *Sinclair Goldsmith v Minero Peru Comercial* (1978) 248 EG 1015.
5 On this point see pp160-161.

reasonable sum at the very figure which such a calculation would have produced, describing this result as "coincidental and irrelevant"! In *Sinclair Goldsmith*, O'Connor J declined even to refer to the scale in question; the figure which he declared to be a "reasonable sum" was approximately one-third of what would have been earned on a scale.[1]

A similar lack of judicial generosity towards estate agents can be seen in cases where no written agreement of any kind has been entered into between agent and client. In *Chaskill Ltd v Marina Developments Ltd*,[2] which concerned the sale of a marina, the judge explicitly costed out the time spent by agents in effecting an introduction, arriving at a figure of £2325, which fell a long way short of the £15,000 which the agents regarded as a reasonable commission. And in *Withey Robinson v Edwards*,[3] although no such costing exercise was carried out, a firm of surveyors who assisted a client in the purchase of a night club found that, because they had not stipulated for payment in accordance with RICS scales, their bill was reduced by approximately one-third.

It is submitted that the approach adopted in these cases is erroneous; if the view of the courts is that an estate agent is not entitled to be paid unless the property is sold, it should logically follow that a "reasonable sum" in respect of a successful transaction must be considerably higher than would be justified by reference to "time and trouble".[4] Unless and until such arguments meet with judicial approval, however, estate agents should ensure that their terms of business are watertight, so that they are not driven to rely on claims for a "reasonable sum".

8　Formalities

(a) *Commission agreements*

It remains to consider the steps which can and should be taken to ensure that an estate agent's commission terms, whatever they

---

1 In *Debenham Tewson & Chinnocks plc v Rimington* [1989] 2 EGLR 26, failure to provide for a particular contingency meant that the plaintiffs received £15,000 for their services instead of £487,500 as commission!

2 [1988] 2 EGLR 241.

3 [1986] 1 EGLR 32.

4 See, further, Murdoch: "Professional Fees – How Much is Reasonable?" [1981] Conv 424.

may be, are binding upon the client. The simplest method of achieving this is to obtain the client's signature to a document in which all the relevant terms are set out; if this is done, then the general principles of contract law suggest that the client is bound, whether or not the document has been read.[1] However, some doubt has been cast upon the effectiveness of this procedure by Lord Denning MR, whose regard for the "common understanding of mankind" (that commission comes out of the purchase price on completion of the sale) has led him to argue that an estate agent who seeks to depart from this understanding must ensure that the client has *actual* notice of the proposed alteration. The learned judge relied upon this principle as one ground for his decision in the case of *Jaques* v *Lloyd D George & Partners,*[2] which concerned one of the widest commission agreements ever to come before the courts. In that case the vendor signed a form which contained the following clause: "Should you be instrumental in introducing a person willing to sign a document capable of becoming a contract to purchase at a price, which at any stage of the negotiations has been agreed by me, I agree to pay you a commission of £250 ..." The estate agents did not explain to the vendor the meaning of this clause and, indeed, their representative had already told him: "If we find a suitable purchaser and the sale goes through, you will pay us £250." The sale did not go through, the landlord having refused his consent to the assignment, and the Court of Appeal rejected the estate agents' claim to have earned their commission by virtue of the clause quoted above.[3] It was held that the vendor was not fixed with notice of what he had signed, as the effect of the document had been misrepresented to him.[4] Lord Denning MR, however, went further, stating that an agent who seeks to depart from the usual understanding of men must explain this to the client:

---

1 *L'Estrange* v *Graucob* [1934] 2 KB 394. Unless of course the client's letter is made conditional, for example by using the phrase "subject to contract": see *Ronald Preston & Partners* v *Markheath Securities plc* [1988] 2 EGLR 23.

2 [1968] 2 All ER 187.

3 For the views of the Court of Appeal on the effect of this clause, see p 147.

4 Following *Curtis* v *Chemical Cleaning & Dyeing Co* [1951] 1 KB 805. The position would be the same if the client had been misled by an estate agent's advertisements: *Homebuyers Estates (Fylde) Ltd* v *Laycock* (1981, unreported).

In the absence of such explanation, a client is entitled to assume that the form contains nothing unreasonable or oppressive. If he does not read it and the form is found afterwards to contain a term which is wholly unreasonable and totally uncertain, as this is, then the estate agent cannot enforce it against the innocent vendor.[1]

If correct, this assertion would impose upon an estate agent a duty more onerous than that imposed upon other categories of agent, namely that of ensuring that a client is given specific notice of the agent's terms of employment. This would be a departure from the normal position under the law of contract and, it is submitted, such an innovation cannot be supported. Indeed, it runs counter to an earlier decision of the Court of Appeal concerning estate agents which, unfortunately, was not cited to the court in *Jaques* v *Lloyd D George & Partners*. The case in question was that of *Pilkington* v *Flack*[2] in which a client, who was busy serving customers in her shop, was induced by an estate agent to sign a printed commission agreement. This document was described as "scandalous" by the Court of Appeal, which none the less held that the client, having signed this document, was bound by what it contained.

(b) *Confirming letters*

Notwithstanding the benefits to be derived by obtaining written instructions signed by the client, many practising estate agents (especially in the residential field) have traditionally preferred to take instructions orally and then to "confirm" these to the client in writing.[3] In so far as such a letter really does confirm points which have been specifically agreed between the parties, it is unlikely to cause any harm,[4] although whether a letter sent by an agent is of much positive value in proving what the agent claims was agreed must be open to doubt. However, very considerable difficulties may arise where the letter is *not* an accurate record of the earlier meeting, either because it contradicts what was actually said or

---

1 [1968] 2 All ER 187 at p190.

2 (1948) 152 EG 366: see p 113.

3 Whether this practice satisfies the Estate Agents Act 1979, s 18 is considered at p 209.

4 However, in *London Commercial & Land Ltd* v *Beazer Lands Ltd* [1990] 1 EGLR 54 the conditional wording of a letter ("we would look to you for payment") was held to negate any obligation to pay!

because it introduces fresh material. The problem lies in producing evidence of the client's *agreement* to the relevant terms, given the basic rule of contract law that silence is not consent.[1] Further, it remains equally intractable whether the relationship be classified as a unilateral or a bilateral contract.[2] After all, if the contract is *bilateral*, it is formed when instructions are first taken, so that a variation introduced by one party alone is not binding. If, on the other hand, the relationship consists of a *unilateral* contract, the offer is made by the client and the "confirming letter" may be seen as a counteroffer from the agent, binding only when positively accepted.

The theoretical difficulties, then, are formidable, but the case law undoubtedly suggests that a confirming letter may none the less be of some effect. In the absence of express agreement to the contrary, it is established that the basis on which an estate agent will be assumed to operate is that of "finding a purchaser" in return for a "reasonable sum". Both these elements have been held by the Court of Appeal to be capable of alteration by means of a "confirming letter". In *Way & Waller Ltd* v *Ryde*[3] the plaintiffs, on being instructed to find a purchaser for the defendant's hotel, wrote to the defendant enclosing a scale of remuneration which they intended to apply to this transaction The defendant did not reply to the agents' letter and, when a sale was effected, claimed that he was not bound by the enclosed scale. The trial judge held that the defendant need pay only a "reasonable sum"; the Court of Appeal, however, took a different view. Lord Greene MR, referring to the agents' letter, said:[4]

The substantial point of it is that in that letter there is enclosed, or set out, a scale of remuneration, and the recipient of that letter must have understood that those were the terms on which the plaintiffs were willing to work for him. With that letter before him he allowed them to continue. He allowed them to do the work ... This was the plaintiffs' scale, be it a usual one or an unusual one, and that is the scale the defendant must be taken to have agreed to accept ... He agreed to it by conduct for better or worse, and whatever it is, be it high or be it low, he is bound by it, in my opinion. That seems to me

---

1 *Felthouse* v *Bindley* (1862) 11 CBNS 869.
2 A question which is considered at pp 99-101.
3 [1944] 1 All ER 9.
4 At p10.

to be a perfectly clear case of a contract to be inferred from the conduct of the parties.

The "confirming letter" which reached the courts in *John E Trinder & Partners* v *Haggis*[1] purported to alter, not the amount of commission, but the circumstances in which it should become payable. The plaintiffs in that case were orally instructed to find a purchaser for the defendant's property; the letter which they sent to their client, however, stated that commission would be due upon the introduction of "a person willing to sign a contract to purchase at an agreed price". This letter was ignored by the defendant, who later disputed his liability to pay commission in respect of an introduction which did not lead to a sale. It was held by a majority of the Court of Appeal that the plaintiffs were entitled to their commission, but a strong dissenting judgment was delivered by Denning LJ, who pointed out that the agents' letter was in law an offer and, as such, became binding upon a client only when it was accepted. Mere silence could not constitute acceptance for this purpose and, as for the client's "conduct" in carrying on negotiations with the person whom the agents introduced, this no more suggested that he agreed to the terms of the letter than that he regarded the original instructions as still applicable.

Notwithstanding Denning LJ's note of dissent, these two cases support quite strongly the idea that an unanswered letter may be of binding force.[2] However, the matter cannot be regarded as settled, for an earlier decision of the House of Lords, which suggests the contrary, was unfortunately not cited to the Court of Appeal on either occasion. The case in question, *Toulmin* v *Millar*,[3] concerned an agent who was instructed to find a tenant for an estate. The agent sent the client a list of the charges appropriate to this work, including a note to the effect that, if a tenant who was introduced by the agent subsequently purchased the freehold, an additional commission would become payable. The client did not reply to this communication, the agent introduced a tenant, and the tenant subsequently purchased the freehold reversion. The House of Lords

---

1 (1951) 158 EG 4.
2 See also the unreported case of *Britton Poole & Burns* v *Theodosiades* (1983), where the appointment of a subagent was held valid by virtue of a confirming letter.
3 (1887) 3 TLR 836.

rejected the agent's claim for commission on this sale, on the ground that he had never been employed to find a purchaser for the property, but only a tenant; nor was the client bound by the agent's attempt to enlarge the scope of his authority, for this was something to which he had not positively assented.

In the light of the foregoing discussion, it must be regarded as doubtful whether the terms of a "confirming letter" really *bind* a client in the legal sense. However, even if it is not actually enforceable, such a document may have a more limited but none the less useful role to play in the event of legal proceedings. After all, the question which has to be decided is upon what terms the parties *in fact* agreed, and a court may give some weight to the fact that the client, when faced with the agent's letter, expressed no dissatisfaction whatsoever with the terms which are now disputed.[1]

The uncertainty as to precisely what formalities are legally necessary, in order for an agent to recover commission, has now been intensified by section 18 of the Estate Agents Act 1979 and the Estate Agents (Provision of Information) Regulations 1991.[2] These statutory provisions oblige an estate agent to notify the client at the outset of their relationship of all potential charges; failure to do so may render the agent's claim unenforceable in court, whether or not the requirements of common law have been met.

B Expenses

As a general rule, every agent has a right to be indemnified by the principal against all losses, liabilities and expenses incurred in the lawful performance of the agent's duties.[3] However, while an estate agent may undoubtedly claim an *indemnity* where carrying out a client's instructions results in legal liability, it is presumed that the agent's *expenses* will be covered by the commission which is earned on successful transactions. In consequence, an estate agent who wishes to ensure that expenses will be met, whether or not a

---

1 See, for example, *Milton Marlowe & Co v Southcut* (1979) 254 EG 293; *Hampton & Sons v Trade & General Securities Ltd* (1978) 250 EG 451; *John D Wood & Co v Bardiger* [1986] 1 EGLR 238; *Colin Buckle & Co v Charterhall Properties (Chesham) Ltd* [1990] 1 EGLR 57.
2 p201.
3 See p54.

sale results, must provide expressly for this in the terms of appointment.[1] Moreover, section 18 of the Estate Agents Act 1979 requires such express provision to give a detailed breakdown of the charges for which the client may become liable.[2]

C Lien

There appears to be no direct authority on the question whether an estate agent may reinforce a claim to commission or expenses by exercising a lien over any property or money belonging to the client which comes into the agent's possession by virtue of the agency. However, it is submitted on principle that there is no reason to treat estate agents any differently from other categories of agent in this respect. If this is correct, it means that an estate agent is entitled to exercise a *particular* lien, that is, to retain possession of the client's goods or money until all charges in respect of those particular items have been met.[3] In practice this right will only be of value to an agent who is given possession of title deeds or who is still holding a deposit at a stage in the transaction when it belongs to the client;[4] until that time there is nothing belonging to the client to which the agent's lien may attach.[5]

D Interest on deposit money

At common law, an auctioneer holding a deposit "as stakeholder" was not liable to pay over to either of the parties the interest which the money earned while it was so held.[6] This was based on the idea that it was the stakeholder who took the risk of any loss or depreciation of the capital; a later judge[7] added the suggestion that

---

1 For a successful claim based on such a provision, see *Bernard Thorpe & Partners* v *Flannery* (1977) 244 EG 129.
2 See p 202.
3 See p 55.
4 This will not usually occur until completion of the sale: see *Skinner* v *Trustee of the Property of Reed* [1967] Ch 1194.
5 For an estate agent's unsuccessful attempt to claim an equitable charge over sale proceeds held by the client's solicitor, see *WA Ellis Services Ltd* v *Stuart Wood* [1993] 31 EG 78.
6 *Harington* v *Hoggart* (1830) 1 B&Ad 577.
7 Harman J in *Smith* v *Hamilton* [1951] Ch 174 at p174.

the interest earned formed part of the stakeholder's remuneration. However, some inferential doubt was cast upon this principle by the decision of the House of Lords in *Brown* v *Inland Revenue Commissioners*[1] that, in the absence of express agreement, a solicitor was bound to account to clients for all interest earned on their money while it was in the solicitor's hands, no matter how small the individual amounts might be, or how great the difficulties of accounting. As Lord Upjohn said:[2]

A professional adviser, whether he be solicitor, factor, stockbroker or surveyor is of course in a fiduciary relationship to his client, and if and when he is entrusted with his client's money he can make no profit out of it.

In 1973, in the case of *Potters* v *Loppert*,[3] Pennycuick V-C held that an auctioneer's freedom from liability to pay interest on a *contract* deposit was also enjoyed by an estate agent holding a *pre-contract* deposit. The legal basis of this decision was that there was no fiduciary relationship, in the *Brown* v *IRC* sense, between a stakeholder and a prospective purchaser; the stakeholder's only obligation was a purely *contractual* one to hand back precisely what was deposited. An ethical justification for this rule was found in the fact that, while holding a pre-contract deposit, an estate agent would have no prospect of earning commission by selling the property to anyone else; it would in effect be "sterilised".

Whatever may be felt about the decision in *Potters* v *Loppert*, it has for most practical purposes ceased to matter since section 15 of the Estate Agents Act 1979 was brought into force. That section, together with the Estate Agents (Accounts) Regulations 1981, lays down a set of rules governing interest which is or should be earned on both contract and pre-contract deposits, the circumstances in which and the persons to whom an estate agent must account for such interest and the amount payable.[4] In relation to pre-contract deposits (the kind held by an estate agent in virtually all cases), these rules effectively mean that, irrespective of whether the agent purports to receive the money "as agent" or "as stakeholder", he or

---

1 [1965] AC 244.
2 At p265.
3 [1973] Ch 399.
4 These rules are discussed in detail at pp 231-233.

she will be liable to account to the prospective purchaser who deposited it for any interest which is or which should be earned. Certain cases, for example those in which the capital sum does not exceed £500 or where the interest is less than £10, do not come within this provision; indeed, the Act specifically states that, if a deposit in such a case is kept in a *general* client account, there is no duty to account for the interest.[1]

As a result of these statutory provisions, it seems that the common law rules will now be of relevance only in cases which fall outside the Estate Agents Act altogether, such as those where the transaction in question does not constitute "estate agency work" as defined by section 1.[2]

---

1 If it is kept in a *separate* account, it seems that a duty *will* arise, because section 13 of the 1979 Act creates a fiduciary relationship where none existed previously.
2 See p 185.

CHAPTER 6

The Estate Agents Act 1979

The title of this chapter might suggest to readers that the estate agency profession is rigorously controlled by statute. However, it will soon be realised that any such suggestion would be highly misleading. What is offered by the Estate Agents Act 1979, and the package of orders and regulations made under the Act in 1991, is a number of limited controls upon the practice of estate agency; these controls fall a long way short of anything resembling an overall code.

A The legislative background

The Estate Agents Act 1979 represents a return on more than 90 years of Parliamentary frustration for, between 1888 and 1978, there were at least 14 attempts by Private Members to secure statutory recognition for and control of the profession. There is little to be gained, in the context of our present enquiry, from an exhaustive analysis of these earlier failures,[1] but it is perhaps worth mentioning three threads which run with remarkable consistency through the story: the Bills presented all envisaged a positive registration scheme (with registration normally restricted to those holding a particular qualification); each scheme in turn, supported by one or more the major professional bodies of the day, was resolutely opposed by "unattached" agents; and the professional bodies themselves were unable to achieve any real consensus over the most suitable form of control to adopt.

A further feature of this period was that successive Governments were constant in their refusal to introduce legislation on the subject of estate agents, or to give any support (other than assistance at the drafting stage) to Private Members' Bills dealing with the matter. The lack of official interest thus demonstrated continued until 1975,

---

1 For the story up to 1967, see FAR Bennion: (1968) 206 EG 427, 543, 661, 779, 887.

when the Department of Prices and Consumer Protection published a Green Paper entitled: *The Regulation of Estate Agency: a Consultative Document*. This found no evidence of frequent malpractice among estate agents, but referred to "a continuing groundswell of complaint" about certain matters, notably some well-publicised cases involving the loss of deposits. The major suggestion contained in this document was that there should be established a scheme for licensing of any person seeking to carry on the business of estate agency, and that this should be administered, not by the profession itself, but by the Director-General of Fair Trading, on whose licensing functions under the Consumer Credit Act 1974 the new proposals were based.

The consultations which were stimulated by the Green Paper convinced the Government that, while the time was ripe for statutory control of estate agents, the desired degree of consumer protection could be achieved without what the Minister termed "a bureaucracy of control involving compulsory registration or licensing". Oddly, detailed proposals then appeared, not in a Government Bill, but in the guise of a Private Member's Bill introduced by Mr Bryan Davies MP. This achieved a fair measure of support from both the main parties but was ultimately "talked out" for political reasons. However, it served to pave the way for a Government Bill in almost identical terms which passed through Parliament in the following session and received the Royal Assent on April 4 1979. Even then the delays were not over; the Estate Agents Act 1979 remained wholly inoperative until May 3 1982, when most of the Act,[1] together with some supporting regulations, was brought into effect.

The scheme of control laid down by the 1979 Act was based upon what may be called "negative licensing". There was in general no requirement for any would-be estate agent to demonstrate any particular qualification or competence before setting up in practice;[2] the powers of the Director-General of Fair Trading (extending to the issue of an order banning an agent from practice altogether) would come into play only when the agent was shown

---

1 Yet to be implemented are sections 16 and 17 (compulsory insurance cover for clients' money); section 19 (restriction on the size of pre-contract deposits); and section 22 (minimum standards of competence).

2 There is power under section 22 to impose such a requirement, but that section is not yet in force.

to be unfit to continue, and when some other condition, such as a conviction for a relevant criminal offence, was also satisfied. True, the Act created a number of new duties with which estate agents must comply in their daily business but these, for the most part, operated only to "trigger" the Director's powers.

In the first six years of its operation, the Estate Agents Act kept a fairly low profile. However, fundamental changes in the estate agency world, due both to the buoyant property market and to the incursions of major financial institutions, created a range of new pressures and new reported abuses. Official interest in estate agency was duly reawakened, and resulted in the publication of two reports within a period of six months. First came a review of the Estate Agents Act which was published by the Director-General of Fair Trading in December 1988. Then, in June 1989, the Department of Trade and Industry published its *Review of Estate Agency*.

It must be said that neither the Office of Fair Trading nor the Department of Trade and Industry was unduly critical of the estate agency profession. The OFT report stated that the OFT had "no evidence to suggest that the majority of estate agents fail to treat consumers fairly and efficiently"; the DTI document acknowledged that much of the public concern related to "a perception of shortcomings in the property transfer system itself rather than estate agents". Perhaps because of this, neither review was in favour of implementing any of the remaining provisions of the 1979 Act; the way forward, it was felt, lay in persuading estate agents themselves to produce a non-statutory Code of Practice. However, it was suggested that certain aspects of estate agency should be curbed by being designated "undesirable practices" under the Act, and, moreover, that the Trade Descriptions Act should be extended to cover land and buildings.

Responsibility for taking these proposals forward was given to the Director-General of Fair Trading. Action followed swiftly: a consultation document was produced in September 1989, and this led in March 1990 to a final report. This acknowledged defeat on a voluntary Code of Practice, confirmed an intention to extend the Trade Descriptions Act and contained draft proposals for the designation of a number of "undesirable practices" (including, as an interim measure, one of property misdescription).

Within a mere 12 months, the necessary orders and regulations to be made under the Estate Agents Act had all been drafted, consulted over and laid before Parliament. These came into force on July 29 1991. As for property misdescription, the Government's intentions in this area had been overtaken by a Private Member's Bill sponsored by the Consumers' Association and this, with Government support, duly received the Royal Assent on June 27 1991. The statutory instrument upon which the Property Misdescriptions Act 1991 depended did not, however, appear until almost 18 months later, and the Act finally came into operation on April 4 1993.[1]

The following description of the current statutory controls[2] falls into three sections. We shall consider, first, the scope of the Act; second, the specific duties which are imposed upon practitioners; and third, the machinery by which these new rules are to be enforced.

B Scope of the Act

It should be emphasised at this point that the Estate Agents Act 1979, even with its 1991 extensions, falls well short of providing a comprehensive system of statutory control for the estate agency profession as a whole. What the Act covers may be described as "estate agency work in relation to freehold and leasehold interests in land, subject to a number of exclusions", a definition which must now be examined in some detail. It will be seen that many of the services commonly provided by estate agents (such as valuations or mortgage-broking) are nevertheless outside the scope of the 1979 Act, either because they do not satisfy the rather limited definition of "estate agency work" or because they have been specifically excluded. As to precisely *why* these matters have been excluded, the detailed reasons vary, but the common thread is that in each case the element of "consumer protection" involved was felt insufficient to justify the public expenditure required to extend the coverage of the legislation.

---

1 The Property Misdescriptions Act is considered in detail in Chapter 7.
2 Based on the account in Murdoch, *The Estate Agents and Property Misdescriptions Acts* (3rd ed, 1993), which includes annotated copies of both the primary and secondary legislation.

1 Estate agency work

An estate agent is easy enough to recognise and fairly easy to describe; a satisfactory *definition*, however, is much harder to achieve, as the instigators of previous attempts at legislative control discovered. Rather than try yet again to attain this difficult objective, the Estate Agents Act adopts an alternative approach, namely that of defining the estate agency *function*. As a result, this definition requires extremely careful study, since any person who carries out the functions described will be caught by the Act, whether or not he or she would otherwise be regarded as an "estate agent".

The crucial definition is contained in section 1(1), which provides:

This Act applies, subject to subsections (2) to (4) below to things done by any person in the course of a business (including a business in which he is employed) pursuant to instructions received from another person (in this section referred to as "the client") who wishes to dispose of or acquire an interest in land –
(a) for the purpose of, or with a view to, effecting the introduction to the client of a third person who wishes to acquire or, as the case may be, dispose of such an interest; and
(b) after such an introduction has been effected in the course of that business, for the purpose of securing the disposal or, as the case may be, the acquisition of that interest;
and in this Act the expression "estate agency work" refers to things done as mentioned above to which this Act applies.

(a) *The basic definition*

It will be clearly seen from the above that the basic definition of "estate agency work" is an extremely wide one. "Things done" is not, perhaps, the most elegant of expressions, but it serves to indicate that the Act is capable of applying to any form of activity, provided that its object is *either* to effect an introduction between potential contracting parties *or* to bring such an introduction, once made, to a successful conclusion. Furthermore, the specific reference to both acquisitions and disposals of interests in land makes it clear that the Act covers estate agents, not only where they act for vendors or landlords who are seeking to dispose of property, but also where they represent purchasers or tenants who are seeking to acquire it.[1] However, it may be noted that certain of the statutory duties are worded in such a way that they can only apply to agents acting for vendors or landlords.

As to the first of the statutory alternatives (the effecting of introductions), few problems of definition seem likely to arise, especially given that persons who do nothing more than publish advertisements are specifically excluded from the operation of the Act by section 1(4). Para (b), however, leaves a curious loophole in relation to post-introduction work, by providing that such work is only covered when it takes place in the course of the same business as the introduction which it follows. If it were not for this restriction, it might perhaps be argued that building societies agreeing to lend money on mortgage, or Land Registry clerks dealing with searches, were doing things for the purpose of bringing transactions to fruition and were therefore within the scope of section 1(1). Common sense suggests that such persons should not come within the Act; however, in seeking to prevent them from doing so, the wording also serves to exclude the work of an estate agent who is instructed to *negotiate* a sale or lease on behalf of one of the parties, at a time when the *introduction* has already been made by another agent or by the parties themselves. Such work is not uncommon; indeed, the meaning of "negotiation" in this context has twice received the attention of the Court of Appeal.[2] Nevertheless, and despite the fact that such an agent, if called in to advise a vendor, might well receive a deposit from the purchaser (control of which is one of the primary objectives of the Act), it is quite clear that this situation is not covered by the statutory definition of "estate agency work".

(b) *Business*

Many of the introductions which lead to a sale of property are made by a mutual acquaintance of the parties on a purely social basis. It would not of course be desirable to subject these to the provisions of the Act and, one might have thought, a simple way to avoid this would be to confine the operation of the statute to cases

---

1 An estate agent who acts for a person seeking the tenancy of a dwelling house is also subject to the Accommodation Agencies Act 1953: see p 258.

2 *Rolfe (FP) & Co* v *George* (1969) 210 EG 455; *Hoddell* v *Smith* (1975) 240 EG 295: see p 160.

where the person concerned is to be paid for this trouble.[1] This, however, has not been done; the Act applies to all work, whether paid or not, provided only that it is done both "in the course of a business" and "pursuant to instructions received".

The first point to be noted in relation to this chosen form of words is that the "business" in question need not be an estate agency business; indeed, it need have little or no ostensible connection with the property world at all. For example, it has been said that bank managers not infrequently mention to one client who is seeking to sell a house the name of another client who may be interested in buying it, and there can be no doubt that any such introduction would fall within the course of the bank manager's business. The same would of course be true of members of other professions, such as accountants, who might well happen to introduce two of their clients and thereby indirectly bring about a sale of property.

As to the meaning of "business" itself, the Act provides no definition. If previous decisions of the courts upon other legislation may be relied upon as a guide, it seems that a "business" connotes both a degree of continuity (ie more than one isolated transaction) and the general idea of gain or reward. However, it is not essential that a person intends to make a gain out of each and every transaction, nor need the "business" show an overall profit; thus, for example, any activities of a local authority, the Housing Corporation or a housing association which satisfy the rest of the definition of "estate agency work" will come within the Act.

(c) *Instructions*

It is not every introduction made by a person in the course of business that will constitute "estate agency work" for the purposes of section 1, but only those which are effected "pursuant to instructions received". "Instructions", like "business", are not defined by the Act, but it seems clear that they may quite validly be given by word of mouth, whether or not they are subsequently confirmed in writing. None the less, there must always be some element of instruction, however informal; if this is lacking, then the person concerned is not engaged in "estate agency work". As a result, the

---

1 The legal profession's so-called "conveyancing monopoly" applies only to work done "for or in expectation of any fee, gain or reward": see p 262.

Act does not apply to sales of land effected by such people as the personal representative of a deceased landowner, a trustee in bankruptcy or the liquidator of a company; all these "officials" act by virtue of their position, rather than pursuant to instructions received.

It has been suggested that the concept of "instructions" will serve to exclude from the Act those other professional persons, such as bank managers and accountants, mentioned above, who may in the course of business introduce one of their clients wishing to sell a house to another client wishing to buy one. No doubt this is true of some cases, where the intermediary acts on his or her own initiative, but equally there must be many occasions where a bank manager is specifically asked by a prospective vendor to keep an ear to the ground, and here the requirement of "instructions" would seem to be satisfied.

(d) *Employees*

Much of an estate agent's work is carried out by employees, who may (depending on their type and status) be remunerated on a salary basis or by the payment of commission on business done. Section 1(1) makes it quite clear that such an employee is engaged in "estate agency work" and is therefore subject to all the provisions of the Act and its supporting regulations. Indeed, it is not necessary for a person to be acting pursuant to instructions which *that person* has received from a client; the instructions may have been received by the employer or by a fellow-employee.

The effect of this is to bring every member of an estate agent's staff[1] within the Act. As a result, each employee must comply with all the various statutory duties;[2] any failure to do so may lead to investigation of the individual employee by the Director-General of Fair Trading, with all the consequences that this may involve. In practical terms, such coverage is essential in order to provide for the case of a firm with branch offices, some of which may be under the sole control of a person who is an employee rather than a principal in the business.

---

1 At least all those who are employed under "contracts of employment": see section 1(5)(c).

2 Except the duty to open a "client account"; section 14(1) permits an employee to pay clients' money into a client account maintained by the employer.

Not only is the employee of an estate agency firm subject to the provisions of the Act; responsibility for what that employee does in the course of business may also be placed upon the firm itself. This may involve criminal liability[1] or, under other legislation,[2] a finding that the firm is guilty of discrimination. Further, in connection with the events which empower the Director-General of Fair Trading to make an order prohibiting an estate agent from practising, section 3(3)(a) imposes vicarious liability upon the employer in respect of those duties under the 1979 Act which do not lead to criminal sanctions and also any "undesirable practices" as defined by statutory instrument.[3]

2 Excluded matters

Section 1(1) defines "estate agency work"; the remainder of section 1 specifies no fewer than nine situations in which work apparently satisfying this definition is nevertheless not covered by the Act. Although these exclusions are not classified by the Act itself, they may be seen as falling into two groups. In the first place, there are a number of things which may well be done by an estate agent, either in connection with the disposal of a particular property or quite independently of it, which have been thought for one reason or another not to warrant statutory control. Second, certain work carried out by persons who are not themselves "estate agents" is also excluded.

(a) Things done by estate agents

Section 1(2)(e) excludes from the operation of the Act things which are done "in connection with applications and other matters" which arise under current planning legislation. The reason for this exclusion, which appears to cover such advice even where it is given in the course of "estate agency work", is not immediately apparent. Presumably it was felt by those responsible for drafting the Act that the need for consumer protection, which was its motivating force, was much less evident in this connection than in

---

1 There may be vicarious liability in respect of crimes which do not require the prosecution to prove guilty intent.
2 Sex Discrimination Act 1975, section 41; Race Relations Act 1976, section 32.
3 Section 3(1)(c) and (d): see pp241-242.

relation to those functions more directly connected with the actual disposal of property.

Things done "in the course of carrying out any survey or valuation pursuant to a contract which is distinct from that under which other things falling within subsection (1) above are done" are excluded by section 1(2)(*d*). This again gives a sharper focus to "estate agency work" by making it clear that it is only when such work is already being done that an *incidental* survey or valuation is included within the definition. This, it is suggested, would cover the case where a valuation forms part of the service which is offered by an estate agent to a prospective vendor. It would not, however, apply to a mortgage valuation carried out on behalf of a building society, even if the valuer's firm had been responsible for introducing the property to the borrower concerned.[1] What, then, of the case where an agent retained by a prospective purchaser, having found a suitable property, then carries out a structural survey of that property on the client's behalf? This is more doubtful, but it would probably be held to fall outside the scope of the Act, as such a survey would normally be done under a separate contract.

"Estate agency work" does not include things done "in the course of credit brokerage, within the meaning of the Consumer Credit Act 1974".[2] The reference is to section 145(2) of that Act, which deals with "the effecting of introductions – in the case of an individual desiring to obtain credit to finance the acquisition or provision of a dwelling occupied or to be occupied by himself or his relative, to any person carrying on a business in the course of which he provides credit secured on land". This clearly applies to the common case of an estate agent who arranges mortgages, and such a person will therefore need to be licensed under Part III of the 1974 Act as carrying on an "ancillary credit business". In view of the strict control which this involves, and the supervisory functions exercised by the Director-General of Fair Trading, to have brought credit brokerage within the Estate Agents Act as well was seen as an unnecessary duplication. It should be noted, however, that mortgage-broking in respect of *non-residential* premises is beyond

---

1 If the firm had not effected the introduction, the Act would in any case not apply, since the valuation would not then follow an introduction made in the course of *the agent's* business.

2 Section 1(2)(*b*).

the scope of the Consumer Credit Act; as a result, an estate agent carrying out this particular function remains within the Estate Agents Act, provided of course that the agent's firm is responsible for introducing the parties.

Similar reasoning underlies section 1(2)(c), which excludes things done "in the course of insurance brokerage by a person who is for the time being registered under section 2, or enrolled under section 4, of the Insurance Brokers (Registration) Act 1977".[1] It should be noted, however, that this provision is of much narrower scope than that relating to credit brokerage. The 1977 Act does not compel all those who *practise* insurance broking to register or enrol; it applies only to those who wish to use the *title* of "insurance broker".[2] Hence, if an estate agent arranges insurance, without using a restricted title or falsely claiming to be registered, these activities will be governed, not by the Insurance Brokers (Registration) Act, but by the Estate Agents Act.

(b) *Things done by other persons*

Five groups of persons are specifically excluded from the statutory controls. In the first place, things which are done "in the course of his profession by a practising solicitor or a person employed by him" are excluded from the operation of the Act by section 1(2)(a). Since the normal conveyancing work of a solicitor, although undoubtedly of assistance in bringing about a completed transaction, does not follow an introduction made in the course of the *solicitor's* business, this would not in any case be covered by the Act. Section 1(2)(a), therefore, is concerned to exclude cases where a solicitor is in effect acting as an estate agent, for example by operating a "property shop". This apparently privileged position has been heavily criticised by estate agents' professional bodies, especially in its application to Scotland, where solicitors have traditionally played a much more active role in the actual selling of property and have therefore been in direct competition with estate agents. The Government's response to such criticism has been to

---

1 Registration applies to individuals, enrolment to companies.
2 For the precise nature of the restrictions which are imposed upon unregistered persons, see the Insurance Brokers (Registration) Act 1977, section 22.

argue that existing controls on solicitors[1] are at least as rigorous as those imposed upon estate agents and that to subject solicitors to both régimes would, from the point of view of consumer protection, be superfluous. Whether or not the Government view is correct depends upon one's assessment of the relative burdens imposed by two different sets of regulations. However, it is interesting to note that one of the main grounds of estate agents' complaints (that solicitors were not obliged to give their clients advance warning of charges for estate agency services) has since been remedied by a guidance note from the Council of the Law Society, which requires a written agreement signed by the client at the time when instructions to negotiate a sale are given and accepted.

Second, in order to avoid an unnecessary extension of statutory control to newspapers, computerised house-finding agencies and the like, whose activities in the estate agency field consists *solely* of the provision of information, it is laid down by section 1(4) that the Act does not apply to "the publication or the dissemination of information by a person who does no other acts which fall within subsection (1)". However, the exemption applies only where the organisation goes no further than merely providing information; any further measures designed to effect introductions for clients *are* governed by the Act.

Third, as a result of anxiety expressed by accountants through their professional bodies, it was suggested that the Estate Agents Act should specifically exclude the activities of liquidators, trustees in bankruptcy, executors and so on who might, in that capacity, sell property belonging to another person. The official view, however, was that, with one exception, such a person would be acting by virtue of an office rather than "pursuant to instructions" and would not therefore in any case be caught by the Act. The exceptional case (which, it was felt, might come within the definition of estate agency work but ought not to) was dealt with by section 1(3)(b), which excludes things done by any person "in relation to any interest in any property if the property is subject to a mortgage and he is the receiver of the income of it".[2]

---

1 Section 1(5)(a) defines solicitors in such a way that those who are *not* subject to their own professional code are caught by the Estate Agents Act.
2 "Mortgage" is defined by section 1(5)(b).

Fourth, section 1(3)(a) excludes from the operation of the Act things done by any person "pursuant to instructions received by him in the course of his employment in relation to an interest in land if his employer is the person who, on his own behalf, wishes to dispose of or acquire that interest". The purpose of this provision may have been simply to avoid the creation of a client-agent relationship between an estate agent and an individual employee[1] where that estate agent seeks to buy or sell a property through the firm, but the effect of the statutory wording appears to be wider than this in at least two respects. In the first place, it seems that, while an estate agent who actually has a personal interest in property will be in breach of section 21 of the Act[2] if this is not disclosed in any negotiations, the employee who actually conducts those negotiations with a third party will owe no such duty of disclosure. This could of course lead to the removal of the Act's protection in the very circumstances in which it is most needed. Second, it is at least arguable that the exemption may also apply where the "instructions" mentioned in section 1(3)(a) come, not from the employer, but from an independent client, and where the employee then carries out those instructions by selling to his or her own employer. This can hardly have been intended, and it is to be hoped that a court would resist this conclusion by interpreting the phrase "the person who, on his own behalf, wishes to dispose of or acquire that interest" as referring back to the person described as a "client" in section 1(1).

It is not only the employees of estate agents who may be removed from the operation of the Act by section 1(3)(a), but anyone carrying out what would otherwise constitute "estate agency work" on behalf of his or her own employer.[3] This means, for example, that office workers may safely assist the employer in arranging a "private" sale of the employer's own house without finding that they have inadvertently become estate agents. More importantly, where a firm of builders or developers sells its houses direct to the public, the activities of its employees in negotiating

---

1 It is clear that an employee is, potentially at least, subject to all the statutory controls: see p 188.

2 And of the Estate Agents (Undesirable Practices) (No 2) Order 1991: see p 212.

3 Provided that the relationship between them is a true "contract of employment": see section 1(5)(c).

sales, collecting deposits, etc are outside the scope of the Estate Agents Act.[1]

Fifth, and less controversially, section 1(3)(c) excludes things done by any person "in relation to a present, prospective or former employee of his or of any person by whom he also is employed if the things are done by reason of the employment (whether past, present or future)". As a result of this provision, a firm which assists its employees in buying or selling their own houses will not be treated as carrying on "estate agency work", and nor will the specific employees whose job it is to provide that assistance. The exemption also covers cases where the "employee" assisted has not yet started work or has ceased to work for this employer (eg where he or she is moving into the area to take up the employment or leaving the area at the end of it).

3 Interests in land

The Estate Agents Act was originally intended to apply only to estate agency work which related to residential property, or at least to property with a substantial residential element. To critics who regarded the buyer of a small business as being as much in need of "consumer protection" as the buyer of a house, the Government made two replies: first, that "small" business deals were difficult to define and there was no evidence to suggest that large ones caused any problems; and second, that the consultations which had been carried out prior to the introduction of the Bill had dealt only with residential property. Unconvinced by these explanations, however, the critics redoubled their efforts to extend the Bill's coverage beyond the residential sector, and these efforts ultimately proved successful during the committee stage in the House of Lords. Political events then denied the Government the opportunity to restore the earlier restriction, so that the legislation in its final form applies to all forms of property, be it residential, commercial, industrial or agricultural or of course any combination of these.[2]

Section 2 sets out the particular *interests* in land whose acquisition or disposal attracts the operation of the Act. The legislation is not concerned with minor interests in land, such as

---

1 Though they will be subject to the Property Misdescriptions Act: see p 251.

2 There is no mention of price, so that the Act will even apply to a wholly gratuitous transfer, provided that an estate agent is involved in arranging it.

rights of way or mortgages;[1] the basic concept is that of *ownership*. First and foremost, therefore, the Act applies to the transfer of "a legal estate in fee simple absolute in possession", that is, to the simple case where a freehold is marketed. About this little need be said, except to note that the restriction to *legal* estates will exclude subsales of property, at least those in which a person is selling the right to acquire the property directly from the original vendor, rather than undertaking to acquire the property and sell it on.[2]

If freehold transactions are relatively straightforward, the same unfortunately cannot be said of those involving the creation or transfer of leases. The first point to be made is that the absence of the word "legal" in section 2(1)(*b*) (by contrast with section 2(1)(*a*)) suggests that equitable as well as legal leases are included. In fact, even if this interpretation were not accepted, those equitable leases which are deemed to arise where the parties fail through lack of the proper formalities (ie use of a deed) to create a legal lease[3] would in any event be brought within the Estate Agents Act by section 2(2), which provides that "the expression 'lease' includes the rights and obligations arising under an agreement to grant a lease".

The major problems in respect of leases arise from the Government's belief that the Estate Agents Act should not apply to agents involved in arranging rents or property management, since it was felt that other statutes governing such activities already offered sufficient in the way of consumer protection. Attempting to define precisely what was to be excluded from the Act was, however, no simple task, and the formulation finally adopted sought to make the crucial question whether or not the lease was one for which a premium could lawfully be charged on either creation or assignment.[4] As we shall see, this formulation may have the unintended effect of excluding leases of *any* property at a full

---

1 Section 2(3)(a) makes it clear that this is so, even where the mortgagee's security consists of a leasehold interest in the property under the Law of Property Act 1925, sections 85 and 86.

2 In the former case what the subpurchaser receives is an equitable right to call for a conveyance of the property.

3 Under the principle of *Walsh* v *Lonsdale* (1882) 21 ChD 9. The vast majority of equitable leases are of this kind.

4 This effectively excluded from the Estate Agents Act the vast majority of transactions involving property within the Rent Act 1977, though that Act does permit the taking of a premium in certain cases (mainly involving assignments).

market rent.[1] However, whether or not this is so, the very idea of defining the scope of the Estate Agents Act by reference to the lawfulness or otherwise of premiums today bears an irrelevant, indeed rather arbitrary, air. This is because the prohibition on requiring or receiving a premium on the grant or assignment of a protected tenancy under the Rent Act 1977 does not extend to an assured or assured shorthold tenancy under the Housing Act 1988. In consequence, the vast majority[2] of residential tenancies created after January 15 1989 will not be excluded from the operation of the Estate Agents Act by this provision. However, it remains generally unlawful[3] to require or receive a premium on the assignment of a protected tenancy (which means most residential tenancies created before that date) and thus an estate agent involved in the assignment of such a tenancy is not subject to the Estate Agents Act.

4   Doubtful areas

The discussion in this chapter of sections 1 and 2 of the Estate Agents Act has highlighted a number of potential uncertainties in the definition of "estate agency work", and thus in the scope of the legislation. We may now examine several areas of estate agency activity where, for various reasons, the applicability of the Act is a matter of some debate.

(a) *Sales by auction or tender*

As we have seen, section 1(1) defines estate agency work by reference to the "introduction" of two parties (the client and another) who wish respectively to acquire and to dispose of an interest in land. It might be suggested that this form of words serves to exclude both auctions and sales by tender from the operation of the Act, on the ground that what is brought about by the agent in such cases is not an *introduction* of the prospective vendor and purchaser, but rather an immediate *contract* between them. However, it seems clear that the Act was intended to cover sales of

---

1 See p 199.

2 In exceptional cases it may still be possible to create a protected tenancy: see for example the Housing Act 1988, section 34.

3 There are some exceptions, most of which are listed in the Rent Act 1977, section 120.

land by whatever method, and it is certainly desirable that it should do so, if only because of the difficulties which might arise where, for example, an agent is instructed to sell land "by auction or otherwise". In any event, it may be suggested that the term "introduction", in the sense of bringing parties together, is wide enough in meaning to include these procedures.

The view that auctions at least are covered by the legislation is certainly shared by those responsible for drafting the Estate Agents (Undesirable Practices) (No 2) Order 1991, which is at pains to provide a specific exemption for auctioneers from one of the duties which it imposes. None the less, it must be acknowledged that some of the specific estate agency rules do not sit too easily in the auction context. In particular, auctioneers may find severe difficulty in complying with the requirement that every offer received for a property is to be communicated to the vendor "promptly and in writing"![1]

(b) *Overseas property*

There is a basic presumption, rebuttable only by very clear words, that the effect of an Act of Parliament does not extend beyond the United Kingdom. In consequence, the legislation now under discussion can only apply to "estate agency work" which is carried out in England, Wales, Scotland or Northern Ireland. However, a separate question, which the presumption does nothing to answer, is whether the Estate Agents Act can apply to UK agents who market overseas property. This is a common enough activity, and it offers as much scope for abuse as does domestic property; none the less, it is doubtful to say the least whether it falls within the Act.

The view that sales of overseas property lie outside this legislation[2] is based largely upon section 2 of the 1979 Act. This section, in describing the interests in land which are covered, adopts the language of English (and Scottish) land law, using phrases such as "legal estate in fee simple absolute in possession" and "Register of Sasines". Such terms may well be inappropriate when referring to immoveable property in other countries whose land law is

---

1 See p 212.
2 A view which is held by both the Department of Trade and Industry and the Office of Fair Trading: see the OFT's *Estate Agency Guide*, published in July 1991, p 3.

fundamentally different from that of the United Kingdom, which suggests that the Act cannot apply to such property.[1]

Although the view outlined above is probably the correct one, it should be pointed out that it is based upon inference, rather than upon any express provision. What is more, some support for the opposing view, that the Act does in fact extend to UK transactions involving overseas property, may be extracted from section 12. This defines "clients' money" as deposits relating to "an interest in land in the United Kingdom". Why, one might ask, is it necessary to place this qualification on the definition in section 12, if the entire Act only applies to UK property? If nothing else, the existence of such doubts leads to the practical conclusion that estate agents handling overseas sales should adhere to the same principles as they adopt in relation to their domestic work.

(c) *Subagency*

The question of how far, if at all, the estate agency legislation applies to subagents is a surprisingly complex and difficult one to answer. It is clearly desirable that subagents should be subject to the statutory controls, especially those which seek to protect members of the public rather than clients, since the various abuses at which these are aimed are just as capable of arising at the subagency level. However, it is clear that the legislation has not been drafted with subagency specifically in mind, and there is consequently some difficulty in bringing it within the statutory wording.

The basic problem lies in the 1979 Act's definition of "estate agency work", which requires the agent's instructions to have been "received from another person (in this section referred to as 'the client') who wishes to dispose of or acquire an interest in land". In considering whether these words apply to subagents, the most natural interpretation is surely that a subagent's "instructions" are received from the main agent, and that the main agent is not a person who wishes to dispose of or acquire an interest in land. If this is correct, then what the subagent does is not "estate agency work" as defined by the Act.

---

1 The wording of section 1(6) of the Property Misdescriptions Act 1991 seems even more clearly to rest on this assumption.

In order to bring subagents within the Act (and, for that matter, within the Property Misdescriptions Act), it might be argued that the main agent *is* a person who wishes to dispose of or acquire land, albeit only as an agent for someone else. This argument, if accepted, would lead to the conclusion that the subagent's "client" is the main agent, and that all the statutory controls therefore apply "one step down". The conclusion is attractive, but the argument itself does not seem very convincing.

A third possible interpretation of the legal position would be to treat the subagent as working pursuant to instructions which emanate from the real client (ie the vendor or purchaser) and which are merely transmitted to the subagent through the main agent. This avoids the need to strain the meaning of the word "client" in section 1; unfortunately, it creates a situation in which the subagent and the "client" do not have a direct contractual relationship with each other. This in turn leads to the conclusion that, while most of the statutory obligations would apply to a subagent, the duty to give the client written notice of charges could not, since that duty requires a direct contract between the "agent" and the "client".[1]

(d) Leases at a rack-rent

As has already been pointed out, the original intention was that the Estate Agents Act should apply in principle to transactions involving leasehold interests, while excluding residential lettings and property management. However, the chosen method of expressing this distinction raises the uncomfortable possibility that the baby may have been thrown out with the bath water. The problem lies in section 2(1)(*b*), which applies the Act to "a lease which ... has a capital value which may be lawfully realised on the open market". Had this description been: "a lease whose capital value *if any* may be lawfully realised", it would have indicated clearly that what mattered was whether any premium value could legitimately be extracted, rather than whether there was any such value to extract. As it stands, however, the wording of this provision suggests that, where a lease has no capital value (because the property is let at

---

1 Section 18(1): see p 208.

full rental value), no transaction involving that lease can fall within the Estate Agents Act.[1]

If this is indeed the true position, it seems to introduce an unnecessary and unproductive complication into what should be a simple matter of deciding whether or not the Act applies.[2] The crucial question, be it noted, is not whether a premium has been paid as part of a transaction, but whether the lease actually *has* a capital value. And this question is of course one which may receive different answers at different times, as fluctuations in the property market determine whether or not the current rent is a rack-rent.[3]

It can hardly have been intended that an estate agent should have to carry out a complex valuation exercise in order to discover whether or not the Estate Agent Act applies. However, unless a somewhat extended interpretation can be given to the term "capital value",[4] that appears to be the inevitable consequence of section 2(1)(*b*).

C Controls on estate agents

From the point of view of the practising estate agent, the most important aspect of the Estate Agents Act 1979, and the orders and regulations made under it, is the imposition of detailed rules governing the way in which day-to-day estate agency business is carried on. The legislation creates a number of specific duties which are owed, not only to clients, but also to third parties with whom an estate agent deals, and breaches of these duties can lead in appropriate cases to penalties ranging from loss of commission through a criminal prosecution to an order from the Director-General of Fair Trading which bans the agent altogether from continuing to practise.

In considering the specific statutory duties of estate agents, we shall not follow the order in which these duties appear in the

---

1 Unless, perhaps, it can be argued that any lease has in principle a capital value, albeit one which, depending on the rent charged, may be "nil" at any given time.

2 The problem would of course have been far less serious if the Act, as was intended, had been limited in scope to residential property.

3 In a falling market, as agents will be painfully aware, leases can rapidly acquire a *negative* value.

4 See note 31.

legislation, but rather the approximate order in which they may be expected to affect a practitioner. Thus, in a straightforward case, an estate agent on obtaining instructions from a client must immediately furnish that client with certain information, concerned largely with the agent's charges. When the property is put on the market, the agent must keep the client informed about certain specified matters, and must also deal in a fair manner with any person with whom negotiations take place. If negotiations reach the point at which the agent is in receipt of deposit money (including a pre-contract deposit), this must be dealt with in accordance with strict statutory rules. We conclude with a reminder that, while the right to practise estate agency is in principle open to anyone, whether qualified or not, there are some special restrictions on that right.

1 Information to clients

In an effort to bring about the maximum possible transparency in dealings between estate agents and their clients, section 18 of the Estate Agents Act requires certain information to be provided by the estate agent as soon as an agency relationship is in view.[1] That requirement has been significantly extended by the Estate Agents (Provision of Information) Regulations 1991 in respect of both the information which is included and the time and manner at which it is to be provided. It should be appreciated, however, that neither the Act nor the Regulations seek in any way to restrict the terms on which an estate agent contracts with the client; all that is required is that those terms are properly set out at the correct time.

(a) Details of charges

The main thrust of section 18 is geared to information about all the charges, whether in the nature of remuneration or otherwise, for which the client may become liable. This information, according to section 18(2), comprises:

(a) particulars of the circumstances in which the client will become liable to pay remuneration to the agent for carrying out estate agency work;

---

1 In principle, the requirement applies as much to agents acting for prospective purchasers or tenants as to those acting for vendors or landlords. However, some of the 1991 provisions make sense only in relation to vendors' agents.

(b) particulars of the amount of the agent's remuneration for carrying out estate agency work or, if that amount is no ascertainable at the time the information is given, particulars of the manner in which the remuneration will be calculated;

(c) particulars of any payments which do not form part of the agent's remuneration for carrying out estate agency work or a contract or pre-contract deposit but which, under the contract referred to in subsection (1) above, will or may in certain circumstances be payable by the client to the agent or any other person and particulars of the circumstances in which any such payments will become payable; and

(d) particulars of the amount of any payment falling within paragraph (c) above or, if that amount is not ascertainable at the time the information is given, an estimate of that amount together with particulars of the manner in which it will be calculated.

If all this information is duly given, a client will know at what point the agent's remuneration is to become payable (whether this is on the mere introduction of a prospective purchaser, the exchange of contracts, completion of the sale or some other specified event), and either the precise amount of that commission or the method by which it is to be assessed (eg professional scales or percentage of the purchase price). It has further been accepted by a Scottish court that, where an estate agent obtains a "secret profit" from the agency work which is concealed from the client (consisting in that case of a discount which the agent was given on newspaper advertising) the agent is also guilty of a breach of section 18(2)(a), since this profit constitutes part of the agent's "remuneration".[1]

Compliance with section 18(2) also means that the client will be informed about any potential payments which do not amount to commission, such as advertising or other out-of-pocket expenses.[2] In relation to such payments, the agent must state either the exact amount which is to be charged or, where this is not possible at the outset, the method of its assessment together with an estimate. The Office of Fair Trading's view of this provision is that it requires the agent to provide as far as practicable an itemised list of expenses for which the client will be responsible, together with an estimate of

---

1 *Solicitors Estate Agency (Glasgow) Ltd* v *MacIver* 1993 SLT 23: see p 210.
2 A payment for abortive work (such as a "withdrawal fee") which exceeds the expenses actually incurred will be regarded as "remuneration" and will therefore fall within paras (a) and (b).

the charges which will arise under each heading. It is emphatically *not* regarded as sufficient for the agent simply to agree a global maximum figure for expenses with the client, even if the agent then keeps within that figure.[1]

(b) *Special commission clauses*

One of the main criticisms of estate agents, in the period leading up to the 1991 legislation, lay in their use of certain restrictive terms of business which might prove unduly onerous to inexperienced clients. Three such terms ("sole agency", "sole selling rights" and "ready, willing and able purchaser") came in for especially heavy criticism, and the Government's response was to require any estate agent using these terms to provide the client with an explanation of their meaning. Not only that; regulations 5 and 6 of the Estate Agents (Provision of Information) Regulations 1991 prescribe the exact words in which the explanation must be couched, subject only to the proviso that, if the circumstances render a statutory explanation misleading, it is the estate agent's responsibility to amend it so as to ensure accuracy.

It might be thought that the new rules could be evaded by the simple expedient of using variations on these terms, such as "exclusive agency" or "person willing to purchase"); however, this potential loophole has been foreseen and duly closed. The 1991 regulations provide that, if an estate agent uses any terms which "have a similar purport or effect" to those listed, the appropriate statutory explanation (again amended as far as necessary to avoid any misunderstanding) must be used.

The clear intention of regulations 5 and 6 is that the relevant statutory explanation should appear in whatever document is used by the agent to satisfy the general requirements of section 18. In any event, the time within which this information is to be given to the client is the same as for all information relating to the agent's terms of business. Furthermore, it is specifically provided that the

---

1 Warning Orders issued on this ground against the firm of *Burling Morrison* and one of its partners were overturned on appeal to the Secretary of State. However, on September 8 1988 the Office of Fair Trading issued a press notice stating that, having taken counsel's opinion, it maintained its original interpretation (which furthermore had been accepted by the RICS, the ISVA and the NAEA).

statutory explanations must be given no less prominence than any other information in the document in which they are contained.

We may now examine the three statutory explanations. What is particularly interesting about them is that they all depart to a greater or lesser extent from the meaning which earlier case law has attributed to the commission terms in question. What is more, the departure in each case appears to be for the benefit of the estate agent. Ironically, therefore, it seems that an estate agent's compliance with statutory rules designed to offer protection to clients may have the effect of entitling the agent to commission, in circumstances where a claim would not have succeeded at common law.

Sole agency

According to the 1991 regulations, "sole agency " means that remuneration will be payable in the following situation:

if at any time unconditional contracts for the sale of the property are exchanged with a purchaser introduced by us during the period of our sole agency or with whom we had negotiations about the property during that period; or with a purchaser introduced by another agent during that period.

A number of points may be made about this clause:

i The agent will be entitled to commission whenever the *sale* occurs, so long as the relevant *introduction* (whether made by the agent or by another agent) takes place during the period of sole agency.[1]

ii There appears to be no requirement for the agent's introduction to be the "effective cause" of the sale in question.[2] Indeed, it is specifically provided that mere "negotiation" with the ultimate purchaser will sufficient.

iii The agent will be entitled to full commission, rather than an award of damages for breach of the sole agency which would normally reflect only the lost *chance* of earning commission.[3]

---

1 Contrast *Fairvale Ltd* v *Sabharwal* [1992] 2 EGLR 27: p 336.

2 Contrast *Sadler* v *Whittaker* (1953) 162 EG 404: p 164.

3 See, for example, *Hampton & Sons Ltd* v *George* [1939] 3 All ER 627 (p 163), where the agents recovered as damages approximately three-quarters of what would have been earned as commission.

Sole selling rights

The definition of "sole selling rights" contained in the 1991 regulations requires a client to pay remuneration in either of two situations. The first of these is:

if unconditional contracts for the sale of the property are exchanged in the period during which we have sole selling rights, even if the purchaser was not found by us but by another agent or by any other person, including yourself.

The second commission-earning situation is:

if unconditional contracts for the sale of the property are exchanged after the expiry of the period during which we have sole selling rights but to a purchaser who was introduced to you during that period or with whom we had negotiations about the property during that period.

Notwithstanding its different layout, the effect of this definition seems very similar to that of "sole agency" (apart, of course, from the fact that it catches private introductions as well as those made by a rival estate agent). In consequence, all the comments made above about the earlier definition apply with equal force to this one.

Ready, willing and able purchaser

The 1991 regulations define a "ready, willing and able purchaser" as a person who "is prepared and is able to exchange unconditional contracts for the purchase of your property". The significance of using such a term is then made clear by a paragraph which states:

You will be liable to pay remuneration to us, in addition to any other costs or charges agreed, if such a purchaser is introduced by us in accordance with your instructions and this must be paid even if you subsequently withdraw and unconditional contracts for sale are not exchanged, irrespective of your reasons.

The first point which may be made about this definition is that the phrase itself appears wholly inappropriate in cases where an estate agent is seeking a *tenant* for property (though it is probably suitable where the agent is acting on behalf of an existing tenant who is seeking to assign the leasehold interest). More serious, however, is the fact that, while the statutory definition appears accurately to reflect the case law on "person ready willing and able to purchase",[1] it is strongly arguable that the use of the word "purchaser" would normally prevent an agent from earning commission unless the transaction proceeded at least as far as exchange of contracts.[2] If this is indeed so, then compliance by an estate agent with the regulations will once again prove to offer additional benefits.

(c) *Services offered to purchasers*

One area where the Estate Agents (Provision of Information) Regulations 1991 break entirely new ground is in connection with the provision, by estate agents acting on behalf of vendors, of "tie-in" services to prospective purchasers. This practice, which is perhaps especially prevalent where the estate agent concerned forms part of a larger organisation (such as a financial institution) has given rise to a range of complaints, some of which have now been addressed in the Estate Agents (Undesirable Practices) (No 2) Order 1991. As far as *clients* are concerned, the majority of complaints centred on the fear that there might be a conflict of interest and, while the general law of agency could offer at least some protection under the doctrine of "secret profit",[3] it is clear that by no means all services offered to purchasers would be caught in this way.

The Government's response to this problem lies in regulation 2 of the 1991 regulations, which requires estate agents to inform their clients (at the same time that they are informed of the agents' terms of business) as to certain services which are to be offered to prospective purchasers. The services in question, which do not include any which are offered free of charge, are defined as "any services to a prospective purchaser ... which are such as would ordinarily be made available to a prospective purchaser in connection with his acquisition of an interest in land or his use or enjoyment of it". The regulation goes on to list by way of example "the provision to that purchaser of banking and insurance services and financial assistance and securing the disposal for that purchaser of an interest in land if that disposal is one which has to

---

1 See *Christie Owen & Davies* v *Rapacioli* [1974] 2 All ER 311: p 140.
2 *Davis* v *George Trollope & Sons* [1943] 1 All ER 501: p 145.
3 See p 44.

be made in order for him to be able to make the acquisition he is proposing or is one which is a result of that acquisition".

This wide definition (which, it is important to emphasise, is in no way limited to the examples given) will clearly include such matters as assisting a prospective purchaser in obtaining a mortgage or a required life insurance policy, or introducing the purchaser to a surveyor or a removal firm. Further, however obvious it might appear to clients who realise that estate agency is a business, an agent must solemnly inform the client that, if a prospective purchaser has a house to sell, the agent will offer to market it.

The obligation of an estate agent under regulation 2 arises in three situations. First, and simplest, there is the case where the estate agent (which, it should be remembered, may be a partnership or a company, as well as an individual) itself intends to offer relevant services. Second, the services may be offered by what the regulations call a "connected person". The meaning of "connected person" for this purpose picks up certain definitions in the Estate Agents Act itself, where they are used in setting out the scope of the agent's duty to disclose any "personal interest". These terms will accordingly be discussed in detail in relation to section 21;[1] for the moment it will suffice to point out that "connected persons" include an estate agent's employer, employee, principal or agent, and also any "associate" of either the agent or of the agent's employer, employee, principal or agent. As for "associates", these include both business associates such as partners (though not, rather oddly, co-directors of a company) and personal associates such as spouses and a wide circle of relatives. What is more, where an estate agency consists of a partnership or company, there are detailed provisions under which it may be regarded as the "associate" of an organisation of equivalent type.

The third situation in which a client must be told about "services" is where these are to be offered by an independent third party, but where the estate agent or a "connected person" will derive a financial benefit from this. This would apply, for example, where an estate agent regularly introduces prospective purchasers to a particular mortgage or insurance broker and receives a commission from that broker for the introduction.

---

1 See p 215.

Although the duty created by this regulation is wide-ranging, it should be emphasised that the estate agent is not obliged to give *details* of the services in question; the regulation states "information ... as to the services", which appears to require no more than a list, and certainly does not compel the agent to reveal the amount of any financial benefit which will accrue. Still less does the regulation demand that the agent should obtain the client's *permission* to offer such services, although a client who objects strongly enough can of course withdraw the agent's instructions altogether.

(d) *Time and manner of compliance*

Somewhat surprisingly, section 18 as enacted did not specify any particular manner in which the required information was to be given to clients. In consequence, while any sensible agent would give the information in writing (so as to be able if called upon to prove compliance), what mattered in law was simply whether or not the client had been informed.[1] However, the power given by section 18(4)(*b*) to issue regulations on this matter has now been utilised, and regulation 4 of the Estate Agents (Provision of Information) Regulations 1991 duly provides that all relevant information within section 18 shall be given by the estate agent in writing.

The manner in which information is to be given is clear enough; the time at which it must be given is less so. Section 18(1) as enacted required this to be done "before any person (in this section referred to as 'the client') enters into a contract with another (in this section referred to as 'the agent') under which the agent will engage in estate agency work on behalf of the client".[2] There were considerable difficulties of analysis in relating this to the generally held view of estate agency as a unilateral or "if" contract;[3] however, these problems can now for practical purposes be ignored, since the time at which section 18 must be complied with has been spelled out more precisely in the 1991 regulations. According to regulation 3(1), the relevant time is "when communication commences between the estate agent and the client or as soon as

---

1 See *Fiesta Girl of London Ltd* v *Network Agencies* [1992] 2 EGLR 28 : p 210.

2 The provision appears not to bite unless a contract is entered into. Hence, an agent who attempts to entice another agent's client cannot be guilty of a breach of section 18 unless the attempt succeeds!

3 See pp 99-101.

is reasonably practicable thereafter provided it is a time before the client is committed to any liability towards the estate agent".

It is important to appreciate that this provision does *not* mean that agents can delay in giving the necessary information to their clients so long as they give it before the client is committed to any liability for fees or expenses. The basic requirement is to give the information as soon as communication commences, which suggests for example that an agent visiting a potential client to measure up the property which is to be marketed should take along a copy of the firm's terms of business; the agent can thus ensure that this is given to the client before any "estate agency work" is carried out. This is not to say that a letter "confirming instructions", if sent out promptly, would fail to satisfy the regulations; however, there is always the risk that such a letter might not be regarded as having been sent "as soon as is reasonably practicable" and, in any event, it can *never* be in time if any charges have already been incurred.

(e) *Sanctions for non-compliance*

Any breach by an estate agent of section 18 (including those matters governed by the 1991 regulations) may have two legal consequences. First, as with the other specific duties which are imposed by the Act, such a breach may operate to "trigger" the enforcement powers of the Director-General of Fair Trading. Second, it is provided by section 18(5) that, unless the information has been given at the correct time and in the correct manner, the contract is unenforceable, either by legal action or by the exercise of a lien over the client's money, without a court order.[1] Where such an order is sought, the court is given a discretion by section 18(6) either to dismiss the agent's claim altogether, where this is justified by "prejudice" caused to the client by the agent's failure to comply with this obligation and the degree of culpability for the failure", or to reduce the amount payable so as to compensate the client for any prejudice suffered (presumably in cases where the agent's failure cannot be described as "culpable").

---

1 But compliance with the Act does not necessarily render the agent's commission claim legally enforceable. In particular, there are doubts as to the status of "confirming letters": see p 174.

Attempts by clients to use section 18 as a ground for refusing to pay fees have come before the courts on several occasions.[1] First, in the Scottish case of *Solicitors Estate Agency (Glasgow) Ltd* v *MacIver*,[2] a client complained that, by not disclosing the discount of 18% which they received on the charge for advertising the client's property in a local newspaper, estate agents were in breach of either section 18(2)(*a*) or section 18(2)(*d*) or both (depending on whether or not the money which thereby accrued to the agents was to be regarded as part of their "remuneration"). This complaint was upheld and, having taken into account both the agents' "culpability" and the client's "prejudice", the court ruled that the commission payable should be reduced by one-half.

In *Fiesta Girl of London Ltd* v *Network Agencies*,[3] a client met with less success. It was clear from the evidence in that case that, although the agent had not set out the commission terms properly in writing, the client had in fact known precisely how much would be charged and in what circumstances. Since the case arose before the 1991 regulations came into force (and therefore at a time when agents were not compelled to give notice of charges *in writing*, it was held that the agents had in fact complied with section 18 and that there was accordingly no justification for challenging their claim for payment.[4]

2   Other duties to clients

As far as estate agents' duties to their clients are concerned, the 1979 Act itself has little to offer other than the information-giving requirement of section 18. However, the 1991 regulations and orders are rather more demanding in this respect, laying down a number of duties which continue throughout the agency relationship. These may now be considered.

---

1 In addition to the two cases discussed below, see *Connell Estate Agents* v *Begej* [1993] 39 EG 125: p 151.

2 1993 SLT 23.

3 [1992] 2 EGLR 28.

4 Similar facts would today amount to a breach of section 18 (which requires the agent's terms to be set out in writing). However, whether this would justify a court in denying the agent commission would depend on whether the client, despite knowing the truth, could be said to be "prejudiced" by the breach.

(a) Variation of terms

As noted above, section 18 of the 1979 Act and the Estate Agents (Provision of Information) Regulations 1991 impose detailed obligations upon estate agents to give their clients written notice of a number of matters at the commencement of the agency relationship. Of course, it is perfectly possible for an estate agent and a client to agree at some point that the terms of their contract shall be varied. If this happens, section 18(3) requires the agent to notify the client of the new terms; the 1991 regulations require the up-dated information to be given in writing at "the time when, or as soon as is reasonably practicable after", the changes are agreed by the parties.

(b) Services requested by purchasers

We noted above the obligation imposed upon an estate agent by the Provision of Information Regulations, to inform the client of any "services" which the agent intends to offer to prospective purchasers. It is further provided by the Estate Agents (Undesirable Practices) (No 2) Order 1991 that, where an estate agent has introduced a prospective purchaser to the client and that purchaser has made an offer,[1] the agent must also inform the client "promptly and in writing" of any services which that purchaser *requests* from the agent, or from a "connected person",[2] or from anyone else in circumstances where the agent or a connected person will derive a financial benefit. This obligation applies to all such requests, except those which are refused outright, which are received at any time before contracts for the sale or lease of the property are exchanged.

It is important to emphasise that this obligation is completely independent of the one discussed earlier. Even if the agent has already warned the client that, for example, the firm will offer to arrange mortgages for prospective purchasers, the client must be told when a purchaser actually requests the firm to do so. Furthermore, where an agent has *not* informed the client at the outset of a particular service (because at that time the agent had no intention of offering it), the agent must nonetheless report any request from a prospective purchaser unless this is immediately refused.

---

1 "Offer" for this purpose is expressly defined to include a conditional offer.
2 See p 207.

(c) *Notification of offers received*

The Estate Agents (Undesirable Practices) (No 2) Order 1991 seeks to ensure that estate agents are completely open with their clients over offers received from prospective purchasers. To this end, Schedule 3 para 2 defines as an undesirable practice any "failure by an estate agent to forward to his client ... accurate details ... of any offer the estate agent has received from a prospective purchaser in respect of an interest in the land". These details are to be forwarded "in writing" and may be sent "by hand, post or fax at the address or to the number given by the client to the estate agent". Whatever method is adopted, the information must be sent "promptly", which is defined to mean "within as short a period as is reasonably practicable in the circumstances, from the moment when what is to be done can reasonably be done".

As to precisely what information must be sent to the client, the 1991 order is not explicit. There is no explanation of what constitutes "details", although it may be suggested that these should include at least the amount of the offer, the identity of the person making it, and perhaps the form in which it is received (whether or not it is in writing). Further, and very importantly, the order makes clear that the agent's duty applies as much to *conditional* offers as to unconditional ones, which suggests that the agent should surely identify any conditions which are attached to an offer (eg whether it is "subject to contract").

An important exception to this "undesirable practice" lies in the fact that it does not extend to categories of offer, or categories of "details", which the client has indicated in writing need not be forwarded. For example, a client might agree that the agent need not pass on offers which are less than a certain percentage of the asking price.

(d) *Disclosure of personal interest in purchase*

Section 21 of the Estate Agents Act imposes a duty of disclosure in respect of certain interests which either the agent or a person connected with the agent has in property to be disposed of or acquired. The main thrust of that provision concerns disclosure to third parties with whom the agent "enters into negotiations"; indeed the extent if any to which it can compel disclosure *to the client* is highly debateable.

This potential loophole has now been directly addressed by Schedule 1 para 2 to the Undesirable Practices Order, which requires an estate agent to disclose to the client "promptly and in writing" that the agent "has, or is seeking to acquire, a beneficial interest in the land or in the proceeds of sale of any interest in the land". A similar obligation arises where the agent "knows that any connected person[1] has, or is seeking to acquire" such an interest.

The duty of disclosure to the client which is imposed by this paragraph appears to arise in four different situations:

i Where an agent acting for a vendor or landlord already has a "beneficial interest" in the property. This would arise, for instance, where a tenant of property instructs an estate agent to market the leasehold interest, and the agent has an existing interest (direct or through a "connected person") in the freehold.

ii Where an agent acting for a vendor or landlord wishes to acquire a beneficial interest in the property.

iii Where an agent acting for a client who is seeking property to rent or buy introduces property in which the agent or a "connected person" has a beneficial interest.

iv Where an agent, acting on behalf of a client who is seeking property to rent or buy, introduces a property to the client but then decides to acquire that property personally or for a connected person (ie the agent intends to compete with the client for the property).

3 Duties to third parties

A combination of the 1979 Act and the Estate Agents (Undesirable Practices) (No 2) Order 1991 means that, in addition to their clients, estate agents also owe certain obligations to third parties with whom they deal in the course of business. Three matters are of particular importance in this respect.

(a) *Disclosure of personal interest*

Once an estate agent accepts instructions to act for a client, a fiduciary relationship comes into existence between them, as a result of which an equitable duty of loyalty is imposed upon the agent.[2] This duty manifests itself in various ways, but these are all related to the principle that an agent's personal interests should not

---

1 The meaning of "connected person" is discussed at p 207.
2 See p 110.

be allowed to come into conflict with the interests of the client. If a potential conflict arises, it is the agent's duty to make full disclosure to the client, so that the latter can make an informed decision on what action to take. Failure to make such disclosure may render the agent liable to pay damages, disgorge any personal profit which has been made and forfeit the agreed commission.

The equitable duty of loyalty arises out of the agency relationship; there is no corresponding obligation owed to a third party with whom the agent deals. As a result, it appears that an auctioneer is quite entitled to sell his or her own property, without revealing its ownership to bidders,[1] Further, although there is no authority on the point, it seems likely that the same would be true of an estate agent. However, such cases are now subject to a *statutory* duty of disclosure by virtue of section 21 of the Estate Agents Act.

The first point to be noted about section 21 is that it is not limited in its application to the carrying out of "estate agency work" as defined by section 1 of the Act. The opening words of section 21(1): "A person who is engaged in estate agency work" might, if taken out of context, mean either someone *generally* engaged in estate agency work (ie someone whom the layman would describe as an "estate agent") or someone so engaged *in the relevant transaction.* However, section 21(3) shows conclusively that the former interpretation is the correct one by providing that subsections 1 and 2 apply "where an estate agent is negotiating on his own behalf as well as where he is negotiating in the course of estate agency work". As a result, this statutory duty of disclosure applies, not only when an estate agent acts pursuant to instructions received from a client, but also when the agent decides to enter the marketplace in a personal capacity.

Before we turn to consider the actual obligations which are imposed by section 21, some attention must be paid to what that section regards as a "personal interest". In one sense, this concept is less widely drawn by statute than in equity, for it is limited to interests in the land itself. In other respects, however, the scope of the section far surpasses any duty created by the courts.

Section 21(5) provides:

---

1 *Flint* v *Woodin* (1852) 9 Hare 618: p 309.

for the purposes of this section, an estate agent has a personal interest in land if –
(a) he has a beneficial interest in the land or in the proceeds of sale of any interest in it; or
(b) he knows or might reasonably be expected to know that any of the following persons has such a beneficial interest, namely –
   (i)   his employer or principal, or
   (ii) any employee or agent of his, or
   (iii) any associate of his or of any person mentioned in sub-paragraphs (i) and (ii) above.

The overall width of this definition is enormous. In the first place, what we may term an estate agent's "direct" personal interests in land will include any interest whatsoever[1] in either the land itself or in the proceeds of sale of any interest in it. Second, the estate agent will have what we may term an "indirect" personal interest in land if any member of a wide class of persons associated with the agent has a "direct" personal interest and the agent is or should be aware of that fact. This class covers not only the estate agent's partner, employer,[2] employee principal and agent, but also his and their "associates", who are defined by section 32 as including spouses and an extensive circle of relatives.

In an effort to provide an exhaustive definition of "personal interest", the Act deals in sections 31 and 32 with the common situation where an estate agency practice is carried on, not by an individual, but by a partnership, company or unincorporated association. In each case, certain natural persons are named as "business associates" of the organisation, which is then under a duty to disclose any direct personal interest of those persons, their spouses and relatives. Further, complex provisions govern the possibility that two partnerships, two companies or two unincorporated associations may be "associates" where certain natural persons are common to both organisations. In any such case, one associate would be under a duty to disclose any direct personal interest of the other. Interestingly, however, no provision is made for the possibility of one type of organisation, such as a

---

1 Not just the freehold or lease included in section 2 but any legal or equitable interest.

2 Note, however, that the agent who is acting on behalf of his own employer may in any case be outside the scope of the Act: see p 193.

limited company, being the "associate" of another type, such as a partnership. Thus, for example, if X, a partner in a firm of estate agents, is also a director of a development company which markets its houses through X's firm, X as director will be deemed to have a personal interest in the houses, and thus a duty of disclosure. However, the partnership as a whole has no such interest or duty. As a result, so long as X does not personally conduct negotiations with any third party but leaves everything to the other partners, there is no breach by anybody of section 21. If, however, X does contravene the section, it must be remembered that the partnership (and the other individual partners) may also be responsible for that contravention as "business associates" under section 3(3)(c), provided that they are guilty of "connivance or consent".

On turning to the actual obligations as to disclosure which are created by section 21, it may be seen that the section attempts to deal with two different situations. First, section 21(1) provides that an estate agent who has a personal interest in land shall not "enter into negotiations with any person with respect to the acquisition or disposal by that person of any interest in that land until the estate agent has disclosed to that person the nature and extent of his personal interest in it". At its simplest, this covers the case where an estate agent is marketing his or her own house; here the truth about ownership must be disclosed to any prospective purchaser before negotiations commence. This, however, is only the tip of the iceberg; the agent's duty of disclosure applies equally where the personal interest is "indirect" (as described above) and also where that interest in the land is not the one which is being sold. For example, an estate agent instructed to sell the freehold reversion on business premises would come within section 21(1) if the agent's nephew happened to be the sublessee of those premises, or if the ex-wife of one of the agent's partners held a mortgage over them (provided in each case that the agent knew or ought to know the relevant facts).

The examples so far given all relate to an estate agent who is instructed to sell property, but the wording of section 21(1) clearly also covers the converse case. It may be unusual for an agent to be negotiating with a third party over land in which they both hold a personal interest without this being obvious but, given the wide definition of personal interest in this section, it is by no means impossible. Suppose, for example, that an estate agent is approached by a client who is seeking leasehold shop premises to rent. Suppose also that an "associate" of that agent is the landlord of a suitable shop. By virtue of the provision under discussion, the agent may not begin to negotiate with the present tenant for an assignment of the lease until the nature and extent of the agent's personal interest in the property have been disclosed to that tenant.

The Estate Agents Act itself does not specify precisely either how or when agent's duty of disclosure is to be fulfilled, beyond stating that this is to be done before "negotiations" commence. However, this matter has now been effectively fleshed out by Schedule 1 to the Estate Agents (Undesirable Practices) (No 2) Order 1991, which provides that any required disclosure is to be made "promptly and in writing". As to what is meant by "promptly", the order defines this as "within as short a period as is reasonably practicable in the circumstances, from the moment when what is to be done can reasonably be done".

If section 21(1) appears nightmarishly complex, what is to be made of section 21(2)? This deals with cases where the estate agent has no initial personal interest in the land in question, but where, as a result of a proposed transaction or series of transactions, such an interest will be acquired.[1] One might regard the case of an estate agent buying a client's property through an undisclosed "associate" as the obvious abuse at which this provision is aimed but, on closer examination, section 21(2) does not appear to catch this situation. Once again, the duty of disclosure is owed to any person with whom the agent "enters into negotiations", and it seems to place an unjustified strain upon the ordinary meaning of these words to suggest that they include the agent's own client. What section 21(2) covers is the case where an estate agent seems to be buying on behalf of an independent client, whereas in reality the agent intends to act personally or for an associate. Even so, it is by no means certain that the common case of an agent bidding at auction would be included, since such conduct might well not amount to "entering into negotiations".

Interestingly, a situation which appears to fall outside both section 21 of the Act and the Undesirable Practices Order, despite having been singled out for adverse comment by the Department of Trade and Industry, is where an estate agent acting on behalf of a vendor

---

1 Note that disclosure in this instance need not be made "promptly and in writing", since the Estate Agents (Undesirable Practices) (No 2) Order 1991 does not apply.

wishes to make a personal bid for the property (or to sell it to a connected person). The agent's intention must in such a case be disclosed to the client;[1] however, it seems that there is no obligation to disclose to prospective purchasers the fact that the agent intends to compete with them for the property.

All in all, it cannot be said that section 21 is happily drafted. In particular, it seems likely that, because the definitions are so widely drawn, many agents will find themselves in breach of its terms in cases where there is not the slightest suspicion of sharp practice. The sole consolation which can be offered is that there are no criminal or civil sanctions for a breach of these provisions;[2] the only effect is that a breach may be used to trigger the enforcement powers of the Director-General of Fair Trading, and one may hope that the Director is unlikely to take any action in respect of trivial or inadvertent breaches.

(b) *Discrimination over services*

One matter which was identified by the Office of Fair Trading in the late 1980s as giving cause for concern related to those estate agents who, while acting for a vendor, sought directly or indirectly to profit from the provision of services (financial or other) to prospective purchasers. It was felt that such practices, which had naturally increased considerably with the move by financial institutions into the estate agency field, could have adverse effects on both purchasers and clients. Unless restrained, an unethical agent might well be tempted for example to favour a prospective purchaser who would require a mortgage from the agent's linked financial services division over one who had already arranged the necessary finance. This would obviously be detrimental to the rejected purchaser; it could also of course work to the disadvantage the client, who might thereby be deprived of a higher offer for the property. True, the client (if able to prove what had occurred) could take action against the agent for any loss suffered and could also refuse to pay commission;[3] however, the enforcement authorities felt that the situation called for legislative intervention.

---

1 See p 212.
2 Section 21(6).
3 See *Henry Smith & Son* v *Muskett* (1977) 246 EG 655: p 167.

We have already noted[1] those provisions in the 1991 orders and regulations which require an estate agent to inform (and keep informed) the client as to services which are provided directly or indirectly to prospective purchasers. However, the legislation goes further by defining as an undesirable practice any "discrimination against a prospective purchaser by an estate agent on the grounds that that purchaser will not be, or is unlikely to be, accepting services".[2]

While "services" for the purpose of this provision bears the meaning which we have discussed earlier, "discrimination" is not further defined in the order. However, other statutory provisions in the fields of sexual and racial equality define discrimination in terms of treating a person less favourably than one treats or would treat others in similar circumstances, and there seems no reason to doubt that such ideas would also be applied in the estate agency context. It would surely be discrimination, for example, to seek to persuade the client to prefer one applicant to another,[3] to delay in passing on an offer from an unfavoured purchaser,[4] or to send out details of suitable properties only to those applicants identified as likely to require services.

(c) *Misrepresentation of offers*

An estate agent acting on behalf of a vendor will naturally try to obtain the best possible price for the client and, to that end, to emphasise the attractions and desirability of the property in question. Such conduct is only to be expected, although a feeling that agents have on occasion been somewhat over-enthusiastic in this respect is what has led to the passing of the Property Misdescriptions Act 1991. However, one type of misdescription which is *not* covered by that Act is any false or misleading statement as to the state of competition for a particular property. This is because claims designed to play off one prospective purchaser against another (for example by suggesting that the other has made a higher offer or is a "cash buyer") do not appear

---

1 See pp 206, 211.
2 Estate Agents (Undesirable Practices) (No 2) Order 1991, Schedule 2 para 1.
3 As occurred in *Henry Smith & Son* v *Muskett* (1977) 246 EG 655.
4 This would of course also be an undesirable practice under Schedule 3 para 2.

on the list of "prescribed matters" which define the scope of the 1991 Act.

This particular matter is addressed by Schedule 3 para 1 to the Estate Agents (Undesirable Practices) (No 2) Order 1991, which provides that it is an undesirable practice for an estate agent to make any misrepresentation "(a) as to the existence of, or details relating to, any offer[1] for the interest in the land; or (b) as to the existence or status of any prospective purchaser of an interest in the land". This applies to all false or misleading statements, whether made in writing or orally; however, an agent is only in breach where the offending statement is made "knowingly or recklessly".

Pretending to one prospective purchaser that a rival has made a higher offer for the property might be regarded by cynics as the equivalent in private treaty sales of an auctioneer's taking of bids "off the wall". While that practice is clearly illegal,[2] an auctioneer may quite lawfully bid *on behalf of the vendor* provided that the right to do so has been properly reserved in the particulars or conditions of sale.[3] The 1991 order accordingly provides that an auctioneer who bids on behalf of the vendor in accordance with the 1867 Act is not to be regarded as guilty of an "undesirable practice".

4   Clients' money

The intention which underlies sections 12 to 17 of the 1979 Act, and the Estate Agents (Accounts) Regulations 1981, is that estate agents should deal properly with clients' money and that, in the event of an agent's default, the public should be protected as far as possible against any resulting loss. In considering this matter, it will be convenient to look first at the statutory definition of "clients' money", before turning to the specific obligations which the Act imposes in respect of such money.

(a) *Definition*

For the purposes of the Estate Agents Act, "clients' money" bears a restricted meaning, as is apparent from the wording of section 12(1):

---

1 Including a conditional offer.
2 See p 370.
3 Sale of Land by Auction Act 1867, section 6.

In this Act "clients' money", in relation to a person engaged in estate agency work, means any money received by him in the course of that work which is a contract or pre-contract deposit –
(a) in respect of the acquisition of an interest in land in the United Kingdom, or
(b) in respect of a connected contract,
whether that money is held or received by him as agent, bailee, stakeholder or in any other capacity.

Of the various sums of money which may be handed over in the course of estate agency work, therefore, the Act controls only the two types of deposit on sales of land and contracts connected to and conditional upon sales of land, such as sales of curtains and carpets. Section 12(2) provides:

In this Act "contract deposit" means any sum paid by a purchaser –
(a) which in whole or in part is, or is intended to form part of, the consideration for acquiring [an interest in land in the United Kingdom] or for a connected contract; and
(b) which is paid by him at or after the time at which he acquires the interest or enters into an enforceable contract to acquire it.

Section 12(3) applies a similar definition to "pre-contract deposit" except that in this case, of course, the sum is paid *before* the interest is acquired or the contract made.

In view of the obligations which attach to "clients' money" and the severe consequences of failure to meet them, the definitions in section 12 are of fundamental importance, and several points are worthy of emphasis. First, since the definition of "clients' money" includes both contract and pre-contract deposits, the question into which of these categories a particular sum falls is one of purely academic interest. Second, it matters not whether the money is received by the estate agent as agent, as stakeholder or in any other capacity;[1] the Act makes it clear that the same rules apply. Third, in cases where a sum of money is paid to an estate agent partly as a deposit and partly for other purposes (eg for transmission to a building society or an insurance company) then,

---

1 The word "bailee" seems inappropriate in this situation, as this usually refers to the deposit of goods rather than money.

if it cannot conveniently be split, the whole sum is "clients' money" and must therefore pass through the "client account".[1]

(b) Clients' money as trust property

The problems caused in the past by estate agents who defaulted with deposit-money[2] were due in no small measure to the common law rule that the legal claim of a person entitled to a deposit against the deposit-holder was a purely personal one. Hence, if the deposit-holders' assets were insufficient to pay off general creditors, the deposit was in no way "earmarked" for the person entitled to it. Nor, if the deposit-holder had wrongfully used the money, could it be traced. In an attempt to alleviate the hardship caused by this rule, section 13(1) provides that where clients' money, as defined above, is received by any person in the course of estate agency work, that money –

(a) is held by him on trust for the person who is entitled to call for it to be paid over to him or to be paid on his direction or to have it otherwise credited to him, or
(b) if it is received by him as stakeholder, is held by him on trust for the person who may become so entitled on the occurrence of the event against which the money is held.[3]

This statutory creation of a trust in respect of clients' money has a number of important effects. First, it means that, if an estate agent becomes insolvent, any money which is in that agent's "client account" cannot be used to pay off general creditors; it is "property held by the bankrupt on trust for any other person"[4] and is therefore payable only to those persons entitled to the deposits.[5] Second, if the estate agent has wrongfully used money impressed with a trust, for example by paying it into his or her own bank

---

1 See p 228.
2 See pp 84-87.
3 If the estate agency work is done in Scotland (no matter where in the United Kingdom the property is located) the money is held "as agent" rather than on trust (section 13(2)); the legal effect, however, is the same.
4 Insolvency Act 1986, section 283(3).
5 If there is not enough money in the client account to meet all claims, the rule in Clayton's case (1816) 1 Mer 572 applies. It is presumed that withdrawals from the account are made in the same order as payments in; hence, "first in, first out".

account or buying goods with it, the person entitled to the money may be able to "trace" it, even into a different form and into the hands of a third party (though not of a *bona fide* purchaser for value without notice).[1] Less importantly, the existence of a trust brings into operation various supervisory powers of the High Court, notably the power to appoint a new trustee where necessary, such as where the sole principal of an estate agency practice dies or becomes insane.[2]

The designation of clients' money as a trust fund would normally lead to a number of other consequences under the general law of trusts. Those responsible for the drafting of the Estate Agents Act, however, adopted a more specific approach; according to section 13(3): "The provisions of sections 14 and 15 below as to the investment of clients' money, the keeping of accounts and records and accounting for interest shall have effect in place of the corresponding duties which would be owed by a person holding clients' money as trustee, or in Scotland as agent, under the general law." Further, it is provided by section 13(5) ("for the avoidance of doubt") that, where an estate agent has a lien over clients' money, this does not affect the trust; equally, the trust does not affect the lien.[3]

The statutory trust created by section 13(1) is expressed to be for the benefit of the person who is entitled to demand the clients' money from the estate agent or, in certain circumstances where nobody is so entitled, to the person who may become entitled. In the vast majority of cases, this will be one of the parties to an actual or proposed sale; which one it is will depend upon the type of

1 The equitable rules on "tracing" are complex, depending mainly upon the status of the ultimate recipient of the money and also upon whether the money remains sufficiently "identifiable". Readers are referred to any of the major works on Equity.
2 In the particular case where an order made by the Director-General of Fair Trading prohibits an estate agent from holding clients' money, it is provided that the order itself may appoint a substitute trustee and make provision for his expenses and remuneration: section 13(4).
3 Although it has never been specifically decided whether or not an estate agent has a lien on clients' money for remuneration and expenses, it seems in principle (by analogy with the case of an auctioneer: *Webb* v *Smith* (1885) 30 ChD 192) that there should be one on money which belongs to the client. In practice, this will only apply to a contract deposit which is still in the agent's hands after the sale is completed or (possibly) to a contract deposit which has been received "as agent" with the authority of the vendor.

deposit in question and the capacity in which it is received and held by the estate agent. In practical terms, it appears that the "person entitled" to a pre-contract deposit is the prospective purchaser who has paid it, irrespective of whether the estate agent purports to receive that deposit "as agent for the vendor", or "as stakeholder", or without any designation.[1] The only exceptions to this general principle are where the vendor has expressly authorised the agent to receive a pre-contract deposit as agent, or where the agent purports (without authority) so to receive it and the vendor subsequently ratifies what the agent has done. If, while an estate agent is holding a pre-contract deposit, contracts are exchanged between vendor and purchaser, the status of that deposit depends upon the terms of the contract. It may well be that the money is expressed to become part of the *contract* deposit; if the contract is silent, however, the rules outlined above will continue to apply.

In relation to a contract deposit, an estate agent may receive the money either "as agent for the vendor" or "as stakeholder". In the former case (assuming that the agent is acting with the vendor's authority), it is the vendor who is the "person entitled" for the purposes of section 13.[2] In the latter case, neither party is immediately entitled to demand the money; which of them subsequently becomes entitled depends upon whether the sale is successfully completed (the vendor) or one of the parties wrongfully fails to complete (the innocent party). Perhaps because estate agents so seldom hold contract deposits, the English courts have never been called upon to decide the capacity in which they are presumed to do so in the absence of any evidence to the contrary. Given that an auctioneer is presumed to be a stakeholder,[3] it would seem appropriate to regard an estate agent in a similar light; however, *dicta* from the Court of Appeal suggest that the presumption is in favour of holding the deposit "as agent".[4]

---

1 *Sorrell* v *Finch* [1977] AC 728: p 86.
2 *Ellis* v *Goulton* [1893] 1 QB 350.
3 *Furtado* v *Lumley* (1890) 6 TLR. 168. By contrast, the vendor's solicitor is presumed to hold a contract deposit as agent for his client: *Edgell* v *Day* (1865) LR 1 CP 80. See p 313.
4 *Ojelay* v *Neosale Ltd* [1987] 2 EGLR 167.

(c) *Restrictions on deposit-taking*

There are four situations in which the Act either curtails or removes altogether the power of an estate agent to accept a deposit. Of these, potentially the most important is probably section 16(1), which provides:

Subject to the provisions of this section, a person may not accept clients' money in the course of estate agency work unless there are in force authorised arrangements under which, in the event of his failing to account for such money to the person entitled to it, his liability will be made good by another.[1]

Surprisingly, perhaps, this "compulsory bonding" provision has not yet been brought into force. Even more surprisingly, if it is implemented, it will not require *all* who engage in estate agency work to be bonded, but only those who accept clients' money. However, in an effort to ensure that members of the public realise when they are dealing with an unbonded agent, section 16(4) makes it a criminal offence for any person who carries on estate agency work to describe himself or herself as an "estate agent", or to indicate in any way that he or she is in business "to act as a broker in the acquisition or disposal of interests in land", unless the relevant information[2] is displayed both at the agent's place of business and in all documents, such as advertisements, notices and the like, which may induce people to use the agent's services.

The details of what constitutes "authorised arrangements" are not set out in the Act; they are to be filled in by subsequent regulations, which may for example specify the circumstances in which the liability of the insurers may be excluded,[3] and provide that any "ceiling" on that liability in an individual case shall not be less than a specified amount.[4] It is, of course, impossible to predict with certainty the content of such regulations, but it seems safe to assume that the insurance required would have to provide total cover, not only for the agent's deliberate misappropriation of clients'

---

1 The person entitled to the money will not of course be a party to these "authorised arrangements", but may none the less make a direct claim against the insurers: section 16(3).
2 The content of which will be specified in regulations.
3 Section 16(2)(c).
4 Section 16(2)(d).

money, but also for the careless mixing of such money with the agent's own funds, which results in its loss on the agent's bankruptcy. It also appears that the insurance schemes presently operated by the major professional bodies would be designated as satisfying the requirements of the statute.

Where estate agency work is carried on by such institutions as banks, building societies or insurance companies, whose funds are adequately protected by other legislation, they may be exempted from the requirements of section 16, either under the regulations or on application to the Director-General of Fair Trading under section 17. Subject to such exemption, however, these provisions are regarded as very important; any breach is a criminal offence.

The second situation in which an estate agent may not hold clients' money is where the agent has a personal interest in the property concerned. Section 21(4) provides:

An estate agent may not seek or receive a contract or pre-contract deposit in respect of the acquisition or proposed acquisition of –
(a) a personal interest of his in land in the United Kingdom; or
(b) any other interest in any such land in which he has a personal interest.

The odd thing about this provision is that it appears *not* to apply to the sale of an agent's own property. Such a case would not normally fall within the Act at all, because section 1 requires the agent to be acting "pursuant to instructions", and one can hardly "instruct" oneself to act. Furthermore, the extension by section 21(3) to private deals applies only to the duty of disclosure imposed by subsections (1) and (2). If this analysis is correct, the ban on seeking or receiving deposits is limited to cases where the estate agent has a "personal interest" in land but is nevertheless selling it *as agent* for a client.

It should be noted that, even where an estate agent accepts a contract deposit in breach of this provision, there is no statutory obligation on the agent to refund it.[1] Section 21(6) provides that no breach of the section shall give rise to any form of legal action, either civil or criminal.

The remaining two restrictions on deposit-taking both relate solely to pre-contract deposits. Where estate agency work is done in

---

1 A pre-contract deposit must in any case be returned on demand.

Scotland (no matter where in the United Kingdom the land itself may be situated), such deposits are banned altogether; section 20 provides that no pre-contract deposit may be sought or received. Where estate agency work is carried out in England, Wales or Northern Ireland, there is no such absolute prohibition, but section 19[1] enables regulations to be made which will limit the size of the sums involved "and such a limit may be so prescribed either as a specific amount or as a percentage or fraction of a price or other amount determined in any particular case in accordance with the regulations".

(d) *Dealing with clients' money*

When an estate agent receives clients' money in circumstances where this is permitted, the Act leaves no doubt as to what should be done with it. Section 14(1) provides:

Subject to such provision as may be made by accounts regulations, every person who receives clients' money in the course of estate agency work shall, without delay,[2] pay the money into a client account maintained by him or by a person in whose employment he is.

Failure to comply with this obligation is a criminal offence carrying a fine of not more than £500.

The definition of a "client account", and the detailed rules which govern its operation, are to be found in section 14 of the Act and the Estate Agents (Accounts) Regulations 1981. According to section 14(2), a client account is a current or deposit account with an authorised institution, which is in the name of a person who is or has been engaged in estate agency work and which contains in its title the word "client". The "authorised institutions", which are listed in the Schedule to the regulations, are, broadly speaking, banks (including trustee savings banks), building societies and the Post Office. It is further provided by regulation 3 that, should any of these institutions themselves engage in estate agency work, they

---

1 Which has not yet been brought into force.
2 Unfortunately perhaps, in view of the severe consequences of any breach of this provision, "without delay" is not further defined in the Act.

and their employees are exempt from the requirements relating to client accounts.[1]

Regulations 4 and 5 govern the precise way in which a client account is to operate. The basic objective is to achieve the rigid separation of "clients' money", as defined by the Act, from all other money in the estate agent's hands; to this end, while clients' money must always be paid into a client account without delay, there are only two other occasions on which other money may lawfully be paid into the same account. These are, first, where the institution in question requires a minimum sum to open or maintain the account (in which case it can and should be withdrawn when it is no longer required for that purpose) and, second, to restore in whole or in part any money wrongfully paid out of the account.[2] The regulations also clarify the position of money which is paid to an estate agent for more than one reason. In such circumstances,[3] the whole sum is deemed to be "clients' money" but, in so far as it is practicable to split that part which may be strictly described as a "deposit" from the rest, only the former may be paid into the client account. If it is not practicable to split it, then the entire sum must be paid into the account and the surplus removed.

The circumstances in which money may lawfully be paid out of the account (apart of the removal of anything which should never have been paid into it) are:

i where money is paid to the person entitled to it;[4]

ii in payment of the estate agent's remuneration or expenses, with the agreement of the person for whom the money is held;

iii in the lawful exercise of a lien;[5] and

iv where money is transferred to another client account.[6]

It follows from these rules that, strictly speaking, a client account should neither be credited with interest earned on the money in it,

---

1 This is on the basis that depositors are given sufficient protection by other statutory codes which govern such institutions.

2 This might seem odd but, without it, every wrongful payment out of a client account (which constitutes a criminal offence) would automatically be followed by another offence when the money was returned.

3 See p 221.

4 As to who is the "person entitled", see pp 223-224.

5 See p 178.

6 In which case the records kept must enable its movements to be clearly traced.

nor debited with any bank charges. The agent must arrange for these payments in and out to be allocated to other accounts.

(e) *Accounts and records*
   In an effort to ensure that there is a means of checking compliance by an estate agent with his duty to open a client account and to operate it properly, section 14 and the Accounts Regulations lay down details of the actual accounts and records which are to be kept.[1] The duty to keep these accounts is imposed by regulation 6 upon "any person who receives clients' money in the course of estate agency work", except an employee who always pays such money without delay into the employer's client account. It is, however, provided that the obligation (which involves keeping records for six years after the end of the accounting period to which they relate) may be handed over by one person to another when the former ceases to be engaged in estate agency work.
   As to the nature of the accounts and records which are to be kept, regulation 6(1) provides generally that these must be sufficient to show that the estate agent's basic duty in respect of clients' money has been discharged, and "to show and explain readily at any time all dealings with the money". This latter requirement involves identifying the account itself, the institution where it is located, and so on. From the point of view of the practising estate agent, however, the more important (and more useful) provision is regulation 6(3), which gives a detailed list of the information which must be made available.[2] In relation to clients' money *received*, this consists of the date of receipt; the amount; the name and address of the depositor; the purpose of the payment (eg pre-contract deposit, contract deposit, payment in respect of a connected contract);[3] the interest in land to which the payment relates (and the identity of the person wishing to dispose of that interest); and the person for whom, and the capacity in which, the money is from

1 Failure to keep such accounts is a criminal offence: section 14(8).
2 The information is to be "indexed" be reference to the interest in land to which it relates: reg 6(3)(b).
3 If part of the sum is paid in only because it cannot be split, the purpose of that payment must be shown.

time to time held.[1] Further, it is provided that the majority of this information must also appear upon the counterfoils or duplicate copies of receipts issued to those who deposit clients' money and that these counterfoils or copies must themselves be kept. Where payments *out of the account* are concerned, the information required to be shown is the date of the payment; the amount; the identity of the payee; the interest in land to which the payment relates; a reference to the corresponding payment in; and the purpose of the payment.[2] Finally, where money is transferred from one client account to another, the records must show the reason for the transfer and enable the original payment in to be traced. However, this last requirement does not apply where sums are transferred between a current and a deposit account kept by the agent, in both of which clients' money is held generally.

(f) *Audit*

The basic obligation imposed by regulation 8 of the Estate Agents (Accounts) Regulations 1981 is to draw up the accounts and records described above in respect of consecutive "accounting periods"[3] and to have them audited within six months of the end of each period by a "qualified auditor".[4] The auditor's report must then, under threat of criminal penalties, be produced on demand to a duly authorised officer of an enforcement authority.

The methods to be adopted by an auditor in this context are clearly defined by regulation 8. Having ascertained from the estate agent in question particulars of all bank accounts maintained by the agent or by employees in the course of estate agency work during

---

1 The regulation acknowledges that the estate agent may not know these matters, since both the person and the capacity may change while clients' money is in the agent's hands.

2 Where payment is made to the estate agent in respect of remuneration or expenses, the records must further identify any information required to be given to the client in respect of those charges under section 18: see p 201.

3 A period not exceeding twelve months. No dates are specified, but an employee who is obliged to keep such accounts must adopt the same accounting period as the employer.

4 Defined by section 14(6) so as to mean, in nearly all cases, either a chartered accountant or a member of the Association of Certified and Corporate Accountants. In the case of limited companies, certain persons such as officers and servants of the company are disqualified from acting as auditors by the Companies Acts, and the Estate Agents Act applies the same disqualifications: section 14(7).

the relevant period, the auditor is to examine the accounts and records kept by that person to see whether or not they comply with the requirements of regulation 6 described above. To this end the auditor may demand further information or explanations from the estate agent, but is not required to pursue enquiries beyond the accounts and records (as supplemented by these further explanations), nor to consider the keeping of the relevant accounts outside the period in question.

Having carried out this investigation, the auditor is required to produce a report to the estate agent, and this report may take one of four forms:

i that all the requirements of regulation 6 have been complied with;
ii that the requirements of regulation 6 have been substantially complied with. This would be appropriate where, in the auditor's opinion, the only breaches are trivial ones due to clerical errors, all of which were rectified on discovery and none of which have caused any loss;
iii that the requirements of regulation 6 have not been complied with. In this case the auditor must specify the relevant breaches; and
iv that the auditor is unable to form an opinion as to whether or not the requirements of regulation 6 have been complied with. In this case the auditor must specify the relevant matters and explain why it is impossible to form an opinion about them.

(g) *Interest on deposits*

Regulation 7 deals with the situations in which a person engaged in estate agency work must account for interest upon clients' money.[1] By providing that such account is to be made to the "person who is for the time being entitled to the money", and specifically excluding any period during which the money is held "as stakeholder on trust for the person who may become entitled to it on the occurrence of" a specified event, regulation 7(1) makes it clear that the same sum of money may attract a duty to pay interest to more than one person, in respect of different periods of time. As we have already seen,[2] the "person entitled" to clients' money (and therefore entitled to interest on it) may be the actual or prospective

---

1 For the common law rules which this regulation overrides, see p 178.
2 pp223-224.

purchaser (pre-contract deposit, or contract deposit once the sale has gone off); the vendor (contract deposit held "as agent", or contract deposit after completion of the sale); or neither party (contract deposit held "as stakeholder").

To avoid the creation of a legal obligation which might necessitate an expensive book-keeping operation in respect of a trifling sum, it is provided by regulation 7 that the duty to pay interest arises only where the clients' money in question exceeds £500 and the relevant interest is at least £10.[1] The relevant interest for this purpose is computed in different ways, according to where the clients' money is held:

i   If the money is held in a separate deposit account (assuming of course that this is a valid client account), the estate agent must account for the interest which it actually earns.

ii If the money is held in a client account which is not a separate deposit account, the agent must account for interest as if it had been so held at the same authorised institution.

iii If (contrary to section 14 of the Act) the money is not held in a client account, the agent is penalised by having to pay interest at the highest rate available on the day when it should have been paid in.[2]

iv In the case of an authorised institution itself, interest must be paid at the appropriate rate for a separate deposit account at that institution.

Section 15 of the Estate Agents Act makes it clear that the obligations described above may be modified or excluded by an "arrangement in writing, whenever made" between an estate agent and any other person who has or may have an interest in clients' money. Exactly what is meant by this is not clear. Presumably the mere giving of notice in writing (for example on the receipt which is issued to a depositor) falls short of being an "arrangement between" the parties, but there is no positive requirement of *signature* by or on behalf of the person concerned. In the absence of such an

---

1 This means, not the total interest earned by the sum in question, but the amount to which the particular person is entitled.

2 If the estate agent has one or more client accounts with authorised institution, payment must be made at the highest rate available at those institutions. If the agent has no such account, payment must be made at the highest rate available at *any* of the authorised institutions.

arrangement, the statutory rules are practically exhaustive; section 15(3) provides that there is no other liability to account for interest on money held in a general client account.[1]

It should be noted that, unlike the other provisions of accounts regulations, those concerned with the duty to account for interest are not backed up by criminal sanctions. However, a breach may of course operate to trigger the powers of the Director-General of Fair Trading, and it is also specifically provided by section 15(5) that any person entitled to interest on clients' money may claim it from the estate agent in the civil courts.

5 Restrictions on the right to practise

It has already been noted that, unlike previous attempts to legislate in the field of estate agency, the 1979 Act does not compel would-be practitioners to obtain a licence before setting up in business. The general philosophy is that there should be no restrictions upon the right to practise estate agency. There are, however, three exceptions to this general principle; two are no more than one would expect, but the third is more controversial.

(a) Prohibition orders

As will shortly be seen, the Director-General of Fair Trading is empowered in certain circumstances to make an order prohibiting a person from engaging in estate agency work, on the ground that that person is unfit to do so. Once such an order is made, it must be obeyed, on pain of criminal sanctions.[2]

(b) Bankruptcy

Section 23(1) provides:

An individual who is adjudged bankrupt after the day appointed for the coming into force of this section or, in Scotland, whose estate is

---

1 This presumably does not preclude the possibility of the money being held in a *separate* client account, in such a case, it seems that any liability to pay interest is governed by common law in so far as it does not fall within the accounts regulations. If so, a liability *will* arise, since section 13 creates a trust where none existed previously.
2 An unlimited fine following conviction on indictment; a fine of up to £5,000 on summary conviction.

sequestrated after that day shall not engage in estate agency work of any description except as an employee of another person.[1]

This prohibition, which ceases to have effect when the bankrupt is discharged, is backed by criminal sanctions.[2] Interestingly, however, a criminal conviction in such circumstances is not a ground on which the Director-General of Fair Trading may make an order banning the agent from practice; as a result, the bankrupt agent could still continue to practise as an employee of someone else.

(c) *Minimum standards of competence*

Somewhat out of place in an Act which firmly eschews any positive system of licensing is section 22(1), which enables regulations to be made prescribing minimum standards of competence for those engaged in estate agency work. This provision, though at first regarded as highly controversial, now commands the support of the major estate agency bodies;[3] however, it has not been brought into force and the present Government has repeatedly stated that there is no intention to implement it.

If regulations *are* ever made under section 22, they must "prescribe a degree of practical experience which is to be taken as evidence of competence" and, in addition, they may provide for alternative qualifications. As to what these alternatives might be, section 22(2) provides that regulations may:

(a) prescribe professional or academic qualifications which shall also be taken to be evidence of competence;

(b) designate any body of persons as a body which may itself specify professional qualifications the holding of which is to be taken as evidence of competence;

---

1 A possible loophole, by which a bankrupt might form a company and work for it under a contract of employment, is closed by section 23(3).

2 An unlimited fine on conviction on indictment; on summary conviction, a fine of (current) maximum of £5,000.

3 Following a U-turn by the Royal Institution of Chartered Surveyors, which was originally concerned that "official recognition" might be given to those holding lesser qualifications.

(c) make provision for and in connection with the establishment of a body having power to examine and inquire into the competence of persons engaged or professing to engage in estate agency work; and

(d) delegate to a body established as mentioned in paragraph (c) above powers of the Secretary of State with respect to the matters referred to in paragraph (a) above.

Of these provisions, para (a) is straightforward, while para (b) assumes that the existing professional bodies with their own examination systems would be designated to set the standards of competence for their own members, so that existing arrangements would continue largely undisturbed. As for para (c), what is envisaged is a body representative of all persons engaged in estate agency work, whether or not holding professional qualifications, to test the competence of those not wishing to join the designated bodies, to prescribe standards for them, and to provide an alternative to the arrangements which are institutionalised by the existing professional bodies. The composition of this body is to be determined by the regulations, but it seems clear that, at least at the outset, the knowledge and expertise of members of the existing professional bodies would be heavily relied upon.

If section 22 is ever brought into force, any person who engages in estate agency work "on his own account" will, unless he or she satisfies the required standard of competence, be guilty of a criminal offence.[1] Further, statutory regulations will provide what proportion of partners must satisfy the minimum standard in order to render the partnership itself "competent", and similar rules will apply to any "body corporate or unincorporated association" which engages in estate agency work.

D Enforcement of the Act

Responsibility for the enforcement of the Estate Agents Act is given by section 26(1) to both the Director-General of Fair Trading and local weights and measures authorities.[2] The latter are

---

1 Carrying, on conviction on indictment, an unlimited fine; on summary conviction, the maximum fine is at present £5,000.

2 In Northern Ireland, the functions of the latter are given to the Department of Commerce.

concerned with local "on the ground" enforcement which, in this instance, means only the investigation and prosecution of specific criminal offences under the Act;[1] breaches by estate agents of the *non-criminal* obligations imposed by the Act and its supporting Regulations and Orders are the concern of the Director alone. Notwithstanding this division of responsibility, however, local weights and measures authorities may be called upon to report to the Director on the carrying out of their functions under the Act.

1 Negative licensing

The overall supervision and enforcement of the Act is made the responsibility of the Director-General of Fair Trading. However, unlike the Consumer Credit Act 1974, which the Director also administers, the Estate Agents Act does not impose any *positive* system of licensing or registration. With very few exceptions,[2] any person may practise as an estate agent until proved unfit to do so. The scheme, therefore, consists of a kind of "negative licensing", and the question of a particular agent's fitness or unfitness is a matter for the Director who may, if the requirements of the Act are satisfied, make various orders, including one which prohibits the agent altogether from continuing to practise.

The taking away of a person's livelihood is of course a drastic form of punishment and, not surprisingly, the Director's powers in this area are hedged about by numerous restrictions, both procedural and substantive.[3] Not only must the Director be satisfied that the agent is generally unfit; there must also have occurred one of a number of specified "trigger" events, such as a criminal conviction, before these powers come into play.

We shall shortly consider the various "triggers" and the procedures (including the question of appeals) which govern their exercise. First, however, we must look at the important matter of the exact range of orders which the Director is empowered to issue.

---

1 But no enforcement authority may prosecute in Scotland: section 26(3). All prosecutions there are initiated by the Procurator Fiscal.
2 See pp 233-235.
3 It has been held that, where a person's livelihood depends upon the decision of a tribunal, the strict test of proof "beyond reasonable doubt" is to be applied: see *R* v *Milk Marketing Board, ex parte Austin* The Times, March 21 1983.

2 Types of order

The simplest and most drastic form of order which may be made under the Estate Agents Act 1979 is one which prohibits a person[1] from doing any estate agency work at all. If, however, the Director feels that the "unfitness" relates to only one aspect of estate agency work, the order may instead prohibit the agent "from doing estate agency work of a description specified in the order".[2] A limited order of this kind might be thought appropriate, for example, where an agent's careless accounting procedures, while not reflecting upon his or her general level of honesty and competence, nevertheless make the agent unfit to hold clients' money. In such a case, the agent might simply be banned from accepting clients' money.[3]

It is further provided[4] that any order, whether general or specific, may be limited in scope to a particular part of the United Kingdom, a useful provision where, for example, complaints of malpractice are restricted to one branch of a larger organisation. There is, however, no power to limit the *time* for which an order is to operate; any ban takes effect (subject to the possibility of revocation following the agent's application)[5] as a life sentence.

The severity of a prohibition order may be tempered under section 4, which empowers the Director in certain cases to issue a *warning* to the estate agent that, if he or she persists in infringing the law, the Director will make a declaration of unfitness to practise under section 3. It is vital to appreciate that this warning power does *not* exist where the grounds for an order under section 3 consist of a criminal conviction (section 3(1)(a)) or either racial or sex discrimination (section 3(1)(b)). It *only* applies where the estate agent is guilty of a breach of one of the non-criminal obligations contained in sections 15 and 18 to 21 (section 3(1)(c)), or has engaged in an "undesirable practice" as defined by a statutory instrument made under section 3(1)(d). Further, it should be

---

1 Or an estate agency partnership or company as a whole: see p 238.

2 Section 3(2).

3 As to money which is already in the agent's possession when the order comes into force, the Director is empowered to appoint a new trustee in substitution for the banned agent: section 13(4).

4 By section 3(5).

5 See p 247.

emphasised that a warning order can only be made where the Director is satisfied that the agent's *general* "unfitness" will justify an order under section 3 if the warning order is not heeded.

A warning order made under section 4 must indicate the type of section 3 order (general or limited) which will be made against the agent if there is a further infringement. If such an infringement does occur,[1] the Director may automatically proceed to make an order under section 3; the agent's failure to comply with the warning is, by section 4(3), to be treated as conclusive evidence of unfitness to practice.

It should be noted that any prohibition or warning order under the Estate Agents Act is made against a "person" which, according to the Interpretation Act 1978, "includes a body of persons corporate or unincorporate". As a result, it seems clear that an order may be made against a partnership or a limited company, as well as an individual estate agent. Indeed, the possibility of dealing *en bloc* with a partnership is expressly envisaged by section 5(2), which provides that the order may also have effect against some or all of the partners individually. Somewhat oddly, however, there is no similar provision in relation to limited companies.

3   Trigger events

The grounds upon which an order may be made by the Director are set out in section 3(1). This requires the Director to be satisfied that the agent:

(a) has been convicted of –
   (i)   an offence involving fraud or other dishonesty or violence, or
   (ii) an offence under any provision of this Act, other than section 10(6), section 22(3) or section 23(4), or
   (iii) any other offence which, at the time it was committed, was specified for the purpose of this section by an order made by the Secretary of State; or
(b) has committed discrimination in the course of estate agency work; or
(c) has failed to comply with any obligation imposed on him under any of sections 15 and 18 to 21 below; or

---

1 If the warning order is based on a breach of the Act itself (ie sections 15 and 18 to 21), a further breach of *any* of those sections may trigger a ban. If it is based on an "undesirable practice", however, it must be the *same* practice which recurs.

(d) has engaged in a practice which, in relation to estate agency work, has been declared undesirable by an order made by the Secretary of State.

These four categories of events which trigger the Director's powers may now be considered.

(a) Criminal convictions

Section 3(1)(a) lists three groups of offences, conviction for which will justify the Director in making an order against the agent. In relation to all of these it should be noted that a conviction which is "spent" by virtue of the Rehabilitation of Offenders Act 1974 "or any corresponding enactment for the time being in force in Northern Ireland" is to be disregarded.[1]

The first group of offences, those involving fraud, dishonesty or violence, is identical to that which would justify the Director-General of Fair Trading in refusing to grant a licence under the Consumer Credit Act 1974. It is important to note that conviction for an offence within this group is a "trigger", whether or not the offence took place in the course of estate agency work. Indeed, the Office of Fair Trading has used this provision to issue orders against persons who were not estate agents at all, but who it was thought might start an estate agency business (and who would be highly unsuitable if they did).

As to the 15 offences created by the Act (most of which are concerned either with the handling of clients' money or with obstruction of the enforcement authorities), all but three rank as "triggers". Of those which do not, section 10(6) (which makes it illegal to disclose information obtained by authorised officers under the Act) is simply irrelevant to the practice of estate agency. The other two (practising without possessing the necessary qualifications[2] or when bankrupt[3]) are such as to render a banning order superfluous. It should be noted, however, that a criminal conviction for disregarding a previous order of the Director is a ground for a subsequent order; this might be relevant where, for example, the first order is limited as to type or work or geographical area.

---

1 Schedule 1 para 1.
2 Section 22 (not yet in force).
3 Section 23.

The third group includes any criminal offence which may be specified by statutory instrument. Under this provision, the Estate Agents (Specified Offences) (No 2) Order 1991 lists more than 40 offences arising under 13 statutes. These offences range from the making of unauthorised disclosures by a computer bureau[1] to the impersonation of a licensed conveyancer.[2] The broad impression is that these offences have for the most part been collected from "consumer protection" statutes, rather than with any real consideration of what it is that estate agents actually do; however, the Estate Agents (Specified Offences) (No 2) (Amendment) Order 1992 is more to the point, in that it adds offences arising under the Property Misdescriptions Act 1991.

The Estate Agents Act contains two provisions which are designed to ensure that, so far as possible, the Director receives information of any relevant convictions. In the first place, when a local weights and measures authority propose to institute proceedings for an offence under the Act it is their duty to notify the Director and to supply a summary of the facts upon which the prosecution is to be based.[3] Second, section 9(5) amends section 131 of the Fair Trading Act 1973 so as to empower courts, both civil and criminal, to notify the Director of any conviction or judgment which is regarded as relevant to the Director's functions under either Act.

(b) *Discrimination*

At first sight, section 3(1)(b) seems to be of enormous scope. This appearance, however, is deceptive; "discrimination" for the purposes of the Estate Agents Act bears only that meaning which is assigned to it by Schedule 1. In effect, this provides that the question whether or not an estate agent has committed discrimination is not one for the Director to answer; it is governed by the outcome of previous proceedings under either the Sex Discrimination Act 1975 or the Race Relations Act 1976.[4] As a result, an agent will only be guilty of discrimination under section 3 where a court has made a finding

---

1 Data Protection Act 1984, section 15.
2 Administration of Justice Act 1985, section 35.
3 Section 26(2).
4 In relation to Northern Ireland, the reference is to the Sex Discrimination (Northern Ireland) Order 1976 and there is *no* provision as to racial discrimination.

to that effect or where a non-discrimination notice served on the agent by the Equal Opportunities Commission or the Commission for Racial Equality has become final; in either event, the agent will have had an opportunity in judicial or quasi-judicial proceedings to contest the allegations.[1]

To constitute a "trigger" for the purposes of section 3, the discrimination in question must have been committed "in the course of estate agency work". Whether or not it is so committed *is* a matter for the Director to decide, but there is an important limitation; an estate agent who discriminates *as employer* rather than *as estate agent* is not to be dealt with under the Estate Agents Act.

The general treatment of discrimination in the Act runs parallel to that which is given to criminal offences, and this similarity is heightened by two procedural provisions. In the first place, a finding or notice of discrimination under Schedule 1 becomes "spent" after five years. Second, section 9(6) makes it the duty of the statutory Commissions to notify the Director of any finding, notice, injunction or order which appears to them to be relevant to the Director's functions under the Act.

(c) *Breaches of the Estate Agents Act*

Of the specific "estate agency" duties which are imposed by the 1979 Act, only those which relate to the keeping of client accounts are backed by criminal sanctions. It is, of course, essential that breaches of the other duties should serve as "triggers" for the enforcement powers of the Director-General of Fair Trading, and this is achieved by section 3(1)(c), which refers to "sections 15 and 18 to 21". The task of deciding whether an agent has failed to comply with any of these obligations is one for the Director's own judgment; it is possible, however, for a breach of sections 15, 18 or 20 to lead to a civil action,[2] in which case the court concerned may notify the Director of its decision under section 131 of the Fair Trading Act 1973.[3]

---

1 For a case of racial discrimination involving a London firm of estate agents, see *R v Commission for Racial Equality, ex parte Cottrell & Rothon* [1980] 3 All ER 265.

2 The same is potentially true of section 19, but this has not yet been brought into effect.

3 As amended by section 9(5) of the Estate Agents Act.

(d) *Undesirable practices*

Section 3(1)(*d*) empowers the Secretary of State to designate as "undesirable" certain practices which may be found in estate agency work, so as to constitute them as additional "trigger" events. The six practices so designated by the Estate Agents (Undesirable Practices) (No 2) Order 1991 have been considered earlier in this chapter.

(e) *Vicarious liability*

An important feature of the last two groups of "trigger" events (statutory obligations and undesirable practices) is the extent to which an estate agent may be held responsible for someone else's default. Section 3(3) lays down three separate types of vicarious liability which can apply in this area. In the first place, a person is responsible for anything done by an employee "in the course of his employment", unless it can be can shown that the employer "took such steps as were reasonably practicable to prevent the employee from doing that act, or from doing the course of his employment acts of that description". Second, a person is responsible for any act of an *agent* (as opposed to an *employee*) which is expressly or impliedly authorised, a provision which could well lead to problems in cases where an estate agent has sub-instructed.

These two kinds of vicarious responsibility are modelled on those found in the Sex Discrimination Act 1975, section 41 and the Race Relations Act 1976, section 32. By contrast, the third situation covered by section 3(3) creates a wider form of responsibility than one is accustomed to see. This lies in the provision that: "Anything done by a business associate of a person shall be treated as done by that person as well, unless he can show that the act was done without his connivance or consent." Given the Act's broad definition of "business associate",[1] the requirement of "connivance or consent" seems a necessary safeguard against an unacceptably onerous obligation. However, it should be stressed once again that, like all "triggers", these events do not *compel* the Director to make an order against an estate agent; they merely enable such an order to be made if the agent is considered to be generally unfit to practise.

---

1 See section 31.

4 Proceedings under the Act

The attention of the Director-General of Fair Trading may become focused on a particular agent or firm for a variety of reasons. There may for example be a complaint from a member of the public (either directly to the OFT or passed on by a trading standards department); a court or tribunal may report a case in which an estate agent has been held guilty of some offence; or a professional body may pass on the result of serious disciplinary proceedings against one of its members. In any of these cases, the Director may decide that further investigation of the agent is justified.

(a) *Investigation*

An investigation by the Director can be extremely wide-ranging; section 3(2) provides that, in addition to "trigger" events, the Director may "also take account of whether, in the course of estate agency work or any other business activity, that person has engaged in any practice which involves breaches of a duty owed by virtue of any enactment, contract or rule of law and which is material to his fitness to carry on estate agency work". Thus, provided that at least one "trigger" can be found, an estate agent's unfitness (leading to the loss of livelihood) may ultimately rest upon the conduct of business activities in a very different field.

In carrying out an investigation, the Director is given far-reaching powers by section 9 of the Act. This empowers the Director, by simple notice, to "require any person to furnish to him such information as may be specified or described in the notice or to produce to him any document so specified or described".[1] Once served, a notice under section 9 must be treated seriously; any positive refusal or deliberate failure to comply with it, or the giving of false or misleading information, is a criminal offence under section 9(4).

The confidentiality of information collected by the Director under the Estate Agents Act is protected by section 10, which makes it a criminal offence to disclose such information without the consent of the person concerned or, if the information is about a business still in existence, without the consent of the person carrying on that business. However, these provisions do not prevent the disclosure

---

1 However, this does not compel any counsel or solicitor to disclose privileged information: section 9(3).

of information for the purpose of criminal investigation or proceedings, civil proceedings under the Act or other consumer protection legislation, or the performance by the Director of any other statutory functions.

(b) *Preliminary proceedings*

It is by no means certain that the investigation of an estate agent will lead to formal proceedings by the Director-General of Fair Trading. However, if the Director is minded to make a prohibition order under section 3 or a warning order under section 4, the procedures which are set out in Part I of Schedule 2 must be followed.[1] The first step is to notify the person concerned[2] of the Director's proposal. This must be done in some detail; notice of a proposed prohibition order must specify any relevant "trigger" on which the Director relies, list other matters which have been taken into account and, if the order is to be based on a previous warning under section 4, make that clear. The notice must give the person affected at least 21 days in which to make written representations to the Director or, if preferred, to notify the Director that an oral hearing is required. Where an oral hearing is requested, this is to be arranged by the Director, and the person affected is to be given at least 21-days notice. The hearing itself is informal,[3] although the estate agent may, if he or she wishes, be represented.[4]

(c) *The making of orders*

If the Director decides (having duly taken into account any oral or written representations) to make the order in the form of the original proposal, this may be done. Alternatively, an order may be made in different form, provided that the grounds for this were contained in

---

1 The Director, in the exercise of these adjudicating functions, is governed by the Tribunals and Inquiries Act 1971: section 24.

2 This initial notice need only be served on a partnership as a whole, even where it is intended that the order shall also take effect against the individual partners. However, all subsequent notices during the proceedings must be served by the Director on the partners as well.

3 Evidence may not be excluded solely on the ground that it would not be admissible in a court of law.

4 By any other person (not necessarily a barrister or solicitor). However, barristers and solicitors have the advantage that communications with them are privileged from disclosure under section 9 or section 11.

the original proposal (for example, the Director may abandon one or more of the original grounds, where others remain). If, however, the Director wishes to rely on new grounds, the person affected must be given a fresh notice of this proposal, whereupon the whole procedure begins again.

When the Director decides to make an order, the person or persons affected must be given notice specifying the type of order, the "trigger" on which it is based, and any other facts which justify it. That person must also be informed of the right to appeal against the order.

As a general rule, an order comes into operation only when there is no further possibility of an appeal against it, either because an appeal has failed or because it is too late for one to be made. If, however, the Director feels it necessary (for example, on the ground of consumer protection) it may take effect immediately upon the giving of the notice. Once the order is in force, it is a criminal offence under section 3(8) not to comply with it, and a conviction under this provision is itself a "trigger" event. An order, once made, remains in force until either the conviction or discrimination upon which it is based becomes "spent"[1] or until it is revoked by the Director on an application made to him under section 6 of the Act.

(d) Appeals and similar proceedings

Once an order is made under either section 3 or section 4, the person affected may try in two different ways to remove its effect. In the first place, it is provided by section 7 that an appeal against the Director's decision lies to the Secretary of State; if this appeal proves unsuccessful, there may be a further appeal on a point of law to the High Court. There is no right of appeal to the court on questions of fact, but it should be remembered that "points of law" include the assertion that a verdict was so contrary to all the evidence that no reasonable tribunal could have reached it.

Details of the machinery governing appeals to the Secretary of State are contained, not in the Estate Agents Act itself, but in the Estate Agents (Appeals) Regulations 1981. Briefly, these regulations (which follow closely those applicable to appeals under the Consumer Credit Act 1974) provide that a person wishing to appeal

---

1 See section 5(4) and (5).

against an order made by the Director[1] must give notice to the Secretary of State within 28 days;[2] if this notice does not itself specify the grounds of appeal (eg disputed reasons or findings of fact relied on by the Director, or points of law), then the appellant must serve another notice specifying these grounds before the 28-day period expires. Once the grounds of appeal are made known to the Director, the latter has 28 days to furnish the Secretary of State with a copy of the original order, together with any representations; the appellant in turn then has 28 days to set out any further representations to be made in the light of the Director's reply.

Assuming that the Secretary of State is not minded at this stage of the proceedings simply to allow the appeal (or, even if so minded, that the Director objects to this), the Secretary of State must make arrangements for the appeal to be heard, unless the appellant within 14 days requests that the matter be disposed of without a hearing.[3] 21 days' notice of the date, time and place of the hearing must be given to both parties.[4]

Appeals will usually be heard by three "appointed persons", a legally qualified chairman together with two other members drawn from a panel made up of people with relevant professional experience. While procedure at the hearing is in the hands of the chairman, the regulations clearly envisage that the parties may be represented (by lawyers or others); may call witnesses (who may be questioned by the other party or the panel); and may make opening and closing statements. Further, it is specifically provided that evidence may be admitted whether or not it would be admissible in a court of law.

---

1 This applies not only to orders under section 3 and section 4, but also to decisions of the Director under section 6 (revocation and variation of orders) and section 17 (exemption from the insurance requirements of section 16).

2 Compliance with this time limit is crucial; it is the only one throughout the appeal procedure which the Secretary of Sate is not empowered to extend: regulation 26.

3 The appellant's wishes are not conclusive; the Secretary of State will decide after hearing from the Director.

4 An appellant who fails to appear runs the risk of the hearing taking place in his or her absence. However, regulations 15 and 17 provide that, in practice, the appellant will be given the opportunity to explain at least a single failure to the Secretary of State.

Once the appointed persons have completed the hearing (or, as the case may be, have considered the matter without a hearing), they are required to furnish the Secretary of State with a reasoned report in writing. On the basis of that report, the Secretary of State notifies the parties of the decision and the reasons for it, together with a reminder to the appellant that a further appeal, on a point of law only, lies to the High Court.

Quite apart from the appeals procedures, a person in respect of whom an order has been made under section 3 or section 4 is permitted by section 6 to make an application to the Director, asking for the order to be revoked or varied.[1] This provision, which is presumably intended for the benefit of the sinner who repents, may lead to a reopening of the whole case for, unless the Director simply accedes to the request, the applicant must be notified of the intention to refuse it (or only to vary the order in a way which does not satisfy the applicant's wishes). Thereafter the position is once again governed by Schedule 2, Part 1 (as to representations, hearings, etc) and by the appeals provisions of section 7.

The Director, on being asked to revoke an order made under section 3, may refuse if it is considered that the applicant remains unfit within the terms of the order. Similarly, an order made under section 4 will be confirmed if the Director considers that the applicant is likely to commit further breaches of whatever obligation formed the basis of the order. Where, however, it is felt that the order may, without detriment to the public, be varied in favour of the applicant (eg by restricting it to a particular area or type of work) the Director may make such a variation.

(e) *Register of orders*

The essence of the Estate Agents Act is consumer protection and, consistently with this philosophy, section 8 imposes upon the Director-General of Fair Trading a duty to "establish and maintain a register on which there shall be entered particulars of every order made by him under section 3 or section 4 above and of his decision

---

1 The form of an application, and the conditions on which it may be made, are governed by section 6 and Schedule 2, Part 2. Repeated applications, especially frivolous ones, will no doubt be discouraged by the non-returnable fee involved, which is set at a swingeing £2,500: Estate Agents (Fees) Regulations 1982, SI 1982 No 637.

on any application for revocation or variation of such an order". The register states the terms of any order and, where an order is not yet in force, the date on which it will come into operation. If an appeal is pending, the order will nevertheless appear (this is a necessary safeguard for the public) but the pending appeal will also be mentioned. The register is open to public inspection, and any person is entitled to take copies or to ask the Director for a certified copy of any entry.[1] The latter is regarded as conclusive evidence of the contents of the register; further, any particulars which are entered on the register are presumed to be correct unless and until the contrary is proved.[2]

It is the duty of the Director to see that the register is kept up to date, and that any change of circumstances is noted. In most cases the Director will automatically have received the information needed for this task, but could be unaware, for example, that an agent has died or that a relevant period under the Rehabilitation of Offenders Act has been extended. In consequence, while the Director's duty only arises when it is known that there is something which requires alteration, section 8(3) and Schedule 2, Part 2 ensure that an aggrieved person has the opportunity to bring such matters to the Director's attention.

5 Criminal offences

As noted at the beginning of this chapter, the criminal offences created by the Estate Agents Act (which relate mainly to the handling of clients' money and failure to co-operate with the enforcement authorities) are "policed" by local weights and measures authorities. In order to assist these authorities in the performance of their duties, section 11 gives them extensive powers of entry and inspection.[3] These powers (all of which are exercisable only by a duly authorised officer of an enforcement authority, only at a reasonable hour and only on production of credentials if demanded) are:

---

1 The fees for these services are modest: inspection costs £1 per file, and taking copies works out at approximately 75p per sheet: Estate Agents (Fees) Regulations 1982, SI 1982 No 637.

2 Section 8(6).

3 Although the powers are highly controversial, it should be remembered that they may *not* be used to investigate any breach of the Act which does not amount to a criminal offence.

i to enter premises (other than purely residential ones) on reasonable suspicion that an offence has been committed.

ii to inspect books or documents, or a legible reproduction of information stored in other forms (eg in a computer) and to take copies, again on reasonable suspicion of an offence.

iii on reasonable belief[1] that they are required as evidence in a prosecution, to seize and detain books or documents. Further, if necessary for this purpose, to break open any container holding such books or documents (but only where the person authorised to open the container has been asked to do so but has not complied).

Where books or documents are seized under these powers, the person from whom they are seized must be informed and, except while they are actually being used as evidence, the person to whom they belong must be given the opportunity to take copies.

The "teeth" of these provisions are to be found in section 27, which makes it a criminal offence to obstruct an authorised officer who is exercising statutory powers or, in some circumstances, to fail to give the officer adequate assistance in the exercise of those powers. However, it does not appear that section 11 justifies an officer in making a *forcible* entry to premises; hence, if admission is refused, the officer must obtain a warrant from a justice of the peace in accordance with section 11(4).[2]

---

1 This denotes something more than mere suspicion of an offence.

2 A warrant will be required in any case where the premises concerned are purely residential.

CHAPTER 7

Other statutory controls on estate agency

In any discussion of the statutes which bear most directly upon estate agency practice, the Estate Agents Act 1979 must naturally take pride of place. However, there are a number of other Acts which are of practical significance, notably the Property Misdescriptions Act 1991. This Act, and other statutes of relevance in everyday practice, are considered in this chapter.

A Property Misdescriptions Act 1991

As mentioned in the previous chapter, the Government's original intention (as stated on several occasions throughout the 1980s) was that the Trade Descriptions Act 1968 should be extended to cover false or misleading statements about land and buildings and that, until such time as this was done, the making of such statements should be designated an "undesirable practice" under the Estate Agents Act. This intention, however, was finally overtaken by events; a Private Member's Bill entitled the Estate Agents (Property Misdescriptions) Bill was introduced into Parliament and this, with Government support, duly passed into law as the Property Misdescriptions Act 1991.[1]

1 Scope of the Act

The area of application of the Property Misdescriptions Act is for the most part similar to that of the Estate Agents Act, although it extends beyond two important respects. According to section 1(1) of the 1991 Act, what is covered is any "false or misleading statement ... made in the course of an estate agency business or a property development business, otherwise than in providing conveyancing services".

---

1 The change of name came about when the Standing Committee widened the scope of the Bill to include statements made in the course of property development as well as estate agency.

(a) *Estate agency business*

The primary target of the Property Misdescriptions Act is undoubtedly the world of estate agency. Section 1(5)(e) provides in effect that, where the making of a statement constitutes "estate agency work" within section 1(1) of the Estate Agents Act 1979, the statement shall also be treated as made "in the course of an estate agency business" for the purposes of the 1991 Act. To this extent, therefore, everything said in the previous chapter about the scope of the 1979 Act is also relevant to property misdescriptions.

(b) *Solicitors*

We noted in the previous chapter that the Estate Agents Act provides a specific exemption for things done by a practising solicitor (or by any employee of a solicitor) "in the course of his profession". The Property Misdescriptions Act confers no such immunity, and thus includes within its definition of "estate agency business" anything which *would* have been caught by the 1991 Act were it not for the solicitor's exemption. As a result, any solicitor who provides estate agency services will be subject to the 1991 Act.

However, the extent of this provision should not be over-estimated. There is no intention to subject solicitors *generally* to the Property Misdescriptions Act, but only in so far as they practise estate agency. The Act achieves this by excluding statements made in the course of providing "conveyancing services", which are defined by section 1(5)(g) as "the preparation of any transfer, conveyance, writ, contract or other document in connection with the disposal or acquisition of an interest in land, and services ancillary to that".

(c) *Property development*

The most important difference between the coverage of the Estate Agents Act and that of the Property Misdescriptions Act lies in the fact that the latter governs property developers as well as estate agents. The Act applies to a statement made in the course of a "property development business" (which is defined by section 1(5)(f) as "a business ... concerned wholly or substantially with the development of land"), provided that the statement is made "with a view to disposing of an interest in land consisting of or including a building, or a part of a building, constructed or renovated in the course of that business".

The latter part of this definition serves to rule out businesses which merely *deal* in property rather than *developing* it. On the other hand, builders and developers who sell houses and flats directly (eg from a sales office on a housing estate) are certainly included.

2 The basic offence

The effect of the Property Misdescriptions Act 1991, which came into force on April 4 1993, is to create a new form of strict liability under criminal law[1] arising out of statements concerning property. The operative provision is section 1(1), which provides:

Where a false or misleading statement about a prescribed matter is made in the course of an estate agency business or a property development business, otherwise than in providing conveyancing services, the person by whom the business is carried on shall be guilty of an offence under this section.

(a) *Statement*

The statutory definition of "statement", contained in section 1(5)(c), is one of considerable breadth. Not only does it extend to written and spoken words (so as to catch both agents' sales particulars and their oral answers to purchasers' enquiries), it also includes pictures.[2] Indeed, the definition specifically refers to "any other method of signifying meaning", which would presumably cover such things as an inaccurate model of a new building, or a "show house" which gives a false impression of the standard of finish to be expected in other houses in the same development.

Notwithstanding the width of this provision, however, it should be emphasised that liability in all cases depends upon the making of something which can be described as a "statement". The Act does *not* impose any positive obligation of disclosure, even where an estate agent actually knows something detrimental about the property (eg that a previous survey has revealed serious defects).

---

1 Section 1(4) provides that contravention of the Act does not in itself give rise to any civil liability.
2 Eg an "artist's impression" of a new development, or a misleading photograph.

(b) *False or misleading*

Section 1(5)(a) provides that a false statement is one which is "false to a material degree", which means that utterly trivial inaccuracies will not be a source of liability. As to what will be regarded as "material", the Act gives no further guidance, but it can safely be assumed that this will take into account all the circumstances of the case, including such factors as the type of property involved and the class of purchaser (residential or commercial).

Of course, words or pictures which are literally true may still convey a wrong impression, and these will fall within the Act if they are "misleading". According to section 1(5)(b), this will occur where "what a reasonable person may be expected to infer from [a statement], or from any omission from it, is false". To this extent only, then, liability can arise from what is *not* said as well as what *is*. A claim that "the property enjoys extensive views over open country" may be perfectly true; but failure to mention the industrial estate which blocks the whole horizon on one side will render the whole statement a misleading one.

One particular way in which a statement can mislead is by being out of date. Under the law of misrepresentation, a person who makes a statement and then discovers it to be untrue is under a legal obligation to inform the person to whom it was made before any contract is entered into.[1] The Property Misdescriptions Act does not go so far, but there is no doubt that an estate agent who continues to issue sales particulars after discovering that they are inaccurate (either because of initial errors or because what they describe has changed) may be guilty of an offence.

(c) *Prescribed matter*

The 1991 Act applies only where a statement is made about a "prescribed matter", and this is defined by section 1(5)(d) to mean "any matter relating to land which is specified in an order made by the Secretary of State". The only such order so far issued, the Property Misdescriptions (Specified Matters) Order 1992, contains a list of 33 items which provides virtually comprehensive coverage of both the physical and the legal aspects of property being sold. As to the former, the order mentions such matters as measurements

---

1 See *With* v *O'Flanagan* [1936] Ch 575.

or sizes, form of construction, condition, environment and survey results. Examples of the latter include lease terms, rent, service charges, rates, easements and planning matters. Other matters which are specified, but which do not fall clearly into either of the above categories, include the property's age and history, its price and the length of time it has been on the market.

(d) *Disclaimers*

Although the Property Misdescriptions Act makes no explicit reference to disclaimer clauses, they are worth a separate mention, if only because such clauses, in one form or another, are routinely found in estate agents' particulars of sale. The Act's reticence on this matter means that it will be left to the courts to determine the extent, if any, to which these clauses may serve to exclude or restrict liability. As to what they are likely to decide, it may be confidently asserted that an exemption clause of the "no liability is accepted" kind will be of no effect whatsoever; it is simply not possible to deny one's liability for criminal offences in this way.

As to those "disclaimers" which do not seek in so many words to deny responsibility, but attempt rather to draw the sting from what would otherwise be a false or misleading statement, the legal position is less clear. Estate agents' particulars have long carried paragraphs stating, for instance, that all statements contained therein are matters of opinion only, or that all measurements are mere approximations, or that accuracy cannot be guaranteed. Can it be said that, by denying any intention on the agent's part to assert positive facts, they effectively prevent anything in those particulars from constituting a "false or misleading statement"?

The answer to this question, it is tentatively suggested, is that matters which are essentially factual in their nature cannot be turned into matters of mere opinion by a statement that this is all they are. Nor will a refusal to "guarantee accuracy" mean that a court is precluded from holding a person liable for making an inaccurate statement.[1] Moreover, even if such terms might prove useful in relation to statements which truly *are* matters of opinion (such as a property's decorative state) or approximations (such as the area of an irregularly shaped garden), they can never amount to a licence to commit fraud. Thus, for example, an estate agent

---

1 See *May* v *Vincent* [1991] 1 EGLR 27: p 413.

who has accurate measurements of a property cannot systematically exaggerate them under cover of a clause which states that they are mere approximations.

Even within their potential field of operation, it appears likely that disclaimers, to be effective, will be required to satisfy the tests laid down by the courts in cases arising under the Trade Descriptions Act 1968. In short, the question to be asked is whether the effect of a false or misleading statement on the mind of the person to whom it is made has been neutralised by an express disclaimer or contradiction of its message. As explained in the leading case of *Norman* v *Bennett*:[1] "To be effective any such disclaimer must be as bold, precise and compelling as the trade description itself and must be as effectively brought to the notice of any person to whom the goods may be supplied. In other words, the disclaimer must equal the trade description in the extent to which it is likely to get home to anyone interested in receiving the goods."

(e) *Incidence of liability*

Interestingly, it is not the *making* of a false or misleading statement which is defined as an offence under the 1991 Act. Instead, section 1(1) provides that, where an offending statement is made in the course of an estate agency or property development business, it is the person by whom that business is carried on who is guilty of an offence. This policy of targeting principals is seen further in section 4(1), which provides that, where the business in question is carried on by a company, liability also attaches to any actual or *de facto* director, manager, secretary or other similar officer who has contributed by "connivance or consent" to the commission of the offence.

The only other person who may be prosecuted under the Act is an employee through whose act or default an offending statement is made.[2] Where an employee is at fault in this way, section 1(2) makes clear that proceedings may be brought against the employee, whether or not the employer is also prosecuted.

---

1 [1974] 3 All ER 351 at p 354, *per* Lord Widgery CJ.
2 Again the wording may impose liability, not only for making a statement, but also for causing one to be made (eg by failing to check sales particulars before publication).

3   The defence of due diligence

The criminal offence created by section 1 of the Property Misdescriptions Act 1991 is in principle one of strict liability, in that the prosecution is not required to prove either intent to deceive or even any negligence on the part of the defendant. However, section 2(1) provides that it shall be a defence for a person prosecuted "to show that he took all reasonable steps and exercised all due diligence to avoid committing the offence".[1]

There are strong echoes here of the defence under section 24 of the Trade Descriptions Act 1968 and, while the analogy cannot be pushed too far (for example because the earlier provision contains some additional elements), there is reason to suppose that the courts will pay attention to cases decided under the 1968 Act when called upon to interpret the new provision. Assuming that this is indeed the case, it is likely that "reasonable steps" and "due diligence" will be treated as cumulative requirements and, moreover, as demanding evidence that the defendant has done something positive to avoid the commission of an offence.

As a general principle, the case law[2] suggests that a defendant wishing to use this defence must prove that a system was set up to avoid contravention of the statute and that this system was subjected to periodic checks to see that it was working satisfactorily. In the estate agency context, such a "system" might involve such things as training staff on how to respond to enquiries, ensuring that sales particulars are always checked before printing, and so on. In this connection it should be noted that it is not enough for an employer merely to give instructions and assume that they will be carried out.[3] However, an employer *is* entitled to delegate responsibility for the firm's compliance system to employees at a senior (supervisory) level, provided that they are not so senior as to rank as the company's "alter ego".[4]

One aspect of the "due diligence" defence is singled out for separate treatment by the 1991 Act, presumably because it is the

---

1 The burden is clearly on the defendant, and will require proof on the balance of probabilities: *R v Carr-Briant* [1943] KB 607.
2 Which is collected in Parry & Rowell (eds), *Butterworths Trading and Consumer Law*, para 250 *et seq*.
3 *Aitchison v Reith and Anderson (Dingwall & Tain) Ltd* 1974 SLT 282: p 414.
4 See *Tesco Supermarkets Ltd v Nattrass* [1972] AC 153.

one which is most likely to arise in practice. This is the question of reliance by the defendant on information given by another person. Section 2(2) provides that, in order to rely on this as a defence against liability, the defendant must prove that reliance on the information was reasonable in all the circumstances. It is further explicitly stated that, in considering the "reasonableness" of reliance, three questions are of particular importance. These are:

i   what steps (if any) were taken to check the information;
ii   what steps (if any) might reasonably have been taken to check it; and
iii   whether there was any reason to disbelieve the information.

Section 2(3) and (4) make additional provision for the situation in which a defendant's plea of "due diligence" amounts in effect to placing the blame on someone else. If the defence involves an allegation that the offence is due to either the "act or default" of, or "reliance on information given by" another person, the defendant must serve notice on the prosecution, at least seven days before the trial, giving as much information as possible to help identify the person concerned.[1] It has further been held, in cases arising under the Trade Descriptions Act, that it is not sufficient for a defendant merely to name all employees and claim that the offence must have been caused by one of them; the defendant must go on to show that all reasonable steps have been taken to identify the culprit.[2]

4   Enforcement of the Act

The enforcement provisions of the Property Misdescriptions Act 1991, which are contained in section 3 and the Schedule to the Act, are based on those of the Trade Descriptions Act 1968. Enforcement of the Act is thus the duty of the trading standards departments of local authorities or, in Northern Ireland, of the Department of Economic Development's Trading Standards Branch.[3]

---

1 Whether that person can then be prosecuted depends on whether he or she comes within the Act, as a principal or employee of an estate agency or property development business.

2 *McGuire* v *Sittingbourne Co-operative Society* (1976) 140 JP 306.

3 However, all prosecutions in Scotland are initiated by the Procurator Fiscal.

The specific powers of investigation given to trading standards officers resemble those which may be used in investigating criminal offences under the Estate Agents Act 1979, although there are some important differences. Briefly, the powers (all of which are exercisable only by a duly authorised officer of an enforcement authority, only at a reasonable hour and only on production of credentials if demanded) are:

i   to enter premises (other than purely residential ones) and to inspect goods, for the purpose of ascertaining whether an offence has been committed.[1]

ii   on reasonable suspicion of an offence, to inspect books or documents, or a legible reproduction of information stored in other forms (eg in a computer) and to take copies.

iii   on reasonable belief[2] that they are required as evidence in a prosecution, to seize and detain any books or documents.

It should be emphasised that the power of entry under this Act does not extend to premises used only as a dwelling, even where an alleged offence concerns a misdescription of that dwelling. Indeed, the power is more restrictive than that contained in the Estate Agents Act, in that, even where a warrant is issued (eg to justify an entry by force), this cannot extend to purely private premises.

It is a criminal offence to obstruct an authorised officer who is exercising any of the statutory powers mentioned above or, in some circumstances, to fail to give the officer adequate assistance in the exercise of those powers.

B Accommodation Agencies Act 1953

This Act, which was originally passed as a short-term measure and was due to expire at the end of 1957, was thereafter renewed on an annual basis and was eventually made permanent.[3] None the less, although contraventions of the Act are widespread, these

---

1 Note that, in contrast to the Estate Agents Act, there is no requirement of reasonable suspicion; these powers can be exercised in order to carry out spot checks.

2 This denotes something more than mere suspicion of an offence.

3 Expiring Laws (Continuance) Act 1969, section 1.

have given rise to legal proceedings on remarkably few occasions. Indeed, it appears that, as Edmund Davies LJ has said: "The provisions of the 1953 Act are not nearly as well known as they ought to be."[1]

As a general rule, of course, an estate agent is at liberty to act either for a vendor/landlord or for a purchaser/tenant and, in either case, to charge the appropriate commission. The only restriction placed upon the agent by the general law is not to act for both sides. The effect of the Accommodation Agencies Act is to place a specific limitation upon an agent's right to act on behalf of a prospective tenant.

Section 1 of the 1953 provides as follows:

(1) Subject to the provisions of this section, any person who, during the continuance in force of this Act,

(a) demands or accepts payment of any sum of money in consideration of registering, or undertaking to register, the requirements of any person seeking the tenancy of a house;

(b) demands or accepts payment of any sum of money in consideration of supplying, or undertaking to supply, to any person addresses or other particulars of houses to let . . . shall be guilty of an offence.[2]

In *McInnes* v *Clarke*[3] the appellant's business was that of finding furnished accommodation for people, in return for a fee equal to one week's rent of the premises taken. His practice was to ask clients how much they were willing to pay as a weekly rent and to take a deposit of approximately half this amount, with an agreement to pay the balance when accommodation was found. The client then received a list of addresses which was revised daily. A client who accepted one of the properties on the list would be asked to pay the balance of one week's rent. If a client did not find accommodation, the deposit would be refunded on demand. The appellant, who had been convicted on two counts of contravening section 1(1)(b) of the Accommodation Agencies Act, appealed to the Divisional Court of Queen's Bench, arguing that the Act was designed to prevent persons being charged for a list of addresses

---

1 *Crouch & Lees* v *Haridas* [1971] 3 All ER 172 at p176.
2 The penalties on summary conviction are a fine of up to one hundred pounds or imprisonment of up to three months, or both: section 1(5).
3 [1955] 1 All ER 346.

which might be totally worthless; it did not apply where, as here, the client would ultimately have to pay only in the event of obtaining the desired accommodation.

The Divisional Court dismissed the appeal and held that there had been a clear breach of the Act. Lord Goddard CJ said:

> The statute might have made some provision for the case where a man is honestly conducting a business, but it has not; what it says is, that he must not demand or accept payment of any sum of money in consideration of supplying, or undertaking to supply, to any person addresses or other particulars of houses to let. That is what the appellant did. That was why he received the deposit, and the deposit was to be treated as part payment if the person took one of the houses on the list supplied.

The principle laid down in *McInnes* v *Clarke* led to the conviction of another agent in *Lawrence* v *Sinclair-Taylor*[1] where, once again, a client's deposit could be refunded if no satisfactory accommodation was found. The agent in this case argued that the deposit was in respect of "services rendered", namely, arranging for the client to view the property and negotiating with the landlord; the Divisional Court, however, agreed with the stipendiary magistrate that the "substantial consideration" for this payment was supplying the client with the address in question.

In *Saunders* v *Soper*[2] the House of Lords had its first opportunity to consider the effects of the Act. In that case the practice of the agent, who appealed against two convictions, was not to demand a deposit, but to ask clients to sign an agreement under which a fee would become payable if and when they took a tenancy of accommodation found for them by the agent. The House of Lords, while approving the decisions in the two previous cases, regarded them as different in an important respect; as Viscount Dilhorne pointed out:[3]

> As in my view it was not proved in this case that any payment was demanded or accepted for the supplying of an address and as it was proved that the payments were accepted or demanded not for that but for finding

---

1 (1973) 228 EG 1922.
2 [1975] AC 239.
3 At p246.

[the client] suitable accommodation and due only on her entering into a tenancy, in my opinion she was wrongly convicted.

Thus, it appears, an agent may legitimately charge for *finding* accommodation for a tenant who actually takes it, but may not demand a fee (even a returnable deposit) for merely supplying a prospective tenant with the address in the first place.

Apart from the criminal liability described above, a breach of the 1953 Act will also render the agency contract illegal. In consequence, the estate agent will forfeit any right to commission and, if money has already changed hands, the client is entitled to recover this. It should be noted that these principles remain valid, notwithstanding that the only reported case in which they have been considered[1] was overruled by the House of Lords in *Saunders* v *Soper* because it could not be distinguished on the facts.

C Control of Advertisements Regulations 1989

The display of advertisements is subject to planning controls under Part VIII of the Town and Country Planning Act 1990. Since an estate agent's "For Sale" board falls within the statutory definition of "advertisement", the erection of a board in principle requires a grant of planning permission. Such a situation would of course be unworkable, and the solution lies in the "deemed consent" provisions of section 222 of the Act. According to that section, planning permission is deemed to have been granted for the display of any advertisement, provided that it complies with regulations made under section 220.[2]

The relevant regulation[3] provides that planning permission is deemed to have been granted for the display of:

---

1 *Crouch & Lees* v *Haridas* [1971] 3 All ER 172, where the Court of Appeal rejected an estate agent's claim for commission on finding an unfurnished flat of which the client took a five-year lease.
2 If it does not, conviction for an offence under section 224(3) carries, on summary conviction, a fine not exceeding level 3 on the standard scale (currently £1,000: Criminal Justice Act 1991, section 17) plus £40 for each day the offence continues after conviction.
3 Town and Country Planning (Control of Advertisements) Regulations 1992 (SI 1992 No 666), regulation 6, Sched 3 Part I.

An advertisement relating to the sale or letting, for residential, agricultural, industrial or commercial use or for development for such use, of the land or premises on which it is displayed.

There are, however, strict limitations on such matters as the size of a board or its lettering, and a board's positioning (including its projection from a building). It is further specifically provided that illumination is not permitted.

The "deemed consent" under the 1992 regulations is designed to permit the advertisement of the property, not the estate agent. Consequently, while "For Sale" boards are allowed, "Sold" boards are not. However, an estate agent is specifically permitted to add to an existing board "a statement that a sale or letting has been agreed, or that the land or premises have been sold or let, subject to contract", provided in any case that "any such advertisement shall be removed within 14 days after the sale is completed or a tenancy is granted".

It should be noted that the regulations limit permission to the display of one advertisement (consisting of a single board or two joined boards). Under a previous set of regulations, it was argued that an agent who quite lawfully put up a board at a client's property could become guilty of a criminal offence without knowing it if a second agent also erected a board. That argument, which convinced the Queen's Bench Divisional Court, was ultimately rejected by the House of Lords in *Porter* v *Honey*, on the basis that Parliament could not have intended that criminal liability might arise in this way.[1] In any event, the 1992 regulations put the matter beyond doubt by providing specifically that "where more than one such advertisement is displayed, the first to be displayed shall be taken to be the one permitted".

D Solicitors Act 1974

Section 22 of the Solicitors Act 1974 is the most recent of a line of statutory provisions in substantially the same form originating in the Stamp Act 1804, the general object of which is to give the legal profession a monopoly in the carrying out of conveyancing work in return for payment.

---

1 [1988] 3 All ER 1045.

Section 22(1) provides:

[A]ny unqualified person who directly or indirectly–
  (a) draws or prepares any instrument of transfer or charge for the
      purposes of the Land Registration Act 1925, or makes any application
      or lodges any document for registration under the Act at the registry,
      or
  (b) draws or prepares any other instrument relating to real or personal
      estate, or any legal proceeding,
shall, unless he proves that the act was not done for or in expectation of
any fee, gain or reward, be guilty of an offence and liable on summary
conviction to a fine not exceeding level 3 on the standard scale.[1]

"Unqualified" for this purpose means anyone who is not a solicitor,
although there are a few exemptions, of which the most important
are barristers, notaries public[2] and licensed conveyancers.[3]

As originally enacted, the prohibition in this section was limited by
its definition of "instrument" as including only agreements made by
deed. In relation to the transfer of freehold property, this meant that
an unqualified person such as an estate agent would be guilty of a
criminal offence in preparing a deed of conveyance, but could
legitimately draw up a contract of sale. However, this opening was
firmly closed by an amendment introduced in 1985,[4] as a result of
which section 22(3) now provides:

For the purposes of subsection (1)(b), "instrument" includes a contract for
the sale or other disposition of land (except a contract to grant such a lease
as is referred to in section 54(2) of the Law of Property Act 1925 (short
leases)), but does not include –
...
(b) an agreement not intended to be executed as a deed other than a
contract that is included by virtue of the preceding provisions of this
subsection.

In relation to the creation of leases, estate agents have attempted
to evade prosecution under earlier statutes by preparing documents
but not affixing a seal to them. However, such attempts have mostly

---

1 Currently £1,000: Criminal Justice Act 1991, section 17.
2 Section 22(2).
3 Administration of Justice Act 1985, section 11(4).
4 Administration of Justice Act 1985, section 6(4).

proved ineffective, as illustrated by the case of *Harte* v *Williams*.[1] An estate agent there, acting on behalf of a landlord, found a person willing to take a 21-year lease of property. The agent then offered to prepare the lease on behalf of the prospective tenant, in order to save him the expense of a solicitor's fee. When this offer was accepted, the estate agent filled in a standard-form document commonly used by solicitors and had a number of copies made; no seal, however, was affixed, although the law required one for a lease of this length. When the agent charged a small fee for this service of "preparing copy lease", he was convicted of an offence under the Stamp Act 1891, section 44. On appeal to a Divisional Court of King's Bench, it was strongly argued that the document in question was "an agreement under hand only" (ie not under seal) but a majority of the court rejected this, preferring the view that "an agreement under hand only means an instrument valid and intended to operate in law as such". What the agent had prepared did not satisfy this definition; it was merely a lease which was void for the lack of a seal.

Of course, there are some leases which may be validly created without using a deed and, where this is so, an estate agent may lawfully charge for preparing the relevant document. It is for this reason that section 22(3) refers specifically to section 54(2) of the Law of Property Act 1925, under which a deed is not required for the creation of a lease which "takes effect in possession for a term not exceeding three years (whether or not the lessee is given power to extend the term) at the best rent which can be obtained without taking a fine".

A periodic tenancy (monthly, yearly, etc) is within this definition, since it may well not last for three years;[2] however, a lease for more than three years must be made by deed, notwithstanding that it may be determined at an earlier date. In *Kushner* v *Law Society*[3] an estate agent, in return for a fee from the tenant, drew up a document which purported to grant him the tenancy of a flat for 14 years, with a provision that the tenant might terminate the agreement by notice at the end of any year. A Divisional Court of King's Bench unanimously held that the estate agent was rightly

1 [1934] 1 KB 201.
2 *Re Knight, ex parte Voisey* (1882) 21 ChD 442.
3 [1952] 1 KB 264.

convicted of an offence under the Solicitors Act 1932, section 47; since the lease was one which could only validly be made under seal, the case was identical to that of *Harte* v *Williams*. As Lord Goddard CJ said:[1]

The offence consists not in procuring the execution of a document, but in drawing or preparing it ... A person who draws or prepares a document which if it is to be a valid document, must have a seal on it at the time of execution, commits an offence; because he has drawn the deed he commits the offence none the less although the document when executed does not have a seal put upon it.

---

1 At p271.

CHAPTER 8

Auctioneers' authority

A Authority to sell

Unlike an estate agent, whose primary function is merely to introduce a prospective purchaser to the client, an auctioneer is normally employed to bring about a legally binding contract for the sale of land or goods. In the vast majority of cases, therefore, an auctioneer will be specifically instructed to sell the vendor's property. However, this chapter is mainly concerned, not with the auctioneer's express authority, but with the extent to which the principal may be bound in the absence of such express instructions. Not surprisingly, we find that authority to carry out a sale is implicit in the nature of the profession. As Lord Ellenborough CJ has said:[1]

If the principal send his commodity to a place, where it is the ordinary business of the person to whom it is confided to sell, it must be intended that the commodity was sent thither for the purpose of sale ... If one send goods to an auction-room, can it be supposed that he sent them thither merely for safe custody? Where the commodity is sent in such a way and to such a place as to exhibit an apparent purpose of sale, the principal will be bound, and the purchaser safe.

In the situation here envisaged, a purchaser will obtain good title, not only where nothing has been said to the auctioneer, but even where the owner of the goods has strictly forbidden a sale. The auctioneer, however, will of course be liable to the owner for any disobedience of express instructions.

1 Sale by private treaty

It is important to note that implied authority to sell (and, for that matter, any express authority which is given in general terms) is not

---

1 *Pickering* v *Busk* (1812) 15 East 38 at p43.

unlimited in scope. The auctioneer is authorised to carry out a sale in accordance with normal trade practice, having regard to the subject-matter of the sale. In particular, an auctioneer has no implied authority to sell by private treaty; unless express instructions to the contrary are given, the sale must be by auction. In *Daniel* v *Adams*[1] the defendant and his wife, who were joint owners of two houses, instructed their steward to sell these by public auction. Two days later, the defendant wrote to the steward, stating that he would not accept less than £120 for the property. The steward, believing that he was authorised to sell, agreed to sell the houses to the plaintiff for £150. It was held that the wife, who had not joined in writing the letter, could only be bound by acts within the steward's original authority, which did not include a private sale.

The principle embodied in this case was applied to an auctioneer as such in *Marsh* v *Jelf*[2] where the plaintiff auctioneer, who had been employed to sell the defendant's property, bought it in at the reserve price. One month later, the property was sold to a person who had attended the auction and the auctioneer claimed commission for negotiating the sale. It was held that, even if this private sale had been negotiated by the auctioneer (and not, as the defendant contended, by his solicitor) he would not be entitled to any payment for this act, since it lay outside the scope of his authority. Moreover, the auctioneer was not permitted to bring evidence of a custom among auctioneers to charge commission in such cases, since a trade custom of this type does not bind the general public.

Although it is clear from the foregoing that the mere placing of property in the hands of an auctioneer does not impliedly authorise a sale other than by auction, a wider authority is frequently contained in the client's instructions[3] and, indeed, the circumstances of a particular case may show that the normal principle has been displaced. In *Else* v *Barnard*[4] certain property was ordered by the court to be sold by auction in two lots. The auctioneer was given a sealed envelope containing a reserve price,

---

1 (1764) Ambl 495.
2 (1862) 3 F&F 234.
3 See, for example, *Green* v *Bartlett* (1863) 14 CBNS 681, where the auctioneer was authorised to sell "by public auction or otherwise".
4 (1860) 28 Beav 228.

which he was to open at the time of the sale. In the event of bidding failing to reach the reserve, the auctioneer was instructed merely to buy it in without revealing the reserve price. The first lot was bought in in this way and the second lot was knocked down to a Mr Courtauld, who thereupon discovered from the auctioneer's clerk the amount of the secret reserve upon lot 1 and offered this sum to the auctioneer, who was still on the rostrum. The auctioneer agreed and Courtauld signed a bidding paper for the two lots. Courtauld later regretted his action, but the court held him bound by the contract. As Sir John Romilly MR pointed out, the bidding paper clearly treated this as a sale by auction; further, there was no reason why the purchaser should not agree to pay the reserve price, despite the curious secrecy over the figure.

A similar conclusion was reached in *Bousfield* v *Hodges*,[1] where a legal action concerning a deceased person's estate was compromised on the terms that it should be sold by public auction and the proceeds divided. The auction having proved abortive, the auctioneer sold privately for the amount of the reserve price to the defendant, who later refused to proceed with the purchase, claiming that the auctioneer had no authority to sell by private treaty. It was held, however, that the clear intention of the vendors was to sell, provided only that the reserve price was obtained; consequently the defendant was bound to complete.

In both *Else* v *Barnard* and *Bousfield* v *Hodges*, where private sales were held to have been impliedly authorised, the vendors raised no objection to what had been done on their behalf; indeed, in each case it was the vendor who sought to enforce the sale. These two cases might equally therefore have turned upon a ratification by the vendor of an unauthorised act by the auctioneer. However, in *Garnier* v *Bruntlett*,[2] where an auctioneer sold a farm privately at its reserve price immediately after an abortive auction, it was the clients who sought to resile. After a detailed consideration of the evidence, Whitford J concluded that the clients' instructions, as communicated through their solicitors to the auctioneer, were that the property should be *sold*; the method of sale was of secondary importance. As a result, the sale was held to be binding. Nevertheless, the decision was a close one, and it is suggested that

1 (1863) 33 Beav 90.
2 (1974) 236 EG 867.

a prudent auctioneer should always obtain express authorisation from the client before entering into a private contract of sale.

2 Terms of sale

A contract of sale entered into at auction must, if it is to be enforced against the vendor, be in accordance with the terms which the vendor has laid down.[1] Thus, it appears, the auctioneer has no implied authority to vary those terms.[2] In *Moore* v *Khan-Ghauri*[3] a purchaser claimed to have been promised by the auctioneer that the fall of the hammer would be merely conditional, and that he would be given the opportunity to inspect the property. The Court of Appeal swiftly rejected this claim, holding that an auctioneer would have no authority to bind the vendor by such an undertaking.

One situation in which this problem surfaces is where inaccuracies in the printed sale particulars are corrected by the auctioneer from the rostrum. In *Manser* v *Back*,[4] for example, the defendant's property was to be sold by auction. The day before the sale was due, it was discovered that the printed particulars and conditions of sale did not reserve to the vendor a right of way, as had been intended. A number of copies were therefore altered and the auctioneer read out the alteration before the bidding started. The plaintiff, who had an unaltered copy of the particulars and who did not hear the alteration, successfully bid for the property. The auctioneer then inadvertently drew up and signed a memorandum of the sale upon an unaltered copy of the particulars. The plaintiff claimed specific performance of the agreement as it appeared in writing (ie with no right of way reserved); this claim, however, was rejected by Wigram V-C, who said that the auctioneer's authority to sell according to the original particulars had clearly been revoked by the vendor and: "The revocation of the authority of the auctioneer is operative *per se*, and therefore ... is binding upon persons not parties to or conusant of it."

---

1 See the judgment of Hullock B in *Jones* v *Nanney* (1824) 13 Price 76 at p110.
2 In *D & M Trailers (Halifax) Ltd* v *Stirling* [1978] RTR 468, where an auctioneer sold a vehicle by private treaty after an auction, it was held by the Court of Appeal that an exemption clause which *would* have formed part of the contract of sale at auction was *not* incorporated into the private sale. However, the vendors did not attempt to argue that this rendered the entire sale unauthorised.
3 [1991] 2 EGLR 9.
4 (1848) 6 Hare 443.

This decision was followed in *Re Hare and O'More's Contract*,[1] where the particulars of sale contained an inaccuracy which was orally corrected by the auctioneer. It was held that, even if the purchaser had not heard the correction (and the evidence on this point was conflicting), it would be inequitable to compel the vendor to complete the sale, since the purchaser would then have to be allowed compensation in respect of the error.

These two decisions are not, it is submitted, conclusive upon the question of the auctioneer's implied authority. Both were actions for specific performance of a contract and in each case the court, in the exercise of its equitable discretion, refused to grant a decree, a refusal which could be justified on the simple ground of hardship to the defendant. Had these purchasers sued for damages (a common law remedy) the courts' discretion would have been removed; a definite decision would then have been necessary as to whether a purchaser is entitled to assume that an auctioneer has authority to sell in accordance with the published particulars and conditions of sale.

3 Sale "without reserve"

An important question, though one which has not yet been satisfactorily answered by the courts, is whether an auctioneer's implied authority extends to selling property "without reserve"; if it does, then a purchaser to whom a lot is inadvertently knocked down at less than the reserve price is entitled to keep it. Some guidance on this matter may be obtained from the old case of *Bexwell* v *Christie*,[2] in which the defendant auctioneer was employed to sell "the goods and effects of a gentleman deceased, at his house in the country, by order of the executor". The conditions of sale stipulated "that the goods should be sold to the best bidder". The plaintiff, who had no other connection with this sale, sent a horse to the auctioneer, asking him to include it in the sale and instructing him not to let it go for less than £15. The defendant knocked down the horse for less than this sum and, when sued by the plaintiff for disobeying instructions, argued that to have bid on the vendor's behalf would, in the light of the conditions of sale, have been a fraud on those bidding at the sale.

1 [1901] 1 Ch 93.
2 (1776) 1 Cowp 395.

This argument was accepted by the Court of King's Bench, which held that the vendor's instruction, being unlawful, was not binding on the auctioneer. Lord Mansfield CJ went on to remark that the vendor might validly have achieved his object by instructing the auctioneer to put the horse up at the relevant price; since, however, he did not consider the effect in such a case of the auctioneer failing to do so, it is not clear whether such an instruction would need to be made public.

The decision in *Bexwell* v *Christie* suggests that the interests of persons bidding at an auction are to be considered when interpreting the auctioneer's instructions, and this judicial attitude is also revealed in the case of *Rainbow* v *Howkins*.[1] The defendant there was instructed to sell a pony at auction for not less than £25; forgetting this instruction, however, the defendant stated that the sale was "without reserve" and duly knocked down the pony to the plaintiff for 15 guineas. Almost immediately the defendant realised this mistake and, pointing it out to the plaintiff and refusing to sign a memorandum of sale, he put the pony up again and bought it in for seventeen guineas. The plaintiff claimed delivery of the pony from the auctioneer, in accordance with the contract of sale which was made at the fall of the hammer; alternatively, the plaintiff claimed damages for breach of the auctioneer's warranty of authority to sell at 15 guineas. A Divisional Court of King's Bench rejected the first claim, on the ground that such an action required written evidence to satisfy section 4 of the Sale of Goods Act 1893.[2] The second claim also failed because there was no breach of warranty of authority; knocking down the pony at 15 guineas was (in the court's view) an authorised act. As Kennedy J said:[3]

The hammer had fallen, and as between the plaintiff as the highest bidder and the auctioneer's principal the right of the plaintiff could not have been defeated by the principal shewing that the auctioneer was authorised by him to sell only subject to a reserved price. The defendant, the auctioneer, had an apparent authority, which his principal, if he had been sued by the plaintiff, would not have been allowed in point of law to repudiate, after a sale had been concluded by the hammer being knocked down, upon the

---

1 [1904] 2 KB 322.
2 Since repealed by the Law Reform (Enforcement of Contracts) Act 1954, section 2.
3 At p326.

ground that his private instructions had been contravened by the auctioneer in selling without reserve.

Thus the auctioneer had made a contract, albeit one which could not be enforced, between the vendor and the purchaser. The question whether the auctioneer might owe an independent duty to the highest bidder to sign a memorandum was expressly left open by the court.[1]

We shall return shortly to this question of written evidence, which was so important in *Rainbow* v *Howkins*. First, however, we must turn our attention to the criticism directed at that decision in the later case of *McManus* v *Fortescue*,[2] the facts of which closely resemble those of *Rainbow* v *Howkins*, but with one crucial distinction. In *McManus* v *Fortescue* one of the conditions of sale was that "each lot will be offered subject to a reserve price". Once again, the auctioneer knocked down the property below the reserve price and, once again, he realised his mistake in time to avoid signing a memorandum of the sale. The plaintiff, to whom the property had been knocked down, claimed that either he had a contract with the vendor which the auctioneer was obliged to render enforceable by signing a memorandum, or he had no contract, in which case the auctioneer was liable for breach of warranty of authority. The Court of Appeal rejected both these claims, holding that where a sale takes place with notice to all concerned that it is subject to a reserve "every bid, including the final one, and the acceptance of that final bid indicated by the fall of the hammer, is conditional"[3] on the reserve being reached. Thus, both the alleged contract, and the auctioneer's alleged warranty that he had authority to make it, were rendered ineffective by the failure of the condition.[4]

It might be thought that these two cases are sufficiently distinguishable to coexist in peaceful harmony and, indeed, Collins MR in *McManus* v *Fortescue* could see no conflict between them. However, Fletcher Moulton LJ based his judgment upon a rather wider ground:[5]

---

1 This question is considered at p 310.
2 [1907] 2 KB 1.
3 At p7, *per* Fletcher Moulton LJ.
4 The decision on the latter point is criticised at p 312.
5 At p6.

A principal, therefore, who gives authority to an auctioneer to sell subject to a reserve price gives no power to the auctioneer, either expressly or impliedly, to accept a less price. The case of *Rainbow* v *Howkins*, so far as it is inconsistent with this view, cannot be regarded as in harmony with well-established principles. It is admitted in this case that the price offered by the bid of the plaintiff was lower than the reserve price. The auctioneer could not effectively accept such a bid, because he could not make a contract so as to bind his principal to accept less than the reserve price.

Although these remarks are, it is submitted, unnecessary for the decision, which can easily be justified on the basis of the publication of the condition relating to reserves, it cannot be denied that they cast some doubts upon the reliance which can now be placed on *Rainbow* v *Howkins*.

McManus v *Fortescue* makes it clear that, where the existence of a reserve is disclosed by the conditions of sale, no action will lie against a vendor in respect of property mistakenly knocked down at a lower price. Indeed, this will apply even where the conditions state merely that there *may* be reserves; this information is sufficient to put bidders on inquiry, and to render their bids conditional upon the reserve price (if any) having been reached. In *Fay* v *Miller, Wilkins & Co*[1] the defendants, a firm of auctioneers, were instructed to sell a certain house. The conditions of sale reserved to the vendor the right to fix a reserve price and a figure of £750 was stipulated by the vendor. The auctioneers, however, inadvertently knocked the property down to the plaintiff for £600 and signed a memorandum "ratifying" the sale which the Court of Appeal held was sufficient to satisfy section 40 of the Law of Property Act 1925.[2] It was held that the vendor was not bound by the contract for, having received notice of the possibility of a reserve being fixed, "the purchaser was put on inquiry, and if she chose to bid without knowing whether or not there was a reserve price, the risk was hers and she could not hold the vendor bound if in fact there was a reserve price which exceeded the amount of her bid".[3] However, the disappointed purchaser was not completely without remedy, being awarded damages against the auctioneers for breach of

---

1 [1941] Ch 360.
2 Since repealed by the Law of Property (Miscellaneous Provisions) Act 1989, sections 2, 4 and Schedule 2: see p 276.
3 At p365, *per* Lord Greene MR.

warranty of authority to sell.[1] The auctioneers' argument (based on *McManus* v *Fortescue*) that everything was conditional, was rejected by the Court of Appeal, since "a memorandum was actually signed by the auctioneers and it is impossible to treat the condition as applying after that was done".[2] As Clauson LJ said:[3] "The contract is a clear contract for a sale for £600, and, when read with the conditions, it appears to imply that the reserve, if any, is not greater than £600."

It seems, then, beyond dispute that a purchaser who has notice of the existence or possible existence of a reserve price can have no action against the vendor if the auctioneer mistakenly knocks the property down at a lower price. This is because the information which the purchaser has is sufficient to override any implied authority on the part of the auctioneer to sell to the highest bidder at whatever price. However, the original question, whether an auctioneer has such implied authority in the absence of any express conditions as to reserves, remains unanswered, although a number of comments may be made upon it.

As we have seen, the plaintiff in *Rainbow* v *Howkins*[4] could not have succeeded in an action against the vendor of the pony, due to the absence of satisfactory written evidence of the contract of sale. This factor enabled the court to say, in effect: "The agent is not liable, for he has procured a valid contract between his principal and the highest bidder; it is, unfortunately for the highest bidder, not enforceable, but that is a different matter."[5] However, this rather convenient formulation is no longer available to the courts in such cases, for written evidence is no longer required for the enforceability of either a sale of goods[6] or a sale of land at public auction.[7] Thus, if the view of Kennedy J[8] is correct, the fall of the hammer would be sufficient to bind the vendor. Of course, an

---

1 The auctioneers' liability is discussed in more detail at p 312.
2 At p364, *per* Lord Greene MR.
3 At p367.
4 [1904] 2 KB 322.
5 See Kennedy J, at p326.
6 Law Reform (Enforcement of Contracts) Act 1954, section 2, repealing the Sale of Goods Act 1893, section 4.
7 Law of Property (Miscellaneous Provisions) Act 1989, sections 2, 4 and Schedule 2, repealing the Law of Property Act 1925, section 40.
8 p271.

auctioneer in such a case who contravened an express direction from the client would be liable in damages for any loss suffered.

Should a future court be thus compelled firmly to grasp the nettle, there is, it is submitted, another way in which the vendor's liability can be justified, at least as far as chattel sales are concerned. As we have seen,[1] a "mercantile agent" (as defined by the Factors Act 1889) who is in possession of goods with the consent of their owner is empowered to pass good title to a third party, notwithstanding any lack of express authority to dispose of the goods. Although the matter does not appear to have come before the courts, there seems no reason to doubt that an auctioneer who is in possession of goods for sale fulfils the definition of a "mercantile agent". If this is so, then a sale by the auctioneer would pass good title to a purchaser, provided of course that the purchaser had no notice of the auctioneer's lack of authority.[2]

There is, however, one hurdle to be cleared if this line of argument is to be accepted. The disposition, to be binding upon the owner of goods, must be made by the mercantile agent "when acting in the ordinary course of business of a mercantile agent".[3] It must therefore be established that a sale "without reserve" is a sale "in the ordinary course of business" and, although this seems at least arguable, the following words of Fletcher Moulton LJ should be borne in mind: "An auctioneer is as frequently employed to sell subject to a reserve as without one, and indeed in certain markets it may be said to be the more usual practice."[4]

B Authority to sign a memorandum

Until recently the law, while permitting a contract for the sale of land to be *created* by word of mouth or even by conduct, none the less regarded such a contract as *unenforceable* in court unless and until there was written evidence of its terms.[5] Such evidence might

---

1 p25.
2 The principles in *McManus* v *Fortescue* and *Fay* v *Miller, Wilkins & Co* would not, therefore, be affected, since the conditions of sale would be sufficient to fix all bidders with notice of the auctioneer's limited authority.
3 Factors Act 1889, section 2(1).
4 *McManus* v *Fortescue* [1907] 2 KB 1 at p6.
5 Law of Property Act 1925, section 40.

take a variety of forms, but an important requirement was that the document which was alleged to constitute a "note or memorandum" of the sale must be signed by the party against whom enforcement was sought, or by that party's duly authorised agent. Not surprisingly, perhaps, in the context of sales by auction it was consistently held that an auctioneer had implied authority to sign a memorandum as agent for the vendor, and thereby render the sale enforceable by the highest bidder.[1] Furthermore, the courts treated this implied authority as irrevocable once the hammer had fallen, so as to prevent a client from escaping from the contract by withdrawing the auctioneer's authority to sign a memorandum of the sale.[2]

While these legal principles no doubt remain valid in those jurisdictions where section 40 or its equivalent still applies, their relevance in England and Wales has been effectively negated by section 2 of the Law of Property (Miscellaneous Provisions) Act 1989.[3] That statutory provision, which repealed section 40 of the Law of Property Act 1925 and replaced it with a requirement that contracts for the sale of land should actually be *made* in writing, specifically excluded from its operation any "contract made in the course of a public auction".[4] In consequence, the contract which comes into existence on the fall of the hammer is henceforth both binding and legally enforceable, and the question of a "note or memorandum" has ceased to be of significance.

C Authority to receive payment

1 General

We have already seen that a contract of sale, made by an agent acting with authority, is binding upon the principal and operates to pass good title to the purchaser. Closely allied to this is the effect of payment to the agent under such a contract. The question to be answered is this: does payment to the agent discharge the purchaser's obligation or (if the money goes astray) can the purchaser be made to pay the vendor direct? As is so often the

---

1 See, for example, *Beer* v *London and Paris Hotel Co* (1875) LR 20 Eq 412.
2 *Day* v *Wells* (1861) 30 Beav 220 at p224.
3 In force from September 27 1989: section 5.
4 Section 2(5)(b). The Act does not further define what is meant by a "public auction".

case in agency transactions, the answer to this question depends on the extent of the agent's authority, whether express or implied: if the agent was authorised by the principal to receive payment, the purchaser's debt is discharged; if not, the purchaser can be forced to pay the principal again.

It might be thought that an implied authority to receive payment of the purchase price would be found wherever an agent had authority to make a contract of sale and, indeed, this was the early view of the courts. In 1698, Lord Holt CJ was reported as saying:[1] "He who has power to sell, has power to receive the money." Similar sentiments were expressed by Lord Tenterden CJ in *Capel* v *Thornton*:[2] "If he, as their agent, had authority to sell goods, so had he (in the absence of advice to the contrary), an implied authority to receive the proceeds of such sale." More recently, however, the courts have regarded these early cases as applying only to certain classes of agents, such as factors, and have stated the general rule to be quite the reverse. Thus, in *Drakeford* v *Piercey*,[3] Lush J said: "that an agent authorised to sell has as a necessary legal consequence authority to receive payment is a proposition utterly untenable and contrary to authority".

Of the cases so far mentioned, none dealt specifically with the case of an auctioneer and, indeed, there is an almost complete lack of authority on the point. This, it may be assumed, results from the use of conditions of sale to make express provision for payment of the price or a deposit to the vendor, the vendor's solicitor or the auctioneer. Where, as is almost always the case, the sale is subject to such conditions, the implied authority of the auctioneer is not material.

Should the question ever arise for decision, it may well receive a different answer according to whether the sale is of land or goods. As to the former, the case of *Mynn* v *Joliffe*[4] lends support to the view that an auctioneer in this respect has no greater authority the general run of agents. The plaintiff there, who had bought land at an auction and had paid a deposit to the auctioneer, sued the vendor to recover this money when the vendor failed to make a

1 *Anon* (1698) 12 Mod 230.
2 (1828) 3 C&P 352: see also *Howard* v *Chapman* (1831) 4 C&P 508.
3 (1866) 7 B&S 515 at p522; followed in *Butwick* v *Grant* [1924] 2 KB 483.
4 (1834) 1 Mood & R 326.

good title to the property. Counsel for the vendor objected that no evidence had been led to establish that the auctioneer had been expressly authorised to receive the deposit, and claimed that, in the absence of express authority, none could be implied. To this Littledale J replied: "I think that an agent employed to sell has no authority, as such, to receive payment."

As for sales of goods, an important point relates to the Factors Act 1889. It has already been suggested that an auctioneer who has actual possession of the goods to be sold fulfils the definition of a "mercantile agent" laid down by this Act; if this is so, then payment to the auctioneer will be a defence to an action by the vendor against the highest bidder for the price.[1]

2 Method of payment

As already stated, the authority of an auctioneer almost invariably derives from the conditions of sale, which commonly provide for payment to the auctioneer of the full purchase price of goods and the deposit on a sale of land. The fact that the auctioneer is so authorised, however, is not the end of the matter; in the absence of any express provision to the contrary, it is assumed that payment will be in cash, and a principal is not bound by an agent's acceptance of any alternative form of payment. As Lord Loughborough CJ said:[2]

In the common course of auctions, there is no delivery without actual payment; if it be otherwise, the auctioneer gives credit to the vendee, entirely at his own risk.

In *Brown* v *Staton*[3] the purchaser of goods told the auctioneer that the vendor owed him money, and the auctioneer allowed him to set this off against the price of the goods. The auctioneer was held liable to account to the vendor for the full sale price of the goods, and Bayley J said: "It cannot be contended that an agent has duly accounted unless he pays over the full price."

Thus an agent employed to sell goods is not authorised to pay off the principal's debts; nor, it seems, is such an agent entitled to take

---

1 Section 12(3).
2 *Williams* v *Millington* (1788) HBl 81 at p84.
3 (1816) 2 Chit 353.

payment in kind.[1] Most of the cases, however, in which the scope of an agent's authority has been considered have concerned payments made by some form of negotiable instrument, and the general rule has emerged that an agent has no implied authority to accept a cheque, bill of exchange, or IOU, at least as payment of the *full* price.[2] In *Earl of Ferrers* v *Robins*[3] the defendant was instructed to sell furniture belonging to the plaintiff by auction for ready money. He accepted a bill of exchange drawn by the purchaser on a third party, which the plaintiff subsequently rejected. The defendant, when sued for breach of his instructions, was forced to admit, not only this specific breach, but also more generally that the vendor was quite entitled to refuse the bill of exchange in payment.

In *Sykes* v *Giles*,[4] likewise, the actual decision turned on the express instructions given to the auctioneer. In that case the conditions governing a sale of growing beech timber laid down that the purchaser of each lot should pay a deposit of 10% to the auctioneer. The remainder of the price was to be paid by a stipulated date and security for the due performance of this obligation was to be given to the vendor. The defendant purchased a particular lot and paid a deposit. Later the auctioneers, who were in financial difficulties, induced the purchaser to give them a bill of exchange for the remainder of the price, which they then cashed. The vendor sued the purchaser for payment and succeeded. In the opinion of the court, the conditions of sale made it clear to all concerned that the balance of the purchase price was to be paid directly to the vendor, and not to an agent. "But even if the auctioneer had had authority to receive the remainder of the purchase-money, he had no authority to receive it in this way, by means of a bill of exchange. Cash payment was intended, and not a bill of exchange."[5]

---

1 In *Howard* v *Chapman* (1831) 4 C&P 508 the defendant, who had sought to discharge a debt by giving the plaintiff's agent a quantity of horse-hair, was held still liable to pay the plaintiff.

2 As to the payment of a deposit by cheque, see p 281.

3 (1835) 2 Cr M&R 152.

4 (1839) 5 M&W 645.

5 At p652, *per* Parke B.

In *Williams* v *Evans*[1] no express conditions obscured the application of the general rule. In that case a vendor, who suspected the auctioneer's solvency, told a purchaser not to pay any money to the auctioneer. The purchaser, however, had already given the auctioneer a bill of exchange for part of the price and this was duly honoured on being presented two days later. The question for decision was therefore whether, when the auctioneer accepted the bill of exchange, he had authority to do so. Blackburn J, delivering the judgment of the Court of Queen's Bench, had no doubts:[2]

I think, on the authority of *Sykes* v *Giles*, payment by a bill of exchange to an auctioneer is not a valid payment for the purpose of discharging the debtor.

The purchaser therefore remained liable to the vendor for the price.

The Irish case of *Hodgens* v *Keon*[3] illustrates the position of all three parties where a purchaser gives the auctioneer a bill of exchange. The defendant bid for leasehold property at an auction and, on being declared purchaser, claimed that he was bidding as agent for someone else. He gave the auctioneer an IOU for the deposit and in due course the auctioneer sued upon this. The defendant argued that, even if he paid the auctioneer, he would still remain liable to the vendor, who had not authorised his agent to accept payment in this way. The defendant was nevertheless held liable. Indeed, as emerged from the judgment of Palles CB, this was only one instance where one person might be liable to two, or might be entitled to sue two. It was said that if the vendor had authorised the auctioneer to receive an IOU, the vendor's sole action for the money would lie against the auctioneer, who would in turn be able to sue the purchaser. If, however, the auctioneer had no such authority, both auctioneer and purchaser would be liable to the vendor, and both vendor and auctioneer could sue the purchaser.

It should be noted that where a payment is made by cheque, and the cheque is duly honoured on presentation, it is the equivalent of

---

1 (1866) LR 1 QB 352.
2 At p355.
3 [1894] 2 IR 657.

a payment in cash.[1] However, it is only so treated from the moment at which it is honoured; thus, as we saw in *Williams* v *Evans*,[2] if the agent's authority to receive payment at all is revoked during the currency of a bill of exchange, and there was no authority at the time to take a bill of exchange, the purchaser's debt is not discharged.

The general rule, that an auctioneer may only accept cash, appears to have been made subject to one qualification by the decision of the Court of Appeal in *Farrer* v *Lacy, Hartland & Co.*[3] Property there was auctioned on behalf of a mortgagee and the auctioneer, with the concurrence of the mortgagee, took a cheque for the *deposit*. When this cheque was dishonoured on presentation, the mortgagor claimed that the auctioneer's negligence was such as to deprive the mortgagee of the right to claim the costs of the abortive sale. It was held that the auctioneer was not guilty of negligence, as he had merely acted in accordance with the common practice at auctions. As Bowen LJ said:[4]

Can it be said that 99 out of every 100 sales are conducted unreasonably because cheques are taken by way of payment of deposit? On the contrary, it was, I think a reasonable thing ... to do.

Furthermore, as Baggallay LJ pointed out:[5] "Persons cannot be expected to come to sales with large sums of money in their pocket."

It appears, then, that an auctioneer may accept a cheque for the deposit, provided always, of course, that it is reasonable to do so in the circumstances; to accept a cheque despite having reason to suspect the creditworthiness of the purchaser would lay the auctioneer himself open to a charge of negligence by the client.

However, the fact that an auctioneer has authority to accept a cheque as payment of a deposit does not entitle the purchaser to insist on paying in this way. In *Johnston* v *Boyes*[6] the plaintiff, a married woman, instructed her husband to bid for a public-house

---

1 *Bridges* v *Garrett* (1870) LR 5 CP 451.
2 (1866) LR 1 QB 352.
3 (1885) 31 ChD 42.
4 At p48.
5 At p46.
6 [1899] 2 Ch 73.

and he did so successfully. The vendor, however, recognised the husband as a man of little resources and refused to accept a cheque, whereupon the auctioneer resold the property. The plaintiff claimed that her husband had been wrongfully prevented from signing the contract of sale; it was held, however, that a purchaser's basic obligation is to pay a deposit in cash and, since this had not been done, no liability attached to the vendor.

D Authority to describe the property

An auctioneer is employed to sell, and owes a duty to the vendor to obtain the best possible price. To this end the auctioneer will describe the land or goods as favourably as possible in advertisements, in the particulars or catalogue of sale and from the rostrum. The legal rules governing false statements made by the auctioneer in any of these ways are discussed elsewhere;[1] for the moment we are concerned solely with the extent to which a statement which is made without the vendor's express authority may nevertheless involve the vendor in personal liability to the purchaser.

In *Payne* v *Lord Leconfield*,[2] a mare which was being sold by auction was observed to have a discharge from her nostrils. The auctioneer, in the plaintiff's hearing, said: "You need not be afraid. The mare comes from Lord Leconfield; she has only got a cold upon her, and I shall sell her as only having a cold." The mare was knocked down to the plaintiff but was found to be suffering from chronic glanders, as a result of which the local authority ordered her to be shot. The plaintiff thereupon sued the vendor for damages for breach of this warranty but his claim was rejected by the Court of Queen's Bench. It was held that an auctioneer, who is simply an agent to sell, has no implied authority to warrant goods and must therefore approach the principal to seek express authority.

In practical terms, the rule that an auctioneer may not bind the client by giving a "warranty" is not likely to cause any great hardship, for alternative forms of redress are available to the purchaser in this situation. There are, for example, a variety of ways in which the auctioneer may become personally liable for making an

---

1 pp383-414.
2 (1882) 51 LJQB 642.

untrue statement about property which is being sold.[1] Nor is the vendor immune from liability, for statements made by an auctioneer, either orally from the rostrum[2] or in pre-sale advertisements,[3] have been held on occasion to form part of the contract of sale. Indeed, many of the cases in this area could today be disposed of on the simple ground of misrepresentation, the remedies for which have greatly improved by statute.[4] That the vendor could be held responsible for an auctioneer's misrepresentation (ie that it is within the auctioneer's implied authority) is established by the case of *Smith* v *Land and House Property Corporation*,[5] where an hotel was described in auction particulars as being let to "a most desirable tenant" who in fact was in arrear with the rent. The purchasers were held entitled to rescind the contract on the ground of misrepresentation, and Baggallay LJ, said:[6]

It is said that these are words of course put in by the auctioneer, but I hold it to be the duty of a vendor to see that the property is not untruly described, and I cannot hold him to be excused because a description which the property will not bear has been inserted by the auctioneer without his instructions.

In *Overbrooke Estates Ltd* v *Glencombe Properties Ltd*[7] it was held by Brightman J that a vendor might avoid liability for an auctioneer's misrepresentations by notifying bidders that the auctioneer had no authority to make statements about the property. The learned judge held further that such notification did not have to satisfy any statutory test of reasonableness", since it was not an "exemption clause". This somewhat questionable decision, and its endorsement by the Court of Appeal in *Collins* v *Howell-Jones*[8] (a case concerning an estate agent) has already been discussed.[9]

---

1 See p 410.
2 *Couchman* v *Hill* [1947] KB 554.
3 *Lockhart* v *Osman* [1981] VR 57.
4 Misrepresentation Act 1967.
5 (1884) 28 ChD 7.
6 At p13.
7 [1974] 3 All ER 511.
8 (1980) 259 EG 331.
9 p91.

E Authority to delegate

As a general rule, an agent's duties are treated in law as personal to the agent, in the sense that there is no implied authority to delegate performance of those duties to any other person. What is not entirely clear is how far this principle applies to the common situation of members of the auctioneer's staff, notably the auctioneer's clerk, playing some part in the conduct of a sale. In the old United States case of *Commonwealth* v *Harnden*,[1] for example, the Supreme Court of Massachusetts held that an auctioneer was entitled to allow the clerk to use the hammer and make the outcry, provided that the auctioneer maintained general supervision of the conduct of the sale. Thus, it was said, in such circumstances the clerk could not be found guilty of a criminal offence in conducting an auction without a licence.

As far as English law is concerned, the question has arisen almost exclusively in connection with the auctioneer's implied authority to sign a memorandum of the sale, so as to render the contract enforceable. As we have seen,[2] such memoranda are no longer necessary on sales of either goods[3] or land,[4] and so the matter can be shortly dealt with. In brief, the courts have regarded an auctioneer in this connection as agent, not only for the vendor, but also for the highest bidder, and as being impliedly authorised by both parties to sign a binding memorandum on their behalf. Where the actual signature on the vendor's behalf was that of the auctioneer's clerk, general opinion was that the vendor would not be bound,[5] although some support could be found for the contrary view.[6] However, the legal position in respect of signature for the highest bidder was quite unequivocal. The auctioneer's authority was incapable of being delegated to the clerk, and thus the purchaser would not be bound,[7] except where there was clear

---

1 (1851) 19 Pick 482.
2 p276.
3 Law Reform (Enforcement of Contracts) Act 1954, section 2.
4 Law of Property (Miscellaneous Provisions) Act 1989, sections 2, 4 and Schedule 2.
5 *Coles* v *Trecothick* (1804) 9 Ves 234.
6 *Dyas* v *Stafford* (1881) 7 LR Ir 601.
7 *Peirce* v *Corf* (1874) LR 9 QB 210; *Bell* v *Balls* [1897] 1 Ch 663.

evidence that the purchaser had given direct authority to the clerk to sign on his or her behalf.[1]

Although a memorandum of the sale is no longer a statutory requirement, sales by auction generate various documents such as receipts which fall to be signed by the auctioneer. In view of the uncertainly as to the extent of the clerk's authority, if any, it is suggested that a prudent auctioneer should make a point of signing personally all such documents.

F Termination of authority

In terms of its duration, the authority of an auctioneer is no different from that of any other agent. The general principles governing the termination of authority by the parties or by operation of law are thus fully applicable to auctioneers, as are the special circumstances in which an agent's authority is rendered irrevocable.

In the course of our earlier discussion of those general principles,[2] we noted that the authority of an agent who is appointed to carry out a particular task will automatically come to an end when that task is accomplished.[3] In the context of an auction, this means that the auctioneer is *functus officio* from the moment the sale is concluded and consequently has no implied authority to conduct any further negotiations. According to Lord Eldon LC:[4]

The moment after the sale the auctioneer was no longer the agent of the plaintiff. He was his agent only to sell, not to deal with the terms upon which a title was to be made.

In *Nelson* v *Aldridge*[5] the defendant auctioneer was employed to sell certain horses for the plaintiff. The advertisement of the sale, which was drawn up under the plaintiff's direction, described them as "fresh and active horses in good condition, which had lately been in constant employ on the Essex road". The purchaser of one of

---

1 *Bird* v *Boulter* (1823) 4 B & Ad 443; *Sims* v *Landray* [1894] 2 Ch 318.
2 pp31-37.
3 *Blackburn* v *Scholes* (1810) 2 Camp 343.
4 *Seton* v *Slade* (1802) 7 Ves 265 at p 276.
5 (1818) 2 Stark 435.

these horses complained to the auctioneer that it did not meet this description, whereupon the auctioneer took it back. It was held that "it was the duty of the auctioneer to sell and not to rescind, to do and not to undo", and the seller was thus able to recover damages from the auctioneer.

Although this seems fairly clear, it should be noted that the case did not specifically raise the question of the auctioneer's implied authority, and thus did not consider whether or not the auctioneer's "rescission" would have prevented the seller from suing the buyer on the contract. What is more, the auctioneer's duty itself appears to be subject to some qualifications, in that Best J suggested that the auctioneer might have avoided liability by proving that the rescission was justified. This suggestion is supported by the later case of *Stevens* v *Legh*,[1] where the purchaser of a horse at an auction claimed that the owner had fraudulently misrepresented its condition, and gave notice to the auctioneer not to hand over the purchase money to the vendor. In due course the vendor sued the auctioneer for the money, but was held not to be entitled to it. As Erle J pointed out, to hold otherwise would lead to circuity of action, for the purchaser also could have sued the auctioneer, who would then be entitled to sue the vendor for an indemnity.[2]

G Authority from the purchaser

In principle, an auctioneer is regarded as an agent for the vendor of land or goods, looking to the vendor for payment of fees and owing the vendor those duties which are normally imposed by virtue of an agency relationship. Nevertheless, it has been recognised for more than two centuries that, in one respect at least, the auctioneer is also to a limited extent the agent of the purchaser. This "agency" consists of the auctioneer's implied authority to sign, for the highest bidder as well as for the vendor, a contract or a memorandum, something which was until recently required to render the sale enforceable.[3] As stated by Romer J in *Sims* v *Landray*:[4]

---

1 (1853) 2 CLR 251: see also *Hardingham* v *Allen* (1848) 5 CB 793; *Murray* v *Mann* (1848) 2 Exch 538.

2 As to the possibility of interpleader by the auctioneer, see p 329.

3 Until 1954 in sales of goods, and until 1989 in sales of land: see p 276.

4 [1894] 2 Ch 318 at p 320: see also *Simon* v *Metivier (or Motivos)* (1766) 1 WBl 599; *Emmerson* v *Heelis* (1809) 2 Taunt 38.

It is settled beyond the probability of now being successfully disputed, that where there is a sale by public auction, and the property is knocked down by the auctioneer to the highest bidder, the auctioneer is not only the agent of the vendor, but he is also the agent of the purchaser, the highest bidder; and that he is the purchaser's agent clearly to this extent, that he is entitled to sign, in the name and on behalf of the purchaser, a memorandum sufficient to satisfy the provisions of the Statute of Frauds, stating the particulars of the contract.

Although this implication of authority was of great practical importance in preventing a person to whom property had been knocked down from evading the obligations of a purchaser on technical grounds, it was never seriously suggested that there was an agency relationship in the full sense between the auctioneer and the highest bidder. Indeed, the authority itself was regarded with considerable circumspection by the courts, who limited its operation to sales which were truly effected by auction,[1] and required the memorandum to reflect accurately the terms of the contract[2] and to be signed by the auctioneer as part of the sale.[3] However, such niceties can now be forgotten, for the enforceability of a contract of sale no longer depends upon the existence of a signed memorandum,[4] a reform which has made the auctioneer's "agency" for the purchaser a redundant concept.

---

1 *Bartlett* v *Purnell* (1836) 4 Ad & E 792; *Mews* v *Carr* (1856) 1 H&N 484.
2 *Van Praagh* v *Everidge* [1903] 1 Ch 434.
3 *Bell* v *Balls* [1897] 1 Ch 663; *Chaney* v *Maclow* [1929] 1 Ch 461.
4 See p 276.

CHAPTER 9

Auctioneers' duties

A Duties to the vendor

The duties owed by an auctioneer to the vendor as client are in essence no different from those of any other agent. In order to appreciate, however, the way in which these general principles are applied to the specific case of an auctioneer, it is necessary to look at decided cases in relation to each of the major duties.

1 Duty of obedience

An auctioneer, like any other agent, must obey without question all express instructions from the principal. Provided that the instructions are clear, the auctioneer is allowed no discretion in deciding whether or not they are in the principal's best interests. Thus, an auctioneer who was instructed to sell for ready money only was held personally liable to the vendor for accepting a bill of exchange.[1] So too, when a chattel auctioneer sold a number of items under his own descriptions, rather than the ones provided by the client, he was held liable for the difference between what the goods realised and what they *should* have realised if properly described.[2]

The only instructions which may safely be ignored by an auctioneer are those which are unlawful, so that to carry them out would make the auctioneer a party to the illegality. In *Bexwell* v *Christie*,[3] for example, where conditions of sale stated that "goods should be sold to the best bidder", it was held that the auctioneer was not liable to the vendor for failing to comply with the latter's order to impose a secret reserve on a particular lot. Similarly, in

---

1 *Earl of Ferrers* v *Robins* (1835) 2 Cr M&R 152.
2 *Brown* v *Draper & Co* (1975) 233 EG 929. In order to avoid such liability, auctioneers' terms of business frequently give them discretion to sell under their own descriptions.
3 (1776) 1 Cowp 395.

Narramore v *Fuller, Hall & Foulsham*,[1] where reserves had validly been placed upon certain lots, the vendor appeared in the sale room and bid in person. The auctioneer, who had been instructed to bid on the vendor's behalf, thereupon refrained from doing so and, as a result, certain items were sold for less than their reserve. The auctioneer was held not liable to the vendor for, once the latter had made a bid, the auctioneer could not lawfully have joined in the bidding.

Where no express instructions have been given with regard to a particular matter, the auctioneer's duty is to act in accordance with trade usage and not to exceed whatever authority arises by implication. An act which is not expressly authorised, and which is not regarded as normal practice, may involve the auctioneer in personal liability to the client. Thus, in *Brown* v *Staton*,[2] an auctioneer who allowed a purchaser of goods to set off a debt alleged to be due from the vendor was held liable to account to the client for the full price. Similarly, in *Nelson* v *Aldridge*,[3] an auctioneer was held liable for allowing the purchaser of a horse to rescind the contract. This, said Best J, was a clear deviation from the normal course of an auctioneer's duty; it was therefore incumbent upon the auctioneer to show some justification for his actions which, in this case, he had failed to do.

Where an auctioneer is guilty of disobeying specific instructions from a client, one would expect the extent of the auctioneer's liability to be measured by the amount of the loss (if any) which the client has suffered. However, the courts have on occasion treated auctioneers rather more harshly than this in assessing damages against them. In the Canadian case of *City of Halifax* v *Miller & Johnson Auctioneers Ltd*[4] the defendants, who were instructed to sell by auction a number of vehicles belonging to the plaintiffs, sold several of these at less than the reserve prices which the plaintiffs had stipulated. The trial judge dismissed the plaintiffs' claim for damages on the ground that, since they had brought no evidence to suggest that the vehicles were worth any more than they had been sold for, they had failed to show that they would have been

---

1 (1932) 76 Sol Jo 289.
2 (1816) 2 Chit 353.
3 (1818) 2 Stark 435.
4 (1980) 40 NSR 35. The decision, it is submitted, is open to serious question.

any better off if their instructions had been obeyed. The Nova Scotia Court of Appeal, however, held (for reasons which are not entirely clear) that the plaintiffs were entitled to recover the difference between the reserve prices and the amounts actually realised.[1]

2 Duty of care

(a) *Scope of the duty*

An auctioneer, like any professional person, has an implied contractual obligation to manage the affairs of clients with the care and skill to be expected of a reasonably competent member of that profession.[2] As Lord Ellenborough CJ said in *Denew* v *Daverell*:[3]

> I pay an auctioneer, as I do any other professional man, for the exercise of skill on my behalf which I do not myself possess; and I have a right to the exercise of such skill as is ordinarily possessed by men of that profession or business. If from his ignorance or carelessness he leads me into mischief, he cannot ask for a recompense; although, from a misplaced confidence, I followed his advice without remonstrance or suspicion.

This skeletal statement of an auctioneer's duty of care was fleshed out in the following highly instructive passage from the judgment of May J in *Fordham* v *Christie, Manson & Woods Ltd*:[4]

> In my view an auctioneer, like any other professional man, is under an obligation to his client to use reasonable care and skill in and about his calling as an auctioneer and to act in accordance with the terms of his contract with his client, the intending vendor. He must, for instance, obtain the best possible price for the property being auctioned. He must not negligently miss the nod of the head, or the wink of the eye or the raise of the hand in the auction room, indicating a higher bid. He must take reasonable care to ensure that he obtains a binding contract with the purchaser for his client, the vendor. In the ordinary auction of anything other than real property, the binding contract is made by the fall of the hammer.

---

1 See also *Hayes* v *Douglas* [1976] 5 WWR 308, in which a similar measure was adopted in the case of an estate agent who sold property at less than the price authorised by the client.

2 An obligation which is now implied by the Supply of Goods and Services Act 1982, section 13.

3 (1813) 3 Camp 451 at p453. The auctioneer there forfeited the right to commission on the ground of negligence; many others have had to pay damages.

4 (1977) 244 EG 213 at p219.

In effecting that contract the auctioneer must take reasonable care that there is no uncertainty in the mind of either the man on the rostrum or the person bidding about what the one is offering and for what the other is bidding. Nor must there be any lack of reasonable care in ascertaining the amount of the final bid for which the property is knocked down. I think also that there is a clear duty on an auctioneer selling in these circumstances to establish to his satisfaction the identity of the buyer to whom the goods have been knocked down.

Where there is an auction of real property, it may well be necessary to go further and, for instance, to obtain the buyer's signature to a sufficient memorandum under section 40 of the Law of Property Act 1925. Also, if the terms of the auctioneer's contract with the vendor require, which will probably be reflected in the conditions of sale at the auction, to obtain the stated, usually 10 per cent, deposit.

It is clear from the passages cited that the duty of care applies to all work carried out by an auctioneer on behalf of the vendor. In practice, however, it is found that the cases which have arisen on this part of the law fall into a number of groups, each applying to a particular area of an auctioneer's work. These groups of cases may now be considered, although it must be borne in mind that the list is in no way exhaustive.

(b) Making a binding contract of sale

If there is one of an auctioneer's normal functions which can be regarded as fundamental, it is surely that of securing a binding and enforceable contract for the sale of the client's property. If, due to the auctioneer's carelessness or lack of skill or knowledge, the sale is ineffective, then the vendor will be entitled to seek compensation. In *Denew* v *Daverell*,[1] for example, the auctioneer's negligence lay in failing to insert in the particulars of sale a proviso common in all sales of that type of property, with the result that the ensuing contract could not be enforced against the purchaser. In *Jones* v *Nanney*,[2] it was the actual conduct of the sale which gave grounds for complaint. The auctioneer there, having offered one lot for sale, then sold others before returning to the original lot, which was sold upon altered conditions. The Court of Exchequer were of the

---

1 (1813) 3 Camp 451.
2 (1824) 13 Price 76.

opinion that these irregularities would have been sufficient to invalidate the sale.

A modern example is provided by the case of *Friedrich* v *A Monnickendam Ltd*,[1] which concerned an international auction of jewellery held in Geneva. The English auctioneer conducted the auction in French, despite having only a limited knowledge of that language, and this led to a misunderstanding as to the amount of the highest bid (which came, ironically, from an Englishman). The mistake led to the sale being set aside under Swiss law, and a majority of the Court of Appeal regarded the auctioneer as having breached the duty of care and skill owed to the client.

As we have seen,[2] the English law which governs sales by auction no longer requires written evidence in order to make such sales legally enforceable, whether they concern goods or land. When such evidence *was* required by law, the courts were in no doubt that it was part of an auctioneer's duty to the client to ensure that there was sufficient evidence to bind the highest bidder.[3] Presumably this will continue to represent the legal position in those jurisdictions where written evidence is still a statutory requirement.

Where an auctioneer's careless misdescription of property results in the vendor either losing the sale or becoming liable to pay compensation, the auctioneer will be responsible to the client for the loss suffered. In *Parker* v *Farebrother*[4] the defendants, a firm of auctioneers, prepared sales particulars for three houses owned by the plaintiff. Two of the houses, which were described as having three floors, had in fact only two, a misrepresentation which caused the plaintiff to pay compensation to the purchaser. The auctioneers were held liable to reimburse their client for this expense.

(c) *Obtaining the best available price*

Although an auctioneer must not positively misdescribe property which is being sold, care must be taken to show all its advantages to prospective purchasers, in order to obtain the best possible price for the client.[5] Failure to advertise the property sufficiently, or in a

---

1 (1973) 228 EG 1311.
2 p276.
3 *Peirce* v *Corf* (1874) LR 9 QB 210.
4 (1853) 21 LT(OS) 128: see also *Cole* v *Christie, Manson & Woods* (1910) 26 TLR 469.
5 See *Brown* v *Draper & Co* (1975) 233 EG 929: p 288.

form designed to attract bidders, may thus amount to negligence. In *Cuckmere Brick Co Ltd* v *Mutual Finance Ltd*,[1] for example, building land was to be sold by auction on behalf of mortgagees. Outline planning permission had been granted for the construction of 33 houses or 100 flats, but the auctioneers, believing that the permission for flats had lapsed, did not mention this in the particulars of sale. Before the sale took place it was learned that the permission for flats was still operative but the auctioneers, who did not regard the area as suitable for this type of development, neither postponed the sale nor published new advertisements. It was held by the Court of Appeal that the auctioneers, by cutting out an important part of the possible market for this land, were guilty of negligence, for which their clients the mortgagees were responsible to the mortgagors.

Two recent cases in which the conduct of auctioneers has been subjected to the most intense and detailed judicial scrutiny are *Alchemy (International) Ltd* v *Tattersalls Ltd*[2] and *Luxmoore-May* v *Messenger May Baverstock*.[3] The first of these concerned a special bloodstock sale of high quality racehorses which was put on at Newmarket by the defendants. A yearling colt belonging to the plaintiffs was knocked down by the defendants for some £450,000, but the highest bidder denied having made the final bid, refused to give his name and address and left the auction. The defendants took the view that to reauction the colt immediately, at the end of a long day's sale, would be unwise; they accordingly put the animal up for sale again two days later, when it was sold for less than one-half the previous price. After a lengthy trial involving a great deal of expert evidence, it was held that the decision taken by the defendants was one which a reasonably competent auctioneer might justifiably make; as a result, the defendants were not liable to their clients for their loss on the resale.

The *Luxmoore-May* case concerned that nightmare of provincial art auctioneers, a "sleeper", in this instance a pair of paintings of foxhounds which were brought to the defendant firm in a dirty and poor condition and accepted by them "for research". The

---

1 [1971] Ch 949: see also *Johnson* v *Ribbins* (1975) 235 EG 757, where an allegation of negligence failed on the facts.
2 [1985] 2 EGLR 17.
3 [1990] 1 EGLR 21.

defendants, through their fine art consultant, valued the pictures at no more than £50 the pair, and an employee also took them somewhat casually to Christie's, where nothing favourable was said about them. When the defendants put the pictures up for auction they in fact reached £840; five months later they were sold again, this time by Sothebys with full attribution to George Stubbs, at a price of £88,000.

The trial judge held that the defendants' failure to spot the "Stubbs potential" of these pictures was negligent; however, the Court of Appeal regarded the judge as having demanded far too high a standard of a "general practitioner" firm, and accordingly reversed the decision. Interestingly, the Court of Appeal specifically refused to express an opinion as to whether the pictures really were painted by Stubbs!

(d) *Security for the client's interests*

In addition to obtaining an enforceable contract of sale at a good price, an auctioneer must protect the client's interests in other ways. It would, for instance, almost certainly be regarded as negligent for an auctioneer to permit a purchaser to take away goods without paying for them in cash or by some other guaranteed means.[1] Indeed, even where items bought are not handed over to the buyer, there are circumstances in which the exercise of reasonable care requires the auctioneer to demand at least a deposit. In *Hibbert* v *Bayley*,[2] for example, a ship was put up for sale upon a condition that the highest bidder should immediately sign a contract and pay a deposit. The highest bidder said that he would return with the deposit money in half an hour and would then sign the contract; he then disappeared without trace. In an action against the auctioneers for negligence, it was held that the latitude given to this purchaser could only have been justified if they had known him personally, or if he had given a genuine London address. However, this does not mean that an auctioneer is in a sense a guarantor of the bidder's

---

1 A "retention of title" clause will be powerless to prevent the buyer from disposing of the goods without paying for them. Indeed, such clauses have no effect at all unless provision is made in the conditions of sale, for title normally passes to the buyer when the hammer falls: *Dennant* v *Skinner and Collom* [1948] 2 KB 164.
2 (1860) 2 F&F 48.

obligations; in *Hardial Singh* v *Hillyer & Hillyer*,[1] where the purchaser of a house simply disappeared without trace from the saleroom, an action for negligence by the vendor failed, for there was nothing which the auctioneers could have done.

It should not be thought that, as a result of the decision in *Hibbert* v *Bayley*, failure by an auctioneer to insist upon a deposit in cash automatically constitutes negligence. All the circumstances of the case must be considered before it can be decided whether the auctioneer has acted unreasonably. Thus, in *Farrer* v *Lacy, Hartland & Co*,[2] where mortgaged property was being sold by the mortgagee, the auctioneer accepted a cheque in payment of the deposit, according to custom. The cheque was subsequently dishonoured, but it was held by the Court of Appeal that the auctioneer was guilty of no default and was therefore entitled to his charges on the abortive sale.

Not only may an auctioneer be justified in accepting a cheque in payment of the deposit; there are circumstances in which it may be reasonable to waive payment of the deposit altogether. In *Cyril Andrade Ltd* v *Sotheby & Co*[3] the plaintiffs instructed the defendants to sell a suit of armour. A condition of the sale was that a deposit of 50% could be demanded, which, if not paid, would entitle the auctioneer to put up the lot again. The armour was knocked down for £5,000 to a person who had previously bid on behalf of an American millionaire. No deposit was demanded, as it was assumed that the purchaser was again bidding as agent. Unfortunately, however, the American millionaire repudiated the bidder's authority and the bidder was unable personally to pay for the armour. The vendors accordingly sought to recover their loss by taking action against the auctioneers for failing to obtain the deposit. It was held, however, that in these circumstances it was reasonable not to insist upon the payment of a deposit, and the auctioneers were accordingly not in breach of any duty owed to their clients.

The extent of an auctioneer's duty in respect of the purchase price was carefully considered in *Fordham* v *Christie, Manson &*

---

1 (1979) 251 EG 951.
2 (1885) 31 ChD 42.
3 (1931) 47 TLR 244.

Woods Ltd.[1] The defendants there sold a picture on behalf of the plaintiff to an Italian dealer who did not actually attend the sale but instead submitted a bid in advance. The picture was never delivered to the buyer for, shortly after the sale, he challenged its authenticity and refused to pay. The plaintiff then sued the defendants, alleging that they should have taken positive steps on his behalf to get in the price. It was held, however, by May J that, although an auctioneer undoubtedly has a right to sue the buyer for the price,[2] there is no implied obligation to the client to exercise this right. Nor could it be said, on the facts of this case, that the defendants were negligent in not demanding a deposit; such a procedure would be unworkable, having regard to the common practice of accepting bids from overseas buyers who are neither physically present nor represented in the saleroom.

(e) Care of the goods

Finally, an important application of the duty of care relates to goods which are placed in the auctioneer's possession for the purpose of sale. It was stated by Lord Kenyon in *Maltby* v *Christie*[3] that an auctioneer is bound to take due care of such goods but would not be liable for loss or damage arising from misfortune or unavoidable accident. Although the standard of liability was put on a subjective basis in that case, as being a duty to exhibit such care as the auctioneer would take of his own goods, it is submitted that the true rule of law is that an auctioneer must take such care of the goods as is reasonable in the circumstances; the degree of prudence required does not vary from one auctioneer to another.

The duty expressed in this way was recognised by the Court of Appeal in *Spriggs* v *Sotheby Parke Bernet & Co Ltd*,[4] where it was said that the status of an auctioneer in relation to a client's goods is that of a bailee for reward. This means that the auctioneer owes a duty of care to the client to safeguard the goods against theft as well as damage, and, moreover, the onus of proving that reasonable care has been taken is on the auctioneer. In the *Spriggs* case itself, where a valuable diamond was stolen from the defendants'

---

1 (1977) 244 EG 213.
2 See pp 350-358.
3 (1795) 1 Esp 340.
4 [1986] 1 EGLR 13.

premises while on view prior to sale, the Court of Appeal regarded the defendants' security arrangements as insufficient, even though four security guards were on duty at all times in the viewing room. However, the defendants successfully avoided liability by means of a clear exemption clause in the conditions under which they agreed to accept items for sale.[1]

3 Duty of loyalty

As an agent, an auctioneer is under a fiduciary obligation to the client, which prohibits the auctioneer from acting against the client's interests or making any secret profit out of his agency. Indeed, one of the leading cases on the subject of secret profit concerned an auctioneer. In *Hippisley* v *Knee Bros*[2] the plaintiff employed the defendants to sell some pictures and agreed to pay, in addition to commission, "all out of pocket expenses", including the cost of printing and advertising. The defendants received trade discounts both from the printers and the newspaper proprietors, but charged the plaintiff at the full rate. A Divisional Court of King's Bench held the auctioneers liable to account for the amounts of these discounts to their client. Since, however, the auctioneers had honestly believed that they were entitled by custom to this money, it was held that they were not also obliged to forfeit their commission.

The duty of loyalty will normally debar an agent from obtaining commission from both parties to a single transaction.[3] However, a profit which is obtained with the knowledge and consent of the client is no longer "secret", and an auctioneer may thus play a dual role provided that the specific consent of each party is obtained. It appears therefore that the practice of leading art auctioneers to charge a "buyer's premium" is lawful, since both sellers and buyers are made aware from the outset that this will be done.

Even where no double commission is in prospect, for an agent to act for both parties to a transaction is not normally permitted, since this is likely to bring about a conflict of interests.[4] However, it is by

---

1 It should be noted that the case arose shortly before the Unfair Contract Terms Act 1977 came into operation, so that the clause in question did not have to satisfy the statutory test of reasonableness.
2 [1905] 1 KB 1.
3 See p 115.
4 See p 43.

no means clear that this rule applies to the practice, common in certain types of auction sale, where prospective bidders notify the auctioneer in advance of the maximum amount which they are prepared to pay for a particular lot. It might well be argued that an auctioneer who knocks down property to such a bidder, without taking the bidding up to the stated maximum, would be guilty of failing to obtain the highest possible price for the vendor, and yet such judicial authority as there is on the point seems to be in favour of this practice. As Lord Mansfield said in *Bexwell* v *Christie*,[1] an auctioneer "may fairly bid for a third person who employs him". May J in *Fordham* v *Christie, Manson & Woods Ltd* was even more direct.[2]

I am quite satisfied on the evidence that this procedure is followed time and time again with auctioneers of the reputation and size of Christies or Sothebys. People come and look at the articles for sale during the period of the view, and then leave with the auctioneers authority to bid on their behalf up to a specified limit when the auction is in progress. This is a very common practice, a practice understood throughout the whole of the auctioneering and art world and about which no criticism whatever can be or is made.

Since both these statements of opinion were *obiter* (in the first case the auctioneer did not actually bid at all; in the second he did but the vendor did not complain), the legal position cannot be regarded as settled. In consequence, a prudent auctioneer who believes that such "bids" are likely to materialise should obtain express authorisation from the client to take them.

Even assuming that bidding on behalf of a third party is legitimate, it is settled that an auctioneer may not bid personally. In *Oliver* v *Court*[3] the defendant and his father carried on business together as surveyors and auctioneers. The father, who was asked to value the plaintiff's estate, did so (upon measurements taken by the defendant) but omitted to include the value of timber. The defendant acted as auctioneer of the estate at an abortive sale and, on the following day, himself agreed to purchase the property at approximately the amount of the valuation. It was held that the

---

1 (1776) 1 Cowp 395 at p397.
2 (1977) 244 EG 213 at p215.
3 (1820) 8 Price 127.

plaintiff was entitled to have this sale set aside, not only because of the under-valuation, but also because the auctioneer had acted wrongfully in purchasing the property. Richards CB said:[1] "I am clearly of opinion, that an auctioneer, while his employment continues, cannot purchase the estate which he is engaged to sell."[2]

4 Duty to account

(a) *The auctioneer's basic obligation*

As a general principle, an agent who is in possession of goods belonging to the principal may or may not be regarded in law as a trustee, depending on the type of agency involved.[3] It is settled, however, that an auctioneer is to be regarded as a trustee for the vendor as client, and that this trusteeship covers both goods which are unsold (before and after the sale) and the proceeds of sale. As a result of this trusteeship, certain equitable remedies are available to the client which could not be used if the relationship between the parties were simply one of debtor and creditor, or bailee and bailor. In *Crowther* v *Elgood*,[4] for example, the defendant was instructed to sell farm stock and effects which formed part of the estate of a deceased person. This person had in fact died insolvent and, before the sale took place, a receiver was appointed. The auctioneer was notified of the appointment but, having sold the property, paid only part of the proceeds of sale to the receiver. When the auctioneer was unable to pay the remainder, it was held by the Court of Appeal that a writ of attachment might issue against him, so that he could be committed to prison for contempt. In deciding that the defendant had acted in this transaction in a fiduciary capacity, Cotton LJ said:[5]

He was an auctioneer, and as such he held the goods in trust to sell them for the benefit of the person who entrusted them to him; and if any deposit was paid at the time of the sale, he held it in trust for the vendor.

---

1 At p160.
2 In sales of land, an obligation to disclose any intention on the auctioneer's part to acquire an interest in the property will also arise under the Estate Agents Act 1979: see p 212.
3 See *Henry* v *Hammond* [1913] 2 KB 515.
4 (1887) 34 ChD 691.
5 At p696.

In *Re Cotton, ex parte Cooke*[1] an auctioneer, who regularly conducted cattle sales, was in the habit of paying all the proceeds of these sales into one account and giving his own cheques to the vendors. After a sale in which cattle belonging to Mr Cooke were sold, the auctioneer committed suicide and his estate was discovered to be insolvent. The Court of Appeal held that the money owed to Mr Cooke was held by the auctioneer in a fiduciary capacity and could therefore be traced to the bank account and paid over.

A strict duty to account to the vendor normally arises only once goods or money are in the auctioneer's actual possession. There is, however, an important exception to this, in that an auctioneer who is at fault in not having received the proceeds of sale is liable to the vendor on the same footing as if they had been received. Thus in *Brown* v *Staton*,[2] an auctioneer who gave credit to a purchaser without any authority from the client was held liable to account for the full price.

The auctioneer's duty to account arises out of the relationship of principal and agent, and it is accordingly the principal to whom payment must be made. This requirement was made quite clear by the decision in *Crosskey* v *Mills*[3] where the plaintiff, who was in possession of an insolvent person's goods under a bill of sale, instructed an auctioneer to sell them. The plaintiff said that he would divide the proceeds among various creditors but, when the goods were sold, the insolvent person's widow told the auctioneer to retain the proceeds for distribution among the creditors. It was held that, notwithstanding his earlier declaration, the plaintiff was entitled to demand payment of the entire proceeds from the auctioneer, whose client he was. A similar decision was reached in the case of *Lowe* v *Gallimore*,[4] where the plaintiff had instructed the defendant to sell certain goods. Another person laid claim to the goods, whereupon the plaintiff told the auctioneer to pay the proceeds of sale into a certain bank to await settlement of the dispute. When the plaintiff later repudiated this agreement, it was

1 (1913) 108 LT 310.
2 (1816) 2 Chit 353; see also *Earl of Ferrers* v *Robins* (1835) 2 Cr M&R 152.
3 (1834) 1 Cr M&R 298.
4 (1852) LT (OS) 63 and 241.

held that the auctioneer's duty to account to him revived and could be enforced by legal action.

(b) *Claims by third parties*

The most difficult cases concerning an auctioneer's duty to hand over goods or money to the client are those where a third party lays claim to the property, either under the contract of sale or quite independently of it. In view of the auctioneer's primary duty, it is clear that great caution is necessary before any such claim is accepted. If, however, the third party's claim is genuine, an auctioneer who accepts it will have a good defence to an action brought by the client. In *Hardingham* v *Allen*,[1] the published conditions at a sale of horses stipulated that, should any horse which was sold with a warranty prove unsound, the price paid would be refunded. When a horse was returned in accordance with this condition, it was held that the proceeds of sale were no longer held by the auctioneer to the use of the vendor, but had become due to the purchaser. The auctioneer was accordingly not liable to the vendor for refunding the price.

In the case of *Murray* v *Mann*,[2] this principle was even applied to a case where the reason why the purchaser of a horse rescinded the contract was because of the selling agent's fraud! Although the seller there was quite innocent, and although he would undoubtedly be entitled to make other claims against the fraudulent agent, it was held that he could not show that the money belonged to him once the purchaser had exercised his right of rescission. It should be emphasised however that the onus of proving that the contract has been justifiably discharged in such cases lies upon the auctioneer, and it is by no means an easy task. Thus in *Nelson* v *Aldridge*,[3] an auctioneer who took back a horse which failed to answer its description was held liable to the seller for the full purchase price, as he had failed to show legal justification for allowing the purchaser to rescind the contract.

Where a third party makes some independent claim to goods which have been placed in the hands of an auctioneer for sale, the auctioneer may consider it prudent not to return those goods to the

---

1 (1848) 5 CB 793.
2 (1848) 2 Exch 538; followed in *Stevens* v *Legh* (1853) 2 CLR 251.
3 (1818) 2 Stark 435.

client on demand, nor to hand over the proceeds of sale. If the vendor then brings legal proceedings in respect of this refusal, the auctioneer may seek to defend by setting up the *ius tertii* or right of the third party.[1] The extent to which this defence is available at common law to an auctioneer or, indeed, to any agent is far from clear, although it has been before the courts on a number of occasions. In *Hardman* v *Willcock*[2] the defendant, who had been instructed to sell goods by the plaintiff, was notified by the assignees of an insolvent person that the goods belonged to them and had been removed by a fraudulent arrangement between the insolvent person and the plaintiff. Upon the assignees agreeing to indemnify him against legal liability, the auctioneer refused to pay the proceeds of sale to the plaintiff. The Court of Common Pleas held this refusal to be justified, for the fraudulent plaintiff could have no better right to the goods or proceeds than the insolvent person, who would certainly not have been entitled to them.

The most important decision on the *ius tertii* at common law was laid down in the case of *Biddle* v *Bond*.[3] The plaintiff there, who had seized goods under a distress for rent, instructed the defendant auctioneer to sell them. As the sale was about to begin, the defendant received notice from the owner of the goods that the distress was void. The auctioneer none the less sold the goods, but then refused to pay the proceeds over to the plaintiff on the basis of the true owner's claim, which in fact turned out to be a valid one. It was held that, in these circumstances, the auctioneer was not estopped as bailee from denying the title of the plaintiff as bailor. In delivering the judgment of the Court of Queen's Bench, Blackburn J said:[4]

We do not question the general rule that one who has received property from another as his bailee or agent or servant must restore or account for that property to him from whom he received it ... But the bailee has no better title than the bailor, and, consequently, if a person entitled as against the bailor to the property claims it, the bailee has no defence against him.

1 As to the relief available to the auctioneer by way of interpleader, see p 329.
2 (1832) 9 Bing 382n.
3 (1865) 6 B&S 225.
4 At p231.

Later, he said:[1]

We think that the true ground on which a bailee may set up the *ius tertii* is that the estoppel ceases when the bailment on which it is founded is determined by what is equivalent to an eviction by title paramount. It is not enough that the bailee has become aware of the title of a third person ... We assent to what is said by Pollock CB in *Thorne* v *Tilbury*,[2] that a bailee can set up the title of another only "if he defends upon the right and title, and by the authority of that person".[3]

Biddle v *Bond* notwithstanding, an auctioneer who accepted instructions to sell in the full knowledge that a third party had made a claim to the goods would not be allowed to set up that claim in an action brought against him by his principal. In such circumstances the auctioneer would be presumed to have elected to serve the client in preference to the third party, and the usual estoppel would therefore apply. In *Re Sadler, ex parte Davies*,[4] for example, an auctioneer took possession of goods belonging to a bankrupt on behalf of the holder of a bill of sale. Later, however, he sold the goods on behalf of the trustee in bankruptcy. It was held that the auctioneer was not entitled to set up, as against the trustee, the claim of the bill of sale holder, since, with knowledge of this claim, he had accepted the trustee's instructions. The legal position was succinctly stated by Lush LJ:[5]

I am of opinion that when a person in such a position, knowing of two adverse claims to goods, elects to take the part of one of the claimants, and to sell the goods as his, he is estopped from afterwards denying that claimant's title. If he had not taken this course he would have been entitled to show that there was a better title in the bill of sale holder; there might have been what is called an eviction of the trustee by title paramount.

---

1 At p233.
2 (1858) 3 H&N 534 at p 537.
3 The bailee must expressly claim that he is defending on this basis; *Rogers, Sons & Co* v *Lambert* [1891] 1 QB 318, where *Biddle* v *Bond* was approved by the Court of Appeal.
4 (1881) 19 ChD 86.
5 At p93.

(c) *Statutory intervention*

The defence of *ius tertii* at common law was surrounded by confusion (exemplified by the difficulty of drawing a line between *Biddle* v *Bond* and *Re Sadler, ex parte Davies*). Unfortunately, it cannot be said that this confusion has been greatly lessened by the enactment of the Torts (Interference with Goods) Act 1977. Section 8(1) of that Act provides:

The defendant in an action for wrongful interference shall be entitled to show, in accordance with rules of court, that a third party has a better right than the plaintiff as respects all or any part of the interest claimed by the plaintiff, or in right of which he sues, and any rule of law (sometimes called *ius tertii*) to the contrary is abolished.

The "rules of court"[1] referred to state that a defendant who seeks to set up the rights of a third party as a defence must identify the third party; it is then for the court to decide whether or not that person should be joined as a party to the action.

The major limitation on section 8 is that, like the rest of the 1977 Act, it applies only to an action for "wrongful interference with goods", which is defined by section 1 as including any tort "so far as it results in damage to goods or to an interest in goods". This creates two problems in the context of auctions. First, it can hardly be suggested that a vendor's claim to the proceeds of sale is based on "damage to goods", so that this will inevitably continue to be governed by the common law with all its uncertainties. Second, even where the vendor lays claim to the goods themselves, such a claim can normally be framed as an action for breach of contract as an alternative to tort. If, as seems strongly arguable, the operation of section 8 can be outflanked by this simple expedient, it appears that this statutory reform will be of little utility where auctions are concerned.

B Duties to the purchaser

The foregoing discussion demonstrates that, as an agent, an auctioneer owes the vendor an extensive list of legal obligations.

---

1 Rules of the Supreme Court, Ord 15, rule 10A; County Court Rules, Ord 15, rule 4.

However, as noted earlier,[1] the legal relationship between an agent and the third parties with whom he or she deals is of a much more limited and fragmented kind. What now falls to be considered, therefore, is the limited range of circumstances in which an auctioneer may become liable to the purchaser.

1 Liability on the contract

Perhaps the most important way in which an auctioneer may become liable to the highest bidder lies in the auctioneer's personal duty to see that the contract of sale is duly carried out.[2] As a general rule, an agent who makes a contract expressly as agent incurs no personal liability on it, as it is assumed that the third party intends to contract, not with the agent, but with the principal. In the case of an auctioneer, however, the position appears to be rather different;[3] the question to be asked is whether the auctioneer has disclosed, not merely the fact of agency, but rather the actual identity of the principal. Thus in *Hanson* v *Roberdeau*,[4] where a purchaser successfully sued an auctioneer for failure to deliver a bond, Lord Kenyon said:

And though where an auctioneer names his principal, it is not proper that he should be liable to an action, yet it is a very different case when the auctioneer sells the commodity without saying on whose behalf he sells it; in such a case the purchaser is entitled to look to him personally for the completion of the contract.

Hanson v *Roberdeau* was followed in *Franklyn* v *Lamond*[5] where the defendant, an auctioneer, sold 300 shares in a company to the plaintiff. When it later proved impossible to procure a transfer of these shares to the plaintiff, as the registered owner had disappeared, the defendant was held personally liable. Wilde CJ said:[6]

---

1 pp56-65.
2 For the legal position where a private sale goes through the auctioneer's books, see *Murphy* v *Jonathan Howlett (a firm)* (1960) 176 EG 311.
3 Perhaps because an auctioneer is always assumed to be an agent; see *Mainprice* v *Westley* (1865) 6 B&S 420 at p 429.
4 (1792) Peake 163.
5 (1874) 4 CB 637.
6 At p644.

The first objection urged in this case is, that the mere fact of the defendants' being announced in the catalogue as "auctioneers" was such an indication of agency as to absolve them from personal responsibility, though their character of agents was not otherwise intimated to the purchaser. I apprehend it to be very old law, that an auctioneer who sells without at the time of sale disclosing the name of his principal, contracts personally.

The duty owed to a purchaser by an auctioneer, in cases where the vendor's name is not disclosed, does not arise from the contract of sale itself, for the auctioneer is seldom if ever a party to this contract. It seems, rather, that the fall of the hammer also serves to create a separate contract between the auctioneer and the purchaser, and it is upon this contract that the purchaser may take action.[1]

The exact extent of the obligations imposed upon the auctioneer by this second contract "depends upon the conditions of sale, upon which is said by the auctioneer at the time, upon the surrounding circumstances, and upon the nature of the subject-matter of the sale".[2] It appears, however, that the auctioneer is only bound to hand over possession of the purchased property; there is no implied guarantee that the client has the right to sell it. In *Salter* v *Woollams*,[3] the defendant auctioneer knocked down to the plaintiff a rick of hay which had been seized under a distress for rent. The tenant had acknowledged the distress in writing, and the auctioneer gave the plaintiff a note requiring the tenant to allow him to remove the rick. When the tenant refused to co-operate, it was held that the auctioneer had fully discharged all responsibility to the purchaser by giving the latter the legal right to possession of the hay.

Detailed consideration was given to the relationship between auctioneer and purchaser in the case of *Wood* v *Baxter*,[4] where a crop of wheat and straw was sold by the defendant on behalf of an unnamed principal, who was in fact a tenant-farmer. The plaintiff, who bought the crop, cut the wheat, but the landlord claimed that by local custom the straw was to remain on the farm. When the plaintiff claimed the value of the straw from the auctioneer, it was held that the latter had fully discharged his duty; having given the

---

1 *Benton* v *Campbell, Parker & Co Ltd* [1925] 2 KB 410 at pp 414-415, *per* Salter J.
2 *Wood* v *Baxter* (1883) 49 LT 45 at p46, *per* Williams J.
3 (1841) 2 M&G 650.
4 (1883) 49 LT 45: see also *Payne* v *Elsden* (1900) 17 TLR 161.

purchaser all proper authority to cut and carry away the crop, he could not further be held to warrant his principal's title. Williams J, who reviewed a number of cases concerning the personal contract entered into by an auctioneer, said:[1]

If he is selling livestock or implements in the market-place, or furniture in a room, the extent of his contract would ordinarily be to deliver the goods to the buyer; if he were selling shares in a joint stock company, it would be to procure a transfer to the purchaser; if he were selling timber stacked in a yard or loaded on board ship, or growing crops on a farm, it would be in each case to give such constructive delivery as according to the nature of the subject-matter was practicable and usual.

In *Benton* v *Campbell, Parker & Co Ltd*[2] auctioneers, who sold a car to the plaintiff, were held not liable when it was discovered that their principal had no right to sell it. Salter J stated that, as a general rule, an agent who does not name the client incurs personal responsibility for the due performance of the contract, for the third party is not willing to contract solely with a person unknown. This general rule applies to a sale of unascertained goods described in a general way,[3] since the agent can procure these if necessary. Where, however, the agent is employed to sell specific goods which are known not to belong to the agent personally, it is unrealistic to infer that such an agent guarantees that anyone has the right to sell them. As to the obligations which an auctioneer does undertake in such a case, Salter J said:[4]

Every agent to contract, when he makes the authorised contract between his principal and the other party, makes also a contract on his own account with the other party; he warrants his authority. If he is an agent for sale he also warrants that he knows of no defect in his principal's title. If he is an auctioneer to whom a chattel has been delivered for sale he gives both these warranties, he undertakes to give possession against the price paid into his hands, and he undertakes that such possession will not be disturbed by his principal or himself.

---

1 At p46.
2 [1925] 2 KB 410.
3 For example "300 shares in a named company": see *Franklyn* v *Lamond* (1847) 4 CB 637: p 305.
4 [1925] 2 KB 410 at p415.

It remains to consider the position of an auctioneer who actually names the client at the time of the sale. The *dictum* of Lord Kenyon in *Hanson* v *Roberdeau*[1] quoted above makes it clear that, in the opinion of that learned judge, such disclosure would absolve the auctioneer of any personal liability. This opinion was endorsed by certain *dicta* in *Mainprice* v *Westley*,[2] where, however, the point was not in issue. In *Woolfe* v *Horne*,[3] on the other hand, where property was sold expressly on behalf of the directors of the Great Western Railway Co, the conditions of sale made provision for compensation to be paid in the event of the auctioneers being unable to deliver any lot; it was held in these circumstances that the auctioneers undertook personal responsibility for the performance of the contract. Finally, although not directly in issue, the point was considered by a Divisional Court of King's Bench in *Rainbow* v *Howkins*[4] where Kennedy J, in delivering the judgment of court, said:[5]

> We are of opinion, on the authority of *Woolfe* v *Horne*, which is a more recent decision than *Mainprice* v *Westley*, that an action for wrongful refusal to deliver a chattel sold at public auction may in some circumstances successfully be brought against the auctioneer, although the principal's name is disclosed to the buyer at the time of the sale.

No further guidance was forthcoming from the court, however, on the question of what circumstances would enable such an action to be maintained.

There appears to be no direct authority upon the personal liability (if any) of an auctioneer on a sale of land. However, in such a case the auctioneer can only bring a personal action against the purchaser if the contract of sale makes it appear that the auctioneer is the vendor.[6] It is accordingly submitted, on the basis that a person's rights and duties should be coextensive, that similar evidence will be necessary before the auctioneer can incur personal liability on the sale of land.

---

1 (1792) Peake 163: p 305.
2 (1865) 6 B&S 420.
3 (1877) 2 QBD 355.
4 [1904] 2 KB 322.
5 At p325.
6 See p 357.

2 The auctioneer as the purchaser's agent

As we have seen, the courts for many years regarded an auctioneer as being impliedly authorised by the highest bidder to sign a memorandum of sale on the latter's behalf, so as to enable the vendor to enforce the sale.[1] What must now be considered is whether this limited authority carries with it any of the other incidents of an agency relationship and, in particular, whether the auctioneer owes to the purchaser any obligations by virtue of being an agent. Two such obligations have been suggested although, as will be seen, these have met with little success in the courts.

In the first place, it has been argued that an auctioneer who sells property in which he or she has a personal interest must, as "agent" for the highest bidder, disclose that interest.[2] However, this argument was rejected in *Flint* v *Woodin*[3] which concerned a purchase by the defendant of three houses. The defendant refused to complete the contract on the ground that they were the property of the auctioneer, a fact which had not been disclosed at the time. On the facts of the case, the defendant's delay in raising this objection clearly disentitled him from relying upon it, but in any case, Turner V-C was of the opinion that the auctioneer had broken no duty:[4]

It is quite true, that the auctioneer is, at such a sale, the agent of the purchaser, but he is not his agent for all purposes. The auctioneer, as it seems to me, may properly hold the character of owner, without any objection being taken to the sale on that ground.

Although, as *Flint* v *Woodin* makes clear, the relationship between auctioneer and bidder is not in itself sufficient to support a duty of disclosure, this does not mean that such a duty may not arise in other ways. Indeed, as noted earlier, there are serious doubts as to whether anyone who purports to act as an agent may lawfully then claim to have been acting personally.[5] Furthermore, where a sale of land is concerned, a duty on the auctioneer to disclose any

---

1 p275.
2 The obligation on an agent is shown by *Gillett* v *Peppercorne* (1840) 3 Beav 78.
3 (1852) 9 Hare 618.
4 At p622.
5 p60: see also *Bowstead on Agency*, 15th ed, Art 115.

personal interest is now imposed by the Estate Agents Act 1979,[1] although it should be noted that a breach of that duty will not provide the bidders themselves with any legal remedy.

The second attempt to conjure some obligation out of the auctioneer's position as "agent" of the highest bidder is now of purely historical interest, at least in England and Wales, since it relates to the former requirement of written evidence to render sales enforceable, something which has been removed by statute.[2] Before the law changed, it was suggested that the ability of an auctioneer to sign on behalf of the highest bidder, however unwilling such a person might be, imposed on the auctioneer a reciprocal duty to obtain a binding contract for the purchaser, by exercising the auctioneer's irrevocable authority to sign on behalf of the vendor.

The validity of this argument has never fallen for direct decision by a court, although it has been the subject of some inconclusive judicial *dicta*. The strongest authority for the existence of such a duty is to be found in the case of *Johnston* v *Boyes*[3] where, it was alleged, the vendors of land had, in breach of the conditions of sale, refused to allow the highest bidder to sign a contract of sale. Cozens-Hardy J, relying on *Warlow* v *Harrison*,[4] held that such an allegation would, if proved, render the vendors liable for breach of an implied promise to keep to the published conditions of sale, and that such an action would not fail for lack of written evidence. The point was left open in *Rainbow* v *Howkins*,[5] where the plaintiff's claim was rested (unsuccessfully) upon other grounds, while in *McManus* v *Fortescue*,[6] it was held by the Court of Appeal that no such implied duty arose where the sale was subject to a reserve which had not in fact been reached.

The most recent judicial discussion of this matter was by Pennycuick J in *Richards* v *Phillips*,[7] where simultaneous bids were made for a property by the plaintiff and a third party. The defendant

---

1 See p 213.
2 See p 276.
3 [1899] 2 Ch 73.
4 (1859) 1 E&E 295.
5 [1904] 2 KB 322.
6 [1907] 2 KB 1.
7 [1969] 1 Ch 39.

auctioneer, who had not observed the other bid, knocked the property down to the plaintiff; then, treating the subsequent argument as a "dispute respecting a bid" within the meaning of the conditions of sale, he put the property up again. Pennycuick J held that the auctioneer had acted in accordance with the conditions of sale, and his decision was upheld by the Court of Appeal.[1] The learned judge went on to say, however, that he doubted in any case whether an auctioneer owed any personal duty to the highest bidder to sign a memorandum of sale binding upon the vendor.

3   Other forms of liability

Apart from collateral contracts and spurious agency relationships, there are undoubtedly ways in which an auctioneer can incur liability to a purchaser in accordance with general legal principles. For example, where the ownership of goods has passed to the purchaser,[2] an auctioneer who remains in possession does so as the purchaser's bailee and will thus owe the purchaser a duty of care to guard the goods against loss or damage. Moreover, although the matter has not come before the courts, there appears no reason to doubt that an auctioneer who makes a negligent statement about property which is being sold may be made liable to pay damages to a purchaser, in the same way as an estate agent.[3]

Like all agents, an auctioneer who acts without authority from the client, or in excess of whatever authority has actually been given, may be personally liable for breach of warranty of authority to anyone with whom a purported contract is made. In the Scottish case of *Anderson v Croall & Sons*[4] the defendants, honestly believing that the owner of a racehorse wished them to auction it, sold it to the plaintiff. In fact the defendants were mistaken as to the owner's intention and, when the latter refused to hand over the horse, were held liable to pay damages to the disappointed purchaser.

---

1 See p 380.
2 This will in principle occur at the fall of the hammer, unless the sale conditions provide otherwise: *Dennant v Skinner and Collom* [1948] 2 KB 164.
3 See p 117.
4 (1903) 6 F (Ct of Sess) 153.

An action for breach of warranty of authority cannot be brought by a third party who has notice, either actual or constructive, of the agent's lack of authority. In this connection it has been held that a condition of sale stating that reserves have been or may be fixed is sufficient to put all bidders on inquiry. Thus in *McManus* v *Fortescue*[1] an auctioneer who, having mistakenly knocked down property below the reserve price, refused to sign a memorandum rendering the sale enforceable against the vendor, was held not liable for breach of warranty of authority. In *Fay* v *Miller, Wilkins & Co*[2] on the other hand, the auctioneer incurred personal liability when, after knocking down the property below the reserved price, he went on to sign the necessary memorandum.

The reasoning embodied in these two decisions of the Court of Appeal, which makes the auctioneer's liability depend upon whether or not a memorandum of sale is signed, is unfortunate, since a memorandum is no longer required to render the sale enforceable.[3] In any event, it is submitted that the approach is quite erroneous. Where a sale is expressly made subject to a reserve, an auctioneer who knocks property down clearly represents that the reserve has been passed; if it has not, the auctioneer should be liable in damages to the highest bidder, irrespective of what happens thereafter.

In another context, it has been suggested that an action for breach of warranty of authority may lie where an auctioneer withdraws property from a sale which is expressed to be without reserve. This argument, together with the possibility that the auctioneer might in such circumstances be in breach of some implied contract with the highest bidder, will be discussed later.[4]

C Duties in respect of the deposit

When land is sold at auction, the conditions of sale almost invariably provide that the purchase shall pay a proportion of the total price as a deposit. According to Lord Macnaghten:[5] "The

---

1 [1907] 2 KB 1.
2 [1941] Ch 360.
3 See p 276.
4 See pp 373-378.
5 *Soper* v *Arnold* (1889) 14 App Cas 429 at p435.

deposit serves two purposes – if the purchase is carried out it goes against the purchase money – but its primary purpose is this, it is a guarantee that the purchaser means business." This "guarantee" may be paid directly to the vendor, but in most cases the contract will provide for it to be handed over to a third party, normally either the auctioneer or the vendor's solicitor. In holding the deposit, the nominated third party may act in one of two capacities; either as agent for the vendor or as stakeholder, ie a person who "does not receive the money for either party, he receives it for both; and until the event is known, it is his duty to keep it in his own hands".[1]

1 Agents and stakeholders

Before considering the duties attaching to the two types of deposit-holder, we may first enquire as to normal status of the auctioneer and the vendor's solicitor. The capacity in which each of these parties holds a deposit naturally depends in the first instance upon the contract of sale itself. Where the contract is silent, it is presumed that the vendor's solicitor holds the deposit as agent for the vendor,[2] although this presumption is in no way conclusive. In *Wiggins* v *Lord*,[3] for example, where the contract of sale provided for the payment of the deposit to certain named persons, who were in fact the vendor's solicitors though not described as such, it was held that they received the money as stakeholders.

An auctioneer, on the other hand is presumed to receive a deposit as stakeholder, and this presumption is a strong one. Thus, in *Furtado* v *Lumley*[4] an auctioneer was held personally liable as stakeholder to refund deposit-money to a disappointed purchaser, notwithstanding that the auctioneer had signed the conditions of sale "as agent" and that the conditions made express provision for the vendor to return the deposit in certain circumstances. Similarly in *Edwards* v *Hodding*,[5] where the auctioneer was also solicitor to the vendors, it was held that the auctioneer must be treated as a stakeholder and thus as owing a personal duty to the purchaser.

---

1 *Harington* v *Hoggart* (1830) 1 B&Ad 577 at p 586, *per* Lord Tenterden CJ.
2 *Edgell* v *Day* (1865) LR 1 CP 80.
3 (1841) 4 Beav 30: see also *Wolf* v *Hosier & Dickinson* [1981] Com LR 89.
4 (1890) 6 TLR 168.
5 (1814) 5 Taunt 815.

Where the person holding a deposit does so as agent for the vendor, either because the contract so provides or because that is the inference drawn from the circumstances by the court, payment to the agent is deemed at the same moment to be payment to the principal. As a result, if the purchaser becomes entitled to the return of the money, the vendor is liable to repay it, whether or not it has been received from the agent.[1] Moreover, the agent is not personally liable to the purchaser in such circumstances, even where the deposit is still in the agent's possession.[2]

A person to whom money is paid as stakeholder, on the other hand, undertakes personal responsibility for its safe keeping. Such a person must await the event on which one party or the other becomes entitled to the money; if, before that event occurs, the money is paid to one party without the express consent of the other, the stakeholder is liable. In *Burrough* v *Skinner*[3] the plaintiff, who had bought an interest in land at an auction, paid a deposit of £50 to the defendant auctioneer. The sale fell through and the auctioneer was held liable to return the deposit. It was said of the auctioneer that: "he was a stakeholder, a mere depositary of the £50 and ought not to have parted with it, till such time as the sale should be finished and completed, and it should appear in the event to whom it belonged."

Although the report of that case does not make it clear, it may be surmised that the auctioneer had paid over the deposit to the vendor. Certainly it has been held in later cases that such a payment by the auctioneer is a breach of his duty as stakeholder, and *Burrough* v *Skinner* has been cited as the basis of the rule. A number of the cases, however, can be explained on other grounds. Thus in *Edwards* v *Hodding*,[4] where the auctioneer was also the vendor's solicitor, he clearly knew before paying over the deposit that the vendor could not make out a good title to the property. Similarly in *Gray* v *Gutteridge*,[5] where *Burrough* v *Skinner* was again relied upon, it appeared that the auctioneer had, immediately after

---

1 *Duke of Norfolk* v *Worthy* (1808) 1 Camp 337.
2 *Bamford* v *Shuttleworth* (1840) 11 A&E 926; *Ellis* v *Goulton* [1893] 1 QB 350.
3 (1770) 5 Burr 2638.
4 (1814) 5 Taunt 815.
5 (1828) 1 Man & R 614.

the sale, entered into a personal contract with the purchaser to see that the sale was completed.

Whether or not these two cases support in any binding fashion the proposition that an auctioneer may not pay the deposit to the vendor until the latter is entitled to it under the contract is uncertain. No such uncertainty arises, however, in respect of the decision of Stephen J in *Furtado* v *Lumley*.[1] In that case the defendant auctioneer paid over to the vendor part of a deposit received on the sale of his property. The sale having fallen through, the defendant returned the remainder of the deposit money to the purchaser, who sued the vendor for the balance. When the vendor proved unable to pay this sum, the purchaser was held entitled to recover it from the defendant.

Precisely what is involved in a stakeholder's obligations has recently been considered in two cases concerning solicitors who received deposits expressly "as stakeholders". In *Hastingwood Property Ltd* v *Saunders Bearman Anselm*[2] it was held that a stakeholder who is convinced that one of the parties has become entitled to the deposit is both bound and entitled to pay it over to that party. The other party cannot prevent this payment by injunction, although a stakeholder whose decision turns out to be wrong will of course incur personal liability for this. On the other hand, where *both* parties instruct the stakeholder to deal with the deposit in a particular way, their instructions must be obeyed; the stakeholder cannot insist on retaining the money, for example because of some claim which the stakeholder is making against one of the parties.[3]

2 Interest on the deposit

Although an auctioneer stakeholder is bound to pay the deposit to a purchaser who has become entitled to it, it seems that at common law there is no liability to pay any interest upon the sum, even though it may have remained in the auctioneer's possession for a considerable time. In *Lee* v *Munn*,[4] Burrough J said:

---

1 (1890) 6 TLR 168.
2 [1990] 3 All ER 107.
3 *Rockeagle Ltd* v *Alsop Wilkinson* [1991] 4 All ER 659.
4 (1817) 8 Taunt 45 at p55. The decision was followed in *Curling* v *Shuttleworth* (1829) 6 Bing 121.

An auctioneer can never be liable to interest, unless two circumstances concur. First, the contract must, on failure of the condition, be rescinded; secondly, a demand of the deposit must be made, and a refusal to return it must be given.

The Court of Common Pleas there made it clear that their decision rested upon the special circumstances of the case; in particular, the fact that the contract was kept open, and negotiations with the auctioneer pursued, for a period of four years. The general principle, however, was made the basis of an express decision of the Court of Exchequer in *Gaby* v *Driver*.[1] The vendor in that case having failed to make a good title, the auctioneer was sued for the return of the deposit with interest. It was held that no interest was payable, and Garrow B said:[2]

I admit that when the contract has been finally broken off, he should return the deposit; but he has a right to notice that his character of stakeholder has ceased, before he can be charged personally with interest, on account of the detention of this money.

It should however be noted that, where the purchaser sues the vendor for breach of contract, the damages recovered will include loss of interest on the deposit while it is in the hands of the auctioneer.[3]

An auctioneer's immunity from liability to pay interest on deposit-money is even more far-reaching than has so far appeared. In *Harington* v *Hoggart*[4] it was held that there is no liability to account even for the interest which is actually earned by the money while it is in the auctioneer's possession as stakeholder. In that case the defendant auctioneer in 1813 sold the plaintiff's estate and received a deposit of £2,000, which he invested in a mixed fund with his own money. In 1816 the plaintiff, who was endeavouring to enforce the contract against an unwilling purchaser, instructed the auctioneer to invest the money for the vendor's benefit. When the purchase was finally completed in 1822, the vendor sued to recover the interest earned by the deposit-money. It was held that the

---

1 (1828) 2 Y&J 549.
2 At p556.
3 *Farquhar* v *Farley* (1817) 7 Taunt 592.
4 (1830) 1 B & Ad 577.

auctioneer, as a stakeholder, was not liable to pay interest, and the express instructions given to him by the vendor did not alter the situation, for "one party was not competent by himself to alter the contract on which the money was placed in the defendant's hands".[1]

As to the reason for the auctioneer's immunity, it was suggested by Taunton J that, until one person became entitled to the deposit under the terms of the contract, the right to it was in abeyance, and that interest earned during this period could not be claimed. It is submitted, however, that the Court of King's Bench attached more importance to the potential liability of the stakeholder in respect of loss of part or all of the money. As Lord Tenterden CJ said:[2]

If he think fit to employ it and make interest of it, by laying it out in the funds or otherwise, and any loss accrue, he must be answerable for that loss; and if he is to answer for that loss, it seems to me he has a right to any intermediate advantage which may arise.

The decision in *Harington* v *Hoggart* has not met with universal approval among judges in later cases.[3] None the less, the principle which it embodies now appears to have been given statutory force by the Estate Agents Act 1979. Under section 15 of that Act, a person holding a contract deposit *as stakeholder* need not account to either the vendor or the purchaser for interest which is or which could be earned on the money during the period when neither of them is entitled to demand that the capital be handed over.[4] Of course, if the auctioneer were holding the deposit *as agent*, the normal duty to account for interest would apply.

3 Loss of the deposit

Although not strictly related to the duties of an auctioneer, this is a convenient point at which to consider the legal position of the parties where a stakeholder absconds with the stake or becomes insolvent, with the result that the money is lost. In such a case the loss must fall upon one of two innocent parties, and it might be

---

1 At p589, *per* Parke J.
2 At p586.
3 See the judgment of Sachs LJ in *Burt* v *Claude Cousins & Co Ltd* [1971] 2 QB 426 at p449.
4 See p 231.

expected that it would simply fall upon the person who ultimately becomes entitled to receive the money from the stakeholder. That is indeed the position taken by the law in cases of true "stakeholding", where the parties to a wager jointly nominate a third party to hold the bet.

Where, however, the stakeholder is the nominee of one party alone (as in the case of an auctioneer) it appears that the nominating party is treated as taking responsibility for the stakeholder's honesty and solvency. In *Fenton* v *Browne*[1] a sale of land took place by private treaty, though under conditions of sale drafted for an auction. A deposit was paid to a stakeholder and, when disputes arose, the purchaser asked for it to be paid into court. The vendor refused to agree to this proposal; consequently, when the agent absconded with the deposit, the vendor was held to have taken the risk upon himself. The decision, then, turned upon the special circumstances of the case; however, Sir William Grant MR took the opportunity to comment upon the general situation:[2]

Upon a sale by auction the vendor determines who is to receive the deposit. The auctioneer is not a stakeholder of the purchaser: at least not of his choice. If he were a stakeholder for both parties, either would have a right to propose to change the stakeholder; and the party refusing takes upon himself the risk.

This *dictum* was quoted with approval in *Smith* v *Jackson*,[3] where a deposit was paid, according to the conditions of sale, as part of the purchase money. It was held that it must be treated, while in the auctioneer's hands, as the vendor's money, so that the purchaser was entitled to credit for the interest which it earned. The case of *Annesley* v *Muggridge*[4] was likewise not directly in point, for it dealt with an auctioneer's claim to deduct charges and expenses from a deposit before paying it into court. In deciding that the auctioneer could lawfully do this, on the ground that the deposit must be treated as the vendor's money, Sir Thomas Plumer V-C said:[5]

---

1 (1807) 14 Ves 144.
2 At p150.
3 (1816) 1 Madd 618.
4 (1816) 1 Madd 593.
5 At p596.

Pending the dispute as to the title, all the risk respecting the deposit rests with the vendor: for though the auctioneer is, to a certain degree, a stakeholder for vendor and vendee, yet so far as respects any risk as to the deposit, the auctioneer is considered as the agent only of the vendor.

The proposition supported by these various *dicta* was placed beyond doubt by the case of *Rowe* v *May*,[1] where a mortgagee put property up for auction in the exercise of a power of sale. The property failed to sell, whereupon the mortgagor instructed the auctioneer to sell it privately on the same conditions. The auctioneer having done so, and having taken a deposit, the sale was adopted by the mortgagee. When it was later discovered that the auctioneer was insolvent and the deposit lost, the mortgagee was held liable to complete the sale upon the purchaser paying only the balance of the price. Sir John Romilly MR said:[2]

Where a purchaser pays a deposit on his purchase-money to the auctioneer, and it is lost, on whom does the loss fall? If the matter goes off, because the vendor cannot make a good title, it is the vendor's duty to repay the deposit, and the loss occasioned by the non-completion; and in case an action were brought against him for breach of the contract, the amount of deposit not repaid would be part of his loss, and the purchaser would be entitled to add it to the damages; so if the contract be completed, and the deposit cannot be recovered from the auctioneer, who for this purpose is the agent of the vendor, it will be the vendor's loss, and not that of the purchaser.

Not everyone would agree that it is morally justifiable to make the vendor responsible for the auctioneer's default. Moreover, the authorities cited above, on which this principle is based, are all of some age. However, such recent judicial reference as there has been to the point suggests that it remains valid.[3]

---

1 (1854) 18 Beav 613.
2 At p616.
3 See *Burt* v *Claude Cousins & Co Ltd* [1971] 2 QB 426 at p450, *per* Sachs LJ; *Barrington* v *Lee* [1972] 1 QB 326 at p335, *per* Lord Denning MR; *Sorrell* v *Finch* [1977] AC 728 at p 754, *per* Lord Russell of Killowen.

D Liability to third parties

Apart from the obligations which may arise out of transactions into which an auctioneer enters with both clients and purchasers, there are certain circumstances in which the ordinary business activities of an auctioneer may involve the risk of legal liability to third parties. The most important of these may now be considered.

1 Conversion

In dealing with the duty of an auctioneer to account to the client for any money received, we noted the possibility that a third party might lay claim to ownership of the goods being auctioned. In that context, we were concerned with the third party's claim solely as a possible justification for the auctioneer's failure to account to the client. What now falls to be considered, however, is the extent to which an auctioneer who chooses to serve the client may thereby incur any liability to the third party. As we shall see, it appears that an auctioneer who deals with goods on behalf of someone who has no right to sell them may thereby commit the tort of conversion against the true owner.

(a) *Nature of conversion*

The tort of conversion has been defined as "an act of deliberate dealing with a chattel in a manner inconsistent with another's right whereby that other is deprived of the use and possession of it".[1] "Dealing" in this context may take a variety of forms. In *Loeschman* v *Martin*,[2] for example, two pianos were sent to the defendant for sale by auction. The plaintiff then claimed that they belonged to him, and that the defendant's client had merely hired them; the auctioneer, however, refused to hand them over unless the plaintiff paid his expenses. This refusal was held to constitute a conversion and the auctioneer was liable.

It should not be thought that, as a result of this case, an auctioneer must immediately deliver goods in his possession to anyone who demands them; the auctioneer owes a duty to the

---

1 *Clerk and Lindsell on Torts*, 16th ed, para 22-10.
2 (1818) 2 Stark 311.

client and is entitled to ask for proof that the claim is genuine. In *Lee* v *Bayes and Robinson*,[1] Jervis CJ stated the law as follows:

Where the servant or agent receives from his master or his principal goods which belong to a third person, on their being demanded of him by such third person he is entitled to say "I received them from my master or my principal; and I require a reasonable time to ascertain whether the party making the demand is the real owner;" and such qualified refusal would not be evidence of a conversion so as to render him liable in trover. But if ... the man who holds the goods chooses to set up the title of his bailor and to rely on it ... he asserts a title adverse to the title of the real owner of the goods, and so is guilty of a conversion.

A refusal to hand over goods is clearly one way of committing conversion. However, the most common way for an auctioneer to become liable under this tort is by actually selling a disputed item. For example, in *Hardacre* v *Stewart*,[2] where the lease of a house was to be sold, the landlord gave notice to the auctioneer that he claimed certain fixtures. The auctioneer nevertheless sold the fixtures and was held liable to the landlord.

Although in that case it was regarded as important that the auctioneer had notice of the adverse claim at the time of sale, it has been consistently held in later cases that this is irrelevant to liability; innocence is no defence to this action. In *Cochrane* v *Rymill*[3] the defendant, an auctioneer, sold a number of cabs on behalf of a client, to whom he paid the proceeds of sale after deducting his commission and expenses. It was then discovered that the cabs belonged to the plaintiff, from whom the client had hired them. The defendant was held liable to the plaintiff in conversion, notwithstanding that he did not know, and could not have been expected to know, of his client's fraud. As Bramwell LJ pointed out,[4] it was a very hard case, but "the defendant keeps them, and finally sells them in such a way as to pass the property in them to the buyers, and if that is not a conversion, then I think there can be no such thing".

---

1 (1856) 18 CB 599 at p607.
2 (1804) 5 Esp 103.
3 (1879) 40 LT 744; see also *Brown* v *Hickinbotham* (1881) 50 LJQB 426.
4 At p746.

A similar decision was reached in *Barker* v *Furlong*,[1] where a man who had inherited a life interest in certain furniture under his wife's will instructed the defendant to sell it by auction. The defendant did so and was held liable to the wife's executor in conversion. Romer J recognised that an auctioneer who merely settled the price between vendor and purchaser would not, without more, incur personal liability. In this case, however, the general rule applied, for the auctioneer had conducted the sale and had delivered the goods with intent to pass the property in them to the purchaser.

The cases concerning an auctioneer's liability in conversion were carefully reviewed by Collins J in *Consolidated Co* v *Curtis*[2] where the defendant, on behalf of a client, sold furniture which unknown to him was the subject of a bill of sale. In holding the auctioneer liable, Collins J said:[3]

It is clear that there can be no conversion by a mere bargain and sale without a transfer of possession ... But, I should have thought it equally clear that a sale and delivery with intent to pass the property in chattels by a person who is not the true owner and has not got his authority is a conversion.

The essence of conversion lies in a denial, albeit an unwitting one, of the plaintiff's title. It has consequently been held that a person who deals with the mere *custody* of goods, without intending to alter the *property* in them, does not commit this tort. Upon this principle a carrier who receives and delivers goods with no knowledge of any adverse claim to them is not liable;[4] nor is a forwarding agent who packs and ships goods in accordance with instructions received.[5] On the other hand, it was held in *Stephens* v *Elwall*[6] that, where the servant of a person who had bought goods from a bankrupt innocently received and forwarded those goods, he was guilty of conversion, for he had dealt with the goods with knowledge of the sale and with the intention of enabling it to be carried out.

---

1 [1891] 2 Ch 172.
2 [1892] 1 QB 495.
3 At p498.
4 *Hollins* v *Fowler* (1875) LR 7 HL 757 at p767, *per* Blackburn J.
5 *Greenway* v *Fisher* (1824) 1 C&P 190.
6 (1815) 4 M&S 259.

In *Cochrane* v *Rymill*,[1] Bramwell LJ considered in passing how this rather difficult principle would apply to the case of an auctioneer:

Supposing a man were to come into an auctioneer's yard, holding a horse by the bridle and to say, "I want to sell my horse; if you will find a purchaser I will pay commission." And the auctioneer says: "Here is a man who wants to sell a horse; will anyone buy him?" If he then and there finds him a purchaser, and the seller himself hand over the horse, there could be no act on the part of the auctioneer which could render him liable to an action for conversion.

The possibility which Bramwell LJ recognised actually came before the Court of Appeal some two years later, in the case of *National Mercantile Bank Ltd* v *Rymill*.[2] In that case certain horses and harness were taken to the defendant's yard for sale by auction and entered in the catalogue. Before the sale the apparent owner sold them privately and the auctioneer handed them over to the purchaser, deducting his commission from the purchase money. The plaintiffs, who were holders of a bill of sale over the goods, sued the auctioneer. It was held, however, that the auctioneer had done nothing which could constitute conversion; he had not claimed to transfer title to the goods, nor had he purported to sell them.

It must be said that this decision is not easy to reconcile with *Stephens* v *Elwall*, and it also appears to conflict with the views expressed by Blackburn J in *Hollins* v *Fowler*.[3] None the less, the same principle was applied by the Divisional Court of Queen's Bench in *Turner* v *Hockey*,[4] where the defendant cattle auctioneer was in possession of a cow for the purpose of sale. Instead of concluding the sale personally, the defendant passed an offer to the client, and this was accepted. When it transpired that the client had no right to sell the cow, the auctioneer was held not liable in conversion.

The status of sales which are not effected under the hammer was considered most recently by the Court of Appeal in *RH Willis & Son*

---

1 (1879) 40 LT 744 at p 746.
2 (1881) 44 LT 767.
3 (1875) LR 7 HL 757 at p767.
4 (1887) 56 LJQB 301.

v *British Car Auctions Ltd.*[1] The defendant auctioneers there bought in a car which failed to reach its reserve but, because the highest bid was not far short of the reserve, they put into operation their "provisional bid" procedure. This involved bringing together the vendor and the highest bidder and, upon their reaching agreement on a private sale, putting it through their books and deducting commission in the usual way. When it was discovered that the car belonged, not to the vendor, but to the plaintiffs, who had let it on hire-purchase to the vendor, the Court of Appeal had no hesitation whatsoever in holding that the auctioneers were guilty of conversion. All three members of the court regarded *Turner* v *Hockey* as wrongly decided. As for *National Mercantile Bank Ltd* v *Rymill*, the position was slightly more equivocal; Lord Denning MR treated it as incorrect but, while the other two judges had their doubts about it, they preferred to skirt the problem by treating the case as easily distinguishable on its facts.

(b) *The limits of liability*

An auctioneer who sells goods on behalf of someone who has no right to sell them is only liable in conversion if the client has no title whatsoever to the goods. If the client is in possession of goods under a voidable contract, ie one which the other party is entitled to repudiate, the auctioneer is not liable if the goods are sold before repudiation takes place.[2] If, however, the contract is void rather than voidable, the auctioneer may not safely sell. In *Higgins* v *Burton*,[3] a rogue named Dix fraudulently obtained goods by purporting to purchase on behalf of his ex-employer, and handed them over to the defendant for sale. It was held that no contract ever existed between the plaintiff, who intended only to sell to the employer, and Dix; consequently the defendant was liable in conversion. Similarly, in *Hardman* v *Booth*,[4] where the auctioneer's client obtained goods by pretending to be someone else, it was held that he did not even have a voidable title to the goods, and the true owner could sue the auctioneer.

---

1 [1978] 2 All ER 392.
2 *Hardman* v *Booth* (1863) 1 H&C 803 at p808, *per* Wilde B.
3 (1875) 26 LJ Ex 342.
4 (1863) 1 H&C 803.

Under the Factors Act 1889, a sale of goods by a person not expressly authorised to sell them may in certain circumstances operate to pass title to a third party, provided that the latter receives them in good faith and without notice of the seller's lack of authority. Section 2(1) of the Act provides:

Where a mercantile agent is, with the consent of the owner, in possession of goods, or of the documents of title to goods, any sale, pledge or other disposition of the goods made by him when acting in the ordinary course of business of a mercantile agent shall, subject to the provisions of this Act, be as valid as if he were expressly authorised by the owner of the goods to make the same; provided that the person taking under the disposition acts in good faith, and has not at the time of the disposition notice that the person making the disposition has not authority to make the same.

Whether this provision could operate so as to protect an auctioneer was considered in *Waddington & Sons* v *Neale & Sons*[1] where the plaintiffs, a firm of piano manufacturers, sent a piano to their agent for sale or hire-purchase. The agent, however, instructed the defendant auctioneers to sell the piano and, claiming that it was his own property, obtained an advance from them. The defendants were later told of the plaintiff's claim but they nevertheless sold the piano, deducted their charges from the proceeds of sale and paid the balance into court. The defendants were held liable in conversion and their defence, based on section 2(1) of the Factors Act, was rejected. Darling J said that the "disposition" of the goods by the mercantile agent to the auctioneers was neither a sale nor a pledge, but rather a deposit for sale; as such it was not a disposition "in the ordinary course of business of a mercantile agent", and the statute did not apply.

Section 9 of the Factors Act 1889[2] provides:

Where a person, having bought or agreed to buy goods, obtains, with the consent of the seller, possession of the goods or the documents of title to the goods, the delivery or transfer, by that person, or by a mercantile agent acting for him, of the goods or documents of title, under any sale, pledge, or other disposition thereof, to any person receiving the same in good faith and without notice of any lien or other right of the original seller in respect

1 (1907) 96 LT 786.
2 Repeated in virtually identical terms by the Sale of Goods Act 1979, section 25.

of the goods, shall have the same effect as if the person making the delivery or transfer were a mercantile agent in possession of the goods or documents of title with the consent of the owner.

In *Shenstone & Co v Hilton*,[1] a person who had agreed to buy a piano under a hire-purchase agreement[2] instructed the defendant to sell it by auction. The defendant was held to be protected against liability to the owner of the piano by section 9, as the delivery to him was "a disposition, something in the nature of a sale".

It is submitted that this decision is incorrect and would not be followed today. Even if the learned judge was justified in treating the deposit of the piano for the purpose of sale as a "disposition",[3] section 9 does not say that such a disposition is valid, merely that it is as good as if it were made by a mercantile agent. In order to decide the validity of a disposition made by a mercantile agent it is necessary, as we have seen, to decide whether it is within the ordinary course of business of such an agent. Thus, despite the obvious artificiality of trying to decide whether a disposition made by someone who is not a mercantile agent would be within the course of business of a hypothetical mercantile agent, this is precisely the approach which has to be adopted.[4] And since, according to *Waddington & Sons v Neale & Sons*,[5] it is not within the ordinary course of business of a mercantile agent to deposit of goods with an auctioneer, section 9 should confer no protection upon the innocent auctioneer.

It may be noted in passing that section 8 of the Factors Act 1889[6] lays down similar provisions in relation to dispositions of goods made by a seller remaining in possession. In this case, however, the disposition shall be as effective as if the seller were authorised by the owner of the goods; its validity is not related to any notional mercantile agent. It is suggested that an auctioneer who sells goods

---

1 [1894] 2 QB 452.

2 Modern hire-purchase agreements do not fall within this section; *Helby v Matthews* [1895] AC 471. Nor do conditional sales: Sale of Goods Act 1979, section 25(2).

3 Which, it is submitted, would itself be incorrect.

4 *Newtons of Wembley Ltd v Williams* [1965] 1 QB 560. The abolition of this artificial rule was recommended by the Law Reform Committee (Twelfth Report, Cmnd 2958, 1966, para 23).

5 (1907) 96 LT 786.

6 Substantially repeated by the Sale of Goods Act 1979, section 24.

on behalf of such a person may thus avoid liability for conversion, provided that a court is prepared to regard the deposit of goods with an auctioneer as a "disposition".

(c) *Damages*

An auctioneer found guilty of conversion is liable like any other person to pay damages to the plaintiff, who "is entitled to the real value of the goods sold, and not merely to what they fetched at auction, which cannot be assumed to be the real value of the goods".[1] Thus in *Davis* v *Artingstall*,[2] where goods belonging to a married woman were sent for sale by her husband, the auctioneers, despite knowing of the wife's claim, sold some of the goods and returned the others to the husband. They were held liable for the full value of all the goods.

As a general rule, the value of goods which have been wrongfully converted is assessed at the date of conversion. It was formerly the case that, where the defendant's act also constituted detinue (the wrongful refusal to hand over a chattel to its true owner on demand) the value might be taken at the date of judgment against the defendant. Detinue has now been abolished,[3] so it is the rules of conversion which are to be applied. It might be thought that the true owner of goods would thereby be effectively deprived of any increase in their value in the period between their conversion and his discovery of it, but it seems that any such increase may be recoverable as consequential damages. In *Sachs* v *Miklos*[4] the plaintiff had been allowed to store his furniture free of charge in the house of the first defendant. After three years, having failed in various attempts to trace the plaintiff, the first defendant, who needed the room, instructed the defendant to sell the furniture by auction. When the plaintiff reappeared three years later he claimed the value of the furniture at that date, which was £115, as against £15 for which it had been sold. The Court of Appeal held that, provided the plaintiff did not know of the proposed sale, he could recover the higher sum; if, however, he had realised the defendant's intention, it would have been his duty to mitigate his loss by making

---

1 *Davis* v *Artingstall* (1880) 49 LJ Ch 609 at p610, *per* Fry J.
2 (1880) 49 LJ Ch 609.
3 Torts (Interference with Goods) Act 1977, section 2(1).
4 [1948] 2 KB 23.

an immediate claim, and so he would not be entitled to the subsequent rise in value.

2 Other forms of liability

(a) *Executorship de son tort*

A type of liability which somewhat resembles conversion is that which arises under the doctrine of executorship *de son tort*. This, it has been said, "implies a wrongful intermeddling with the assets, a dealing with them in such a way as denotes an usurpation of the functions of an executor, an assumption of authority which none but an executor or administrator can lawfully exercise".[1] Any person who deals with a deceased person's assets without the authority of a duly appointed executor or administrator will thus be treated as an executor, and may, if the estate is insolvent, incur a certain amount of personal liability. In the Irish case of *Nulty* v *Fagan*[2] an auctioneer sold some of the assets of a deceased person and retained the proceeds, on the instructions of a person who was named as executor in the will. It was held that, since the will had not been proved, the auctioneer became an executor *de son tort* and was liable jointly for rent owed by the deceased at the time of his death.

On the other hand, in *Peters* v *Leeder*,[3] where an auctioneer made preparations for a sale of a deceased person's assets, but did not sell them until an administrator had been appointed, and then paid the proceeds over to him, it was held that the auctioneer was not an executor *de son tort*.

(b) *Negligence*

In conducting a sale, an auctioneer owes a duty of care as regards the safety of all who attend. As Atkin J said in *Walker* v *Crabb*,[4] where the plaintiff was kicked by a horse which was being demonstrated before the sale:

An auctioneer is a skilled agent to whom the complete control of the sale is given by the owner of the goods to be sold, whether the sale be held at the

---

1 *Peters* v *Leeder* (1878) 47 LJQB 573 at p574, *per* Lush J.
2 (1888) LR 22 Ir CL 604.
3 (1878) 47 LJQB 573.
4 [1916] WN 433.

premises of the owner of the goods or at the auctioneer's own premises, and it is the auctioneer, not the owner of the chattels, who is liable if injury results from the negligent handling of those chattels.

The type of liability considered in that case arose under the tort of negligence; today an action might equally be based upon the provisions of the Occupier's Liability Act 1957.

E Interpleader

In the course of this chapter we have noted a number of circumstances in which conflicting claims may be made to goods or money in an auctioneer's possession. For example, both vendor and purchaser may demand the deposit; or some third party may claim to be the owner of goods which the auctioneer has been instructed to sell. Where such a situation arises, the auctioneer is faced with the possibility of having to defend two legal actions, with the certainty that one of these will result in defeat and a consequent liability to pay costs. The potential hardship which this involves may, however, be alleviated by means of a court procedure known as interpleader. This procedure, though it can hardly be described as a duty of the auctioneer, may conveniently be discussed at this point.

Interpleader has been defined by Lord Cottenham LC as follows:[1]

It is where the plaintiff says, I have a fund in my possession in which I claim no personal interest, and to which you, the defendants, set up conflicting claims; pay me my costs and I will bring the fund into court, and you shall contest it between yourselves.

The rules which govern interpleader are to be found in Rules of the Supreme Court, Ord 17, in the case of the High Court; in relation to the county court the relevant provisions are those of the County Court Rules 1981, Ord 33.

The court normally encourages interpleader applications, since these tend to prevent circuity of action; nevertheless, interpleader will only be permitted to where the court is satisfied that:

---

1 *Hoggart* v *Cutts* (1841) Cr & Ph 197 at p204.

i   The applicant claims no interest in the subject-matter in dispute, other than for charges or costs. Thus an auctioneer's claim to deduct commission from a disputed fund is not a bar interpleader.[1]

ii The applicant does not collude with any of the claimants. This does not necessarily involve any element of moral wrong, but simply an identification with the interests of one party. Thus, an auctioneer who obtained an indemnity from one party would not be allowed to interplead.[2]

iii The applicant is willing to pay or transfer the subject-matter of the application into court, or to dispose of it as the court or a judge may direct.

It is important to note that interpleader is only available in cases where the two or more claims which have been made, or are about to be made, against the applicant are in respect of the same subject-matter. In *Wright* v *Freeman*[3] the plaintiff, who had bought a horse at auction, sought damages from the auctioneer for breach of a warranty that it was quiet to ride. The auctioneer sought to interplead, on the ground that the owner was demanding the price from him. It was held, however, that the two claims against the auctioneer were quite independent, since one was for the price and the other for damages. Relief was therefore refused. So too, in *Ingham* v *Walker*,[4] where a horse was returned to the auctioneer because it did not answer its description in the catalogue, it was held that the purchaser's true claim was for damages. Thus the auctioneer, from whom the seller was demanding the price, could not interplead.

The case of *Hoggart* v *Cutts*[5] provides a further illustration of the principle that interpleader is only available where the adverse claims are truly co-incidental. In that case the plaintiff auctioneer sold property on behalf of a vendor and took a deposit from the purchaser. Disputes arose concerning the title and the vendor, who

1 *Best* v *Hayes* (1863) 1 H&C 718.
2 *Tucker* v *Morris* (1832) 1 Dowl 639. However, the party who gives the indemnity is not entitled to object to the interpleader on that ground: *Thompson* v *Wright* (1884) 13 QBD 632.
3 (1879) 48 LJCP 276.
4 (1887) 3 TLR 448.
5 (1841) Cr & Ph 197.

claimed to forfeit the deposit, instructed the plaintiff to resell the property. This the plaintiff did, and took a deposit from the second purchaser. When the vendor demanded both deposits, the auctioneer sought to interplead. It was held, however, that although interpleader was possible as between the vendor and the first purchaser, the second purchaser's claim was quite independent and could not be avoided in this way.

The court has a discretion or not to grant an interpleader order; further, the court may make such orders as to costs as are just and reasonable. In general, the costs of an applicant who has acted with fairness and propriety as an innocent stakeholder will be paid out of the fund in question, the deficiency ultimately being made good by the unsuccessful claimant.[1] However, even an innocent auctioneer may finish out of pocket, as occurred in *Deller* v *Prickett*[2] where a deposit was claimed by both vendor and purchaser. The vendor owned no other property, and so the Court of Queen's Bench made the auctioneer's claim to interplead conditional upon the giving of security for the costs of the action, since these might otherwise fall unjustly upon the purchaser.

---

1 *Pitches* v *Edney* (1830) 6 Scott 582.
2 (1850) 20 LJQB 151.

CHAPTER 10

Auctioneers' rights

A Remuneration

Whenever an auctioneer claims to be entitled to remuneration from a client, two questions fall to be answered. In the first place, it must be asked whether the event has occurred upon which the contract has arranged for commission to be paid. Assuming that this is answered in the affirmative, so that the auctioneer is undoubtedly entitled to receive something, the amount of that remuneration remains to be ascertained.

1 Commission on sale

As in the case of estate agents, whatever contract has been made between auctioneer and client must be carefully construed, in order to establish exactly what is required to happen before commission becomes payable. In *Peacock v Freeman*[1] the plaintiffs asked the defendants, a firm of auctioneers, what commission they would require for selling certain property. After some dispute a scale of charges was settled which would apply in the event of a sale and it was further agreed that, if the property were not sold, a fee of 30 guineas together with out-of-pocket expenses would be payable. The property was duly knocked down at the sale, and a deposit paid to the auctioneers. Later, however, the purchaser objected to the title and the vendors, in accordance with the conditions of sale, rescinded the contract and repaid the purchaser the amount of the deposit. The vendors then sought to recover the deposit money from the auctioneers; they, however, claimed to deduct from it their full commission, as the property had been "sold". The Court of Appeal held that the auctioneers were entitled only to the agreed fee of 30 guineas and expenses, as the commission agreement contemplated a completed sale and not merely the fall of the

---

1 (1888) 4 TLR 541.

hammer. Further, since the vendors had acted in accordance with the conditions of sale in rescinding the contract, they could not be said to have wrongfully deprived the auctioneers of their commission.

It must be emphasised that the decision in *Peacock* v *Freeman* was based, not on any rule of law, but on the interpretation of the agreement made by the parties. This point is illustrated by the case of *Skinner* v *Andrews & Hall*[1] where the terms upon which the auctioneers were to be paid commission were contained in letters to and from their client. These stipulated that half-commission would be payable if the property, though not sold at the auction, were sold within two months thereafter to a person introduced by the auctioneers. It was also stated that commission would be payable on any sale taking place before the sale under the hammer or before October 30 but that, if the property remained unsold at that date, no charge of any description would be made. The property was knocked down at the auction but the vendor then rescinded the contract, as he was entitled to do under the conditions of sale. It was held nevertheless that the auctioneers had earned their commission, for it was clear that in this case the parties had used the word "sale" to mean the knocking down of the property to a purchaser, rather than the completion of the transaction by a formal conveyance.

It sometimes happens that, after an abortive auction, the property is purchased privately by a person who either has been introduced to the vendor by the auctioneer or who has at least learned about the property from advertisements of the sale. In such a case the auctioneer may be entitled to commission on the sale but, once again, this depends upon the terms of the agreement with the client. What is certain is that an auctioneer who is not authorised to sell by private treaty cannot earn commission by purporting to sign a contract on behalf of the vendor. Thus in *Marsh* v *Jelf*,[2] an auctioneer who negotiated a private sale of the property was not allowed to bring evidence of a custom among auctioneers that commission should be payable; as Keating J said: "Auctioneers could not among themselves make such a custom to bind the rest of her Majesty's subjects."

---

1 (1910) 26 TLR 340.
2 (1862) 3 F&F 234: see p 267.

Where an auctioneer *is* authorised to sell by private treaty, any claim to commission will depend on the same principles as those which govern the claims of estate agents.[1] In *Green* v *Bartlett*,[2] for example, the plaintiff was instructed to sell an island for the defendant "by public auction or otherwise". The plaintiff was held to be entitled to commission upon a private sale which was proved to have been negotiated by him, although the sale was concluded by the defendant personally.

The commission clause which came before the House of Lords in *Bayley* v *Chadwick*[3] was of an unusually wide nature, in that it provided for payment to the auctioneer upon a private sale to any person "led to make an offer in consequence of your mention or publication for auction purposes". The purchaser never met the auctioneer, nor did he see any advertisement of the sale; he was merely told by a third party, who attended the sale, that the property (a ship) had not been sold. The House of Lords, reversing the decision of the Court of Appeal and restoring that of the Court of Common Pleas, held that the jury were quite entitled to find that this purchaser came within the clause, so as to entitle the auctioneer to commission.

2   Commission on direct sales by vendor

The cases discussed above all relate to sales effected, directly or indirectly, by the auctioneer. A rather different problem arises where property which has been put into the hands of an auctioneer for sale is sold privately by the vendor, either before the date of the auction or after the auction has failed to produce a purchaser. A claim by an auctioneer for commission in such circumstances was successful in the old case of *Rainy* v *Vernon*,[4] in which an auctioneer was employed to sell certain ground rents. The client sold these ground rents personally before the date of the auction, whereupon the auctioneer brought an action for commission, calling as witnesses three other members of the profession, who said that the custom in these circumstances was for commission to be

---

1 As to which see chapter 5.
2 (1863) 14 CBNS 681.
3 (1878) 39 LT 429.
4 (1840) 9 C&P 559.

payable. In summing up to the jury, Lord Denman CJ said:[1], "If, however, you think that the witnesses called for the plaintiff have, by their evidence, made out a case of usage so notorious that the defendant was aware of it, then the custom is engrafted on the contract, and the plaintiff is entitled to his commission". The jury was clearly persuaded by these witnesses, for it decided in favour of the auctioneer.

The custom which was established to the satisfaction of the jury in *Rainy* v *Vernon* does not appear to have formed the basis for any subsequent successful claims by auctioneers. Indeed, the whole trend of decisions since that time has been against awarding commission to an auctioneer who is not in some way personally responsible for bringing about a sale. In *Green* v *Hall*[2] the auctioneer's instructions provided for the payment of commission if the client's estate were sold. After an abortive auction, the client sold the property privately through another firm of agents. It was held that, since "sold" meant "sold by the auctioneer himself",[3] no commission was payable; the auctioneer was entitled only to the fee which had been agreed as payable in the event of no sale resulting.

In *Williams* v *Tuckett*[4] where the defendant, having instructed the plaintiff to sell property by auction, withdrew it from the sale and sold it privately, the jury were again asked to find a custom that commission was payable in these circumstances. However, although *Rainy* v *Vernon*[5] was referred to, the jury found that no such custom existed, after a summing-up by Lawrence J which indicated that requiring the auctioneer to have brought about the sale was "consistent with common law and common sense".

In the light of such judicial attitudes, it is hardly surprising that auctioneers have sought to include in their standard terms of business a clause to safeguard their commission in the event of the client withdrawing property for private sale. The following clause, versions of which were adopted by both the Royal Institution of

---

1 At p562.
2 (1848) 12 LT (OS) 151.
3 A similar construction has been placed upon estate agents' agreements: see *Sadler* v *Whittaker* (1953) 162 EG 404.
4 The Times, March 9 1900: see also *Watson* v *Newton* (1920) 96 EG 140.
5 (1840) 9 C&P 559.

Chartered Surveyors and the Chartered Auctioneers and Estate Agents Institute, is typical:[1]

Commission will amount to [a specified percentage of the sale price] and will be payable if a sale of the property, whether arranged by the auctioneers or not, is effected after the acceptance of instructions and before the auction, or within [a specified period] after the auction.

In *Bernard Thorpe & Partners* v *Snook*,[2] where a vendor sold his farm privately shortly after it had failed to reach its reserve at auction, it was held by Nolan J that a clause of this kind was effective to secure the auctioneers' commission. This decision was approved by the Court of Appeal in *Barnard Marcus & Co* v *Ashraf*,[3] where the defendant's property was sold through another estate agent some three weeks before it was due to be put up for auction by the plaintiffs. The defendant argued that this constituted a "withdrawal" of his property, for which the plaintiffs would have been entitled under a separate clause to a mere £200 plus expenses, but the Court of Appeal ruled that commission was payable on the full price realised.

Although it would seem sensible for auctioneers to adopt terms of business similar to those under discussion, it must be appreciated that these do not cover every eventuality. In *Fairvale Ltd* v *Sabharwal*,[4] for example, where the defendant's hotel failed to reach its reserve price and was bought in, the plaintiff auctioneers introduced their client to one of the unsuccessful bidders. This introduction, which was made immediately after the sale, led to a private sale of the property to that bidder. When the auctioneers sought commission on this sale, relying on a clause which required a sale to be effected within 28 days of the abortive auction, it was held that their claim must fail; the word "effected" meant that, to qualify, the actual contract of sale must be entered into within the 28 day period.

A second limitation on such clauses, albeit one which is unlikely to cause frequent problems, was exposed by the case of *John*

---

1 See *Barnard Marcus & Co* v *Ashraf* [1988] 1 EGLR 7; *Fairvale Ltd* v *Sabharwal* [1992] 2 EGLR 27.
2 (1982) 266 EG 440.
3 [1988] 1 EGLR 7.
4 [1992] 2 EGLR 27.

Meacock & Co v Abrahams.[1] The plaintiffs there were instructed to sell property by the defendant, who was second mortgagee. Immediately before the auction, the mortgagor sold the property and paid off the mortgage, which of course left the defendant with nothing to sell. The county court judge held that the plaintiffs were entitled to their commission under a clause of the kind under discussion, but this decision was reversed by the Court of Appeal, by a majority. The Court of Appeal's ruling was that this clause applied only to cases where the property was sold by the vendor or with his concurrence; it did not protect the auctioneer where (as here) the sale was effected by a third party over whose actions the vendor had no control.

3 Remuneration in the absence of a sale

It appears from the foregoing discussion that an auctioneer's commission becomes payable only when a sale actually takes place, either under the hammer or by private treaty. Further, this sale must be effected by the auctioneer personally or (under certain commission clauses) by the vendor. Does it follow from this that an auctioneer who fails to secure a purchaser is entitled to nothing whatsoever for the time and trouble expended, something which, if an auction has actually been held, may be considerable?

There is a dearth of authority on this point, largely because in practice the position is usually provided for in the agreement between auctioneer and client. Thus, for example, in *Skinner v Andrews & Hall*[2] it was agreed that, if the property had not been sold by a certain date, there would be no charge of any description. More commonly, provision is made for the payment of a sum of money (often modest in amount), which may be inclusive or exclusive of expenses, if the sale proves abortive or the property is withdrawn by the vendor. In *Green v Bartlett*[3] the amount was to be £25; in *Green v Hall,*[4] the figure was £200 plus all advertising expenses. And, of course, where the commission agreement contains a clause similar to that used in *John Meacock & Co v*

---

1 [1956] 3 All ER 660.
2 (1910) 26 TLR 340.
3 (1863) 14 CBNS 681.
4 (1848) 12 LT (OS) 151.

Abrahams,[1] it will be argued that a withdrawal of property by the vendor for the purpose of selling privately entitles the auctioneer to the full agreed commission.

Even where no express agreement has been made as to a possible failure of the sale, many vendors are willing to pay a reasonable sum to the auctioneer for trouble and expense, and this too has undoubtedly helped to prevent litigation. In *Rainy* v *Vernon*[2] where, as we have seen, an auctioneer claimed to be entitled to full commission when the client withdrew property from the sale and sold it privately, the vendor was prepared to make a payment of 50 guineas for the auctioneer's services. So too, in *Frank Swain (a firm)* v *Whitfield Corporation Ltd*,[3] where the liquidator of a company withdrew an auctioneer's authority some 10 minutes before the sale was due to commence, it was agreed on all sides that the auctioneer should receive reasonable remuneration for his labours.

The few occasions on which a court has considered the position of an auctioneer, who has not in fact sold the property, have produced a remarkable diversity of judicial opinion. Some slender support for the view that a vendor who revokes the auctioneer's authority is liable to pay a reasonable sum may be found in the case of *Chinnock* v *Sainsbury*.[4] In that case an auctioneer, who had advanced money to the defendant, sued to enforce a promise to allow him to sell certain property and recoup himself from the proceeds. It was held that the promise was not of a type which equity would enforce, but that the parties were "subject to any claim which is due to the auctioneer or agent in that character, which must be ascertained at law".[5]

Chinnock v *Sainsbury* notwithstanding, it is well settled that an *estate agent* who has not succeeded in earning commission cannot recover a reasonable sum on a *quantum meruit*, and it seems probable that an auctioneer is in a similar situation. In *John Meacock & Co* v *Abrahams*[6] the auctioneers, whose sale on behalf of mortgagees had been prevented by the mortgagor, claimed

---

1 [1956] 3 All ER 660.
2 (1840) 9 C&P 559.
3 (1962) 183 EG 479.
4 (1860) 30 LJ Ch 409.
5 At p411, *per* Romilly MR.
6 [1956] 3 All ER 660.

against their clients for commission or a reasonable remuneration. The claim for commission failed, for reasons which have already been considered.[1] The Court of Appeal was unanimous in rejecting the alternative claim, on the ground that, where an express agreement as to payment has been made, there is no room to imply a promise to pay a reasonable sum if the condition for payment is not fulfilled. Both Denning and Hodson LJJ likened the instant case to that of an estate agent, and Hodson LJ quoted with approval a passage from the speech of Lord Wright in *Luxor (Eastbourne) Ltd v Cooper:*[2]

In the case of the commission agent, to whom payment is dependent on completion or the like condition, the principal does not promise that he will complete the contract for reasons which I have explained. His only promise is that he will pay commission if the contract is completed. There is no promise to pay a reasonable remuneration if the principal revokes the authority to the agent. And it is a further objection to a claim on a quantum meruit that the employer has not obtained any benefit. The agent has earned nothing until the event materialises.

The applicability of this principle to the case of an auctioneer was questioned by Upjohn LJ in *Frank Swain (a firm) v Whitfield Corporation Ltd.*[3] The matter did not, strictly speaking, arise for decision, since the client conceded that a reasonable sum was due,[4] and the sole question to be answered therefore was what amount would be "reasonable" in the circumstances. Nevertheless, in approving the client's admission of liability (which was based on counsel's opinion), Upjohn LJ said:[5]

It is clear that an auctioneer is in rather a different position from an estate agent who contracts with his principal to introduce a purchaser. Until he introduces a purchaser who purchases, he has no right to any commission whatever; but with an auctioneer the law is different, if the properties are withdrawn from auction he is entitled to a quantum meruit for the services thrown away.

---

1 p337.
2 [1941] AC 108 at p 141.
3 (1962) 183 EG 479.
4 A very questionable concession, in the light of what has been discussed.
5 (1962) 183 EG 479.

In the light of *John Meacock & Co* v *Abrahams*,[1] which does not appear to have been cited in *Frank Swain's* case, it is submitted that this *dictum* cannot be supported. Accordingly, if an auctioneer wishes to be able to claim for time and trouble expended on an abortive sale, this intention should be made plain in the commission agreement.

4 Amount of commission

In certain types of sale, the scale on which an auctioneer is to be remunerated is laid down by legislation, either primary or secondary. The most important of these are as follows:

- Sales of goods taken by a landlord under a distress for rent.[2]
- Sales of goods seized by a sheriff under a writ of fieri facias.[3]
- Sales of goods taken under an execution issued by the county court.[4]

In addition, where land is sold by order of some (but not all) courts, special application must be made in order to justify a fee which exceeds the normal "sole agency" rate or 2½%.[5] However, this "scale" does not apply to sales of investment, business or farm property, nor to property which is sold in lots.

Where no statutory scale applies, the amount of commission payable depends upon the agreement between the auctioneer and the client. This may stipulate for a fixed sum, or provide that the auctioneer is to receive any excess over a certain amount which the property realises, or it may incorporate a scale of charges issued by a professional society.[6]

---

1 [1956] 3 All ER 660.
2 Law of Distress Amendment Act 1888, section 8(2); Distress for Rent Rules 1988, SI 1988 No 2050.
3 Sheriffs' Act 1887, section 20(2); Writs of *Fieri Facias*, Sheriffs' or Sheriffs' Officers' Fees Order 1920, SR & O 1920 No 1250, amended by SI 1956 Nos 502, 2081, SI 1962 No 2417, SI 1971 No 808, SI 1988 No 1384.
4 County Courts Act 1984, section 128; County Court Fees Order 1982, SI 1982 No 1706, amended by SI 1983 No 1681, SI 1985 Nos 574, 1834, SI 1986 Nos 633, 2143, SI 1988 No 509, SI 1992 No 2762.
5 Practice Direction [1983] 1 All ER 160: see p169.
6 The restrictions on scale fees imposed by SI 1970 No 1696 are discussed at p 170.

If the contract is silent as to commission, a mere request for services from a professional person raises the implication that these will be paid for at a reasonable rate of remuneration.[1] In *Miller* v *Beal*[2] the defendant, an auctioneer, who had advanced £1,500 to a man named Elliott, was empowered to sell Elliott's property to recover his money. The plaintiff, another creditor, laid claim to part of the property, whereupon it was agreed that the sale should take place and the money should be held in trust for the parties jointly. No express provision was made for the defendant to receive commission on the sale, but the court held that a reasonable fee could be charged.

In deciding what is a "reasonable" amount, regard may well be had to what is customary in the profession, and this can be established either by the evidence of other practitioners or, perhaps, by reference to the scales of charges issued by the professional societies. In *Re Page*,[3] for example, a solicitor employed an auctioneer to sell a client's house, without making any express agreement as to the amount of commission payable. The client's executor challenged the auctioneer's charges, but these were allowed upon the evidence of several other auctioneers which showed that, if anything, the fees were below the average. However, the court's discretion in this matter is unfettered. In *Re Wolfe, Heller* v *Wolfe*,[4] where land was sold by order of the court for £192,500, the relevant scale did not extend beyond £25,000. The judge's attention was drawn to the scale for sales in bankruptcy; nevertheless, he awarded the auctioneers approximately 80% of what they would have earned on that scale, describing this as a "proper figure".

Reference to what is usual in the profession does not always work in favour of the auctioneer at the expense of the client. In *Newman* v *Richardson*,[5] for example, the plaintiff claimed commission upon the sale of a dry dock. The defendant was willing to pay the normal scale fee for the sale of property, but the plaintiff claimed to be

---

1 *Manson* v *Baillie* (1855) 2 Macq 80. This implied term now has statutory force: Supply of Goods and Services Act 1982, section 15.
2 (1879) 27 WR 403.
3 (1863) 32 Beav 487.
4 [1952] 2 All ER 595.
5 (1885) 1 TLR 348.

entitled to approximately five times this amount, on the ground that the property was of a special nature and difficult to sell. The jury had no hesitation in finding that the scale represented a perfectly adequate remuneration for the plaintiff's services.

The practice of assessing what it is "reasonable" to pay by reference to the prescribed professional fees seems quite acceptable in cases where an auctioneer has earned commission by successfully carrying out a sale. Where, however, no sale results and the auctioneer is, by agreement, to receive something for the abortive work involved,[1] it is suggested that a substantially smaller sum would be appropriate. This is because scale fees are not related to the amount of work required to earn them; they are higher than this, in order to make up for the large number of sales on which effort is expended but no commission is earned.

This aspect of professional scales is effectively recognised by the courts in cases involving the breach of a "sole agency" agreement, in that the damages awarded to the agent are usually rather less than the commission which has been lost.[2] However, in exceptional circumstances it may be justifiable to use professional scales of charges as a basis for reasonable remuneration for services which are of no benefit to the client. In *Frank Swain (a firm)* v *Whitfield Corporation Ltd,*[3] for example, the plaintiff's authority to sell certain property was withdrawn some ten minutes before the sale was due to commence, by which time there were fifty bidders present. The evidence showed that a sale would almost certainly have resulted; accordingly Phillimore J,[4] whose decision was unanimously affirmed by the Court of Appeal, awarded the plaintiffs the scale commission on the reserve prices, which was felt to constitute a reasonable sum for their services.

B Expenses

In the absence of any express provision, an auctioneer is not entitled to make a claim for advertising and other out-of-pocket

---

1 Whether he is entitled in the absence of such agreement, has already been doubted; see p 340.
2 See p 163.
3 (1962) 183 EG 479.
4 (1962) 182 EG 11.

expenses, over and above the commission which is payable on a sale of the property. This is because the general presumption which applies to all commission agents is that their agreed fee is inclusive of expenses.[1] Notwithstanding this general principle, however, there is at least some authority for the view that an auctioneer who fails to earn any commission (because no sale has resulted) may have a legitimate claim against the client for expenses incurred. This is based partly on the *dictum* of Romilly MR in *Chinnock v Sainsbury*,[2] to which reference has already been made.[3] Indeed, in one report of that case,[4] the Master of the Rolls is said to have referred expressly to the auctioneer's expenses. There is also a *dictum* of Denning LJ in *John Meacock & Co v Abrahams*,[5] to the effect that, while the auctioneers were not entitled to any *fees* on a quantum meruit basis, they would have been entitled to their expenses.

Despite this slender authority, a claim that auctioneers are to be treated differently from other commission agents seems an inherently weak one, and prudent auctioneers will ensure that the position in respect of expenses is specifically dealt with in their agreement with the client.[6] Indeed, the majority of auctioneers do precisely that, which is presumably why this issue has so seldom reached the courts.

C Indemnity

In principle, every agency relationship contains by implication a promise on the part of the principal to indemnify the agent against any legal liability to which the agent may become subject as a result of carrying out the principal's instructions. As Vaughan Williams LJ said in *Williams v Lister & Co; Llewellyn Bros, Third Parties*:[7]

The law does imply an undertaking to indemnify the agent for injury incurred in the course of carrying out his duty as agent.

---

1 *Marshall v Parsons* (1841) 9 C&P 656.
2 (1860) 30 LJ Ch 409 at p411.
3 p338.
4 (1860) 3 LT 258 at p 259.
5 [1956] 3 All ER 660.
6 In sales of land, this is also a requirement under the Estate Agents Act 1979: see p 202.
7 (1913) 109 LT 699 at p700.

The types of legal liability which may form the subject matter of an indemnity claim are many and varied. One of the most important is where an auctioneer sells goods on behalf of a client who, it transpires, had no right to sell them. As we have seen, in such a case the auctioneer is personally liable in the tort of conversion to the true owner of the goods. In *Adamson* v *Jarvis*[1] the plaintiff auctioneer, who was employed by the defendant to sell cattle and other goods, effected the sale and paid over the net proceeds to the defendant. It was then discovered that the defendant had no right to sell the goods, and the plaintiff was successfully sued by the true owner. On these facts the Court of Common Pleas held that the defendant was liable to indemnify the plaintiff against the damages and costs incurred in the action.

In reaching this decision, the court appears not to have considered the earlier case of *Farebrother* v *Ansley*[2] in which an auctioneer, who sold goods which had been wrongfully seized by a sheriff, was held not to be entitled to an indemnity from the sheriff. It is submitted, however, that that case is of doubtful authority, for it appears to rest on the old rule of common law that no duty of contribution existed between joint tortfeasors, a rule since abolished by statute.[3]

An auctioneer who receives, as stakeholder, a deposit from the highest bidder, will incur personal liability for handing this over to the vendor before the latter becomes legally entitled to it.[4] Should this occur, so that the auctioneer has to pay the amount of the deposit to the purchaser, the auctioneer can then recover this sum from the vendor under the indemnity principle. Furthermore, if an auctioneer who is still holding the deposit is successfully sued by the purchaser for its return, the vendor is liable to indemnify the auctioneer against the legal costs incurred.[5]

Other examples of the right to indemnity include *Brittain* v *Lloyd*,[6] where an auctioneer recovered from the vendor the amount of auction duty which the Commissioners of Excise required the

---

1 (1827) 4 Bing 66.
2 (1808) 1 Camp 343.
3 See now the Civil Liability (Contribution) Act 1978.
4 See p 314.
5 *Spurrier* v *Elderton* (1803) 5 Esp 1.
6 (1845) 14 M&W 762.

auctioneer to pay on property bought in. And in *Warlow* v *Harrison*,[1] where the Exchequer Chamber held that an action would lie against an auctioneer for failing to knock down property which was advertised as "without reserve", Martin B said:[2]

If the auctioneer had contracted any liability in consequence of his employment and the subsequent revocation or conduct of the owner, he is entitled to be indemnified.

To be entitled to an indemnity from the client, an auctioneer must establish that the legal liability in question was incurred during the course of employment. In *Sweeting* v *Turner*[3] the plaintiff and his partner occupied business premises, under an agreement by which part of the rent was paid by the firm and the remainder by the other partner. The partnership was eventually dissolved and the defendant, an auctioneer, was instructed to sell the stock on the premises. This he did, under conditions of sale which stipulated that, after the fall of the hammer, all lots were at the risk of the purchaser. After the sale, the landlord threatened to distrain upon the goods (the partner's share of the rent being in arrear) whereupon the auctioneer paid off the arrears. The Court of Queen's Bench held that the plaintiff was entitled to receive the proceeds of sale from the auctioneer, without any allowance in respect of this payment. Blackburn J said:[4]

When once we understand that the loss would have fallen on the buyers of the goods had they been distrained, it is evident that it would have been a loss not sustained by the auctioneer or his employer, the plaintiff; consequently the promise of the auctioneer, although one that it was natural for him to give, was really made in order to save damage, which would not have befallen his client, but another person; therefore I think he had no authority, either express or implied, from the plaintiff, to make such a promise, and that the plaintiff is entitled to recover.

---

1 (1859) 1 E&E 295: p 374.
2 At p317.
3 (1872) LR 7 QB 310.
4 At p314.

If, however, the auctioneer had taken the same action before the sale, an indemnity could have been claimed, for in this situation the auctioneer would have been protecting the interests of the client.

The right of an auctioneer to be indemnified against legal liability is based upon an implied term in the contract of employment. As a result, it may be overridden by an express term to the contrary; and in any event, the circumstances of the case may preclude any such implication. In *Barker* v *Furlong*,[1] for example, goods were consigned to the plaintiff auctioneers for sale by an agent of the seller. It transpired that the seller in fact had no right to sell these goods, and the auctioneers in consequence incurred liability in conversion, but their claim for an indemnity against the agent who had instructed them failed. It was held that, since the auctioneers knew that they were dealing with a mere agent, the latter could not be made liable so long as he had acted with authority from his own client; he could not be treated as guaranteeing his client's right to sell.

As originally expressed, the rules relating to an agent's indemnity appeared to require some wrongful act on the part of the principal. In *Adamson* v *Jarvis*,[2] for example, Best CJ said:

Every man who employs another to do an act which the employer appears to have a right to authorise him to do undertakes to indemnify him for all such acts as would be lawful if the employer had the authority he pretends to have.

In *Halbronn* v *International Horse Agency & Exchange Ltd*[3] the plaintiff auctioneer was instructed by the defendants to sell, in Paris, a thoroughbred mare named "Pentecost", which appeared in the *English Stud Book*. Due to an error some years previously, another mare had been sold in France under the same name and description and had been entered in the *French Stud Book*. The owner of this mare successfully sued the plaintiff for damages, on the ground that the latter's actions had reduced the value of his mare. The plaintiff duly sought an indemnity from the defendants but this was refused by the court, on the grounds that the

---

1 [1891] 2 Ch 172.
2 (1827) 4 Bing 66 at p72.
3 [1903] 1 KB 270.

defendants had been guilty of no wrong; the auctioneer's loss was said to arise, not out of his employment, but from a mistake as to the identity of the mare.

The decision in *Halbronn*'s case was emphatically disapproved by the Court of Appeal in *Williams* v *Lister & Co, Llewellyn Bros, Third Parties*.[1] The third parties in that case let certain furniture to the plaintiff on hire-purchase and, when he defaulted, instructed the defendants to seize it. The plaintiff, alleging wrongful seizure of the goods, sued the defendants, who in turn claimed an indemnity from their clients. The plaintiff's action was dismissed for want of prosecution, but the defendants remained out of pocket as regards certain legal costs. It was held that the auctioneers were entitled to an indemnity from their clients in respect of these costs, notwithstanding that the clients had not acted wrongfully; the important point was that the auctioneers had incurred loss in carrying out their duties as agents, and this was held to be all that the law requires.

D Lien

As we have seen, an auctioneer who acts within the authority given by the client becomes entitled to commission, an indemnity against any legal liability and, in some circumstances, out-of-pocket expenses. These rights may, of course, be enforced by legal action, but the auctioneer has a further means of pressing the client, namely, by exercising a lien. Such a lien covers goods belonging to the client which are in the auctioneer's possession, and also the proceeds of sale of goods or land. In *Williams* v *Millington*[2] Lord Loughborough LC said:

The auctioneer has also a special property in him, with a lien for the charges of the sale, the commission, and the auction duty, which he is bound to pay.

This lien lasts only so long as the auctioneer retains possession of the goods[3] but, while this is so, it matters not whether the sale

---

1 (1913) 109 LT 699.
2 (1788) 1 HBl 81 at p85; approved in *Woolfe* v *Horne* (1877) 2 QBD 355.
3 *Coppin* v *Walker* (1816) 7 Taunt 237.

takes place on the auctioneer's own premises or on those of the vendor.[1]

It should be noted that an auctioneer's lien only arises automatically where what is done for the client falls within the normal course of an auctioneer's business. If the auctioneer performs special services, the question whether or not a lien may be exercised in respect of charges depends upon the rules of common law. In *Sanderson v Bell*[2] for example, an auctioneer was handed a mortgage deed and asked to obtain payment from the mortgagor. It was held that, since the auctioneer was not employed to do any work upon the deed or to enhance its value by his labours, he could not exercise a lien upon it for his charges.

Unlike a factor's lien, that of an auctioneer is a particular one, which means that it applies only to charges in respect of the actual goods or moneys which are being held, and not to the general balance of account between the parties. In *Palmer v Day & Sons*[3] the defendants, who had sold a house and certain furniture for a client, were authorised by his trustee in bankruptcy to sell some pictures on behalf of the estate. The defendants did so, retaining out of the proceeds of this sale their charges in respect of the earlier ones. It was held, on a technical point of bankruptcy law that the auctioneers were entitled to do so, but the Divisional Court of Queen's Bench made it plain that the auctioneer's lien could not in itself have justified this action.

The case of *Webb v Smith*[4] offers a good illustration of an auctioneer's lien in operation. In that case the defendant auctioneer sold a brewery on behalf of a client, retaining part of the proceeds of sale. The defendant had previously sold some furniture for the same client, and was also still holding the balance of this purchase money. The plaintiff, to whom the client was indebted, claimed to have a charge over the brewery proceeds, and this was acknowledged by the auctioneer; despite this acknowledgment, however, the auctioneer handed over to the client the proceeds of the sale of the furniture. It was held that the auctioneer was still

---

1 *Williams v Millington* (1788) 1 HBl 81.

2 (1834) 2 Cr & M 304.

3 [1895] 2 QB 618; *Dirks v Richards* (1842) 5 Sco NR 534: see also *Webb v Smith* (1885) 30 ChD 192.

4 (1885) 30 ChD 192.

entitled, as against the plaintiff, to a lien over the proceeds of sale of the brewery; he could not be compelled to take his payment from the other fund, over which he had no lien.

Webb v *Smith* indicates that an auctioneer's lien is enforceable, not only against the client, but also against other parties who lay claim to goods or purchase monies. One important consequence of this is that the auctioneer in exercising a lien can refuse delivery of the goods to the purchaser. Thus, in *Lane* v *Tewson*,[1] an auctioneer who had sold 50 trees, but who had not received any commission for so doing, was held not liable to the disappointed purchaser for refusing to hand over the trees to him.

Although an auctioneer's lien may thus be enforceable against a purchaser, its main purpose is to enable the auctioneer to enforce rights against the vendor; consequently the lien only attaches to goods and money which are the property of the vendor. This was made clear in the case of *Skinner* v *The Trustee of the Property of Reed*[2] which concerned the sale by auction of a farm. The farm, which was mortgaged, was stated to be sold free from encumbrances. It was knocked down at the reserve price of £30,000, and a deposit of £3,000 was paid to the auctioneer as stakeholder. Upon completion of the contract it was discovered that the amounts outstanding upon the mortgages were greater in total than the purchase price. Since the vendor was bankrupt, the purchaser called upon the auctioneers to apply the whole of the deposit towards discharging the mortgages. Cross J held that the auctioneers must comply with this demand; the deposit money had never become the property of the vendor, as it was required to discharge encumbrances according to the conditions of sale; consequently there was nothing to which the auctioneer's lien could attach.

It is important to note that a lien of this nature does not entitle the auctioneer to sell the goods and recoup what is owed out of the proceeds; it is merely a right of retention. However, the High Court has jurisdiction to order a sale of any property which is the subject-matter of an action and which it is desirable to sell forthwith.[3] This discretion would probably be exercised, for example, in a case

---

1 (1840) 12 A&E 116n; see also *Robinson* v *Rutter* (1855) 4 E&B 953.
2 [1967] Ch 1194.
3 RSC Ord 29, rule 4.

where goods held by the auctioneer were perishable. It was certainly exercised in *Bartholomew* v *Freeman*,[1] where the purchaser of a horse returned it to the auctioneers for alleged breach of warranty. During the ensuing dispute, the horse consumed its value in food, whereupon a court ordered it to be sold.

E Rights of action against the purchaser

1 On a sale of goods

Unlike most agents for sale, whose relationship with the purchaser ceases when the transaction is carried out, an auctioneer has a personal involvement which extends beyond this time.[2] In *Williams* v *Millington*[3] the plaintiff auctioneer sold goods for a named vendor on the vendor's premises. The defendant bought goods at the sale and paid part of the price; as to the remainder, the defendant claimed to set off a debt owed to him by the vendor. The auctioneer, having paid the vendor in full, was held entitled to recover the full amount from the defendant. Lord Loughborough CJ said:[4]

An auctioneer has a possession, coupled with an interest, in goods which he is employed to sell, not a bare custody like a servant or shopman. There is no difference, whether the sale be on the premises of the owner, or in a public auction room, for on the premises of the owner, an actual possession is given to the auctioneer and his servants by the owner, not merely an authority to sell: I have said a possession coupled with an interest: but an auctioneer has also a special property in him, with a lien for the charges of the sale, the commission, and the auction duty, which he is bound to pay.

(a) *Nature of the right*

The personal right of an auctioneer to sue for the price of goods sold has been endorsed by the courts on numerous subsequent

---

1 (1878) 3 CPD 316.
2 For the legal position where a private sale goes through the auctioneer's books, see *Murphy* v *Jonathan Howlett (a firm)* (1960) 176 EG 311.
3 (1788) 1 HBl 81.
4 At p84.

occasions.[1] The principle on which the right is based was, however, given a slight gloss by Salter J in *Benton* v *Campbell, Parker & Co. Ltd*:[2]

The auctioneer sues for the price by virtue of his special property and his lien, and also, in most cases, by virtue of his contract with the buyer, that the price shall be paid into his hands, and not by virtue of the contract of sale.

In order to maintain an action against the purchaser, the auctioneer must be shown to have had actual possession of the goods at the time of the sale. It appears from the *dictum* of Lord Loughborough CJ quoted above[3] that this can be established notwithstanding that the sale took place on the vendor's premises and, in the Scottish case of *Mackenzie* v *Cormack*,[4] where Lord Mackay referred to this *dictum* as "a classical passage which has now received at least sixfold approval in England", the Court of Session allowed an auctioneer to sue for the price of a carpet which was sold at a castle as part of the furnishings.

It is nevertheless possible for an auctioneer's possession to fall short of what is required. In *Holmes* v *Tutton*,[5] for example, goods were sold on the vendor's premises and the vendor, after the sale, remained in sole charge of them. Lord Campbell CJ said:[6] "There may be some doubt whether the auctioneer, not having possession of the goods, and it not appearing whether he sold in his own name, and his lien for the price having been covered by the money he received, so that he might be found to have paid himself out of the proceeds received, could have sued the plaintiffs for the price of the goods."

Where a sale of goods is effected by private treaty upon conditions drawn up for a sale by auction, the auctioneer has the

---

1 However, the auctioneer is under no duty to the vendor to exercise this right: *Fordham* v *Christie, Manson & Woods Ltd* (1977) 244 EG 213 (p 296).

2 [1925] 2 KB 410 at p416. This appears to have met with some degree of approval from the Court of Appeal; see *Wilson & Sons* v *Pike* [1949] 1 KB 176 at p182, *per* Tucker LJ.

3 See also the judgment of Heath J: (1788) 1 HBl 81, 85.

4 1950 SC 183.

5 (1855) 5 E&B 65.

6 At p81.

same right as if there had been an auction. In *Freeman* v *Farrow*[1] a horse which had been put up for auction was bought in and then sold privately by the owner on the premises. The conditions of sale provided that the auctioneer should receive his normal commission on the sale and, having paid the net proceeds of sale to the vendor, he was held entitled to receive the full price from the purchaser.

Since the personal right of action exists primarily to protect the auctioneer's interest in the purchase money, it might be expected to terminate if, for any reason, the auctioneer's lien came to an end. In *Coppin* v *Walker*,[2] an auctioneer who allowed the purchaser to take away goods without paying for them was held to have abandoned his lien, as he had not made it clear that he had rights over the purchase money. However, this case may be explained on the much narrower ground that the auctioneer was precluded by his own misrepresentation from enforcing his rights,[3] and this more limited view of the case was taken by the Court of Queen's Bench in *Robinson* v *Rutter*.[4] It was there held that a purchaser who seeks to evade liability must show that the terms of the sale, or subsequent facts, have brought the auctioneer's right to an end.

Although the claim to be paid commission is the main factor underlying both the auctioneer's lien and the right to sue for the purchase price, the fact that commission has been paid is not in itself a defence to an action brought by the auctioneer against the purchaser. In *Chelmsford Auctions Ltd* v *Poole*[5] the plaintiffs knocked down a car to the defendant for £57. The plaintiffs' commission on this sale was £3.50, and so, when the defendant paid a deposit of £7, the plaintiffs' own claim was adequately met. The plaintiffs, however, having satisfied the vendor from their own funds, sued the defendant for the balance of the purchase price. It was held by the Court of Appeal that they were entitled to recover this amount, there being nothing to remove the case from the operation of the general rule.

The fact that an auctioneer's own claims have been met may, however, be of relevance where a purchaser claims to be

---

1 (1886) 2 TLR 547.
2 (1816) 7 Taunt 237.
3 On this point, see p 355.
4 (1855) 4 E&B 953.
5 [1973] QB 542.

discharged from liability by virtue of having paid the purchase money to the vendor, either in cash or, more usually, by setting off the price against a debt which the vendor owes to the purchaser. The normal rule is that an auctioneer's right to sue is not affected by such a payment. In *Robinson* v *Rutter*,[1] for example, where an auctioneer sued for the price of a horse, the defence was simply that the purchase price had been paid to the vendor. Lord Campbell CJ said:[2]

As auctioneer, the plaintiff must be supposed to have had the possession of the horse before and at the time of the sale, to have had a lien upon the horse for the price, and to have had a right of lien on the price, when paid, for his commission and charges. It must be presumed that the plaintiff had a debt due to him from the vendor in respect of the sale, to be satisfied from the proceeds of the sale. The plea does not allege that this debt was paid, nor shew how the plaintiff had no longer a right to sue, nor even aver that he had notice of the payment being made to the vendor.

An auctioneer who specifically agrees that the purchaser shall pay the vendor direct is, of course, bound by any set off which may be made.[3] Further, it appears that the auctioneer will also be bound by a set off, even without notice, in cases where the auctioneer's own charges have been satisfied and where the action is thus in reality brought on behalf of the vendor. In *Holmes* v *Tutton*[4] there was, as we have seen, some doubt whether, in the circumstances of the case, the auctioneer could maintain an action against the purchaser. Having expressed these doubts, Lord Campbell CJ continued:[5]

In an action for the price of the goods so sold, it would be a good answer, either at law, or at all events by way of equitable defence, to show for the defendant that the lien of the auctioneer was satisfied, and that he was suing merely for the principal, and that there was a set-off as between the principal and the vendee of the goods.

---

1 (1855) 4 E&B 953.
2 At p956.
3 *Jarvis* v *Chapple* (1805) 2 Chit 387.
4 (1855) 5 E&B 65: p 351.
5 At p82.

This *dictum* of Lord Campbell CJ was, strictly speaking, *obiter*, since the point did not fall to be decided. Nevertheless, it was made the subject of a decision in the case of *Grice* v *Kenrick*.[1] In that case the plaintiff had sold certain goods on behalf of a man named Weir. Unknown to the plaintiff, Weir, who owed the defendant £60, agreed that the defendant might buy at the auction in satisfaction of the debt. This the defendant did, and was allowed by the plaintiff to remove the goods which he had purchased. The plaintiff, who had collected enough money from other lots to pay his commission and charges for the whole sale, handed over the balance to the vendor and sued the defendant in respect of the lots which he had purchased. The Court of Queen's Bench, distinguishing *Robinson* v *Rutter*,[2] pointed out that, since the auctioneer's charges had been paid, he would be bound to hand over this money to the vendor, who had already agreed with the defendant not to receive it. Accordingly the auctioneer's action failed.

In *Manley & Sons Ltd* v *Berkett*[3] a cattle-owner, who was indebted to the plaintiff auctioneers, instructed them to sell certain cattle and to pay themselves and other creditors from the proceeds. The owner also owed money to the defendant, whom he induced to bid at the sale by promising to set off any purchases he might make against what he was owed. The proceeds of the sale were only sufficient to satisfy the auctioneers' claims provided that the defendant's purchases were included, and the auctioneers accordingly sued the defendant upon these. It was held that the auctioneers were entitled to recover as much as was necessary to meet their own claims; they were not bound by the defendant's right of set-off, for they had no notice of it. The defendant was, however, entitled to retain the small amount which remained in his hands after the auctioneer's personal demands had been met; this sum was due to the vendor himself, and the defendant's set-off was valid against him.

(b) *Loss of the auctioneer's right*

We must now consider a number of cases in which, for one reason or another, an auctioneer's right of action against a

---

1 (1870) LR 5 QB 340.
2 (1855) 4 E&B 953.
3 [1912] 2 KB 329.

purchaser is lost. In *Dickenson* v *Naul*[1] the plaintiff was employed to sell farm stock by a woman who was believed to be the farmer's widow and executrix. The defendant, who bought the stock, was allowed to remove it only after he expressly promised to pay. It was later found that the property in truth belonged to the farmer's real widow, and not to the auctioneer's client. Accordingly, it was held, the plaintiff could not sue the purchaser, for his right to do so depended on his interest in the goods which he was employed to sell. This interest in turn could only be derived from the interest of the auctioneer's employer which, in this case, was non-existent.

When the contract of sale made by the auctioneer cannot be enforced against the purchaser, it might be expected that the auctioneer would be equally unable to maintain a personal action for the price. Support for this proposition is to be found in the cases of *Coppin* v *Walker*[2] and *Coppin* v *Craig*,[3] which arose out of the same sale. The auctioneer said that all the goods in the sale belonged to one Appleton, against whom both defendants wished to exercise set-offs. In fact some of the goods belonged to a man named Appleby. It was held that the auctioneer, by his misrepresentation, was precluded from claiming that the goods did not belong to Appleton, and so was bound by the defendants' rights of set-off.

In *Hindle* v *Brown*,[4] however, an auctioneer succeeded in an action against a purchaser, notwithstanding that the contract of sale itself could not have been enforced. In that case the plaintiff was instructed to sell some pictures which the vendor had fraudulently attributed to certain artists. These false attributions were innocently repeated by the plaintiff in the sale catalogue. The defendant, to whom the pictures were knocked down, gave a cheque for the price to the plaintiff, who duly settled with the vendor. On discovering the fraud, however, the defendant stopped the cheque, and the plaintiff sued him upon it. At first instance[5] Pickford J held that, as the auctioneer's misrepresentations were innocent, and the contract between the auctioneer and the purchaser had been completed, the

---

1 (1833) 4 B & Ad 638.
2 (1816) 7 Taunt 237.
3 (1816) 7 Taunt 243.
4 (1908) 98 LT 791.
5 (1908) 98 LT 44.

remedy of rescission was no longer available, in accordance with the rule laid down in *Seddon* v *North-Eastern Salt Co.*[1] The Court of Appeal affirmed the decision of Pickford J, but on rather different grounds; it was held that the auctioneer's right to sue on the cheque was unaffected by the fraud of his principal, a fraud of which he was personally innocent. As Farwell LJ said:[2]

It is not the same as if the auctioneer were suing to recover cash, the price which became due upon the sale of the goods. He is suing upon the cheque given to him and not upon the contract of sale at all.

It should be noted that the facts of *Hindle* v *Brown* would probably justify a different decision today. The rule in *Seddon* v *North-Eastern Salt Co* has been abrogated by statute[3] so that the auctioneer's claim would now be met by the defence that he had, by his own innocent misrepresentation, entitled the purchaser to rescind the contract and therefore to refuse payment. If, however, the auctioneer were guilty of no misrepresentation of any kind (as, for example, where the auctioneer is completely unaware that the vendor has made any statement about the goods) it would appear that an action on the cheque would be sufficiently independent of the contract of sale to remain enforceable. That, at any rate, was the view of the Court of Appeal in *Hindle* v *Brown*.

The conditions of sale at auctions commonly provide that, if the purchaser does not pay for his goods within a certain time, they may be resold and the loss, if any, be recovered from the defaulter. The existence of such a condition does not in itself preclude the auctioneer from suing the purchaser for the full price, even if it states that the goods "shall" be resold.[4] If, however, the option to resell is exercised, it has been held[5] that the original sale is thereby avoided and the auctioneer is consequently not entitled to sue the defaulter for the full price.

1 [1905] 1 Ch 326.
2 (1908) 98 LT 791 at p792.
3 Misrepresentation Act 1967, section 1(*b*).
4 *Robinson, Fisher & Harding* v *Behar* [1927] 1 KB 513.
5 *Lamond* v *Davall* (1847) 9 QB 1030.

2   On a sale of land

In the Irish case of *Cherry* v *Anderson*[1] the plaintiff sold certain leasehold property for a named vendor, under a contract which made the purchaser responsible for the auctioneer's fees. An action by the auctioneer to enforce this obligation was unsuccessful, for reasons explained by Palles CB:[2]

Upon the sale of real estate the auctioneer has no right to sue in his own name, analogous to his right on the sale of goods. In the latter case he has, or is deemed to have, a possession of the goods and a qualified property in them. On the sale of real property the right to sue depends on the written contract alone; and unless that contract be so framed as to render the auctioneer the ostensible vendor ... he cannot on the sale of real estate maintain in his own name an action against the purchaser.

The principle thus clearly enunciated had been the basis of two earlier English decisions which concerned the practice of letting land by auction. In *Evans & Thomas* v *Evans*[3] the plaintiff auctioneers let certain fields by auction, the defendant being the highest bidder. The conditions of sale stated that the land was let by, and the rent was payable to, the auctioneers; but the words "Approved by me, David Jones" appeared at the bottom of the conditions. On these facts it was held that the auctioneers could not sue on the contract, which was clearly made with the real lessor, David Jones. In *Fisher* v *Marsh*[4] on the other hand, the plaintiff was employed by a committee responsible for organising the Oxford races to let by auction small plots of land for the erection of booths. The conditions, which were signed by the auctioneer, gave no indication that anyone else was the true lessor; accordingly the auctioneer was held entitled to maintain an action for use and occupation against a successful bidder.

Although an auctioneer is not usually likely to succeed in an action against a purchaser of land which is based on the contract of sale, there may in some circumstances be an alternative means of redress. In *Cleave* v *Moore*[5] the defendant bought certain

---

1 (1876) IrR 10 CL 204.
2 At p209.
3 (1835) 3 A&E 132.
4 (1865) 6 B&S 411.
5 (1857) 28 LT (OS) 255: see also *Hodgens* v *Keon* [1894] 2 IR 657.

premises at auction and signed a contract stating that he had paid a deposit. In fact no deposit was paid but the defendant gave the auctioneers an IOU for the amount in question. The auctioneers were held entitled to recover upon this IOU; the effect of the transaction, in the opinion of the Court of Exchequer, was that the deposit had been paid by means of a loan from the auctioneers to the purchaser.

A somewhat similar point arose in *Pollway Ltd* v *Abdullah*,[1] where the Court of Appeal reached a decision of great practical importance to auctioneers. In that case, which concerned the sale of certain ground rents, the conditions of sale provided for a 10% deposit to be paid to the auctioneers as agents for the vendors. The defendant, who signed a memorandum of purchase as the highest bidder, made out a cheque for the auctioneers for the deposit, which they accepted. The cheque was subsequently dishonoured, whereupon the vendors rescinded the contract and resold the property. When sued upon the cheque, the defendant claimed that there had been a total failure of consideration, in that the vendors were no longer liable to complete the sale to him. The Court of Appeal, however, upheld the auctioneers' claim on the ground that they had given consideration, either by warranting their authority to sign a memorandum and accept a deposit, or by agreeing to accept a cheque in place of the cash which, strictly speaking, the defendant was bound to provide.

F Rights against third parties

The special property in goods, which forms the basis of the auctioneer's right to maintain a personal action against a purchaser, is also legally effective against third parties. As a result, an auctioneer may take action against anyone who commits torts such as trespass to goods or conversion. As Heath J said in *Williams* v *Millington:*[2]

It is the same thing, whether goods be sold on the premises of the owner, or in an auction room; the possession is in the auctioneer, and it is he who

---

1 [1974] 2 All ER 381.
2 (1788) 1 HBl 81 at p85.

makes the contract; if they should be stolen, he might maintain trespass, or an indictment for larceny: he therefore has a special property in them.

The right to sue a third party in tort requires the auctioneer to have possession of the goods in question; thus in *Holmes* v *Tutton*,[1] where it was doubtful whether the vendor had relinquished possession, Lord Campbell CJ thought that the auctioneer could not have sued in conversion. A similar conclusion was reached in *Davis* v *Danks*,[2] where the plaintiff auctioneer was instructed to sell certain fixtures attached to a freehold house. At a sale which took place on the premises, the defendant bought some items and removed these without payment, since he claimed to have a right of set-off against the vendor. It was held that the plaintiff could not maintain an action in trespass against the defendant, for the fixtures, while unsevered, remained part of the freehold and therefore outside the possession of the auctioneer.

---

1 (1855) 5 E&B 65 at p82.
2 (1849) 3 Exch 435.

CHAPTER 11

The conduct of auctions

This chapter is concerned for the most part with the legal rules which control the procedures of sales by auction, in an attempt to strike a fair balance between the competing interests of sellers and buyers. Before turning to such matters, however, mention may be made of a preliminary formal obligation imposed upon auctioneers by statute, with the object of ensuring that certain information is made available to the company. The Auctioneers Act 1845, section 7 provides:

Every auctioneer, before beginning any auction, shall affix or suspend, or cause to be affixed or suspended, a ticket or board containing his true and full christian and surname and residence painted, printed, or written in large letters publicly visible and legible in some conspicuous part of the room or place where the auction is held, so that all persons may easily read the same, and shall also keep such ticket or board so affixed or suspended during the whole time of such auction being held.

In addition to this requirement, section 3 of the Auctions (Bidding Agreements) Act 1927 provides that a copy of that Act shall also be exhibited, a provision now extended to include the Auctions (Bidding Agreements) Act 1969.[1] Failure to comply with any of these requirements renders the auctioneer liable to a fine of £20.

A Control of the bidding

Under this heading we shall examine various legal principles which govern the bidding process at auctions. Where everything runs smoothly, the bidders make a series of offers of steadily increasing amounts, the last of which ripens into a contract when the auctioneer signifies acceptance by bringing down the hammer. However, this simple picture conceals a number of possibilities of

---

1 These Acts are discussed at pp 419-421.

things not running smoothly, largely because the very nature of an auction presupposes a conflict of interest. On the one hand, bidders are naturally concerned to purchase property as cheaply as they can; on the other hand, the vendor will wish to obtain as much as possible for the property and may, in addition, have a minimum price in mind below which the property cannot be sold at all.

In taking any positive steps to achieve their objectives, the bidders are hampered by the fact that they are in competition with each other, as well as with the vendor; and concerted action may, in any case, be illegal.[1] None the less, bidders can and do on occasion seek to withdraw bids, raise disputes over bids which they and other bidders have made, or claim that their bids are based on some mistake.

A vendor, by contrast, has a clearly defined interest to protect, and two long-established means of protecting it: the imposition of a reserve price, below which the property may not be sold, and the reservation of a right to bid. The second of these methods has the advantage of being more flexible, since a vendor who bids personally is in a position to assess the market and to decide at what point to cease bidding. There has never been much doubt as to the legality of these methods of self-protection for vendors, provided that their existence is brought to the attention of prospective bidders before the commencement of the sale. The problem arises when such action is taken secretly on a vendor's behalf.

1 Reserves and bidding rights

Where it is made clear to bidders at auction that reserve prices have been (or may have been) set, the legal position appears fairly straightforward.[2] The auctioneer has no authority of any kind to sell for less than the reserve and if, through inadvertence, property is knocked down at below its reserve, the vendor is not bound by the sale.[3] In such circumstances it is thought that the auctioneer incurs personal liability to the highest bidder for breach of warranty of authority.[4]

---

1 See pp 417-421.
2 The legal problems surrounding unannounced reserves are dealt with at pp 373-378.
3 See pp 272-274.
4 See p 312.

As to vendors' bidding rights, common law established at an early stage that these required explicit notification in order to be valid. In consequence, where a vendor had not expressly reserved the right to bid personally or through an agent, any such bid would constitute a fraud upon those bidding at the sale. In *Bexwell v Christie*,[1] for example, a sale of goods was held under conditions of sale which stated "that the goods should be sold to the best bidder". The plaintiff sent his horse for inclusion in this sale, with an instruction to the defendant auctioneer that he should not let it go below a certain price. The auctioneer disobeyed this instruction, and the Court of King's Bench held that he was justified in so doing, for to have bought in the horse in these circumstances would have been a fraud upon the sale.

In accordance with this principle, a person who was induced to pay an inflated price at an auction by bids which, though apparently independent, were actually made on behalf of the vendor, was not bound by the sale and could recover any deposit paid.[2] In *Green v Baverstock*[3] the defendant bought goods at an auction, a condition of which was that the highest bidder should be the purchaser. Upon later discovering that a puffer employed by the seller had bid against him, the defendant refused to remove or pay for the goods and the auctioneers failed in their action against him. Byles J stated the common law principle:[4]

Upon a sale by auction where the highest bidder is to be the purchaser, the secret employment of a puffer by the vendor is a fraudulent act. The sale is vitiated by the fraud, and void.

Although the common law position was thus quite clear, that of equity was less so. The courts here, while equally anxious to suppress fraud, were also concerned to prevent the sale of property at a gross undervalue. Accordingly, the rule developed in equity that, even without disclosing the fact, a vendor might validly appoint

---

1 (1776) 1 Cowp 395: see also *Narramore v Fuller, Hall & Foulsham* (1932) 76 Sol Jo 289.

2 *Thornett v Haines* (1846) 15 M&W 367.

3 (1863) 14 CBNS 204: see also *Howard v Castle* (1796) 6 TR 642; *Crowder v Austin* (1826) 3 Bing 368; *Wheeler v Collier* (1827) 1 Mood & M 123; *R v Marsh* (1829) 3 Y&J 331.

4 At p208.

one person to bid provided that this was not otherwise inequitable.[1] This rule, however, did not apply where the sale was expressly stated to be "without reserve";[2] nor did it permit the secret appointment of more than one puffer, since the effect of this would clearly be to enhance the price rather than merely to prevent a sale at an undervalue.[3]

(a) *Sales of land*

The conflict between law and equity, although limited in scope, was none the less undesirable and its resolution, at least as far as the sale of land was concerned, was one of the reasons for the enactment of the Sale of Land by Auction Act 1867. The Act gave priority to the rule of common law, which was generally accepted as being preferable.[4]

Section 4 of the Act provides:

And whereas there is at present a conflict between Her Majesty's Courts of law and equity in respect of the validity of sales by auction of land where a puffer has bid, although no right of bidding on behalf of the owner was reserved, the courts of law holding that all such sales are absolutely illegal, and the courts of equity under some circumstances giving effect to them but even in courts of equity the rule is unsettled: and whereas it is expedient that an end should be put to such conflicting and unsettled opinions: Be it therefore enacted that from and after passing of this Act whenever a sale by auction of land would be invalid at law by reason of the employment of a puffer, the same shall be deemed invalid in equity as well as at law.

Had the Act stopped at this point, the position would simply have been that the rules of common law (which were reasonably clear) prevailed over those of equity (which were not). As Lindley J said in *Parfitt* v *Jepson*:[5] "With regard to the statute, it seems to me that the object of the 4th section is not to restrict the legal doctrine, but to leave it as it was and to make the equitable doctrine correspond

---

1 *Conolly* v *Parsons* (1797) 3 Ves 625n; *Bramley* v *Alt* (1798) 3 Ves 620; *Smith* v *Clarke* (1806) 12 Ves 477; *Woodward* v *Miller* (1845) 2 Coll 279.
2 *Meadows* v *Tanner* (1820) 5 Madd 34.
3 *Mortimer* v *Bell* (1865) 1 Ch App 10.
4 Even by some Chancery judges: see the remarks of Lord Cranworth LC in *Mortimer* v *Bell* (1865) 1 Ch App 10 at p16.
5 (1877) 46 LJCP 529 at p533.

with it." Unfortunately, however, the opportunity was taken to restate the common law rules and the results, contained in sections 5 and 6, were so clumsily drafted[1] that they have merely increased the confusion which they were intended to prevent.

Section 5 provides:

And whereas as sales of land by auction are now conducted many of such sales are illegal, and could not be enforced against an unwilling purchaser, and it is expedient for the safety of both seller and purchaser that such sales should be so conducted as to be binding on both parties: Be it therefore enacted by the authority aforesaid as follows: that the particulars or conditions of sale by auction of any land shall state whether such land will be sold without reserve, or subject to a reserved price, or whether a right to bid is reserved; if it is stated that such land will be sold without reserve, or to that effect, then it shall not be lawful for the seller to employ any person to bid at such sale, or for the auctioneer to take knowingly any bidding from any such person.

Section 6 provides:

And where any sale by auction of land is declared either in the particulars or conditions of such sale to be subject to a right for the seller to bid, it shall be lawful for the seller or any one person on his behalf to bid at such auction in such manner as he may think proper.

In requiring any reserve price or bidding right to be stipulated in the particulars or conditions of sale, the Act has clearly altered the common law, which allowed this information to be given to bidders by other means, most commonly by an announcement from the auctioneer. However, the Act does not mention any sanction for failure to furnish this information in the stipulated manner. It is submitted that, since the purpose of the Act was to clarify the law relating to puffers, rather than to amend conveyancing techniques, such default would not render the sale itself invalid; what it would mean is that the sale would then be treated as being "without reserve", so as to preclude any bidding or other interference on behalf of the vendor.

---

1 The Act is hardly a model piece of drafting; section 3 provides a definition of "agent", a word which makes no other appearance in the Act!

Exactly what must be included in the particulars or conditions of sale, in order to satisfy section 5 of the Act, has been a matter of some controversy as yet unsettled by the courts. It is not clear whether a vendor who wishes to reserve a right to bid must, in addition to making express provision for such a right, also state that the sale is subject to a reserve, or whether the reservation of a right to bid automatically carries that implication. Support for the former view[1] is to be found in *Gilliat v Gilliat*,[2] the first case to be decided upon the Act. In that case property was put up for sale under a decree of the court. The conditions of sale state: "The sale is subject to a reserved bidding which has been fixed by the judge." The property was knocked down to a purchaser for £29,000, the amount of the reserved bidding, after a person employed by the auctioneer had bid up to £28,900. Although, in the absence of the puffer, the purchaser could not have obtained the property at a lower price, the sale was none the less set aside. Lord Romilly MR said:[3]

I think the Act makes a distinction between a reserved bidding and a reserved right to bid. It say that you must state whether there is a reserved price or not, and further, if you state that there is a reserved price, you must also state that a right to bid is reserved in order that you may employ a person to bid on your behalf.

The second possible interpretation of section 5 is that, since it lays down three possibilities, each one separated by the word "or", it is sufficient if any one of these is mentioned in the particulars or conditions of sale.[4] In this connection some assistance may be gained from the case of *Dimmock v Hallett*,[5] although this is not of direct authority since it was decided prior to the Act. In that case, which concerned the sale by a mortgagee of the mortgaged property, the auctioneer announced that the sale was without reserve, but that the parties interested in the estate were at liberty to bid. The defendant bought the property for £19,000 but refused

---

1 Which is held by D Macintyre, *Law Relating to Auctioneers and Estate Agents*, pp 64-66.
2 (1869) LR 9 Eq 60.
3 At p62.
4 See *Bateman's Law of Auctions*, 11th ed, pp 143-148.
5 (1866) 2 Ch App 21.

to complete the sale on the ground that, from £14,000, the only other bidder had been the mortgagee himself. It was held that the purchaser could not avoid the sale on this ground. Turner LJ said:[1]

The question then remains, what meaning is to be attributed to the statement that a sale is without reserve, but that the parties interested are at liberty to bid. The two branches of the statement are not very consistent, but I think that they may be read together by taking the second as a qualification of the first; and if a purchaser knows that parties interested have liberty to bid, he cannot be entitled to be discharged on the ground that they have bid against him.

It is submitted that the formal requirements of the Act are to be interpreted in the light of its intention, which was clearly to prevent purchasers of land at auction from being defrauded. This object is satisfactorily achieved, as *Dimmock* v *Hallett* clearly shows, by an express reservation of a right to bid, either with or without a further statement that the sale is subject to a reserved price. The view of Lord Romilly MR[2] to the contrary is, it is submitted, no more than an *obiter dictum* since, in the case before him, no right to bid had been reserved, and the employment of a puffer was therefore unlawful.

Whether or not it is strictly necessary, the prudent auctioneer will ensure that, wherever a right to bid is reserved, the particulars or conditions of sale also contain an express statement to the effect that the sale is subject to a reserve. It has been suggested that the reservation of the right to fix a reserve price would not be sufficient, as this would not inform bidders whether such a reserve had in fact been fixed;[3] however, in other circumstances such a condition has been held sufficient to put a purchaser on inquiry,[4] and it is submitted that a similar conclusion would be reached in this context.

The Sale of Land by Auction Act 1867 has come before the courts on two subsequent occasions. In *Parfitt* v *Jepson*,[5] the lease of a brickyard was auctioned under conditions which stipulated that the

---

1 At p26.
2 *Gilliat* v *Gilliat* (1869) LR 9 Eq 60 at p62: p 365.
3 Macintyre, *op cit*, p63.
4 See *Fay* v *Miller, Wilkins & Co* [1941] Ch 360: p 273.
5 (1877) 46 LJCP 529.

highest bidder should be the purchaser, but that the vendor or his agent should have the right of bidding once for the property. The auctioneer bid three times in competition with a third party, the last bid being £320, and then asked the vendor, who was present at the sale, to state his reserve price. The vendor said that his reserve was £350; the defendant, at the auctioneer's request, bid £351, whereupon the property was knocked down to him. The Court of Common Pleas held that the defendant was entitled to refuse to complete the sale, both on common law principles (as preserved by section 4 of the Act) and in accordance with the provisions of section 5 and 6. As far as the common law was concerned, it was held that the bids made by the auctioneer were to be treated as made by a puffer. Furthermore, the court gave short shrift to the argument that the effect of these unlawful bids had been wiped out by the subsequent statement of the reserve price:[1]

It is impossible to say to what extent a purchaser may not be influenced by bids, whether made earlier or not. People at a public auction are often influenced by the amount of competition going on, and where they assume the bids to be bona fide they are often willing to give more for the property than they would if they knew them to be sham bids.

With regard to the statutory provisions, it was held that, although the reservation of a right to bid once did not come within the express words, it was within the spirit and meaning of sections 5 and 6. In consequence, any action in excess of the rights which were expressly reserved was void. Moreover, Grove J was of the opinion that a right to bid once was very like a reserve price, something which does not of itself entitle the seller to bid, either personally or through an agent.

It may also be noted that, although the issue did not arise for the decision in the case itself, Grove J also stated his opinion that the Act had abolished altogether the practice of employing more than one puffer, since this would create a false appearance of competition.

The only other case concerning these statutory provisions is *Hills & Grant Ltd* v *Hodson*,[2] in which Luxmoore J had to consider what

---

1 *Per* Lindley J at p533; see also Grove J at p532.
2 [1934] Ch 53.

precise form of words is required to satisfy section 5 of the Act. In that case freehold building land was being sold in three lots, of which the present action concerned Lot 2. The Special Conditions of Sale incorporated by reference the National Conditions of Sale (11th ed); these provided that, subject to a right of the vendor to bid up to a reserved price, the highest bidder should be the purchaser. The Special Conditions further provided that, in the event of lot 2 remaining unsold or being bought in by the vendors, the vendors should be entitled to withdraw lot 3 from the sale. The defendant, to whom lot 2 was knocked down, refused to complete the sale on the ground that a puffer had bid against him, claiming that this was illegal in the absence of a clear statement that the property was subject to a reserved price. In dealing with this contention, Luxmoore J said:[1]

In my judgment the Act does not require that the words 'with reserve' or "without reserve", and no others shall be used in the particulars or conditions of sale ... the conditions of the Act are complied with so long as it is made plain, by whatever words may be chosen, that the sale is subject to a reserve.

When the conditions of sale were looked at, it was quite clear that a reserve had been fixed, as only in that event could the property possibly be "bought in". Thus the employment of a puffer was valid, and the defendant was bound by his purchase.

The overall effect of the Sale of Land by Auction Act 1867 appears to be as follows:

1. A puffer (including the auctioneer) may not bid on behalf of the vendor unless a right to bid is expressly reserved in the particulars or conditions of sale.
2. It is submitted that a similar restriction will be imposed upon a vendor who wishes to bid personally.[2] However, it may be noted that, while section 6 of the 1867 Act makes it lawful for "the seller or any one person on his behalf" to bid where a right to do so is reserved in the appropriate manner, section 5 merely provides that, where no such right is reserved, the seller may

---

1 At p61.
2 *Dimmock* v *Hallett* (1866) 2 Ch App 21 proceeded on this assumption.

not "employ any person to bid". It is thus possible to argue, albeit faintly, that personal bidding is not ruled out.
3. As to the possibility that the Act also requires a clear statement (in whatever form) that a reserve has been fixed, this question remains to be decided in some future case.

(b) *Sales of goods*

The unsatisfactory drafting of the Sale of Land by Auction Act 1867 is emphasised by the relative clarity of the statutory provisions governing chattel sales. Section 57 of the Sale of Goods Act 1979 provides:

(3) A sale by auction may be notified to be subject to a reserve or upset price, and a right to bid may also be reserved expressly by or on behalf of the seller.

(4) Where a sale by auction is not notified to be subject to a right to bid by or on behalf of the seller, it is not lawful for the seller to bid himself or to employ any person to bid at the sale, or for the auctioneer knowingly to take any bid from the seller or any such person.

(5) A sale contravening subsection (4) above may be treated as fraudulent by the buyer.

(6) Where, in respect of a sale by auction, a right to bid is expressly reserved (but not otherwise) the seller or any one person on his behalf may bid at the auction.

The general tenor of these provisions is similar to those which have already been considered in relation to the sale of land. Thus, for example, the seller's right will be limited to the employment of only one puffer, and a sale which contravenes this or any other rule will be voidable by the purchaser.[1] Moreover, whatever rights are reserved to the seller will be closely scrutinised by the court, in order to ensure that they have not been exceeded.[2]

Notwithstanding these similarities, however, the statutory rules relating to chattel sales are different in two (and possibly three) respects from their land sales counterparts. In the first place, the Sale of Goods Act does not require a seller to reserve any right to bid by means of the catalogue or conditions of sale. In this way the

---

1 An auctioneer may not bid on the seller's behalf where the seller himself is bidding: *Narramore* v *Fuller, Hall & Foulsham* (1932) 76 Sol Jo 289.

2 As in *Parfitt* v *Jepson* (1877) 46 LJCP 529.

old common law is preserved; an oral statement by the auctioneer at the commencement of the sale is sufficient, although written notification is naturally preferable for evidential reasons. Second, it is made clear that, where no reservation of a right to bid has been made, the seller is not entitled to bid personally.[1] Third, even if the earlier suggested interpretation of section 5 of the Sale of Land by Auction Act is incorrect, so that a seller who wishes to reserve a right to bid must also state expressly that the sale is subject to a reserve, this is certainly not the case in sales of goods.

(c) *Fictitious bids*

What remains to be considered is the legal position where an auctioneer, whether or not in the purported exercise of a right to bid as the vendor's agent, calls bids which have not really been made at all. In *Heatley* v *Newton*,[2] leasehold property was sold at auction under conditions of sale which stated that, subject to a right of the vendor or his agent "to bid once or oftener", the highest bidder should be the purchaser. After an apparently brisk and eager competition the plaintiff, who had made no previous bids, offered £13,000 and the property was knocked down to him at that price. The plaintiff subsequently discovered that all bids above £8,000 had been made on behalf of the vendor, and that a number were entirely fictitious, having been taken "off the wall" by the auctioneer. On realising this, the plaintiff sued the seller and the auctioneer for the return of his deposit with interest. The case as reported did not deal in any detail with the merits of the plaintiff's claim, being mainly concerned with whether the auctioneer was entitled to pay the deposit into court and have proceedings against him stayed. Nevertheless the Court of Appeal was clearly of the opinion that the auctioneer's conduct was wrongful and that, assuming the alleged facts to be true, an action would lie against him.[3]

Notwithstanding *Heatley* v *Newton*, it is sometimes asserted by practising auctioneers that it is perfectly legitimate to "trot" the bidding, or to take bids "off the wall", provided only that the property has not reached its reserve. It is submitted that this is a dangerous

---

1 See p 368.

2 (1881) 19 ChD 326.

3 Presumably the employment of more than one puffer would have been another ground for invalidating the sale, although this was not expressly mentioned.

fallacy, for at least three reasons.[1] First, there can be no doubt that inducing someone to buy property by pretending that others have made offers for it is a misrepresentation; if this is done knowingly, it is fraud.[2] Second, as we have already seen, unlawful conduct by vendor or auctioneer is no less unlawful where it takes place below the reserve, because it may continue to influence bidding above this figure.[3] Third, provided the necessary element of "dishonesty" can be established, there seems no reason to doubt that "calling" a bid which the auctioneer knows has not been made will constitute the criminal offence of obtaining (or attempting to obtain) property by deception.[4]

The principle which underlies all the cases mentioned above is that the purchaser is to be protected against any unfair interference with the bidding. To this end, relief has been given where the interference in question did not take the form of puffing as such, but where the court felt that the overall result was much the same. In *Robinson* v *Wall*[5] Lord Mostyn wished to purchase certain connected estates, one of which was to be auctioned "without reserve". It was accordingly agreed with the vendors that Lord Mostyn should attend the sale and bid for the property; that he should pay £35,000 for it even if it were knocked down for less; and that, if the price exceeded this figure, Lord Mostyn should be free to bid higher or not, as he wished. The defendant, to whom the property was knocked down for £49,800, discovered this arrangement and refused to complete the purchase. It was held that the defendant was justified in his refusal; as Lord Langdale MR said,[6] the auction "was, from the beginning, tainted with reserve, whilst it professed to be 'without reserve'." Lord Cottenham LC, in affirming this decision, said:[7]

Now, what took place in this case, although the arrangement is rather complicated, appears to me to amount to a reserve, or at least to precisely

---

1 Of course, the difficulties involved in proving such allegations may be considerable.
2 *Mullens* v *Miller* (1882) 22 ChD 194: p 89.
3 *Parfitt* v *Jepson* (1877) 46 LJCP 529: p 366.
4 Theft Act 1968, section 15. The maximum penalties are a fine (unlimited in amount) or imprisonment for up to 10 years.
5 (1846) 10 Beav 61; affirmed (1847) 2 Ph 372.
6 (1846) 10 Beav 61 at p72.
7 (1847) 2 Ph 372 at p376.

the same thing, so far as the public is concerned, which is the only way you can look at it. For it is quite immaterial what are the precise terms of the arrangement between the vendor and any other person, that being only the machinery by which the effect is produced. We must look to see what is the effect of what took place as regards the public – as regards those who attended the sale.

The rule preventing interference with the bidding is thus a fairly strict one, in that it does not apply only where the vendor intends to defraud bidders at the sale. However, it appears that the purchaser can only avoid the sale where the vendor is proved to have known of the bids in question. Thus in *Parfitt* v *Jepson*,[1] counsel for the defendant contended that the authority of a puffer to bid for the vendor must be expressly proved,[2] and this was accepted by both Grove J and Lindley J. The point arose specifically in the case of *Union Bank* v *Munster*,[3] where mortgaged property was sold at auction by its equitable mortgagees. The defendant, having already bid more than the reserved price, was forced considerably higher by a person who, with no intention of completing a purchase, was bidding on behalf of the mortgagor. The defendant claimed to avoid the sale on the ground of fraud, but the mortgagees were granted a decree of specific performance was awarded against him. As Kekewich J said:[4]

For a man to go into an auction room and bid either a large or a small sum for a property when he knows that it is impossible for him to perform the contract is, of course, dishonest. But there is no question here of any privity of the vendors either in person or through the auctioneer or otherwise, with that dishonesty.

Thus the independent fraud of a third party, even where it causes hardship to a genuine bidder, is not the responsibility of the vendor.

---

1 (1877) 46 LJCP 529.
2 Relying on *Thornett* v *Haines* (1846) 15 M&W 367, which proceeded on this assumption.
3 (1887) 37 ChD 51.
4 At p53.

The latter's duty is merely to see, as far as possible, that the auction is properly and honestly conducted.[1]

2 Withdrawal of property

In the type of case discussed above, a bidder complains of being forced by the undisclosed intervention of the vendor to pay more than is necessary for property which is put up for sale. A different aspect of the problem is seen where the intervention of the auctioneer, as agent for the vendor, *prevents* the highest bidder from securing the property. The auctioneer can achieve this (and thereby give effect to a secret reserve) either by refusing to bring down the hammer at all, or by bidding for the vendor until all genuine bidders have dropped out. The question is whether, when bidders have been led to expect a sale to be without reserve, such actions on the part of the auctioneer are lawful.

Before turning to examine the English cases in which this question has been discussed, it may be of interest to note the straightforward approach which was adopted by the Scottish Court of Session in *Fenwick* v *Macdonald, Fraser & Co Ltd*.[2] In that case, where a herd of cattle was offered in lots "for unreserved sale", the plaintiff bid 42 guineas for a particular bull. The auctioneer, however, intimating that there was a reserve of 150 guineas on this animal, withdrew it from the sale. The court held that the plaintiff could not recover damages from either the auctioneer or the seller, and Lord Trayner stated the reason for decision succinctly:[3]

If it is the power of any competitor at an auction sale to retract his bid before the fall of the hammer, it follows that the exposer is equally entitled to withdraw his subject, because if the competitor is not bound the exposer is not bound either.

It was also held in that case that the auctioneer, who had at all times been acting upon the instructions of a named principal, incurred no personal liability to the plaintiff.

---

1 The chaos which may be caused by someone who bids wildly and then simply disappears is shown by a celebrated incident at Sotheby's: see The Times, Feb 5 1983.
2 (1904) 6 F 850.
3 At p854.

The Scottish position, though logical, seems somewhat questionable in moral terms, since it enables a vendor to impose a reserve price on property, while at the same time obtaining whatever benefit there may be in advertising the sale as "without reserve". Faced with this problem, the English courts have struggled to find some way of giving effect to a "without reserve" undertaking, while recognising that any liability must necessarily arise before a contract of sale is made; that is to say, before the hammer falls.

In the leading case of *Warlow* v *Harrison*,[1] the defendant auctioneer advertised and put up for sale a mare described as "the property of a gentleman, without reserve, Janet Pride, a brown mare". The plaintiff bid 60 guineas for this mare; there was then a bid of 61 guineas but the plaintiff, upon learning that this bid had been made by the seller, refused to bid further. The mare was accordingly knocked down to the seller whereupon the plaintiff, having tendered 60 guineas to the auctioneer and demanded the mare, sued the auctioneer for damages. The plaintiff's case alleged that, since he was the highest bidder, the auctioneer had become his agent for the purpose of completing the contract, and was liable for breach of this agency. The existence of the alleged agency was denied, both at first instance and on appeal, on the ground that whatever limited authority is possessed by an auctioneer as agent for the purchaser[2] arises only when the hammer falls. The defendant was therefore not liable on the case as pleaded; however, the judges took the opportunity to consider, *obiter*, the merits of the situation.

The judgment of the Court of Queen's Bench was delivered by Lord Campbell CJ, who said that, however the case was pleaded, the defendant could not be liable to the plaintiff upon any contract, since this would contradict the well-established principle of *Payne* v *Cave*.[3] When the plaintiff appealed, however, the five judges of the Exchequer Chamber all thought that an auctioneer could be liable in such circumstances, although they were divided in their reasoning. In giving the decision of the majority, Martin B likened the situation to a "reward case", in which a general offer ripens into

---

1 (1859) 1 E&E 295.
2 To sign a memorandum of the sale on his behalf: see pp 286.
3 (1789) 3 TR 148: see p 378.

a contract with anyone who performs the stated conditions. He continued:[1]

Upon the same principle, it seems to us that the highest bona fide bidder at an auction may sue the auctioneer as upon a contract that the sale shall be without reserve. We think the auctioneer who puts the property up for sale upon such a condition pledges himself that the sale shall be without reserve; or, in other words, contracts that it shall be so; and that this contract is made with the highest bona fide bidder; and, in case of a breach of it, that he has a right of action against the auctioneer ... We think the auctioneer has contracted that the sale shall be without reserve; and that the contract is broken upon a bid being made by or on behalf of the owner, whether it be during the time when the property is under the hammer, or it be the last bid upon which the article is knocked down; in either case the sale is not "without reserve", and the contract of the auctioneer is broken.

The two minority judges, Willes and Bramwell JJ, preferred to rest their decision as to the auctioneer's potential liability upon the ground of breach of warranty of authority, that is to say, upon the auctioneer's untrue claim that he was authorised by the vendor to sell "without reserve".

Before considering the merits of these two lines of reasoning, one point should be noted: no action was brought against the seller in this case and the courts made no mention of this possibility, preferring to treat any liability which might arise as attaching to the auctioneer. It would seem, however, as a matter of principle, that a vendor who causes the conditions of sale to be violated, either by making an unlawful bid or by instructing the auctioneer to withdraw property from the sale, should be equally liable to the disappointed highest bidder. In any event, it was made clear that the legal responsibility would ultimately rest with the seller. As Martin B said:[2]

We entertain no doubt that the owner may, at any time before the contract is legally complete, interfere and revoke the auctioneer's authority: but he does so at his peril; and if the auctioneer has contracted any liability in consequence of his employment and the subsequent revocation or conduct of the owner, he is entitled to be indemnified.

---

1 (1859) 1 E&E 295 at p316.
2 At p317.

While the minority view in *Warlow* v *Harrison*, that the auctioneer is liable for breach of warranty of authority, is superficially attractive, the case does not in truth appear to fall within the normally accepted limits of that principle. Breach of warranty of authority typically arises where an agent, who purports to make a contract on behalf of a client, is later found to have acted without authority. In such circumstances the alleged contract is not binding upon the agent's principal, and the other party is entitled to sue the agent personally for breach of an implied representation of authority.[1] In the *Warlow* v *Harrison* situation, the highest bidder's complaint is not that the auctioneer has done something without authority, but that the auctioneer has refused to exceed that authority.

It is therefore apparent that, if the disappointed bidder is to have a right of action, this must depend upon some form of contractual obligation, which is created by making a bid on the faith of the statement that the sale will be "without reserve".[2] This is the principle which was laid down by the majority in *Warlow* v *Harrison*, and it has been the subject of judicial consideration in a number of later cases.

In *Mainprice* v *Westley*,[3] the defendant auctioneer advertised that a shop was to be "offered for peremptory sale by auction, by direction of the mortgagee with a power of sale". The advertisement named the mortgagee's solicitor as the person from whom further particulars could be obtained. The plaintiff bid for the shop but, after bidding had started, it was announced that there was a reserve price on the property, and the mortgagee's solicitor bought it in at this price. The plaintiff brought an action against the auctioneer on the basis of *Warlow* v *Harrison*, but this claim failed. The court ruled that, having identified the client, the auctioneer could not be said to have made any implied contract with the plaintiff.

It is submitted that the ground of distinction between the two cases on which the court in *Mainprice* v *Westley* relied is, on closer inspection, not valid, and that the cases are in truth irreconcilable.

---

1 See, for example, *Fay* v *Miller, Wilkins & Co* [1941] Ch 360: p 273.
2 It is not of course contended that the contract of *sale* is created then; see the Sale of Goods Act 1979, section 57(2). In *British Car Auctions Ltd* v *Wright* [1972] 3 All ER 462 it was specifically held, for the purposes of criminal law, that an auctioneer does not "offer" goods for sale.
3 (1865) 6 B&S 420.

There are two reasons for this. First, the principal in *Warlow* v *Harrison* was not undisclosed, but merely unnamed, and it is well established that an agent does not automatically incur personal liability merely by failing to name his principal.[1] Second, two of the three judges in *Mainprice* v *Westley* itself expressly doubted whether an auctioneer could ever be said to act for an undisclosed principal:

Inasmuch as the character of an auctioneer as agent is unlike that of many other agents, as to whom, so long as the fact of there being a principal is undisclosed, it remains uncertain whether the contracting party is acting as principal or agent; while in the employment and duty of an auctioneer the character of agent is necessarily implied, and the party bidding at the auction knowingly deals with him as such, and with the knowledge that his authority may be at any moment put an end to by the principal.[2]

The majority decision in *Warlow* v *Harrison* received a degree of support in two later English cases. In *Harris* v *Nickerson*,[3] the defendant auctioneer advertised that certain brewing materials, plant and office furniture would be sold by him on a certain date. The plaintiff obtained a commission to purchase the furniture and travelled from London to Bury St Edmunds, only to find that the furniture had been withdrawn from the sale. In rejecting the plaintiff's claim for loss of time and expenses, the Court of Queen's Bench distinguished *Warlow* v *Harrison* on the ground that the present advertisement was not an offer, but merely a declaration of intention giving rise to no legal rights on the part of anyone who relied upon it. However, both Blackburn J and Quain J thought that a contract might arise between an auctioneer and the highest bidder in the circumstances of *Warlow* v *Harrison*, although Blackburn J appeared to prefer the argument based on breach of warranty of authority.

In *Johnston* v *Boyes*,[4] an action was brought against a vendor of land for refusing to allow the highest bidder, to whom it had been knocked down, to sign a contract of purchase and to pay a deposit by cheque. If this refusal could not be justified[5] it would clearly

1 See *Benton* v *Campbell Parker Co Ltd* [1925] 2 KB 410: p 307.
2 (1865) 6 B&S 420 at p429, *per* Blackburn J.
3 (1873) LR 8 QB 286.
4 [1899] 2 Ch 73.
5 In fact it was; see p 281.

amount to a breach of the conditions of sale, which provided that
the highest bidder should be the purchaser. In dealing with this
possibility, Cozens-Hardy J said:[1]

A vendor who offers property for sale by auction on the terms of printed
conditions can be made liable to a member of the public who accepts the
offer if those conditions be violated: see *Warlow* v *Harrison*.

It appears, therefore, that the balance of authority in English law
favours the imposition of liability upon a seller or an auctioneer who,
having put up property "without reserve", refuses to knock it down
to the highest bidder. This liability is based, it seems, on a second
contract, collateral to the intended contract of sale, made by the
seller or auctioneer with each person who gives consideration by
attending the auction and making a bid.[2]

3 Withdrawal of bids

The conventional analysis of a sale by auction is that it consists
of a series of offers from bidders, culminating in a contract when the
highest bid is accepted by the auctioneer. This would suggest that,
until the hammer falls, any bid may validly be withdrawn. Such
reasoning is indeed supported by the old case of *Payne* v *Cave*,[3]
where the defendant bid 40/- for a worm-tub and a pewter worm.
When the auctioneer "dwelt on the bidding", claiming that the worm
was worth much more, the defendant asked the auctioneer to
warrant its weight and, upon the auctioneer's refusal to do so,
withdrew his bid. The defendant purchased the goods for 30/- at a
later sale, whereupon the seller sued him for the difference in price.
Rejecting the plaintiff's argument that each bidder becomes a
conditional purchaser, subject to the possibility of being overbid, the
Court of King's Bench said:[4]

The auctioneer is the agent of the vendor, and the assent of both parties is
necessary to make the contract binding; that is signified on the part of the
seller by knocking down the hammer, which was not done here till the
defendant had retracted. An auction is not unaptly called *"locus*

---

1 [1899] 2 Ch 73 at p77.
2 See the lucid and persuasive argument of Prof LCB Gower (1952) 68 LQR 457.
3 (1789) 3 TR 148.
4 At p149.

poenitentiae". Every bidding is nothing more than an offer on one side, which is not binding on either side till it is assented to. But according to what is now contended for, one party would be bound by the offer, and the other not, which can never be allowed.

The actual decision in *Payne* v *Cave*, that a bid may validly be retracted before it has been accepted, has been given statutory force by the Sale of Goods Act 1979, section 57(2). This provides:

A sale by auction is complete when the auctioneer announces its completion by the fall of the hammer, or in other customary manner; and until the announcement is made any bidder may retract his bid.

Although there is no equivalent statutory provision applicable to sales of land, it is not suggested that they are to be treated differently. None the less, the basic principle cannot be regarded as entirely free from qualification. What, for example, is the effect (if any) of the frequently encountered condition of sale which states that no bid may be retracted? The conventional answer is that such a condition is meaningless, since it only becomes enforceable when it is contained in a contract, and if a bid is withdrawn before the hammer falls then there *is* no contract. However, there is some attraction in the argument that, if the vendor is legally obliged to adhere to the published conditions of sale,[1] then bidders should be bound as well. Nevertheless, there is little support in the case law for this argument, except perhaps for the rather special situation which came before the court in *Freer* v *Rimner*.[2] Property there was sold by order of the court, and the mortgagee of the property, although not a party to the law-suit in question, gave his consent to the sale. At the auction, a condition of which was that no bid could be withdrawn, a bid was made (and then retracted) by the mortgagee's solicitor. It was held that, having bid in full knowledge of the conditions, the solicitor was bound to complete the purchase.

4 Disputed bids

As mentioned previously, the essence of an auction is that a contract of sale is created when the auctioneer signifies acceptance

---

1 See pp 373-378.
2 (1844) 14 Sim 391.

of the last of a series of bids. It follows that, once the hammer falls, both vendor and purchaser are in principle bound by their contract, and that the auctioneer has no power to reopen matters, for example because a hitherto unnoticed bidder would like to enter the contest.

However, in the hubbub of a crowded saleroom, things are not always so clear-cut. The task of identifying who is actually bidding at any given moment is an art in itself and, not surprisingly, the fall of the hammer is sometimes closely followed by an argument. It may be, for example, that the person identified by the auctioneer as the highest bidder claims not to have made the bid in question; or that someone else claims to have made a bid which the auctioneer has ignored. In order to avoid such problems it is sensible to provide, and auction conditions commonly do provide, for any bidding dispute to be settled at the absolute discretion of the auctioneer.

The efficacy of such a condition fell to be tested in the case of *Richards* v *Phillips*,[1] which arose out of what a member of the Court of Appeal described as "a comedy of errors of a remarkable kind". In that case, which concerned the sale of a London theatre at the London Auction Mart, the auctioneer bid close to the reserve price on behalf of the vendors, whereupon two genuine bidders simultaneously bid above the reserve. The auctioneer saw only one of these bids, that of the plaintiff, and duly knocked the property down to him; however, the other bidder, a Mr Drummy (who had thought that it was *his* bid which had been accepted), then came forward to protest. The auctioneer, on hearing from members of his staff that Mr Drummy had indeed made a bid, decided to put the property up for sale again, relying on a condition of sale which stated that "if any dispute arises respecting a bid, the auctioneer may determine the dispute, or the property may, at the vendor's option, either be put up again at the last undisputed bid or be withdrawn". The two rivals then bid against each other until the plaintiff was again successful, but this time at a price almost 50% higher than on the first occasion.

The plaintiff duly sued the auctioneer for the difference between the two hammer prices, asserting that the auctioneer owed him a

1 [1969] 1 Ch 39.

duty to provide an enforceable contract.[1] When the auctioneer sought in defence to rely on the condition of sale quoted above, the plaintiff claimed that, since Mr Drummy had never succeeded in attracting the auctioneer's attention, he had not in fact made any bid and there was thus no "dispute". This argument failed to convince the Court of Appeal, which held that this was precisely the kind of situation which the auction condition was intended to cover, and that the auctioneer was accordingly entitled to deal with the matter as he had.

5 Mistaken bids

The reluctance of English law to release a party from contractual obligations on the ground of some mistake is well known. At common law, a contract which is entered into on the basis of some fundamental mistake can be declared void, but a mistake of sufficient significance is very difficult to establish. Equity takes a somewhat more relaxed view over this issue, but the relief which equity can offer is in most cases less complete than that of common law.

The basic position outlined above is as applicable to sales by auction as to contracts formed in any other way. As Baggallay LJ pointed out in the auction case of *Tamplin* v *James*:[2]

Where there has been no misrepresentation, and where there is no ambiguity in the terms of the contract, the defendant cannot be allowed to evade the performance of it by the simple statement that he has made a mistake. Were such to be the law the performance of a contract could rarely be enforced upon an unwilling party who was also unscrupulous.

When the Court of Appeal affirmed Baggallay LJ's decision, James LJ said:[3]

For the most part the cases where a defendant has escaped on the ground of a mistake not contributed to by the plaintiff, have been cases where a hardship amounting to injustice would have been inflicted upon him by holding him to his bargain, and it was unreasonable to hold him to it.

---

1 The nature of this alleged duty is discussed at p 310.
2 (1879) 15 ChD 215 at p217.
3 (1880) 15 ChD 215 at p221.

The practical result of such judicial attitudes may be seen in *Van Praagh v Everidge*,[1] where the defendant, who had wished to purchase lot 2 at a sale of land, bid by mistake for lot 1. Kekewich J, having reviewed the relevant case law, held that there was no reason to relieve the defendant from his contract and awarded specific performance to the vendor.

Notwithstanding the general principle, there are undoubtedly circumstances in which a bidder may obtain relief from the consequences of a mistaken bid. It seems in particular that, where a bidder's mistake is in some way induced by the vendor or the auctioneer, for example through misleading sale documents, specific performance of the resulting contract will not be decreed.[2] Nor will equity permit a person to snap up an offer which, it must be realised, is not intended, even though that person may not have been responsible for the mistake. Thus in *Webster v Cecil*[3] the defendant, who had already refused an offer of £2000 for a property from the plaintiff, wrote to the plaintiff offering to sell it to him for £1,250! When the plaintiff purported to accept this offer, notwithstanding the obvious mistake which it contained, a decree of specific performance was refused.

In *Hartog v Colin & Shields*,[4] where a somewhat similar attempt was made to snap up an unintended offer, a judge went so far as to hold the resulting "contract" void at common law.[5] However, such an extreme result is normally reserved for cases where the effect of a mistake is so fundamental that there is in truth no agreement at all between the parties.[6] In *Scriven Bros v Hindley*,[7] for example, bales of hemp and bales of tow were put up for auction on behalf of the plaintiffs. Each set of bales bore the same shipping mark, for the entire consignment had arrived on the same ship (a unique occurrence, according to the expert evidence) and the defendants'

---

1 [1902] 2 Ch 266; reversed on other grounds [1903] 1 Ch 434. Common law is even less likely to grant relief: see *Robinson, Fisher & Harding v Behar* [1927] 1 KB 513.

2 See, for example, *Manser v Back* (1848) 6 Hare 443.

3 (1861) 30 Beav 62.

4 [1939] 3 All ER 566.

5 The duty of an auctioneer in relation to surprising bids was considered by the Court of Appeal in *Friedrich v A Monickendam, Ltd* (1973) 228 EG 1311.

6 The classic case is *Raffles v Wichelhaus* (1864) 2 H&C 906, where the parties were irreconcilably at cross-purposes.

7 [1913] 3 KB 564.

buyer, who had not inspected the samples at the sale room, thought that all the bales contained hemp, which was a much more valuable commodity. The catalogue merely referred to the bales by numbers so that, when the auctioneer put up the tow, the buyer made an extravagant bid for it. The defendants were held not liable to accept the goods or pay the price, for, as AT Lawrence J said:[1]

The parties were never *ad idem* as to the subject matter of the proposed sale; there was therefore in fact no contract of bargain and sale.

Very occasionally, a mistaken bid may qualify for some relief, even though the fault is entirely that of the bidder. In *Malins* v *Freeman*,[2] for example, where the defendant was employed to bid up to the reserved price on a particular lot, he bid for a different lot by mistake. Notwithstanding that the defendant alone was to blame for this error, a decree of specific performance was refused, and the vendor was left to pursue his common law claim for damages.

B Liability for misstatements

A person selling land or goods must not mislead prospective purchasers as to the nature or quality of what is offered, either by erroneously describing the property in the contract of sale or by making false statements about it during the course of negotiations. Any breach of this duty is likely to result in the contract being set aside or in an award of compensation to the disappointed purchaser. Further, a seller of land is treated as misleading the buyer where certain hidden defects in the property (or, more accurately, the title to the property) are not disclosed.

In the case of a sale by auction, much of the information sought by prospective bidders is obtained from the auctioneer, acting as agent for the vendor. Thus, queries raised at the sale itself are usually answered personally by the auctioneer, who is also frequently responsible for drafting preliminary advertisements. The catalogue, which contains a description of goods to be sold, is commonly the work of the auctioneer; likewise the particulars, which

---

1 At p568.
2 (1837) 2 Keen 25.

fulfil the same function in the case of a sale of land, although here the auctioneer is more likely to act on legal advice.

Where information furnished to bidders by an auctioneer is inaccurate or insufficient, the legal liability is primarily that of the vendor, although the auctioneer may incur some personal liability.[1] In any case, a vendor who has lost a sale or who has had to pay compensation through the carelessness of his agent is entitled to be reimbursed. It is therefore of the utmost importance that an auctioneer should not make any misleading statements and should ensure that, when drafting the particulars on a sale of land, all necessary facts are disclosed.

In cases dealing with liability for false statements, the terms "misdescription" and "misrepresentation" are used indiscriminately (even by judges).[2] In reality, however, they are quite distinct, both conceptually and in the remedies to which they give rise. A misdescription occurs where property is inaccurately described in the contract itself (usually in the particulars of sale). A misrepresentation, by contrast, is a false or misleading statement which, though not itself forming part of the contract of sale, none the less induces the purchaser to make that contract. These areas of liability may accordingly be separately considered.

1 Misdescription

Where misdescription is concerned, there are significant differences between sales of land and sales of goods. It will thus be convenient to deal separately with these two topics.

(a) *Sales of land*

The legal effects of misdescription are discussed in more detail below; at this stage it is sufficient to bear in mind that, generally speaking, a substantial misdescription renders the contract unenforceable against the purchaser, even if the vendor is willing to pay compensation in respect of it. For the present, then, we are concerned with the question of how serious an error must be to be treated as "substantial" for this purpose.

---

1 See p 410.
2 See *Registered Holdings Ltd* v *Kadri* (1971) 222 EG 621; *Laurence* v *Lexcourt Holdings Ltd* [1978] 2 All ER 810.

Possibly the most "substantial" misdescription which can be envisaged is a false statement of the identity of the property. If the particulars of sale refer to one piece of land, when the vendor is really selling another piece, there can be no question of enforcing the contract against the purchaser. Thus in *Leach* v *Mullett*,[1] auction particulars described a house as no 4, instead of no 2. The highest bidder wanted the house as an investment and, although both were let at the same rent, no 4 was in a better state of repair. It was held that the purchaser could not be compelled to accept compensation and complete the contract.

As a general rule, any misdescription of the interest which the vendor holds in the property is treated as "substantial". In *Re Arnold*,[2] for example, a farm which was being auctioned included a certain field, of which the vendor only owned four undivided sevenths. This fact was not made clear in the particulars of sale, although the reduced acreage was correctly stated. The purchaser established that he needed the whole field, whereupon the Court of Appeal refused to enforce the contract against him. A similar result was achieved in *Re Russ & Brown's Contract*,[3] where property described as "eight leasehold dwelling-houses" was in fact held by underlease. In *Ridley* v *Oster*,[4] where four houses were described as "freehold de-controlled properties", the purchaser recovered his deposit on proving that two rooms in one of the houses were still controlled at the date of the contract.

Any statement made on behalf of a vendor which effectively conceals the existence of an incumbrance to which the property is subject will render the contract unenforceable against a purchaser. Thus in *Jones* v *Edney*,[5] where a public-house was being sold, the auctioneer, genuinely believing (albeit erroneously) that a tying covenant was unenforceable, sold the property as a free house. The purchaser successfully sued for the return of his deposit. Similarly, in *Dykes* v *Blake*[6] the plaintiff purchased two adjoining lots on the sale of an estate. One of these was subject to a right of way which,

---

1 (1827) 3 C&P 115.
2 (1880) 14 ChD 270.
3 [1934] Ch 34.
4 [1939] 1 All ER 618.
5 (1812) 3 Camp 285.
6 (1838) 4 Bing NC 463.

according to the particulars and an annexed plan, was only for the benefit of the plaintiff's other lot. In fact this second right of way was of more general use and, as a result, the plaintiff was held entitled to avoid the contract of sale.

Where property is bought as an investment rather than for personal occupation, any inaccuracy in the stated rents or profits accruing from it will be fatal to the validity of the contract. In *Swaisland* v *Dearsley*,[1] for example, an ambiguity in the particulars of certain property led a purchaser to believe that the annual income was £16 instead of £8. On this ground the vendor was refused a decree of specific performance. The need for precision in this context is further illustrated by the case of *Lee* v *Rayson*,[2] which concerned a sale of 13 dwelling-houses, let to various tenants. The aggregate annual rent was correctly stated, but the particulars made it appear that the houses were let in pairs rather than singly. This misdescription was held to be sufficiently substantial to entitle the purchaser to the return of his deposit.

A particularly common form of misdescription is one which concerns the size or extent of the property sold; the case of *Mustafa* v *Baptist Union Corporation Ltd*[3] provides a fascinating, even bizarre, example. The plaintiff there bought at auction a rambling four-storey terraced house in East London, which at the time was converted into two maisonettes. The plaintiff inspected the property before the sale, but failed to realise that, within the "box" of the house, there was a room to which he had no access and which in fact formed part of the adjoining property. The particulars of sale, which the plaintiff had seen, accurately described those rooms which *were* included in the sale, but made no mention of the blocked-off part of the premises. It was held that a reasonable purchaser, on seeing the photograph of the front of the house which appeared on the particulars, would assume that everything behind it was included in the sale; it was accordingly the vendors' responsibility positively to correct this "misdescription".

Whether a false statement on matters of size or extent can be adequately remedied by the payment of compensation is largely a question of degree; a purchaser who, in the opinion of the court, is

---

1 (1861) 30 LJ Ch 652.
2 [1917] 1 Ch 613.
3 (1983) 266 EG 812.

getting substantially what was bargained for, will be held to the contract, albeit with a reduction in the purchase price to take account of the error. In *King* v *Wilson*,[1] the defendant agreed to purchase a house of which he was tenant and occupier. The depth of the property was stated in the particulars to be 46 ft, whereas it was in fact only 33 ft. Despite this misdescription, it could hardly be denied that the purchaser was getting what he expected, and therefore the contract was enforced against him at a reduced price. In *Re Fawcett & Holmes' Contract*,[2] a plot of land was sold by the trustees of a will. The boundaries of the land were clear to everyone, including the purchaser; however in stating the area of the property as 1,372 sq yds, the trustees failed to realise that this figure included a well-fenced field of 339 sq yds which the testator had sold off. The Court of Appeal held that, since the purchaser never expected to obtain this field, the discrepancy in area was a matter for compensation only, not for refusal of specific performance.

The effect of an inaccurate statement of the area of property is often complicated by the use in the particulars of sale of such phrases as "be the same more or less" or "or thereabouts". Such a qualification may make the vendor's statement so vague as to deprive the purchaser of any remedy, as in *Winch* v *Winchester*,[3] where an estate "containing by estimation 41 acres, be the same more or less" was found to contain only 35 acres. In *Hill* v *Buckley*,[4] on the other hand, the phrase "be the same more or less" was held not to excuse a deficiency of 26 out of 217 acres; it did, however, help to make the deficiency a fit subject for compensation.

A large error in the stated size of land to be sold is a substantial misdescription enabling the purchaser to refuse the property. Thus in *Shackleton* v *Sutcliffe*,[5] land sold for building purposes was subject to a number of undisclosed easements which affected 4½ acres out of a total plot of 30 acres. The deficiency was held too great to be adequately remedied by the payment of compensation.

---

1 (1843) 6 Beav 124.
2 (1889) 41 ChD 150.
3 (1812) 1 Ves & B 375.
4 (1811) 17 Ves 394.
5 (1847) 1 De G & Sm 609.

So too, in *Aberaman Ironworks* v *Wickens*[1] purchasers were held entitled to recover their money on account of a deficiency of 430 acres out of 1,530.

The types of misdescription so far referred to are in no way exhaustive but are merely used as examples of what is commonly found in practice. Any description of property which is erroneous in a material respect may lead to the award of compensation or, if sufficiently serious, to the loss of the sale. Thus a purchaser of a two-storeyed house described as three-storeyed successfully claimed compensation for the error, notwithstanding that he lived next door to the property![2] So too, in *Stanton* v *Tattersall*,[3] where a house was described as "a freehold estate, being no 58, on the north side of Pall Mall, opposite Marlborough House" it was held that the purchaser could not be forced to accept a property situated behind no 57 and connected to Pall Mall by a narrow passage. In contrast, where a house situated in a road off Regency Square was always known as "39, Regency Square", the vendor was held entitled to sell it by that description without any further explanation.[4]

In describing the qualities and advantages of property which they are trying to sell, vendors and their agents are allowed a certain degree of latitude. In "puffing" the property by stressing (and perhaps rather exaggerating) its good points, no liability is incurred while what is expressed is a matter of opinion rather than fact. The rather patronising attitude of the courts to the natural enthusiasm of a selling agent is well illustrated by the modern case of *Watson* v *Burton*,[5] where property was described as "valuable and extensive premises . . . situated in a first-class position" and "very suitable for development". This description, said Wynn-Parry J,[6] was "what I may describe, with no disrespect, as typical auctioneers' 'puff'".

There are many examples in the law reports of statements falling on either side of the line which separates "puff" from misdescription

---

1 (1868) 4 Ch App 101.
2 *Parker* v *Farebrother* (1853) 21 LT (OS) 128.
3 (1853) 1 Sm & G 529.
4 *White* v *Bradshaw* (1851) 18 LT (OS) 183.
5 [1956] 3 All ER 929.
6 At p931.

(and, therefore, legal liability). In *Scott* v *Hanson*,[1] land described as "fourteen acres of uncommonly rich water-meadow land" was in fact imperfectly watered. It was held that, provided the description of it as a water meadow was accurate, its "richness" was merely a matter of opinion. Similarly, in *Dimmock* v *Hallett*,[2] a statement that land was "fertile and improvable" was disregarded, even though part of the land had been abandoned as useless. On the other hand, where a farm was described as being "in a high state of cultivation", the purchaser was awarded compensation for its very impoverished state.[3]

It is perhaps in relation to houses that estate agents and auctioneers wax mostly lyrical; Sachs J has described purchasers' "recurrent joy of comparing the realities of some property with the benign description in the estate agent's particulars".[4] However, a purchaser who challenges their description must show more than a difference of opinion in order to obtain a remedy. Thus it is merely a "puff" to describe property as "a residence fit for a family of distinction"[5] or a "substantial and convenient dwelling-house".[6] Where, however, a house is described as "in good repair"[7] or "not damp"[8] these are treated as statements of fact and, if they are untrue, the purchaser is entitled to compensation or to avoid the sale. In *Registered Holdings Ltd* v *Kadri*,[9] the defendant successfully bid for what was described from the rostrum as a "nice house" in Battersea, only to discover that his standards of "niceness" went some way beyond those of the auctioneer. In holding that the vendors were not entitled to enforce the sale, Goff J said:[10]

By no stretch of the imagination can a house the whole of which is subject to a compulsory purchase order, albeit provisional, and the basement of

---

1 (1826) 1 Sim 13.
2 (1866) 2 Ch App 21.
3 *Dyer* v *Hargrave* (1805) 10 Ves 505.
4 *Goding* v *Frazer* [1966] 3 All ER 234 at p238.
5 *Magennis* v *Fallon* (1829) 2 Moll 561.
6 *Johnson* v *Smart* (1860) 2 Giff 151.
7 *Dyer* v *Hargrave* (1805) 10 Ves 505.
8 *Strangways* v *Bishop* (1857) 29 LT (OS) 120.
9 (1971) 222 EG 621.
10 At p625.

which, including the kitchen, is subject to a closing order be described as "nice". In my view, this goes beyond the realm of puff and is a misrepresentation.

Although, as has been stated, neither a vendor nor a selling agent will usually be liable for holding opinions, it should be remembered that liability may arise where the known facts conflict with the opinion and these facts are not revealed. Thus, in *Smith* v *Land and House Property Corporation*,[1] an hotel which was being sold by auction was described as let to "a most desirable tenant". In fact the tenant was in arrear with the rent, and the previous quarter's rent had only been paid under threat of distress. In these circumstances the Court of Appeal refused to treat the description as a matter of opinion and held the purchasers entitled to rescind the contract.

Effects of misdescription

In practice, modern contracts for the sale of land usually make express provision for the possibility that the property is inaccurately described. The efficacy of such conditions will be considered in due course; for the moment, however, we are concerned with the treatment of misdescription at common law and in equity, where the issue is not clouded by an express condition of sale.

The most important legal effect of misdescription is that, where it is substantial, it renders the contract of sale unenforceable by the vendor. There can be no question of compelling the purchaser to accept the property, even with compensation, where it differs materially from what he or she has been led to expect. This principle was first expressed in a coherent form in the case of *Flight* v *Booth*,[2] which concerned the sale of a lease of certain business premises. The particulars of sale stated that, under the terms of the lease, "no offensive trade is to be carried on; they cannot be let to a coffee-house keeper or working hatter". In fact the lease prohibited many other inoffensive trades. The Court of Common Pleas ordered the vendor to return the purchaser's deposit, and Tindal CJ stated the rule of law as follows:[3]

---

1 (1884) 28 ChD 7.
2 (1834) 1 Bing NC 370.
3 At p377.

Where the misdescription, although not proceeding from fraud, is in a material and substantial point, so far affecting the subject-matter of the contract that it may reasonably be supposed that, but for such misdescription, the purchaser might never have entered into the contract at all, in such case the contract is avoided altogether, and the purchaser is not bound to resort to the clause of compensation. Under such a state of facts, the purchaser may be considered as not having purchased the thing which was really the subject of the sale.

Where the misdescription is not substantial it will not prevent the vendor from enforcing the contract, although of course compensation must be paid for the deficiency in the property.[1]

In all cases of misdescription the position of the purchaser is a strong one. A purchaser who wants the property "may elect to take all he can get, and to have a proportionate abatement from the purchase-money".[2] This, it appears, applies whether or not the misdescription is substantial, so that the purchaser is entitled to demand, at a reduced price, something materially different from what was originally contracted for. However, in such a case the purchaser is seeking a decree of specific performance which, as an equitable remedy, lies within the discretion of the court. Thus if the result of such a decree would be to inflict severe hardship upon the vendor, the purchaser's claim may well be unsuccessful. In *Earl of Durham* v *Legard*,[3] for example, an estate of some 11,000 acres was stated in the particulars of sale to be almost twice this size. The contract price, however, had been arrived at by the computation from the annual rent, which was accurately stated. It was held that to allow the purchaser to enforce performance of this contract at approximately one-half the agreed price would be grossly unfair; thus, if he wanted the estate, he must take it without compensation. Specific performance with compensation will also be refused to a purchaser in circumstances where the compensation is impossible of assessment. In *Rudd* v *Lascelles*[4] the vendor failed to disclose the existence of restrictive covenants of which she was unaware. Farwell J held that the purchaser must accept the property at the agreed price, or not at all.

---

1 See *Dyer* v *Hargrave* (1805) 10 Ves 505: p 389.
2 *Rutherford* v *Acton-Adams* [1915] AC 866 at p870, *per* Viscount Haldane.
3 (1865) 34 Beav 611.
4 [1900] 1 Ch 815.

It sometimes happens that a misdescription of property may operate in favour of the purchaser rather than the vendor, as when the particulars of property for sale include other property not intended to be sold. In such a case, in the absence of an express stipulation, the vendor is not entitled to any increase on the agreed price to take account of the extra land. However, if the purchaser seeks to enforce the contract, including the disputed portion, this claim may well fail on the ground of hardship to the vendor. In *Alvanley* v *Kinnaird*[1] the vendors of an estate intended to exclude the mines and minerals from the sale, but inadvertently failed to make this clear in the particulars. It was held that the purchaser could neither enforce the sale including the mines and minerals nor claim compensation for their exclusion. Since, however, the purchaser was prepared to take what the vendors had intended to sell, specific performance was granted on this basis.

Conditions relating to misdescription

It is common on the sale of land, particularly where a standard-form contract is used, to find an express provision to the effect that errors of description shall not annul the sale. Such a condition usually goes on to stipulate either that any misdescription shall be the subject of compensation between the parties or, alternatively, that no compensation shall be allowed.

The former type of condition, providing for compensation instead of rescission, has been so treated by the courts that it adds little if anything to the rights of the parties under the general law. Thus, a vendor can never rely upon it where the misdescription is fraudulent. In *Duke of Norfolk* v *Worthy*,[2] for example, where an estate was described as "about one mile from Horsham" when it was in fact over three miles from Horsham, the contract was held to be unenforceable against the purchaser. Even where there is no fraud, the vendor cannot use such a clause to compel the purchaser to take something substantially different from what was bargained for. The rule in *Flight* v *Booth*[3] applies; indeed in that

---

1 (1849) 2 M&G 1; *Neep* v *Abbott* (1838) CP Coop 333: see also *Manser* v *Back* (1848) 6 Hare 443: p 396.
2 (1808) 1 Camp 337.
3 (1834) 1 Bing NC 370.

case the court overrode a clause of this nature in the contract of sale.

The only effect of a clause providing for the payment of compensation in all cases of misdescription appears to be that, where the error is in the purchaser's favour, the vendor may claim an increase in the purchase price, something which would not otherwise be permitted.

A condition which provides that a misdescription shall neither vitiate the sale nor be the subject of compensation appears, at first sight, formidably in favour of the vendor. Once again, however, it cannot be used in a case of substantial misdescription,[1] and it seems reasonable to suppose that a court, knowing that compensation is not to be paid, would take a more liberal view of what is "substantial". If, however, the deficiency is truly a trifling one, the purchaser will be bound to complete without any compensation. Thus, in *Re Courcier & Harrold's Contract*,[2] a freehold dwelling-house was sold subject to certain standard-form restrictive covenants, including a prohibition against its use for public worship. Due to poor drafting, the particulars of sale stated that the property could not be used as a "public workshop" and did not reveal the true restriction. This discrepancy was held to be so trivial that the vendor was entitled to enforce the contract without any compensation.

A condition excluding compensation for misdescription has been held to be effective where it is the purchaser who seeks specific performance of the contract of sale, with compensation for the deficiency. In *Re Terry & White's Contract*[3] the purchaser of a plot of land complained that it was smaller in area than the particulars stated, and claimed a proportionate abatement of the price. The Court of Appeal, by a majority, held that a clause excluding compensation was effective to prevent the purchaser's claim. Had the vendor sought specific performance he would not, of course, have succeeded; but that was not what had occurred.

---

1 *Jacobs* v *Revell* [1900] 2 Ch 858.
2 [1923] 1 Ch 565.
3 (1886) 32 ChD 14.

Oral corrections by the auctioneer

When a contract has been reduced to writing, it is a general rule of law that oral evidence is inadmissible to contradict, vary or add to the written terms. However, while a party may generally resist an action for specific performance of a contract which is inaccurately expressed in writing, the equitable discretion which resides in the court is usually sufficient to prevent enforcement of the contract in its erroneously stated form. In consequence, the effect of any attempt by an auctioneer, at the time of the sale, to correct an error in the particulars of sale will depend upon which of the parties is taking action upon the contract.

It is well settled that a vendor may not enforce a contract which has been orally varied, either by the vendor personally or by the auctioneer as the vendor's agent. In *Townshend* v *Stangroom*[1] the tenant of a farm negotiated with his landlord for a new lease. The agreement drawn up included the property held under the existing lease, but the landlord gave evidence of an oral agreement by which the tenant was to relinquish part of his farm in return for some other land. It was held that the landlord could not enforce the contract subject to this oral variation. So too, in *Higginson* v *Clowes*,[2] where land was sold with timber upon it, the particulars of sale did not make clear whether the timber was included in the price or whether it was to be separately paid for at a fair valuation. Evidence was offered that the auctioneer had stated, before putting up each lot, that the latter was the case; Sir William Grant MR, however, said:[3] "In this case the written agreement leaves the question as to the timber in so much obscurity, that I wish I were permitted to resort to other evidence to elucidate it: but my opinion is, that I cannot admit the parol evidence for the purpose of explaining this agreement". The vendor, therefore, was not permitted to enforce his version of the agreement.

Although oral evidence is inadmissible to vary the terms of a written agreement, it may be used in cases of ambiguity to show that the purchaser has not in fact been misled. This "loophole" in the general rule is of a highly uncertain nature, since it is extremely difficult to distinguish a correction from a variation; however, the

---

1 (1801) 6 Ves 328.
2 (1808) 15 Ves 516.
3 At p521.

possibility has been recognised at least since the case of *Gunnis* v *Erhart*[1] where property sold was stated to be free from incumbrances. Evidence that the auctioneer had, at the time of the sale, disclosed a charge on the property was held to be inadmissible; but the Court of Common Pleas appeared to suggest that if the defendant had been given "particular personal information" of the incumbrance in question he would not be entitled to complain of it. The point was taken in *Ogilvie* v *Foljambe*,[2] which concerned the sale of a leasehold house. The contract did not mention title but oral evidence was admitted to show that the purchaser knew, from reading conditions drawn up for an abortive auction, that the vendor would not prove his landlord's title. Similarly, in *Farebrother* v *Gibson*[3] a house was described as being in the occupation of a named insurance company under a lease. In fact the lease was held by three individuals as trustees for the company and this was made clear at the time of the auction by the vendor's solicitor. The vendor was granted a decree of specific performance since, as this oral evidence showed, the purchaser had not been misled by the particulars of sale.

A vendor who seeks to establish that the purchaser was not misled by some inaccuracy or ambiguity must show very clearly that the purchaser was aware of the correction. As Romilly MR said in *Swaisland* v *Dearsley*:[4]

If it appears upon the evidence that there was in the description of the property a mistake which a person might bona fide make, and he swears positively that he did make such mistake, the evidence not being contradicted, this court cannot enforce the specific performance of the agreement against him.

Where a purchaser seeks to enforce a contract as written and to ignore an oral variation introduced by the vendor or the auctioneer, evidence is admissible to show that such enforcement would be unfair. Thus in *Townshend* v *Stangroom*[5] where, as we have seen, a landlord failed to enforce an agreement for a lease while

---

1 (1789) 1 HBl 289.
2 (1817) 3 Mer 53.
3 (1857) 1 De G&J 602.
4 (1861) 30 LJ Ch 652 at p654.
5 (1801) 6 Ves 328: p 394.

incorporating an oral amendment in it, the tenant was equally unsuccessful in enforcing the agreement as it stood. So too, in *Clowes* v *Higginson*[1] the purchaser, having successfully resisted the vendor's attempt to enforce an orally-varied contract of sale, failed in his own attempt to enforce what was in writing.

In admitting oral evidence to resist the purchaser's action for specific performance, the courts are making use of the wide discretion which they possess in all cases where equitable remedies are sought. Indeed, acting upon general notions of equity, specific performance has even been refused where the purchaser did not hear the oral variation of the written contract. In *Manser* v *Back*[2] the particulars of sale of certain property did not mention that the vendor was reserving a right of way across part of the land for the benefit of other property which he retained. The mistake was discovered before the sale, and suitably altered copies of the particulars were deposited in the auction room. The auctioneer read out the amended particulars, but without specifically drawing attention to the alteration. The purchaser did not hear the amendment and, by mistake, the contract of sale was signed on an unaltered copy of the particulars. It was held that to enforce the contract against the vendor without the reservation of the right of way would cause severe hardship and therefore specific performance was refused to the purchaser. *Manser* v *Back* was followed in *Re Hare & O'More's Contract*,[3] where lot 5 of certain property was described as similar to lot 4, whereas it was inferior in a material respect. The auctioneer orally corrected the misdescription but the purchaser, who denied hearing this, sued for specific performance with compensation. Joyce J refused to award such a decree.

The rule that a plaintiff may not bring oral evidence to vary a written contract applies, not only where equitable remedies are sought, but also where the plaintiff's claim is for damages at common law. In *Powell* v *Edmunds*,[4] for example, a purchaser of timber claimed to withhold part of the purchase price for breach of an oral warranty given by the auctioneer as to the weight of the

---

1 (1813) 1 Ves & B 524.
2 (1848) 6 Hare 443.
3 [1901] 1 Ch 93.
4 (1810) 12 East 6: see also *Winch* v *Winchester* (1812) 1 Ves & B 375.

timber. Lord Ellenborough CJ held this oral evidence to be inadmissible, remarking that the purchaser should have had the warranty reduced to writing at the time.

It is not certain whether a vendor who is sued by the purchaser at common law may call evidence of an oral variation of the contract. As we have seen, such evidence may provide a defence to an action of specific performance, but that may well be a result of the discretionary nature of equitable remedies. In theory at least, evidence should at common law be as inadmissible for the defendant as it is for the plaintiff. Some support for this view is given in the case of *Bradshaw* v *Bennett*,[1] where the particulars of sale stated that certain property was held on three lives. The auctioneer made it clear at the start of the sale that one of the three persons had died, but evidence of this declaration was rejected by Lord Tenterden CJ and the purchaser succeeded in his action to recover the deposit.

Whether or not a vendor may set up an oral variation as a defence at common law, such evidence may undoubtedly be used to show that the purchaser has not been misled by what at first glance appears to be a misdescription. In *Re Edwards & Daniel Sykes & Co Ltd*[2] the particulars of sale of a leasehold shop named the "annual rental" at which it was held. The purchaser of the reversion claimed to have taken this to mean that the tenant had a yearly tenancy, paying the rates. In fact the tenancy was monthly, at a weekly rent equivalent to the stated "annual rental", and the rates were paid by the landlord. The purchaser claimed compensation for this misdescription but his claim failed when evidence was admitted to show that the true position had been clearly explained by the auctioneer, so that the purchaser could have been left in no real doubt as to what he was buying.

(b) *Sales of goods*

Section 13 of the Sale of Goods Act 1979 provides:

(1) Where there is a contract for the sale of goods by description, there is an implied condition that the goods will correspond with the description.

---

1 (1831) 5 C&P 48.
2 (1890) 62 LT 445.

(2) If the sale is by sample as well as by description it is not sufficient that the bulk of the goods corresponds with the sample if the goods do not also correspond with the description.

Any breach of this implied condition entitles the buyer to reject the goods or, if they have already been accepted, to claim damages.

As with misdescription in the sale of land, so with section 13 of the Sale of Goods Act, liability arises only where the offending statement forms part of the contract of sale, all other statements taking effect (if at all) as misrepresentations. However, whereas in relation to sales of land the distinction is usually fairly clear-cut, it is less so in relation to sales of goods. Three particular points are worth making.

In the first place, an oral statement made by an auctioneer of goods may on occasion be held to be a term of the contract, so as to form part of the description of the goods within the meaning of section 13. In *Couchman* v *Hill*,[1] for example, the conditions of sale provided that all lots were sold with all errors of description. The plaintiff, who intended to bid for a heifer, asked the seller and the auctioneer to confirm its catalogue description as "unserved". This they did honestly but mistakenly, for the heifer was already in calf, and it later died in giving birth. The plaintiff claimed damages (not then available in respect of a misrepresentation) and the Court of Appeal held that the contract of sale included the oral statements as well as the printed conditions and, further, that since there was an inconsistency, the specific statement from the rostrum overrode the general printed exemption clause.

Although *Couchman* v *Hill* was followed by the Court of Appeal in *Harling* v *Eddy*,[2] it may be doubted whether future courts will find it necessary to pursue this particular line of authority. As we have already seen, damages are now available in respect of a misrepresentation, and clauses excluding liability for misrepresentation are effective only at the discretion of the court. Thus, if the facts of these cases were to recur, they would probably

---

1 [1947] KB 554.
2 [1951] 2 KB 739.

come before the court as claims under section 2 of the Misrepresentation Act 1967.[1]

Second, it may be noted that the courts are fairly flexible in their approach to written documents such as catalogues.[2] Whereas the particulars in the sale of land almost invariably form part of the contract of sale, no such general principle may be applied to a catalogue at a sale of goods.[3] Once again, however, the importance of this point is diminished by the improvement of the remedies which are available in respect of a misrepresentation.

Third, while a written contract of sale may not be altered otherwise than in writing,[4] a contract which is made orally may be altered in the same way. This point, an important one where an auctioneer draws attention to some error in the catalogue, was recognised as early as 1845 in *Eden* v *Blake*.[5] That case concerned the sale of a dressing-case which was described in the catalogue as having silver fittings; before the sale commenced, however, the auctioneer stated that the catalogue was incorrect and that the fittings were plated. It was held that the auctioneer's oral correction of the catalogue was admissible to show that the contract was for the dressing-case with plated fittings, and the buyer was accordingly held to this bargain.

One final matter falls to be mentioned in relation to a seller's liability under section 13 of the Sale of Goods Act 1979. Section 55 of that Act provides that any attempt to exclude or restrict such liability is subject to the Unfair Contract Terms Act 1977, of which the relevant provision is section 6. This in turn states than any contract term which seeks to exclude or restrict liability under, *inter alia*, section 13 is void as against a person dealing as consumer and, in all other cases, may be relied upon only in so far as the term satisfies the requirement of reasonableness.[6] Since, on a sale by auction, the buyer is not in any circumstances to be regarded as

---

1 Unless the buyer wanted to recover for loss of bargain, a measure of damages not available under section 2: see p 407.
2 In the Australian case of *Lockhart* v *Osman* [1981] VR 57, a statement in a pre-sale advertisement was held to be a contractual description of cattle to be sold.
3 See, for example, *Eden* v *Blake* (1845) 13 M&W 614.
4 See p 396.
5 (1845) 13 M&W 614.
6 Defined by the Unfair Contract Terms Act 1977, section 11: see p 408. For present purpose, certain "guidelines" are laid down in Schedule 2.

"dealing as consumer",[1] this provision has the effect of placing misdescription and misrepresentation at auctions on virtually the same footing, as far as the exclusion of liability is concerned.[2]

2 Misrepresentation

(a) *The meaning of misrepresentation*

A misrepresentation, in legal terms, may be defined as a false statement of fact made by one contracting party to another which, though not forming part of the ensuing contract, induces that party to enter into that contract. The offending statement may be made in writing or by word of mouth, but these are not the only possibilities. A misleading photograph (which suggested that an investment property was a thriving wine bar, when in truth the tenant had lost the licence) has been held to constitute a misrepresentation.[3] And a statement may be made by conduct, as where a landlord deliberately covers up dry rot in a flat before letting it.[4]

It will be noted that the definition makes no mention of whether the person making the representation knew, or should have known, that it was false. Such factors are irrelevant to the question of what constitutes a misrepresentation although, as will be seen, they may affect the legal remedies which may be obtained in respect of it.

A number of other matters contained in the above definition call for further explanation. In the first place, the requirement that the statement be made by a party to the contract means that only a contracting party may be liable for misrepresentation as such.[5] Where the offending statement is made by an authorised[6] agent, liability falls initially upon the client, who may in turn seek reimbursement from the agent who has caused this loss. Thus an agent who (as usual) is not a party to the contract of sale can incur liability only in this second-hand form. This is not to say that a selling agent may never be directly responsible to a purchaser in

---

1 Section 12(2).
2 See p 408.
3 *Atlantic Estates Ltd* v *Ezekiel* [1991] 2 EGLR 202.
4 *Gordon* v *Selico Co Ltd* [1986] 1 EGLR 71.
5 *Resolute Maritime Inc* v *Nippon Kaiji Kyokai* [1983] 2 All ER 1.
6 The client may limit the agent's authority: see *Overbrooke Estates Ltd* v *Glencombe Properties Ltd* [1974] 3 All ER 511: p 409.

respect of an untrue statement; it means, however, that any such liability must be based on tort, the relevant ones being fraud and negligence.

The description of a misrepresentation as a false statement which is not included in the contract serves to distinguish it from a misdescription, which, as we have seen, is an error in the contractual description of property for sale. Furthermore, since failure of a vendor to disclose some defect of title which should have been disclosed amounts to a breach of an implied term of the contract for the sale of land, liability for non-disclosure is more closely related to misdescription than to misrepresentation.

The distinction between contractual and non-contractual mis-statements was rigidly adhered to at common law, and indeed the latter attracted only the rather limited and uncertain relief of equity. One consequence of this strict separation was the rule that where a misrepresentation was repeated in the contract, it could no longer be sued upon as a misrepresentation.[1] In practice, this rule did not operate too harshly, since the remedies for breach of contract were usually more desirable; nevertheless, it has now been abolished by section 1 of the Misrepresentation Act 1967, which provides:

Where a person has entered into a contract after a misrepresentation has been made to him, and –
(a) the misrepresentation has become a term of contract ... then, if otherwise he would be entitled to rescind the contract without alleging fraud, he shall be so entitled.

By virtue of its non-contractual nature, misrepresentation is likely to occur in three main areas of the work of estate agents and auctioneers. First, the "particulars" of property intended for sale by private treaty, which are drawn up and circulated by estate agents, frequently contain a clause expressly denying that those particulars form part of the subsequent contract of sale. As a result, any legal action arising out of their inaccuracy will rest upon misrepresentation and not misdescription.[2] Second, of course, oral statements made during negotiation or from the auctioneer's

---

1 *Pennsylvania Shipping Co* v *Compagnie National de Navigation* [1936] 2 All ER 1167.
2 Auction particulars by contrast are normally part of the contract of sale.

rostrum are seldom treated as part of the contract of sale, at least where a written contract is produced.[1] Third, where property is advertised for sale, whether by auction or private treaty, it is very unusual for the advertisements to be regarded as forming part of the contract of sale;[2] thus any false claims made therein are actionable, if at all, as misrepresentations.

At this point it may be noted that the advertisement in good faith of a forthcoming auction imposes no liability on the advertiser to hold the sale. In *Harris* v *Nickerson*[3] an auctioneer advertised a sale of office furniture to be held at Bury St Edmunds. The plaintiff, having obtained a commission to buy certain lots, travelled from London, but the lots were withdrawn. It was held that the plaintiff could not maintain an action against the auctioneer for the cost of his abortive journey. The good faith of the auctioneer in that case was an important factor, as was made clear by the Court of Queen's Bench in *Richardson* v *Silvester*,[4] which was decided some six months later. There the defendant, without any authority, advertised a large farm to let. The plaintiff, who was eager to take a tenancy of the farm, incurred expense on the faith of the advertisement. It was held that an action for damages in the tort of deceit would lie on these facts.

It is important to remember that an actionable misrepresentation is a statement of existing fact. A promise as to future conduct, however important it may be, cannot give rise to liability unless it forms part of a valid contract, which means in particular that the person to whom the promise is made has given some consideration in return for it. Similarly, an honest statement of opinion, however erroneous it may be, is not a misrepresentation[5] although liability may arise where the facts upon which the "opinion" is based indicate that it is not genuinely and reasonably held.[6]

To give rise to liability, it is essential that the false statement of fact is at least partly responsible for inducing the other party to enter into the contract, since only then can it be shown to have

---

1 See p 398.
2 See, however, the Australian case of *Lockhart* v *Osman* [1981] VR 57.
3 (1873) LR 8 QB 286.
4 (1873) LR 9 QB 34.
5 *Bisset* v *Wilkinson* [1927] AC 177.
6 *Smith* v *Land & House Property Corporation* (1884) 28 ChD 7: p 390.

caused any loss.[1] The results of this particular requirement are felt in two important respects. In the first place, a person who chooses not to rely on what has been said can have no complaint if it turns out to be untrue. In *Attwood* v *Small*,[2] for example, the vendor of a mine greatly exaggerated its earning capacity. The purchasers appointed experts to check these assertions and, upon being told that they were accurate, agreed to purchase the property. The House of Lords decided that the vendor could not be held liable for misrepresentation, since the purchasers had clearly placed no reliance on his statements. This principle is obviously of great importance in the field of property sales, where the purchaser commissions a survey of the premises before entering into a contract. In such a case, provided the surveyor is given a full opportunity to inspect the property, it is difficult to resist the conclusion that the purchaser has chosen to rely solely upon the surveyor, at least in respect of those defects which the surveyor's inspection ought to reveal.

The second main result of the rule that a misrepresentation must induce the contract is that a person who knows a statement to be untrue at the time the contract is made cannot sue in respect of it.[3] In such a case, the false assertion can be assumed to have had no effect at all. However, the onus of proving that the plaintiff knew of the error is on the person making the statement, and it is not an easy one to discharge. In particular, it must be proved that the plaintiff had actual knowledge, for:

No one is entitled to make a statement which on the face of it conveys a false impression and then excuse himself on the ground that the person to whom he made it had available the means of correction.[4]

In *Charles Hunt Ltd* v *Palmer*[5] leasehold shops were described in the particulars of sale as "valuable business premises". The

---

1 See *Swingler* v *Khosla* [1991] 1 EGLR 245.
2 (1838) 6 C&F 232.
3 The position is the same where the person's solicitor knows the truth: *Strover* v *Harrington* [1988] 1 EGLR 173.
4 *Nocton* v *Lord Ashburton* [1914] AC 932 at p962, *per* Lord Dunedin; see also *Laurence* v *Lexcourt Holdings Ltd* [1978] 2 All ER 810 at p819.
5 [1931] 2 Ch 287. This was a case of misdescription, but the principle involved is identical.

conditions of sale provided that the purchaser should be deemed to have knowledge of the contents of the leases, which were available for inspection. The defendant, who did not inspect the leases, purchased the shops for his dairy business, only to find that covenants in the leases restricted the use of the premises to the trades of ladies' outfitter, fancy draper and manufacturer of ladies' clothing. It was held that to describe property thus restricted as "valuable business premises" was a substantial misdescription, which was in no way cured by giving the defendant an opportunity to discover that it was false. The purchaser, therefore, was entitled to avoid the contract and recover his deposit. It is worth noting in relation to this case that, had the description of the premises not been positively misleading, the availability of the leases for inspection would have been a complete answer to any charge of failing to disclose the onerous covenants; however, a vendor who chooses to make an actual statement is responsible for its accuracy.

(b) *Remedies for misrepresentation*

Once it is established that a person's consent to a contract has been induced by a misrepresentation as defined above, there will generally be some redress at law. The form which such redress will take is, however, dependent upon a further variable factor, namely the state of mind of the person responsible for making the false statement.

To take the simplest case first, a *fraudulent* misrepresentation entitles the person to whom it was made to rescind the contract and, whether or not this is done,[1] to sue for damages in the tort of deceit. Such damages, it appears, may well include consequential loss which could not reasonably have been foreseen, provided only that it results directly from the fraud.[2] In this connection it should be noted that fraud is not an easy thing to prove, especially since the courts draw a rigid distinction between a dishonest statement and one which the maker honestly, although wholly without grounds, believes to be true.[3]

---

1 See *Production Technology Consultants Ltd* v *Bartlett* [1988] 1 EGLR 182.
2 See *Doyle* v *Olby (Ironmongers) Ltd* [1969] 2 QB 158; *Archer* v *Brown* [1984] 2 All ER 267.
3 *Derry* v *Peek* (1889) 14 App Cas 337.

As regards *non-fraudulent* misrepresentation, at common law this gave rise to no remedies, even if the maker had no reasonable grounds for believing it to be true. However, equity was prepared to allow rescission of a contract on the basis of innocent misrepresentation, subject to certain qualifications considered below. The consequent illogicality of a situation in which a comparatively unimportant misstatement could be remedied only by cancelling the entire contract led to the drafting of section 2(2) of the Misrepresentation Act 1967, which provides:

Where a person has entered into a contract after a misrepresentation has been made to him otherwise than fraudulently, and he would be entitled, by reason of the misrepresentation, to rescind the contract, then, it if is claimed, in any proceedings arising out of the contract, that the contract ought to be or has been rescinded, the court or arbitrator may declare the contract subsisting, and award damages in lieu of rescission, if of opinion that it would be equitable to do so, having regard to the nature of the misrepresentation and the loss that would be caused by it if the contract were upheld, as well as to the loss that rescission would cause to the other party.

As we shall see, the nature of rescission has led to its being hedged about with restrictions, and the rather clumsy drafting of this provision does not make clear whether these also affect the ability of a court to award damages. Nevertheless, it cannot be denied that the greater flexibility offered by these alternative remedies represents a significant advance on the pre-Act legal position.

The old common law division of misrepresentations into "fraudulent" and "innocent" must today be regarded as too simplistic. Innocent misrepresentations must be further divided, according to whether or not their maker had reasonable grounds for believing what was said to be true. For convenience, we may retain the term "innocent misrepresentation" to cover the case where the maker's belief is reasonable; where it is not, there is a "negligent misrepresentation".

A negligent misrepresentation, where it exists, may first render its maker liable to damages in the tort of negligence. This principle, as laid down by the House of Lords in the case of *Hedley, Byrne & Co*

Ltd v Heller & Partners Ltd[1] has already been discussed, in relation to both estate agents and auctioneers;[2] here it will suffice merely to remind ourselves that a "special relationship" must exist between the maker of the statement and the person who suffers loss in reliance on it, in order for liability to be established. Furthermore, of course, since this is an action in tort, an agent who makes a negligent statement may incur personal liability, notwithstanding that the agent is not party to the resulting contract.

The second legal development concerning negligent misstatements is section 2(1) of the Misrepresentation Act 1967, which provides:

Where a person has entered into a contract after a misrepresentation has been made to him by another party thereto and as a result thereof he has suffered loss, then, if the person making the misrepresentation would be liable to damages in respect thereof had the misrepresentation been made fraudulently, that person shall be so liable notwithstanding that the misrepresentation was not made fraudulently, unless he proves that he had reasonable ground to believe and did believe up to the time the contract was made that the facts represented were true.

Despite its curious drafting, the intention of this provision is reasonably clear; it is to make damages available as of right in respect of a negligent misrepresentation.[3] Its method of achieving this object departs from that of Hedley, Byrne & Co Ltd v Heller & Partners Ltd in three important respects: first, liability falls only upon a contracting party, so that if the statement is made by an agent, it is the principal who is primarily liable;[4] second, no "special relationship" need be established under section 2(1); and third, the burden of proving the reasonableness of the belief is placed upon the person who makes the statement.

For many years, the major uncertainty surrounding section 2(1) was just how far the "fiction of fraud" could be taken in interpreting the effect of the statutory provision. This fiction was held insufficient to impose personal liability upon an agent who was not a party to

---

1 [1964] AC 465.
2 See pp 117, 311.
3 The injured party may in addition claim to rescind the contract under section 2(2), but this remedy lies within the discretion of the court.
4 Gosling v Anderson (1972) 223 EG 1743.

the contract of sale,[1] but its effect upon the appropriate measure of damages to be adopted was far less clear. While there was some support for a measure of damages equivalent to that for breach of contract,[2] the better view was that a tortious measure would be appropriate.[3] The courts in these cases would probably have settled for an assessment of damages reflecting the tort of negligence (which is after all what the defendant is made liable for), but the Court of Appeal has now gone even further. In *Royscot Trust Ltd v Rogerson*[4] it was held that the statutory wording is clear and that, as far as remoteness of damage is concerned, it is the rules relating to the tort of deceit which must be applied.[5]

Perhaps the most important effect of the Misrepresentation Act 1967 is that it makes available the remedy of damages in areas where this could not previously be obtained. Despite this availability, however, there will be many cases in which the offended party prefers to rescind the contract altogether, and it is therefore important to remember that the remedy of rescission may be barred on a number of grounds. In the first place, a person who, with full knowledge of the facts and of the misrepresentation, elects to proceed with the contract, is barred by this affirmation from subsequently rescinding it. In this connection, a person who takes no steps at all upon discovering the false statement would probably be held to have affirmed the contract. Second, since the principle underlying rescission is *restitutio in integrum* it will only be allowed where both parties can be substantially returned to their pre-contractual positions. Thus, if the property involved has substantially deteriorated or been consumed, there can be no rescission of the contract. Third, a contract cannot be rescinded in such a way as to

---

1 *Resolute Maritime Inc v Nippon Kaiji Kyokai* [1983] 2 All ER 1.
2 *Jarvis & Swan's Tours Ltd* [1973] QB 233; *Davis & Co (Wines) Ltd v Afa-Minerva (FMI) Ltd* [1974] 2 Lloyd's Rep 27; *Esso Petroleum Co Ltd v Mardon* [1976] QB 801; *Watts v Spence* [1976] Ch 165.
3 *F & B Entertainments Ltd v Leisure Enterprises Ltd* (1976) 240 EG 455; *Andre & Cie SA v Ets Michel Blanc & Fils* [1977] 2 Lloyd's Rep 166; *McNally v Welltrade International* [1978] IRLR 497; *Chesneau v Interhome Ltd* (1983) 134 NLJ 341. For interesting applications of this measure, see *Hussey v Eels* [1990] 1 EGLR 215; *Naughton v O'Callaghan* [1990] 3 All ER 191.
4 [1991] 3 All ER 294.
5 For these rules see *Doyle v Olby (Ironmongers) Ltd* [1969] 2 QB 158: p 404.

injure a third party who has acquired, in good faith and for value, an interest in the subject-matter.

In the case of innocent (in the sense of non-fraudulent) misrepresentation, equity further refused to grant rescission after the contract had been completed, for example by a formal conveyance of land. This restriction, however, has been removed by section 1(b) of the Misrepresentation Act 1967.

(c) Exclusion of liability

The Misrepresentation Act contains one further section which is of great practical importance to estate agents and auctioneers. As we have seen, provisions in a contract for the sale of land designed to prevent the loss of the sale, or even the payment of compensation, for *misdescription*, are of rather limited effect, at least where the misdescription is of a substantial nature. No such rule, however, applied at common law to clauses which excluded liability in respect of *misrepresentation*. Such clauses are now governed by section 3 of the Misrepresentation Act 1967,[1] which provides:

If a contract contains a term which would exclude or restrict:
(a) any liability to which a party to a contract may be subject by reason of any misrepresentation made by him before the contract was made; or
(b) any remedy available to another party to the contract by reason of such a misrepresentation,
that term shall be of no effect except in so far as it satisfies the requirement of reasonableness as stated in section 11(1) of the Unfair Contract Terms Act 1977; and it is for those claiming that the term satisfies that requirement to show that it does.

This provision provokes a number of comments. First, it applies only to exclusion or limitation clauses which are contained in a contract, and not to extra-contractual notices such as those commonly found in estate agents' particulars. As a result, if clauses of the latter kind are effective in principle to exclude liability for misrepresentation (and it should be noted that, in the opinion of Bridge LJ,[2] they are not), then they will clearly constitute a very powerful weapon in the armoury of vendors and their agents.

---

1 As substituted by the Unfair Contract Terms Act 1977, section 8.
2 *Cremdean Properties Ltd* v *Nash* (1977) 244 EG 547 at p551.

Second, unlike the earlier version of section 3, this one requires the *term* to be proved reasonable, rather than the party's *reliance* on it; thus it is in the light of circumstances at the time of making the contract that "reasonableness" falls to be assessed. Third, it appears that the courts will not adopt an over-technical approach to the question of what constitutes a "term which would exclude or restrict". In *Cremdean Properties Ltd v Nash*,[1] for example, a footnote to the conditions which governed the sale of a large block intended for office development stated: "These particulars are prepared for the convenience of an intending purchaser ... and their accuracy is not guaranteed. Any intending purchaser must satisfy himself by inspection or otherwise as to the correctness of each of the statements contained in these particulars." When it was alleged that the particulars contained a serious misrepresentation as to the amount of lettable office space which would result from the proposed development, the court was asked to decide, as a preliminary issue, whether the footnote was caught by the Misrepresentation Act. The Court of Appeal, affirming the trial judge, held that, whatever the *wording* of the clause, its *intention* was to exclude liability, and it therefore fell within section 3.

Surprisingly, perhaps, Bridge LJ in *Cremdean v Nash* expressed his approval of the decision of Brightman J in *Overbrooke Estates Ltd v Glencombe Properties Ltd*,[2] where it was held that a condition of sale stating that auctioneers had no authority "to make or give any representation or warranty" did not fall within section 3. In rejecting the argument that this condition was in effect an exclusion clause, Brightman J said:[3]

In my view the section only applies to a provision which would exclude or restrict liability for a misrepresentation made by a party or his duly authorised agent, including of course an agent with ostensible authority. The section does not, in my judgment, in any way qualify the right of a principal publicly to limit the otherwise ostensible authority of his agent.

The problems inherent in this decision, and the subsequent case law, have already been considered.[4]

---

1 (1977) 244 EG 547.
2 [1974] 3 All ER 511.
3 At p517.
4 pp91-93.

Where a term is subject to section 3, it is for the party who seeks to rely on it to satisfy the court that it is reasonable, that is, "that the term shall have been a fair and reasonable one to be included having regard to the circumstances which were, or ought reasonably to have been, known to or in the contemplation of the parties when the contract was made".[1] In the context of the sale of land, standard-form conditions have twice been struck out as failing to meet this requirement. In *Walker* v *Boyle*,[2] Dillon J held unreasonable a condition of sale which had been in common use for many years, apparently because, on its strict wording, it would exclude liability even for *fraudulent* statements by the vendor (the statement actually made in that case was not fraudulent, but that was irrelevant to the "reasonableness" of the clause). In *South Western General Property Co Ltd* v *Marton*,[3] too, a number of auction conditions in standard form were held by Croom-Johnson J to be unreasonable and therefore invalid; given that many people attend auctions at short notice, it was, in the opinion of the judge, not reasonable to place upon such bidders the responsibility for discovering errors in the particulars of sale. On the other hand, auction conditions excluding liability for misrepresentation were held *obiter* to satisfy the requirement of reasonableness in *Swingler* v *Khosla*.[4]

3 Personal liability of the auctioneer

The foregoing discussion concerns a purchaser's rights against the vendor of land or goods, where there has been misdescription or misrepresentation. These legal remedies can rarely if ever be pursued against an auctioneer personally, even where it is the auctioneer who has made the offending statement. This is because these remedies are only available as between contracting parties, and it is very unusual to find that an auctioneer is a party to the contract of sale. What is more likely to occur is that the vendor, having been held liable to the purchaser in respect of a misstatement falling within the auctioneer's implied authority,[5] will

---

1 Unfair Contract Terms Act 1977, section 11(1).
2 [1982] 1 All ER 634.
3 (1982) 263 EG 1090.
4 [1991] 1 EGLR 245.
5 See p 282.

in turn sue the auctioneer for breach of the latter's professional duty of care and skill.

Notwithstanding what has just been said, there are ways in which an auctioneer who gives false information about property may incur direct liability to the purchaser. If a deliberate intention to deceive the purchaser can be proved, then there will be liability in the tort of deceit. If the evidence does not establish fraud, then it may be possible to hold the auctioneer liable in the tort of negligence. The position seems directly analogous to that of an estate agent, and the reservations which we expressed in that context are equally relevant here.[1]

A third possible cause of action against an auctioneer, albeit one which does not appear to have been tried in an English court, lies in an action for breach of warranty of authority. This is a well-established form of liability for any agent, which arises where the agent exceeds the authority given by the client, with the result that the client is not bound to the third party by the agent's act. In the present context, one might argue that, where an auctioneer's statement about property is not binding on the client, the auctioneer can be held directly liable to the purchaser for purporting to make it on the client's behalf.

In *Payne v Lord Leconfield*,[2] where it was held that an auctioneer had no implied authority from the client to give a contractual guarantee about a horse, Grove J stated *obiter* that the auctioneer could have been made personally liable for breach of warranty of authority. However, an obstacle which arises out of modern standard conditions of sale should not be overlooked. An action for breach of warranty of authority will not in principle succeed where the third party is aware that the agent in fact has no authority, and the prevalence today of auction conditions which specifically deny the auctioneer's authority to make statements may well mean that this cause of action will seldom be available to purchasers.

4 Criminal liability

An auctioneer selling real property is subject to the provisions of the Property Misdescriptions Act 1991, which is considered in detail in chapter 7. A chattel sale, on the other hand, is governed by the

---

1 See pp117-120.
2 (1882) 51 LJQB 642.

Trade Descriptions Act 1968, which imposes an even more comprehensive code of liability in respect of misdescriptions.[1]

The particular provision of the 1968 Act which is most likely to affect the practising chattel auctioneer is section 1(1). This provides:

Any person who, in the course of a trade or business,
  (a) applies a false trade description to any goods; or
  (b) supplies or offer to supply any goods to which a false trade description is applied;
shall, subject to the provisions of this Act, be guilty of an offence.[2]

In relation to the first of these offences,[3] section 4(2) expressly provides[4] that an oral statement may amount to the use of a trade description, something which is clearly of importance to auctioneers. As to the second offence, the scope of this is considerably increased by section 6, which provides that "a person exposing goods for supply or having goods in his possession for supply shall be deemed to offer to supply them". Thus, notwithstanding that putting up goods for sale does not, in the general law, amount to an offer to sell,[5] an auctioneer is clearly within the definition of one who "offers to supply" goods for the purposes of this Act.[6]

The definition of a "trade description" laid down by the Act is of enormous scope. Section 2(1) provides that it includes any indication of:

(a) quantity, size or gauge;
(b) method of manufacture, production, processing or reconditioning;
(c) composition;
(d) fitness for purpose, strength, performance, behaviour or accuracy;

---

1 For a detailed discussion of this Act, see Parry & Rowell (eds), *Butterworths Trading and Consumer Law.*

2 The penalties are, on summary conviction, a fine of up to a present maximum of £5,000; upon conviction on indictment, an unlimited fine and up to two years' imprisonment: section 18.

3 Which applies to auctioneers: see *Aitchison v Reith & Anderson (Dingwall & Tain) Ltd* 1974 SLT 282; *May v Vincent* [1991] 1 EGLR 27.

4 By section 4(2).

5 A principle which has protected auctioneers against criminal liability under other statutes: see, eg, *British Car Auctions Ltd v Wright* [1972] 3 All ER 462.

6 See *Zawadski v Sleigh* [1975] RTR 113.

(e) any physical characteristics not included in the preceding paragraphs;
(f) testing by any person and results thereof;
(g) approval by any person or conformity with a type approved by any person;
(h) place or date of manufacture, production, processing or re-conditioning;
(i) person by whom manufactured, produced, processed or re-conditioned;
(j) other history, including previous ownership or use.

A "false trade description" means a statement about any of these matters which is either false or misleading to a material degree.[1]

Although liability in respect of false trade descriptions is *prima facie* strict, in that the prosecution need prove neither intent to deceive nor even carelessness, the Act does offer certain specific defences. Section 24(1) provides:

In any proceedings for an offence under this Act it shall ... be a defence for the person charged to prove –
(a) that the commission of the offence was due to a mistake or to reliance on information supplied to him or to the act or default of another person, an accident or some other cause beyond his control; and
(b) that he took all reasonable precautions and exercised all due diligence to avoid the commission of such an offence by himself or any person under his control.

Furthermore, where a person is charged with supplying or offering to supply goods to which a false trade description is applied, section 24(3) provides:

[I]t shall be a defence for the person charged to prove that he did not know, and could not with reasonable diligence have ascertained, that the goods did not conform to the description or that the description had been applied to the goods.

The application of the Trade Descriptions Act 1968 to auctioneers has been considered in relatively few reported cases, of which two are of particular significance. In *May* v *Vincent*[2] the defendant auctioneers sold, on behalf of a client, a picture which they described in the catalogue as "JMW Turner RA, a watercolour of moorland, stream, bridge and people". This attribution, which the

---

1 Section 3.
2 [1991] 1 EGLR 27.

auctioneers had copied from the frame of the picture, turned out to be false; the picture was not a Turner. When charged with applying a false trade description to goods, the defendants argued that the 1968 Act could not apply to the world of art auctions, which deals in opinions rather than facts; that they were protected by a comprehensive disclaimer in the catalogue (repeated in the Conditions of Sale); and that they had acted throughout merely as agents for the seller.

The Divisional Court of Queen's Bench rejected all these defences and held that the auctioneers were guilty of an offence under the Act. Alliott J could see no reason whatsoever for excluding art auctions from the legislation; the auctioneers had applied a false trade description to goods in the course of their business (a ruling which also disposed of the "agency" defence). As to the disclaimer, the court found a clear distinction (established in previous cases) between section 1(1)(*a*) and section 1(1)(*b*); while a disclaimer, if clear enough, could provide a defence to someone charged with merely *supplying* goods under the latter provision,[1] it could never afford protection to someone who actually *applied* the false trade description in question.

The earlier Scottish case of *Aitchison* v *Reith & Anderson (Dingwall & Tain) Ltd*[2] sheds some light on the defence provided by section 24. The defendants there were an established firm of auctioneers who were, however, conducting their first car sale. The defendants' managing director gave strict instructions that no information as to the condition of any vehicle was to be given to bidders, but one of the firm's clerks put a description on each car. The defendants were found guilty of an offence under section 1(1)(a) of the 1968 Act, and there attempt to rely on section 24 failed. Although the managing director had given instructions, he had taken no steps whatever to ensure that these were duly carried out by the staff.

5 Misconduct by bidders

Since the vast majority of the information which is made available at auction sales flows from the vendor to the bidders, one tends to think of "misstatement" as something for which purchasers will seek

---

1 Accepted in relation to an auctioneer in *Zawadski* v *Sleigh* [1975] RTR 113.
2 1974 SLT 282.

a remedy. In normal circumstances this is undoubtedly the case, but one should not overlooked the fact that information flowing in the other direction *can* have an influence on the proceedings, and that a vendor may require legal protection against misstatements and other examples of sharp practice.

(a) *False statements*

An unscrupulous bidder, by misrepresenting the state of property which is put up for sale, may dissuade others from bidding and thereby have the property knocked down at an advantageous price.In such circumstances, the successful bidder will not be entitled to specific performance against the vendor.[1] Indeed, there seems no reason to doubt that the vendor in such circumstances will be entitled to whatever remedies are appropriate for misrepresentation, both at common law and under the Misrepresentation Act 1967.

In cases where, as a result of a bidder's denigration of property, it fails to sell altogether, an action for misrepresentation will not lie.[2] However, assuming that the statement has been made fraudulently, as it usually will have been, the person making it is guilty of the tort of malicious falsehood, more commonly (though less accurately) known as slander of title. In *Mayer* v *Pluck*[3] the defendant, an estate agent who had made previous unsuccessful offers for the plaintiff's house, attended the auction at which the property was to be sold and asked the auctioneer publicly whether he was aware that the house was built on an underground stream and had 6 ins of water in the cellar. Not surprisingly, no bids were forthcoming and the plaintiff was forced to remain in the house and to lose money by calling off the purchase of a new house, negotiations for which had reached an advanced stage. Milmo J told the jury that, in order to find in favour of the plaintiff, they must be satisfied on four points: that the defendant made the statements; that they were untrue; that they were made maliciously, with a dishonest or improper motive; and that the plaintiff had suffered financial loss as

---

1 *Howard* v *Hopkyns* (1742) 2 Atk 371.
2 Such an action requires the misrepresentation to have brought about a contract between the parties.
3 (1971) 223 EG 33 and 219.

a result. Upon the jury finding all these matters proved, the plaintiff was awarded damages.

(b) Damping the sale

Even where there has been no misrepresentation as such, the fact that property has been knocked down at an artificially low price may persuade a court of equity, in the exercise of its discretion, to refuse a decree of specific performance of the sale. In *Twining* v *Morrice*,[1] for example, the defendants, as executors of a deceased person's estate, put some land up for sale, having agreed to a reserve of £2,000 on the first lot. The defendants' solicitor knew of the reserve, although he was not instructed to bid; consequently, when the plaintiff asked the solicitor to bid for him, the latter bid the amount of the reserve and the property was knocked down. Evidence was given that other persons at the sale refrained from bidding against the solicitor since they believed him to be a puffer. On this evidence the plaintiff was refused a decree of specific performance, although there had been no fraud.

A similar decision was reached in *Mason* v *Armitage*,[2] where the plaintiff, a friend of the defendant vendor, had told him that he would not buy the defendant's property at the reserve price. When the plaintiff subsequently bid at the sale, the defendant's puffer assumed that he did so as agent for the vendor. The puffer therefore did not puff, and the property was knocked down to the plaintiff at less than its reserve. Specific performance was again refused.

A more direct means of damping the sale was employed in *Fuller* v *Abrahams*[3] which concerned the sale of a barge taken in execution of a debt due from its owner. The plaintiff, who had built the barge, told the company that the owner had never paid him for it, whereupon no one bid against him. The auctioneer having refused to knock the barge down on a single bid, a friend of the plaintiff made an intervening bid, and the barge was then knocked down to the plaintiff at about one-third of its true value. The Court of Common Pleas held that, in these circumstances, the sale could not be treated as valid.

---

1 (1788) 2 Bro CC 326.
2 (1806) 13 Ves 25.
3 (1821) 6 Moo CP 316.

C Illegal auction practices

1 Bidding rings

If a vendor is not permitted to inflate the price obtained at auction by secretly bidding in person, one might have thought that the law would similarly prohibit collusion among bidders who, by agreeing not to compete with each other, could thereby artificially depress the hammer price. Surprisingly, perhaps, this is not the position taken at common law although, as will be seen, certain bidding agreements are now outlawed by statute.

(a) *Common law*

As mentioned above, there appears in principle to be nothing unlawful in an agreement between intending bidders at an auction, whereby only one of them bids, so as to reduce the price at which the lot is purchased. Despite an early *dictum* of Gurney B[1] that such an agreement constituted a criminal conspiracy, the courts of equity have consistently refused to allow a vendor to avoid a contract of sale by proving that the highest bidder was party to such a "knock-out" arrangement. Thus in *Re Carew's Estate*,[2] where land was being sold by order of the court, two owners of adjoining land agreed that only one of them should bid and that, if his bid proved successful, the land should then be divided between them. The property was knocked down to this bidder for little more than the reserve price; nevertheless the sale was held to be valid.

In *Heffer* v *Martyn*[3] the plaintiff offered a prospective rival bidder for a plot of land £500 to refrain from bidding, provided that the plaintiff then obtained the land for not more than £6,300. In fact, the land was knocked down to the plaintiff for a mere £3,000, which was its reserve price. Despite this clear undervalue, the sale was upheld, and Lord Romilly MR said:[4]

---

1 *Levi* v *Levi* (1839) 6 C&P 239 at p240. This view was disapproved by Park B in *Doolubdass* v *Ramloll* (1850) 7 Moo PC 239 at p263, and by Bankes and Atkin LJJ in *Rawlings* v *General Trading Co* [1921] 1 KB 635 at pp 641, 649.
2 (1858) 26 Beav 187.
3 (1867) 36 LJ Ch 372.
4 At p373.

The intending buyers may arrange between themselves which lots they will bid for and which not, and agree not to compete with each other; and if they may do so in that case I think also they may take money for abstaining to compete as well as arrange to take one lot against another ... This is, no doubt, very hard upon a vendor, that if he combines with others to keep up the price, it should be illegal and the sale void, but that the purchaser may combine together with others to get the property at less than its value; but the real remedy in such a case as this is in fixing the reserved bidding: it is, no doubt, a very important matter, and requires very careful previous consideration.

Not only is the vendor bound in such cases to go through with the sale; the bidding agreements are themselves enforceable as between the participants. In *Galton* v *Emuss*,[1] for example, where the plaintiff abstained from bidding for certain land in return for an option granted by the successful bidder, it was held that the option was enforceable.

The most common type of bidding agreement is one under which the spoils are divided, either in agreed proportions or by a subsequent auction among the parties (the true "knock-out"). It is well established that, in such a case, specific performance will be available to ensure that the division is duly carried out.[2] In *Rawlings* v *General Trading Co*[3] two dealers, who attended a sale of surplus property belonging to the Ministry of Munitions, agreed that only one should bid and that the goods should be equally divided between them. The Court of Appeal, after a review of the authorities, reversed the decision of Shearman J and held the agreement to be enforceable. In a notable dissenting judgement, however, Scrutton LJ was of the opinion that the agreement, while reasonable as between the parties, was contrary to the public interest (since this was a sale of public goods) and could therefore be treated as an unlawful restraint of trade. This argument might well have pointed the way for future development of the law, but it has not been adopted in later cases. Thus in *Harrop* v *Thompson*,[4] for example, Templeman J upheld the legality of an agreement whereby a

---

1 (1844) 1 Coll 243.

2 *Chattock* v *Muller* (1878) 8 ChD 177; *Pallant* v *Morgan* [1953] Ch 43; *Du Boulay* v *Raggett* [1989] 1 EGLR 229.

3 [1921] 1 KB 365; followed in *Cohen* v *Roche* [1927] 1 KB 169.

4 [1975] 2 All ER 94. Templeman J regarded himself as bound by the *Rawlings* case.

purchaser of land had induced another person not to bid against him, and thus granted a decree of specific performance against the vendor. Similarly, in *Du Boulay* v *Raggett*,[1] where part of a country estate was being sold at auction, a number of neighbouring landowners agreed that one of their number should bid as agent for all, and that the land should then be divided in an agreed manner. This agreement was held specifically enforceable against the appointed agent.

(b) *Statute*

The decision of McCardie J in *Cohen* v *Roche*,[2] which highlighted the legal immunity of "rings", received an amount of adverse publicity and led directly to the passing of the Auctions (Bidding Agreements) Act 1927. Section 1(1) of this Act provides:

If any dealer agrees to give, or gives, or offers any gift or consideration to any other person as an inducement or reward for abstaining, or for having abstained, from bidding at a sale by auction either generally or for any particular lot, or if any person agrees to accept, or accepts, or attempts to obtain from any dealer any such gift or consideration as aforesaid, he shall by guilty of an offence.

In order not to invalidate legitimate joint purchases, however, it is further provided that:

Where it is proved that a dealer has previously to an auction entered into an agreement in writing with one or more persons to purchase goods at the auction bona fide on a joint account and has before the goods were purchased at the auction deposited a copy of the agreement with the auctioneer, such an agreement shall not be treated as an agreement made in contravention of this section.

It is clear that the central figure under the 1927 Act is the "dealer", who is defined by section 1(2) as a "person who in the normal course of his business attends sales by auction for the purpose of purchasing goods with a view to reselling them". This definition has two important consequences. First, it means that a bidding agreement (or even, in a rare case, a full-scale "ring") entered into

---

1 [1989] 1 EGLR 229.
2 [1927] 1 KB 169.

by private individuals is not illegal. Second, and of greater practical significance, it leads to the conclusion that the Act has no application to sales of land. True, the Act does not say in so many words that land sales are excluded but, given the statutory definition of "dealer", to include them would be manifestly absurd. The effect would be that, while two property developers could quite lawfully agree not to bid against each other for a building plot, an identical agreement made by two art dealers would constitute a criminal offence!

The 1927 Act had little obvious effect, in that only one prosecution for its breach was mounted during 40 years of its operation. Then, in the late 1960s, continuing doubts as to its effectiveness as a preventive measure were brought to a head by a well-publicised affair in which a painting, bought for £2,700 at a country-house auction in Somerset, was shortly afterwards sold to the National Gallery for £150,000. Widespread suspicions that a dealers' ring had been in operation were never substantiated, but the resulting outcry led to an attempt to strengthen the existing law which was embodied in the Auctions (Bidding Agreements) Act 1969.[1]

Section 1 of the 1969 Act allows summary proceedings in respect of an illegal bidding agreement to be commenced at any time within five years of the commission of the offence, provided that it is also within three months of the date on which the Attorney-General (whose consent to a prosecution is required) is given sufficient evidence of the offence. Further, if the penalties which can be obtained on a summary conviction (a fine of £1,000[2] or up to six months' imprisonment or both) are thought by the prosecution to be insufficient, offences may be tried on indictment, in which case the penalties are up to two year's imprisonment or a fine of unlimited amount, or both.

Section 2 of the 1969 Act introduces a new sanction which may be applied to any person convicted of an offence in respect of a bidding agreement. The court is empowered to order that, for a certain period,[3] a convicted person or his representative may not

---

1 Copies of both Acts must be displayed at any auction sale to which they relate: 1927 Act, section 3: 1969 Act, section 4.

2 Increased from £400 by the Criminal Law Act 1977.

3 Up to one year on summary conviction; up to three years in the case of a conviction on indictment.

"enter upon any premises where goods intended for auction are on display or attend or participate in any way in any sale by auction".

One of the main shortcomings of the 1927 Act lay in its failure to provide an adequate civil remedy to a seller who suffered at the hands of a bidding ring. Such a person was entitled to treat the sale as fraudulent if, and only if, a criminal conviction had been obtained. In order to improve the seller's position, the 1969 Act provides that, where goods are purchased at auction by a party to an illegal bidding agreement, the contract of sale is voidable at the option of the seller.[1] If the seller exercises this right, but the goods are nevertheless not returned, it is further provided that all the parties to the agreement are jointly and severally liable to compensate the seller for any loss suffered.

All in all, it cannot be said that the Auctions (Bidding Agreements) Acts have proved to be a very effective weapon. True, two successful prosecutions of dealers' rings have been reported: in one the "knockout" sale took place on the beach;[2] in the other, it was held in the cocktail bar of a local hotel, where it was captured on video by the police![3] However, a decision of the chief metropolitan magistrate in a case involving Thomas Agnew & Sons, a leading firm of art dealers, has seriously restricted the scope of the Act.[4] This case arose when Agnews, in an undisclosed partnership with two other dealers, bought an Algardi bust at a Christie's auction. When prosecuted under this legislation, the dealers argued that their agreement had not induced anyone to refrain from bidding, since none of the participants could have afforded to bid as individuals. This argument was upheld, the prosecution failed, and the Director of Public Prosecutions decided not to pursue an appeal. It thus appears that no offence is committed under the Act unless the prosecution can prove that, were it not for the bidding agreement, the parties would have competed against each other. This burden, added to the considerable difficulty of proving the existence of a "ring" in the first place, should ensure that prosecutions under these Acts continue to be objects of considerable rarity.

---

1 Auctions (Bidding Agreements) Act 1969, section 3.
2 See The Times, September 1 1983.
3 *R* v *Jordan* [1981] CLY 131.
4 See The Times, April 10 and May 1 1981.

2   Mock auctions

It is impossible to make any sense of the Mock Auctions Act 1961, unless it is realised from the outset that a "mock auction" is really no more than a particular type of confidence trick, one which was at one time especially prevalent in London and seaside resorts. As Kenneth Jones J pointed out in *R* v *Ingram*:[1]

The average holidaymaker going into one of these premises with his eyes open would realise that these proceedings have really as much to do with a true auction as a visit to the shooting gallery further down the street has to do with participation in the rifle championships at Bisley.

The technique employed to perpetrate this trick, although varying from one place to another is broadly speaking as follows.[2] Having collected a crowd of people by displaying attractive goods to be sold at specified low prices, the auctioneer puts up a sealed package and knocks this down cheaply. Then, stating that buying such a sealed package is a pre-condition of bidding at the auction proper, the auctioneer sells several more at the same price. However, by not handing over the packages at this stage, the attendance of the victims is ensured. The goods originally displayed are auctioned and, in each case, most of the money paid is refunded, so that the net price paid is that stated at the outset. However, these bids are made by accomplices or fictitious bidders, a fact obscured by the simultaneous disbursement of free gifts by the auctioneer. Finally, a number of expensive-looking articles, which have not been displayed, are put up and sold to the victims for many times their real value, without the expected refund.

In 1924 it was estimated that £8m worth of specially manufactured shoddy merchandise was distributed in this way.[3] Nevertheless, an attempt in 1929 to legislate against this practice was defeated, since the Government took the view that the existing law was already competent to deal with the situation. Whether this was an accurate view is debatable, but it is to be noted that, between 1869 and 1960, only seven convictions were obtained.

---

1 (1976) 64 Cr App R 119 at p121.
2 See the speech of Lord Denham, introducing the Bill: HL Parl Deb, Vol 214, cols 1121-1128.
3 Lord Crook, HL Parl Deb, Vol 214, col 1141.

The criminal offences created by the 1961 Act apply to mock auctions of certain types of goods. These include plate, plated articles, linen, china, glass, books, pictures, prints, furniture, jewellery, articles of household or personal use or ornament or any musical or scientific instrument or apparatus.[1] A "mock auction" of such goods is defined as a "sale of goods by way of competitive bidding" provided that, during the course of the sale, one or more of three specified events occurs. As to what is meant by "competitive bidding", it should not be thought that this requires anything like the sequence of offers to be found in a true auction; it has been held by the Divisional Court of Queen's Bench that, so long as the number of "bidders" exceeds the number of items for sale, an "auctioneer" who sells at a previously announced price to the first person to raise his hand is within the terms of the Act.[2]

The three events mentioned above, which turn a sale of goods by way of competitive bidding into a "mock auction", are where:

(a) any lot ... is sold to a person bidding for it,[3] and either it is sold to him at a price lower than the amount of his highest bid for that lot, or part of the price at which it is sold to him is repaid or credited to him or is stated to be so repaid or credited, or

(b) the right to bid for any lot ... is restricted, or is stated to be restricted, to persons who have bought or agreed to buy one or more articles, or

(c) any articles are given away or offered as gifts."[4]

The basic offence under section 1(1) of the Mock Auctions Act 1961 is that of promoting, conducting, or assisting in the conduct of, a mock auction of the specified goods. The penalty for this on summary conviction is a fine not exceeding £100 or imprisonment not exceeding three months, or both; on conviction on indictment, the fine may be up to £1,000 and the imprisonment up to two years.[5]

---

1 Section 3(2).
2 *Clements* v *Rydeheard* [1978] 3 All ER 658; *Allen* v *Simmonds* [1978] 3 All ER 662. For further variations, see *Lomas* v *Rydeheard* (1975) 237 EG 801; *R* v *Pollard* (1983) 148 JP 679.
3 Including a fictitious bidder: section 3(4).
4 Section 1(3).
5 Section 1(2).

Index

A

B

E

G

H

I

M

T

U

W